I0813631

Seaforth WORLD NAVAL REVIEW 2025

Seaforth

WORLD NAVAL REVIEW

2025

Editor
CONRAD
WATERS

Seaforth
PUBLISHING

Frontispiece: The lead *Paolo Thaon di Revel* class multi-role offshore patrol vessel – essentially a frigate in all but name – pictured during sea trials in the Ligurian Sea. *(Fincantieri)*

Copyright © Seaforth Publishing 2024
Plans © John Jordan 2024

First published in Great Britain in 2024 by
Seaforth Publishing
An imprint of Pen & Sword Books Ltd
George House, Beevor Street,
Barnsley, South Yorkshire S71 1HN

www.seaforthpublishing.com
Email info@seaforthpublishing.com

British Library Cataloguing in Publication Data
A CIP data record for this book is available from the British Library

Hardback 978-1-3990-7888-7

ePub 978-1-3990-7889-4

PDF 978-1-3990-7890-0

All rights reserved. No part of this publication may be reproduced or transmitted in any form or by any means, electronic or mechanical, including photocopying, recording, or any information storage and retrieval system, without prior permission in writing of both the copyright owner and the above publisher.

The right of Conrad Waters to be identified as the author of this work has been asserted in accordance with the Copyright, Designs and Patents Act 1988

Pen & Sword Books Limited incorporates the imprints of Atlas, Archaeology, Aviation, Discovery, Family History, Fiction, History, Maritime, Military, Military Classics, Politics, Select, Transport, True Crime, Air World, Frontline Publishing, Leo Cooper, Remember When, Seaforth Publishing, The Praetorian Press, Wharncliffe Local History, Wharncliffe Transport, Wharncliffe True Crime and White Owl.

Typeset and designed by Stephen Dent
Printed and bound in India by Replika Press Pvt. Ltd

MIX
Paper | Supporting responsible forestry
FSC™ C016779

CONTENTS

Note on Tables: Tables are provided to give a broad indication of fleet sizes and other key information but should be regarded only as a general guide. For example, many published sources differ significantly on the principal particulars of ships, whilst even governmental information can be subject to contradiction. In general terms, the data contained in these tables is based on official information updated as of June 2024, supplemented by reference to a wide range of secondary and corporate sources, such as shipbuilder websites.

1.1 OVERVIEW

INTRODUCTION

Author:
Conrad Waters

'Those who expect to reap the blessings of freedom must, like men, undergo the fatigue of supporting it', wrote the English-born philosopher and political revolutionary Thomas Paine, widely regarded as one of the Founding Fathers of the United States.[1] His words have particular resonance as the Western World adapts to the end of the post-Cold War era and the steady erosion of the 'peace dividend' that was drawn down after the conclusion of the previous period of East-West hostility.

The last year has seen an ongoing deterioration in the global security situation as the challenges faced by the 'Western' nations have expanded. The Russo-Ukrainian War has continued to grind on into its third year without either side gaining a definitive advantage. Whilst remaining a primarily land-based conflict, the war has encompassed a significant maritime element that holds out a number of potential lessons for navies worldwide. These are explored by first-time contributors Brad and Josiah Martin in an opening chapter extending beyond the usual analysis of the weapons systems and tactics used by the two countries to encompass matters of maritime strategy and operational deployment. Given the overwhelming importance of seaborne trade to the world economy, their conclusion stresses the imperative of maintaining flexible naval forces that can operate effectively in the face of fast-evolving technological changes.

The re-ignition of other trouble-spots over the last 12 months has served to reinforce this conclusion. Pre-eminent amongst these has been the resumption of wholescale hostilities between Hamas and Israel following the Islamic Resistance Movement's murderous assault on Israeli territory from the Gaza Strip on 7 October 2023. Whilst efforts to contain the conflict's spread have been largely successful to date, the ongoing attacks on Red Sea shipping mounted by rebel Houthi forces in sympathy with the plight of the Palestinians in Gaza in the face of harsh Israeli reprisals have further added to the overstretch faced by the US Navy and its allies. As in the Black Sea, the challenge of combatting large numbers of uncrewed systems in a littoral environment has been a major test that is further explored in the pages that follow.

Table 1.1.1: COUNTRIES WITH HIGH NATIONAL DEFENCE EXPENDITURES: 2023

RANK 2023	(2022)	COUNTRY	TOTAL US$BN 2023[1]	SHARE OF GDP 2023	WORLD SHARE 2023	TOTAL US$BN 2022[1]	REAL CHANGE 2022–2023[2]	REAL CHANGE 2014–2023[2]
1	(1)	United States	916.0	3.4%	37.5%	860.7	2.3%	9.9%
2	(2)	China	[296.4]	[1.7%]	[12.1%]	[292.0]	[6.0%]	[60%]
3	(3)	Russia	[109.5]	[5.9%]	[4.5%]	[102.4]	[24%]	[57%]
4	(4)	India	83.6	2.4%	3.4%	80.0	4.2%	44%
5	(5)	Saudi Arabia	[75.8]	[7.1%]	[3.1%]	[70.9]	[4.3%]	[-18%]
6	(6)	United Kingdom	74.9	2.3%	3.1%	64.1	7.9%	14%
7	(7)	Germany	66.8	1.5%	2.7%	56.2	9.0%	48%
8	(11)	Ukraine	64.8	37.0%	2.7%	41.2	51%	1272%
9	(8)	France	61.3	2.1%	2.5%	53.6	6.5%	21%
10	(9)	Japan	50.2	1.2%	2.1%	46.9	11%	31%
-	(-)	**World Total**	**2,443**	**2.3%**	**100%**	**2242**	**6.8%**	**27%**

Information from the Stockholm International Peace Research Institute (SIPRI) – https://www.sipri.org/databases/milex
The SIPRI Military Expenditure Database contains data on countries over the period 1949–2023.

Notes:

1. US$ totals for 2023 and 2022 are based on then current (i.e. non-inflation adjusted) prices and exchange rates for the years in question. Exchange rate movements, in particular, can therefore result in significant movements in the US$ figures and explain apparent discrepancies in the table. SIPRI also adjust previous year calculations when more accurate data becomes available, potentially impacting prior year rankings.
2. The 'real' change figure is based on constant (2022-based) US$ figures. Figures over 10% have been rounded to the nearest percentage.
3. Figures in brackets are SIPRI estimates.

DEFENCE PLANS AND BUDGETS

The clearest evidence of the rapid deterioration in international stability is provided by the sharp uptick being experienced in global defence spending. This is now starting to feed through to the annual data produced by the Stockholm International Peace Research Institute (SIPRI), which published its annual report covering military expenditure in 2023 on 22 April 2024.[2] World military spending increased by 6.8 percent in real terms to US$2.44bn; the highest level that SIPRI has ever recorded. Total expenditure as a share of global economic output – as measured by gross domestic product (GDP) – was still somewhat lower than at the height of the United States' 'War against Terror'. However, world military spending of US$306 per person was the most that has been seen since the end of the Cold War in 1990. Nan Tian, Senior Researcher with SIPRI's Military Expenditure and Arms Production Programme, noted in the press release accompanying the new data that, 'The unprecedented rise in military spending is a direct response to the global deterioration in peace and security'.

SIPRI's latest figures are heavily influenced by the outbreak of the Russo-Ukranian War. Most obviously, Ukraine has now entered the list of the top ten global military spenders – summarised in Table 1.1.1 – as it fights for national survival against an existential threat. A 24 percent year-on-year increase in estimated Russian spending was the other side of the coin. However, there was a broader surge in defence expenditure across the European continent as Russia's neighbours looked to their own defences. The provision of military aid to Ukraine by many European nations also had a major impact on SIPRI's data.

As previously noted, the Russo-Ukrainian War has largely been a land-based conflict. However, there is little tangible evidence to date that this is leading to a broader shift of emphasis away from naval investment. This probably reflects the ongoing rivalry between the United States and China, which – taken together – account for almost half of all global military spending. The *2022 National Defense Strategy* continues to be regarded as the 'North Star' of US Department of Defense decision-making. This prioritises China as the United States' key strategic competitor and pacing challenge despite what is perceived as the acute threat posed by Russia.[3] Given the likely nature of any future conflict in the Pacific, this emphasis tends to favour spending on naval, as opposed to land-based, forces.

Regional concerns over China's growing power are also influencing defence policy across the broader Indo-Pacific region, spawning often large and complex naval construction programmes that will impact spending for decades to come. A primary example is the SSN-AUKUS (SSN-A) nuclear-powered attack submarine programme; first announced in September 2021 as part of the trilateral Australia-United Kingdom-United States security pact, SSN-A – which will see new submarines of a British design that incorporate some American technologies built in both Australia and Britain – is now starting to gain traction. The project is expected to cost Australia alone between AU$268bn (c. US$180bn) and AU$368bn (c. US$245bn) over the next three decades.

Personnel from the Royal Australian Navy, United States Navy and Royal Navy pose against the backdrop of the nuclear-powered attack submarine *Indiana* (SSN-789) during operations in the Arctic in March 2024 in a symbol of the trilateral collaboration between the three nations that has been solidified by the AUKUS security pact. The huge amounts involved in establishing the infrastructure needed to build the new SSN-AUKUS submarines that are being acquired under the agreement demonstrate the heavy burden that will need to be paid to ensure the West's security as the post-Cold War 'peace dividend' is steadily reversed. *(US Navy)*

The example of AUKUS also demonstrates the vast challenges posed by the need to resurrect defence and expand industrial capacity after years of neglect. Understandably, much attention has been focused on the urgent recapitalisation of depleted stocks of munitions, a requirement that has encompassed naval weapons' inventories.[4] However, an equal challenge is the lack of modern and efficient infrastructure to sustain the larger and more active force structure that many countries now envisage. Having shrunk to a low of fewer than 5,000 in the Cold War's aftermath, the workforce of Britain's sole submarine construction yard at Barrow-in-Furness has already expanded to around 13,500 to meet the demands of the *Dreadnought* strategic submarine programme. It will now need to grow further to at least 17,000 as work on SSN-A picks up. The BAE Systems-owned shipyard's facilities will also double in size. Further investment is being made in extending the Rolls-Royce factory at Raynesway, Derby that will manufacture the nuclear reactors installed in both the British and Australian submarines, creating well over 1,000 additional jobs. Meanwhile, in the Southern Hemisphere, Australia estimates that up to 4,000 workers will be involved in building the facility in Osborne, South Australia that will assemble the Royal Australian Navy's submarines. Between 4,000 and 5,500 additional jobs will be created once their construction is underway. Recruiting and training this workforce will inevitably be a major national endeavour that will need to be sustained over many years.

FLEET STRENGTHS AND REVIEWS

Given the complexity involved in realising these projects, it is readily apparent that any expansion of existing naval force structures will also take years to accomplish. In the short term, at least, many of the major NATO fleets face continued decline as life-expired ships are retired well in advance of their intended replacements' arrival. The current status quo is illustrated in Table 1.1.2. In contrast to the usual year-on-year comparison, this provides a more meaningful picture by looking at changes over the 15 years since *Seaforth World Naval Review* (*WNR*) was first published.

China's new aircraft carrier *Fujian* makes an impressive sight as she undertakes initial sea trials in May 2024. Although not yet officially admitted into service, she represents the impressive progress made by China's People's Liberation Army Navy in the 15 years since *Seaforth World Naval Review* was first published. *(China Military Online)*

TABLE 1.1.2: MAJOR FLEET STRENGTHS 2009–2024[1]

REGION	THE AMERICAS				EUROPE & RUSSIA										ASIA								IND. OCEAN	
COUNTRY	**USA**		**BRAZIL**		**UK**		**FRANCE**		**ITALY**		**SPAIN**		**RUSSIA**		**CHINA**		**JAPAN**		**KOREA(S)**		**AUSTRALIA**		**INDIA**	
	2009	**2024**	**2009**	**2024**	**2009**	**2024**	**2009**	**2024**	**2009**	**2024**	**2009**	**2024**	**2009**	**2024**	**2009**	**2024**	**2009**	**2024**	**2009**	**2024**	**2009**	**2024**	**2009**	**2024**
Carriers & Amphibious																								
CV/CVN	11	11	1	–	–	2	1	1	–	1	–	–	1	1	–	2	–	2	–	–	–	–	–	2
CVS/CVH	–	–	–	–	3	–	1	–	2	1	1	–	–	–	–	–	1	2	–	–	–	–	1	–
LHA/LHD/LPH	10	9	–	1	1	–	2	3	–	–	–	1	–	–	–	3	–	–	1	2	–	2	–	–
LPD/LSD	21	23	2	1	6	5	2	–	3	3	2	2	1	–	1	8	3	3	–	–	–	1	1	1
Submarines																								
SSBN	14	14	–	–	4	4	3	4	–	–	–	–	16	12	3	6	–	–	–	–	–	–	–	1
SSN/SSGN	57	54	–	–	8	6	6	5	–	–	–	–	20	20	5	6	–	–	–	–	–	–	–	–
SSK	–	–	5	4	–	–	–	–	6	8	4	2	20	20	55	50	16	22	11	21	6	6	16	16
Surface Combatants																								
BB/BC	–	–	–	–	–	–	–	–	–	–	–	–	2	2	–	–	–	–	–	–	–	–	–	–
CG/DDG/FFG	107	87	9	6	24	15	18	15	16	17	10	11	35	35	45	100	43	42	19	28	12	10	20	24
DD/FGS/FS	1	24	5	2	–	–	15	11	8	–	–	–	55	45	30	55	8	6	28	3	–	–	8	10
FAC[2]	–	–	–	–	–	–	–	–	–	–	–	–	50	25	65	75	6	6	1	18	–	–	12	7
Other (Selected)																								
MCMV	14	8	6	3	16	7	16	11	12	10	6	6	45	40	20	35	29	18	9	12	6	3	10	–

Notes

1 Numbers are based on official sources, where available, supplemented by news reports, published intelligence data and other 'open sources' as appropriate. Given significant variations in available data, numbers should be regarded as indicative, particularly with respect to Russia, China and minor warship categories (which can exclude non-operational vessels and are sometimes rounded). There is also a degree of subjectivity with respect to warship classifications given varying national classifications and this can also lead to inconsistency.

2 FAC numbers relate to ships fitted with or for surface-to-surface missiles.

The table clearly illustrates the eastward shift in naval power that has been a constant theme in *WNR*'s annual analysis. In general terms, the leading navies in the Indo-Pacific have seen a marked growth in their strength and capabilities over the past 15 years; a trend that is more marked when qualitative factors are also taken into account. Inevitably, it is China's People's Liberation Army Navy (PLAN) that has been in the vanguard of this shift, gaining new naval aviation and amphibious capabilities whilst doubling its force of major surface combatants. By contrast the US Navy – still by far the world's most powerful when the unique capabilities of its nuclear-powered aircraft carriers and submarines are taken into account – has essentially stood still despite ongoing efforts to expand overall fleet numbers. The major European fleets are typically smaller than at the start of the period.

Other points of note that the editor draws from the table include:

- The general expansion in the numbers of aircraft carriers and major amphibious vessels. This is likely a reflection of the emphasis placed on acquiring warships suitable for expeditionary stabilisation operations that became popular after the Cold War's end but which has taken decades to bring to fruition.
- Conversely, the widespread drawdown in the number of mine countermeasures vessels. This is a clear demonstration of the influence of technological change, with navies increasingly disposing of conventional minehunters in favour of autonomous solutions.
- A less universal but still apparent trend favouring the acquisition of larger surface combatants in preference to smaller, less capable types, particularly if the US Navy's seemingly abortive experiment with the Littoral Combat Ship type is excluded. This has arguably been driven by a number of factors, including the greater technical demands being placed on front-line warships and the replacement of second-tier vessels with specialised patrol ships purpose-built for constabulary missions.[5]
- The continued 'blue water' capacity of the major European fleets despite their relative decline. Notably, France's *Marine Nationale* and Britain's Royal Navy are still the only naval forces other than the US Navy and PLAN capable of deploying a full spectrum of large aircraft carriers, amphibious shipping and nuclear-powered attack submarines.

Needless to say, a table can only provide a snapshot of headline figures that omits many nuances. The growing significance of uncrewed assets of various sizes and capabilities – analysed on several occasions in this annual – is certainly a case in point. Another is the development of mid-sized navies, which are tending to expand in capacity and regional significance. In this regard, Mrityunjoy Mazumdar's ongoing analysis of Asia's naval forces turns to the Philippine Navy, which is in the course of implementing progressive capacity upgrades in the face of China's efforts to impose its infamous 'nine-dash line' territorial claim across the South China Sea. Meanwhile, another first-time contributor, Jean François Auran, provides an assessment of the Portuguese Navy's force structure and plans. Now in its eighth century of operations, the fleet is acquiring innovative new assets to help support the critical role it plays in both NATO and European Union missions.

SIGNIFICANT SHIPS

The continuing dominance of the US Navy in spite of the remarkable rise of China's PLAN is in no part due to its ability to project maritime power across all parts of the globe. An important linchpin in this capacity is the US Navy's Combat Logistics Force, which operates the replenishment vessels tasked with supplying the fleet at sea. The oilers that form the mainstay of this force are currently being replaced with the new *John Lewis* (T-AO-205) class, which are described by Sidney E. Dean in the first of this year's Significant Ship chapters. There is likely to be increasing demand for such vessels to support the navy's Distributed Maritime Operations concept, with additional smaller oilers now planned.

Another type of vessel essential in projecting global naval influence is the nuclear-powered attack submarine. Such vessels – still the preserve of only a handful of navies – contain many closely-guarded secrets. Bruno Huriet returns to lift the veil of mystery in his analysis of France's *Suffren* class, which are now starting to enter service after a long period of gestation. The new submarines have been heavily influenced by France's leadership in the civil nuclear sphere and make an interesting contrast to the American and British designs described in previous editions. Meanwhile, the editor turns his attention to the Italian Navy's *Paolo Thaon di Revel* class of multi-purpose offshore patrol vessels, which are essentially frigates in all but name. Incorporating

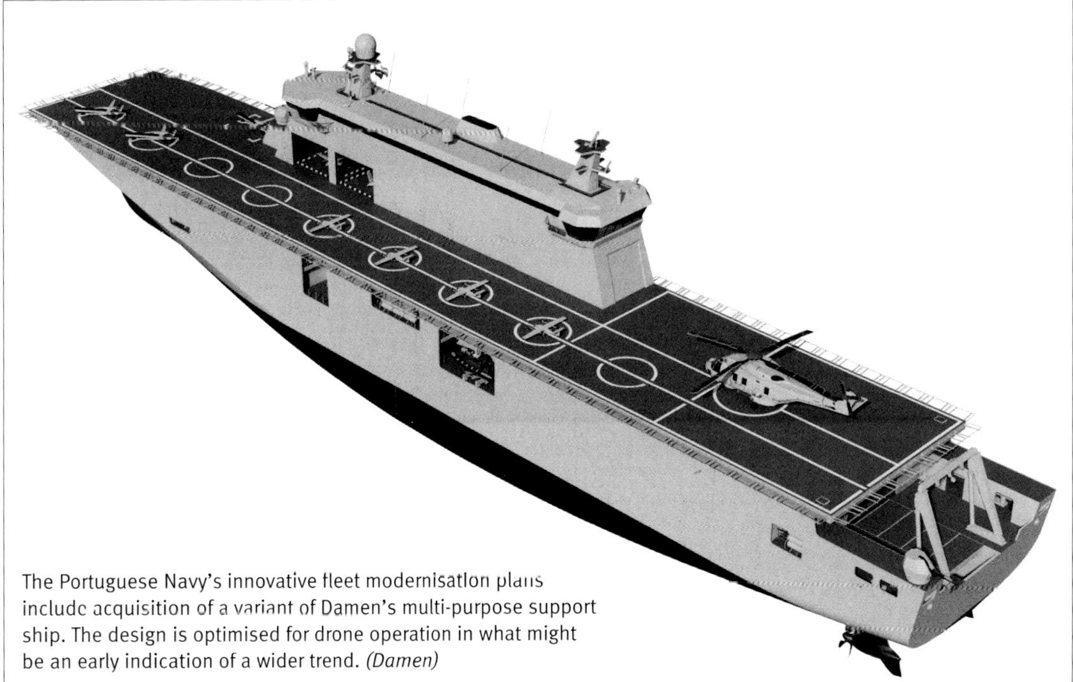

The Portuguese Navy's innovative fleet modernisation plans include acquisition of a variant of Damen's multi-purpose support ship. The design is optimised for drone operation in what might be an early indication of a wider trend. *(Damen)*

Duguay-Trouin, the second of France's six *Suffren* class nuclear-powered attack submarines, pictured entering the harbour of Fort-de-France in Martinique in March 2024 during the course of her lengthy 'shakedown' cruise. The new French submarines make an interesting comparison with contemporary American and British designs. *(Marine Nationale/Défense)*

a host of leading-edge technology supplied by Italian industry, they bring complementary qualities to those provided by the navy's existing FREMM type frigates.

TECHNOLOGICAL DEVELOPMENTS

Our final section commences, as always, with David Hobbs' review of developments in world naval aviation. In addition to providing a detailed analysis of the lessons learned from the crash of British F-35B strike fighter ZM 152 during the course of the CSG-21 deployment on 17 November 2021, he focuses on developments in unmanned naval aviation since *WNR* was first published. His chapter is followed by Richard Scott's description of the development of the new US Navy AN/SPY-6 family of radars, which will see widespread introduction across the fleet in the course of the next decade. Its

Uncrewed vehicles of all types are playing an increasingly important role in the conduct of a wide range of naval operations. This photograph shows the Royal Australian Air Force's (RAAF's) first MQ-4C Triton Remotely Piloted Aircraft System arriving at RAAF Base Tindal in the Northern Territory on 16 June 2024. *(Australian Department of Defence)*

initial Air and Missile Defence Radar (AMDR) iteration was subject to early competitive concept studies in June 2009 – the month that the first edition of *WNR* was completed – in a further indication of the length of time required to bring new capabilities into service.

The pace of delivery of the British Royal Navy's much-needed new frigate programmes has been subject to much criticism, sometimes by your editor. In truth, much of this criticism has been based on imperfect knowledge of the shipbuilding process, as well as a lack of understanding of the extent of the investment in infrastructure and skills required to rebuild long-neglected capabilities. The editor's chapter on the work of the Naval Ships Delivery Group, which is tasked with working with industry to bring the new Type 26 and Type 31 classes to delivery, aims to set the record straight. In particular, it explores how the progress that is being achieved will serve not only to ensure the Royal Navy's rejuvenation in the immediate future but also lay the foundations for the longer-term revitalisation of Britain's shipbuilding sector.

We conclude with another retrospective chapter that provides an overview of how navies have evolved since the Cold War's end. Norman Friedman examines the interface between technological change, geopolitical shifts and operational experience to assess the most important challenges faced by navies today. His description of current naval operations to protect shipping in the Red Sea highlights the practical consequences of the proliferation of drone and ballistic missile technology, as well as the steps that are being taken to mitigate them. It seems likely that these themes will continue to occupy *WNR*'s attention in the years ahead.

The Royal Canadian Navy *Halifax* class frigate *Charlottetown* pulls into US Naval Station Mayport for a scheduled port visit on 27 October 2023. The US Navy *Arleigh Burke* (DDG-51) class destroyer *Donald Cook* (DDG-75) and an unidentified *Freedom* (LCS-1) variant Littoral Combat Ship form part of the backdrop. Whilst surface combatants will remain central to future fleet structures, their capabilities will require continuous evolution to meet new challenges. *(US Navy)*

ACKNOWLEDGEMENTS

The editor remains grateful to the small team comprising publisher Rob Gardiner, designer Stephen Dent and proof reader Stephen Chumbley that has supported *WNR*'s production from the start. Equally important have been the high quality contributions provided by a range of authors. Many have written for *WNR* since its first edition. Another significant factor in assisting *WNR*'s longevity has been the assistance provided by governments and industries worldwide in supplying information and illustrations. The editor particularly appreciates the assistance of Harland Quarrington, the UK Ministry of Defence's Chief Photographic Advisor & Deputy Defence Imagery Editor, for his rapid clearance of the use of official imagery after changes in policy excluded *WNR* from reproducing photographs under the Ministry of Defence's News Licence. The private images supplied by Lorenz Amiet, Derek Fox, Vincent Groizeleau, Michael Leek, Marc Piché, Bernard Prézelin, Arjun Sarup and Devrim Yaylali have over recent years added greatly to the breadth of photographic coverage. Finally, the continued help provided by my wife Susan in reading and correcting initial drafts of the text is appreciated more than she probably realises.

The author continues to welcome engagement with *Seaforth World Naval Review*'s ever-widening readership. Please send any comments marked for my attention at info@seaforthpublishing.com.

Conrad Waters, Editor
30 June 2024

Notes

1. Thomas Paine (1737–1809) is best known for a number of pamphlets that helped inspire American colonists during the American War of Independence. The quotation forms the opening of the fourth of the *American Crisis* series and was published in Philadelphia in September 1777. Paine was later a prominent apologist for the French Revolution.

2. See Nan Tian, Diego Lopes da Silva, Xiao Liang and Lorenzo Scarazzato, *Trends in World Military Expenditure 2023* (Stockholm: SIPRI, 2024) and available on sipri.org

3. The 2022 *National Defense Strategy of the United States of America* (Washington DC: US Department of Defense, 2022) and overarching *National Security Strategy* (Washington DC: The White House, 2022) were both made public in October 2022. They are readily accessible by searching the web.

4. For example, the US Department of the Navy FY2024 budget request sought to increase weapon procurement by around a third from US$5.1bn to US$6.9bn. Moreover, The FY2025 request envisages an average investment of US$9.4bn p.a. over the five years of the Future Years Defense Program (FYDP).

5. A major exception is the Russian Navy. For reasons of both doctrine and industrial capacity it has tended to focus recent construction on smaller vessels that are optimised for deployment in the littoral but incorporate a powerful, long-range strike capability.

1.2 SPECIAL REVIEW

NAVAL LESSONS OF THE UKRAINE CONFLICT

Authors:
Brad Martin and Josiah Martin

Learning from the experience of the Battle of the Black Sea

The 2023 Russo-Ukrainian War has been primarily land-based, with relatively few maritime components. It has been fought largely on land, with the vast majority of reported casualties suffered on both sides being among ground forces. Nevertheless, its naval element is not without significance. The naval portions of the campaign have involved attacks on ports – and on ships in ports – by both sides; the seizure and recapture of Snake Island; attacks on ships underway; and at least some restriction on the flow of commodities.

Ukraine essentially has no navy. The 2014 annexation of Crimea by Russian forces deprived Ukraine of around 75 percent of its naval force. Since then it has relied on a 'Mosquito Fleet' concept, based around large numbers of small vessels, with an eye toward increasing interoperability with NATO naval forces. The intellectual pedigree of this is the *Jeune École* concept originally developed by the French in the nineteenth century.[1] While an ambitious goal, this did not translate to impressive outcomes. For all intents and purposes, the Ukrainian Navy was practically non-existent at the start of the conflict despite the material support of the United Kingdom and other NATO partners. The Ukrainian Navy was mostly a theoretical organisation as of 2022.

Nevertheless, as of the time of writing in mid-2024, Ukraine, with no navy, has in some respects 'won' the naval battle of the Black Sea. It has denied

The Ukrainian Navy's Project 58155 'Gyurza-M' class gunboats *Nikopol* (P176) and *Akkerman* (P174) pictured operating with the Ukrainian Sea Guard's Project 58130 'Orlan' class patrol boat *Balaclava* in July 2020. Ukraine's efforts to create a 'Mosquito Fleet' of numerous small ships along the lines of the French nineteenth-century *Jeune École* concept proved largely ineffective in the opening stages of the Russo-Ukraine War. *(President of Ukraine)*

the Russian Federation Navy's (RFN's) Black Sea Fleet freedom of movement whilst simultaneously keeping the Black Sea sufficiently clear to allow grain shipments. The RFN's Black Sea Fleet can still fire long-range missiles but it has become vulnerable, even in port. Ukrainian officials claim that they have sunk or disabled a third of Russian warships operating in the Black Sea since the conflict began. Approximately twenty-seven Russian vessels have been reported as damaged or sunk; the heaviest losses incurred by the Black Sea Fleet since the Second World War.

These outcomes were accomplished over several months, rather than in one decisive engagement. They may not be critical in the ultimate outcome of the war. But, for now, Ukraine can keep the Russian Navy from using much of the Black Sea and has preserved its own ability to use it for some purposes. What can we learn from these outcomes?

A photograph of the Russian Project 1164 cruiser *Moskva* taken in Sevastapol Bay during happier times in July 2012. The cruiser's loss to surface-to-surface missiles in April 2022 appears to have shown malpractice, poor training and complacency rather than providing any significant insights into the future of naval warfare. *(George Chernilevsky)*

EXAMINING THE LESSONS LEARNED

As we examine lessons learned from the Ukraine conflict, it should be noted that some are sufficiently obvious that they should actually have been learned long ago. For example, in a confined space, a ship failing to set an adequate defensive posture and failing to impose control over its various emissions is virtually certain to be detected, engaged and sunk. The RFN cruiser *Moskva* found this to her cost in April 2022. The *Moskva* episode appears to have shown malpractice, poor training and complacency rather than providing a source of particular insight about naval warfare. 'Don't be dumb' qualifies as good advice, but not necessarily as advice significant to the future of naval warfare.

However, there may be some lessons that prove useful as navies contemplate operations in confined waterways. The Black Sea is home to several major ports, and both Ukraine and Russia have historically used these ports extensively. Ukraine might depend more on Black Sea ports than Russia, but both have an interest in ensuring relative freedom of navigation. The challenges to maintaining freedom of navigation are also present in other chokepoints of relevance to the world. The Black Sea is unique in many ways, but the Black Sea's distances and targeting opportunities are similar to those in the Red Sea, the Arabian Gulf, and indeed, in some scenarios, to the Chinese littoral. The Ukraine-Russia conflict might show how interactions between forces in multiple domains affect the ability to secure critical areas for ocean shipping.

Additionally, Ukraine – without a navy – has used a variety of weapons and tactics that have made the Russian Navy's Black Sea Fleet largely ineffective. It has at the same time been largely able to keep some critical commerce flowing. Unmanned systems have made manned ships – some very capable – highly vulnerable. Some of this effectiveness may be unique to the particular characteristics of this conflict. Some may have more general application.

In order to explore these potential lessons learned, this chapter divides them into three broad categories, viz.:

- Maritime strategy.
- Maritime operational employment.
- Weapons systems and tactics.

This is not to imply that the categories are, in reality, readily separable. Lessons in one area are likely to be related to others.

MARITIME STRATEGY

As previously stated, the Russo-Ukranian War is predominantly a land battle. However, the naval portions of the battle have had a strategic effect. Nations require resources to wage war, and navies have historically been used to wage economic warfare, even in conflicts where the centre of gravity is considered to be ground-based.

A significant portion of Ukraine's national income comes from grain exports. Ukraine has historically exported most of its grain – up to 90 percent – for the world market through Black Sea ports.[2] Absent sea-based export through the Black Sea, Ukraine would be forced to rely on land-based transportation. This has nothing like the capacity of ships and requires cooperation with Poland and other neighbours. Given the ongoing political tensions with Poland over land-based transportation, this would be suboptimal. Inability to export grain through Black Sea ports could consequently have a serious impact on Ukraine's ability to support a war.

Russia has also used the Black Sea for a portion of its grain and other raw material exports, including liquid natural gas. Ukraine has periodically interdicted ships carrying such cargo but, for the most part, the flow continues unimpeded. Ukraine has largely succeeded in preventing interference with its

The patrol vessel *Sloviansk* – formerly the US Coast Guard 'Island' class cutter *Cushing* (WPB-1321) – seen off the port city of Odessa before the outbreak of the Russo-Ukrainian War. *Sloviansk* was sunk by a Russian air-to-surface missile in March 2022 but maritime traffic has continued to flow relatively freely from Odessa and other western Ukrainian ports. *(President of Ukraine)*

A US Coast Guard detachment based on the cruiser *Antietam* (CG-54) seen boarding a foreign fishing vessel during maritime security operations in the Pacific. The Russian Federation Navy's apparent inability to conduct similar operations to impose an effective blockade on Ukraine's maritime traffic has highlighted a major strategic weakness. *(US Navy)*

merchant traffic, but it has not elected to attempt to keep Russian commerce from flowing.

Nations also need international support – or at least acquiescence – to continue fighting. Dramatically increased prices for grain might have resulted in international pressure to end the conflict. Russia's initial calculation appears to have been that potential grain shortages would drive the global south toward Russia as a supplier of grain and toward a demand that Ukraine come to a rapid settlement. The continuity of Ukrainian grain exports has therefore precluded this as a path to victory.

Thus, the most significant strategic outcome to date with respect to the maritime domain may be that Ukrainian grain has largely continued to flow through the Black Sea. From July 2022 to July 2023, this was due to agreement to allow such shipments for humanitarian purposes. More recently, however, shipments have been maintained because Russia has not achieved sufficient maritime dominance to stop the flow in a manner that does not cause it to suffer at least equivalent damage. While Mykolaiv, Kherson and Mariupol remain closed or captured, maritime traffic is flowing relatively freely from Odessa, Chornomorsk and Pivdennyi.

The simple ability to sink merchant shipping is not necessarily an effective means of imposing a blockade. An effective blockade should include the option of querying, boarding and diverting shipping. This, in turn, requires a persistent presence of surface combatants. Previous Russian blockade operations against Georgia in 2008 indicate an ongoing deficiency in this regard. While the Black Sea Fleet was able to seal Georgian ports, it could only do so by sinking Georgian shipping, such as the coast guard cutter *Georgy Toreli*. Either by preference or necessity, the Russian blockade was dependent on the relatively crude methods of sinking and firing warning shots. In many cases, the weaknesses that have been exploited by Ukrainian forces were already evident in Russian operations against Georgia.

Moreover, Ukraine has succeeded in making the

Black Sea sufficiently hazardous to the Russian Navy that Russia has avoided carrying out operations that would place blockading forces at risk. Heavy losses of Russian ships have compelled the fleet to refrain from most offensive operations, falling back to its ports. The construction of a new port in Abkhazia in response to these losses has added new tensions to the Georgian-Russian relationship, suggesting potential larger implications of the navy's tactical shortcomings. Ukraine's ability to hold the blockade force at risk means that – for all intents and purposes – Russia cannot impose a blockade.

Russia still has the ability to fire missiles at merchant ships, as does Ukraine. Such an exchange would likely devolve into both sides simply trading merchant-ship losses. Sinking ships filled with grain or liquid natural gas carries consequences that stopping and diverting them would not. For example, international shipping is usually manned by third-party nationals from states such as India. The deaths of these nationals to Russian action could strain ties already facing challenges. Similarly, the tendency in global shipping toward flags of convenience means that most Ukraine-bound shipping will not be flagged as Ukrainian. The *Kuroglu-3*, for example, which was sunk by Russian forces in the port of Kherson in February 2024, was a Turkish-flagged and owned vessel. Turkey and Greece currently own 34 of the 100 vessels trapped in port by Russian action. While the Turkish government and the *Kuroglu-3*'s owners (the Istanbul-based Kuruoglu Denizcilik transport service) have not publicly criticised Moscow for the sinking, the door to such criticism was opened in a way that it would not have been if the vessel had simply been diverted or confiscated.

Additionally, the environmental damage caused by indiscriminate sinking – as well as the imagery of something akin to Second World War U-Boat warfare – could further galvanise global opinion against Russia in a way that diversion or confiscation would not. For example, the potential threat to Black Sea fisheries through the destruction of LNG-carrying vessels could strain Russian relations with Black Sea states such as Romania, Bulgaria, Moldova and Turkey. While relations are generally already poor with these states owing to their NATO membership (or links with NATO, in the case of neutral Moldova), it would be a questionable choice for Russia to antagonise them directly through collateral damage.

Russia's Project 11356R *Admiral Grigorovich* class frigate *Admiral Essen* – pictured here at Saint Petersburg in August 2016 soon after completion – is one of the Black Sea Fleet's major surface combatants. Although ships like *Admiral Essen* have provided the Russian Navy with an ability to conduct kinetic strikes, the fleet's overall lack of versatility has hindered its capacity to undertake blockade operations. More broadly, missions of littoral sea control generally do not favour easily-targeted large combatants. *(Conrad Waters)*

As a more general matter, the vast majority of the world's commerce – around 90 percent – moves by surface ship. To the extent that trade is important to a nation, the ability to maintain that trade is a national interest. In nearly any war we might contemplate among major powers, the ability to send and receive cargo by sea will be an important part of the protagonists' supply chains. However, any navy hoping to interdict or secure supply chains will contend with vulnerability from shore-based systems.

So, in summary, while sinking enemy shipping is important to a navy, the versatility to deny access to shipping without sinking it is also a significant capability. The Russian Navy currently appears not to possess this capacity, or has been denied it by Ukraine's ability to target its combatant ships. As a result, it put itself in a position of either starting a campaign of mutual destruction or ceding to Ukraine the ability to move critical cargo. It has up to now opted to allow Ukraine to continue shipping its agricultural products. The strategic lessons that can be said to have been learned from this are:

- It is important not merely to have a navy but to have a navy that can perform missions besides kinetic strikes. The Russian Black Sea Fleet is hampered in its attempt to conduct blockade operations by a lack of versatility. This may reflect larger training and doctrinal deficiencies within the Russian Navy. For example, there may be an overemphasis on the destruction of enemy ships as the key to victory, without sufficient attention paid to other aspects of naval warfare.
- Maritime dominance depends on the ability to at least neutralise littoral areas or, absent that, be composed of ships and other craft that complicate detection and multiply targeting problems. The requirements for ship protection will be assessed in more detail in the operational and tactical sections below. However, the strategic point is that missions of littoral sea control generally do not favour easily targeted large combatants.

MARITIME OPERATIONS

As noted above, Russia lost a strategic opportunity in being unable to stop Ukraine from exporting grain. Stopping these exports would have created tremendous economic pressure on Ukraine. Russia could not stop that flow. Although that failure has not directly hampered Russia's war effort, Russia's failure to decisively stop the flow may have prolonged Ukraine's ability to continue the war. The question is which operational factors contributed to this strategic missed opportunity.

From a joint combat operations standpoint, neither side has made extensive use of the Black Sea for military resupply. Ukraine's military resupply is coming over land through Europe, Russia's largely from within its own territory. The ability or inability to move commercial cargo is strategically critical. But, lack of maritime dominance does not appear to have directly impacted either side's ability to carry out military operations. If sea-based military resupply were essential for military operations, Ukraine's military situation, in particular, might have been dire from the outset of the conflict.

However, as already discussed, maritime operations have had a strategic effect, and there are undoubtedly factors relating to operational employment that contributed to these outcomes. The Black Sea is a confined waterway. Submarines can operate in this environment, but the water-space is crowded and in places strewn with mines and obstacles, making submarine operations challenging.[3] Submarines, moreover, do little in this environment except provide one more way to sink commercial shipping. Russian submarines could do little to mitigate Ukrainian ability to threaten Russian surface ships and could not add to Russia's ability to conduct surface operations, of the kind needed to have a strategic effect. Surface combatant ships, which could conceivably offer strategically-relevant options, face their own limitations. A ship on the surface in the Black Sea must contend with the strong possibility of detection and tracking by shore-based sensors. Any surface ship in the Black Sea is also within range of numerous land-based weapons systems, including missiles, aircraft, unmanned aerial vehicles and unmanned surface systems. As noted earlier, the RFN has lost numerous combatants and auxiliary support ships to Ukrainian missile and drone attacks. Many of these ships were pier-side or in dry dock. An obvious lesson learned is that being immobile in the face of an enemy with weapons that can reach most of the target area invites an attack.

The Project 636.3 'Kilo' class submarine *Krasnodar* was one of six of the type ordered to rejuvenate the Russian Black Sea Fleet's underwater capabilities. Although – like the *Admiral Grigorovich* frigates – Russian submarines have been involved in targeting Ukrainian infrastructure with Kalibr cruise missiles, they have been able to do little to mitigate Ukrainian ability to threaten Russian surface ships. Moreover, they cannot add to Russia's ability to conduct surface operations of the kind needed to have a strategic effect. *(Conrad Waters)*

Even assuming that the RFN's Black Sea Fleet could have sortied most of its force out of port, there would still be limitations on what its surface-ship combatants could realistically do once underway. Operations involving a large concentration of surface ships – such as amphibious landings – would be hazardous to the point of foolhardiness. Probably as a result, Russia has made little effort to seize territory with amphibious forces. This would suggest some degree of lessons learned, as the Black Sea Fleet was able to effectively put three battalion tactical groups of the 7th Airborne Division ashore during the 2008 Georgian War. The decision to not attempt to duplicate the relative success of the Abkhazia landings suggests a possible awareness on the part of Russian policymakers of the risks involved.

Operational restrictions extend beyond challenges with large multi-ship operations. As we have already discussed, an effective Russian blockade of Ukrainian ports could have had a major strategic impact. The RFN did for a while attempt to impose a blockade. However, a blockade that does more than simply sink merchant shipping requires the blockade force to be in particular places for extended periods. Blockading ships must be able to query, stop, board, search and potentially divert shipping. This means that the movement and locations of the blockading ships will be impossible to conceal.

For example, if a ship were attempting to carry out visit, board, search and seizure (VBSS) in support of a blockade, it would hail the merchant vessel, order the vessel to lie to, send a boarding team and provide protection for the boarding team during the boarding and search. For an hour or more, the location of the blockading ship will be precisely known. Although it is unlikely that an adversary would attack the blockade ship while it is actually carrying out VBSS in close proximity to a merchant vessel, in the period it approaches the target and the period after it completes the operation, the ship will be precisely located and highly vulnerable. Blockade thus becomes something that can only be attempted under an extensive defensive umbrella. One set of ships would provide air defence; another would carry out actual stopping and diversion of merchants. Although a formation of large numbers of ships is vulnerable, so too is a single ship trying to carry out multiple missions in a confined area.

In short, the operational lessons to be taken from the RFN's ineffectiveness include:

- Immobility is a sure way of being detected and engaged. Ships sitting pier-side are remarkably easy to detect and difficult to defend. If a conflict is imminent, getting ships out of port is critical.
- Once ships are underway, their movements cannot be so predictable nor their signatures so obvious that finding them requires little to no effort. As previously noted, *Moskva* was operating in a manner that made tracking it trivially easy. Like many Russian actions in the early stages of the war, it showed a neglect of basic best practices that implied extreme complacency.
- In a confined water-space, disrupting detection and targeting continuously might not be possible. Indeed, some missions (such as VBSS) require that a ship's location be known. In such cases, multiple ships may be required, one to perform the mission and possibly several to provide active defence.
- However, active defence can only go so far. The defenders are themselves vulnerable, particularly if the adversary can use a variety of different weapons and tactics. Operational concepts should emphasise disciplined electronic emissions control and unpredictable movement. Reliance should be placed on active defence only in cases where avoiding detection is impossible.

WEAPONS, COMBAT SYSTEMS AND TACTICS

The final set of lessons learned addresses the instruments each nation has used to carry out the Black Sea campaign. Ukraine has no navy of note; Russia has the overwhelming advantage in conventional force tonnage ratios. Ukraine has, however, used a variety of different systems and tactics to overcome this disparity and render the Russian Navy ineffective.

Before considering these systems more fully, we should recognise that geography can have a major impact on the relative value of conventional naval platforms. Nelson's maxim that 'A ship's a fool that fights a fort' conveys that land-based systems have some inherent advantages over naval systems in terms of vulnerability, ease of defence and ease of resupply. The RFN Black Sea Fleet has been attempting to operate in conditions where it faced hundreds of land-based weapons and multiple means for detection and tracking. Any navy would be challenged to operate in such conditions.

However, Ukraine has developed innovations that multiply the ways that ships may be attacked and thus must be considered as navies contemplate operations in confined areas. Some of these are theatre and geography-specific, but many have broader applications, especially when combined with already used capabilities. These include:

The Russian Federation Navy has lost numerous combatants and auxiliary support ships to Ukrainian missile and drone attacks, many alongside or in dry dock. These include the Project 22800 'Karakurt' class corvette *Askold*, which was targeted by MBDA SCALP/Storm Shadow cruise missiles whilst completing at the Zaliv shipyard in Kerch on 4 November 2023. These photographs show the corvette under construction and the extensive damage caused by the missile strike. *(President of the Russian Federation – kremlin.ru – under CC BY 4.0/Ukraine Ministry of Defence)*

Amphibious operations have not been a major feature of the Russo-Ukrainian War, possibly because operations in littoral conditions potentially face hundreds of land-based weapons and multiple means for detection and tracking. Ukraine has, however, targeted numerous Russian amphibious and logistic support vessels, particularly in pier-side attacks. One early casualty was the Project 1171 'Tapir' class landing ship *Saratov* – seen here off Istanbul in 2016 – that was destroyed in the captured Ukrainian port of Berdiansk in March 2022. *(Devrim Yaylali)*

- Using small unmanned aerial vehicles (UAVs) to provide near-constant surveillance over some areas. Readily-available commercial UAVs can carry sophisticated optical sensors and locating devices that can provide real-time information on the location and identity of maritime targets. Individual UAVs may be limited in range and endurance, and may thus be of less value in wide areas, but in the Black Sea, they can, with only general cueing from other sensors, maintain a near-continuous track over some targets. They are, moreover, difficult to shoot down and inexpensive to replace. Such UAVs can also be equipped with explosives that turn them from surveillance assets into weapons. They might not be able to hold a large enough explosive charge to sink a ship, but they certainly can damage topside radio antennas and radars.[4]
- Anti-ship cruise missiles (ASCMs) are not new, but Ukraine has engineered its own ASCMs and used them to effect in conjunction with UAVs. These provide a warhead big enough to significantly damage a ship, to the point of sinking it. The tactic is to use enough attack systems that the target ship defence systems become overwhelmed, both in available numbers of interceptors and in the ability of battle management systems to accurately present a picture.
- Ukraine has also used unmanned surface vehicles (USVs) to attack both ships in port. USVs can be very difficult to detect and if directed against a stationary target, such as a moored ship, they can be stopped only by obstacles such as nets or by gunfire once they are detected. They are hampered by range and, if not largely autonomous, by spotty connectivity for vessels operating very near to the surface of the water. If wholly autonomous, they will go to where they are directed. They will, however, not be responsive to changes in the tactical situation, such as the target ship moving.[5]
- USVs have also been used against ships underway, to significant effect. If a USV is receiving updated location information – which it receives passively with no requirement for it to transmit – it can locate and then apply logic similar to what is already applied in torpedoes to track and engage surface ships. The target ship, conversely, may have difficulty locating and then engaging the USV. The ship will have a speed advantage, but if several USVs are being used, running away from one might result in running into another's path. USVs have range and speed limitations, but in a confined area such as the Black Sea, these kinds of weapons may be uniquely valuable.

Ukraine has engineered its own anti-ship cruise missiles and used them to effect in conjunction with UAVs. This is a prototype missile launching unit for the R-360 'Neptune' missile, which is widely credited with sinking the cruiser *Moskva*. There are six launch units, each equipped with four missiles, along with a command vehicle and additional missile transporting vehicles in a typical Neptune missile battery. *(Ministry of Defence of Ukraine)*

A general point about weapons and tactics is that the Black Sea environment inherently favours land-based systems, but the strategic imperative is to assert sea-based dominance. Countering inexpensive land-based systems requires different defensive systems, different operational concepts and possibly different platforms. The Black Sea maritime campaign is providing some very clear signals on what's needed for a future navy.

CONCLUSIONS

Despite a pronounced material advantage, the Russian Navy has, to date, failed to secure a victory in the Black Sea. Not only has the Russian Black Sea Fleet suffered losses of expensive-to-replace ships, but it has also become strategically impotent. It is largely stuck in port, a fixed asset requiring protection rather than an effective offensive capability. If its ships attempt to get underway, they are readily tracked and readily engaged by Ukrainian land-based assets. It retains the ability to sink civilian ships by firing missiles – some from ships, some from ashore – but overall the Black Sea Fleet lacks the ability to interdict civilian shipping without sinking it.

This impotence has not cost Russia the war but it probably did give Ukraine a reprieve from what could have been a serious vulnerability. Ukraine was able to generate revenue to fight another day. It was able to do this by exploiting geography and short-range but accurate unmanned systems. The only way the Russian Navy could have made itself operationally relevant would have been by attacking Ukrainian sensors and weapons delivery platforms, which was, and remains, a major challenge for targeting and weapons systems capabilities.

The war is still ongoing and its outcome is uncertain. There are, however, some clear lessons for warfare in contested littoral areas, which will likely

The use of small UAVs and USVs for surveillance, targeting and strike purposes have become a defining feature of maritime operations in the Russo-Ukranian War. Their utility reflects the proliferation of such systems in navies across the world; the photographs show a L3 Harris Arabian Fox MAST-13 unmanned surface vessel and VBAT vertical take-off and landing unmanned aerial vehicle during US Navy operations. *(US Navy)*

apply in any war. While some of these lessons – most notably the sinking of the *Moskva* – are reflective of specific Russian deficiencies, many of them may be of more general relevance to future Great Power conflicts. In summary:

- As long as the majority of world commerce moves on the ocean, sea lanes are going to be points of conflict.
- The simple ability to sink commercial shipping is not enough for a nation to stop commerce effectively. The need for versatility in training and doctrine that allows navies to use a range of options aside from lethal force in interdicting and/or diverting civilian shipping is relevant in any conflict in which control of civilian trade is a strategic imperative.
- The capacity to carry out sea control at levels other than the simple ability to sink ships needs both a force structure that is able to operate in a high-threat environment; both by evading targeting in most circumstances and by having active force protection in cases where detection is inevitable.
- Unmanned systems able to operate in large numbers from land bases can give a nation without a navy a decisive advantage over forces trying to operate at sea. The capability and operational concept challenges involved in countering these systems are paramount. To date, the Russian Navy has come nowhere near solving them.

Some of the lessons seen in the Black Sea have surfaced elsewhere, but with different outcomes. US Navy surface combatants in the Red Sea have, in fact, done a credible job minimising threats from shore-based systems. However, even with this success, the threat of attack has still resulted in a change to shipping patterns. Discussions of the possible disruption of shipping into Taiwan or into the People's Republic of China (PRC) recognise that the volume of shipping is so high and the economic interdependence so intense that the mere threat to sink shipping is almost an empty threat. Overall, however, the lessons from the Black Sea conflict are rather clear. From the perspective of the United States and its allies, the message of needing a versatile fleet could not be clearer.

Notes

1. The *Jeune École* ('Young School') concept was essentially an asymmetric warfare strategy developed by French naval strategists to counter the dominance of the British Royal Navy. It advocated the use of, inter alia, torpedo-armed vessels and commerce raiders to counter the strength of the British battlefleet and disrupt the Empire's commerce. The 'Mosquito Fleet' updated this idea in the context of Russia's domination of the northern part of the Black Sea. There are, however, some questions as to Ukraine's commitment to the Mosquito Fleet before the outbreak of the current war. For example, see Ihor Kabanenko, 'Ukraine's New Naval Doctrine: A Revision of the Mosquito Fleet Strategy or Bureaucratic Inconsistency?' posted to the *Jamestown Foundation's* site – jamestown.org – on 25 May 2021.

2. See the US Department of Agriculture's Foreign Agricultural Service Factsheet, Ukraine Agricultural Production and Trade: April 2022 available by searching the department's website at: fas.usda.gov.

3. Analysis of the nature of Russian submarine potential in the Black Sea and the best way of countering it was provided by Sidharth Kaushal and Kevin Rowlands in an article, 'Tackling the Underwater Threat: How Ukraine Can Combat Russian Submarines' posted to the *RUSI* website – rusi.org on 7 March 2023.

4. An interesting assessment of the wider course of drone warfare in the Russo-Ukrainian conflict was produced by Kristen D Thompson in 'How the Drone War in Ukraine Is Transforming Conflict' posted to the *Council on Foreign Relations* site – cfr.org – on 16 January 2024.

5. One of the most prominent Ukrainian USVs is the 'Magura V5' sea drone, which is claimed to have sunk a number of Russian warships. Further detail of the USV was provided by Barry Hatton in, 'Meet Ukraine's small but lethal weapon lifting morale: Unmanned sea drones packed with explosives' posted to AP News – apnews.com – on 5 March 2024.

2.1 REGIONAL REVIEW

Author:
Conrad Waters

NORTH AND SOUTH AMERICA

On 11 March 2024, the United States' Biden Administration published its FY2025 Presidential Defense Budget Request. If implemented by Congress, core Department of Defense spending will amount to US$849.8bn. This increases to US$895.2bn once other defence-related activities are included. Both these figures represent cash increases of around one percent, reflecting the constraints of the budget caps contained in the bipartisan Fiscal Responsibility Act (FRA) of 2023.[1] Whilst substantial figures, these numbers actually represent a reduction in defence spending when inflation is taken into account; an outcome that is seemingly at odds with the deteriorating international backdrop that the United States finds itself facing. Inevitably, this has resulted in very difficult decisions as to what elements of defence spending to prioritise.[2]

The US Department of the Navy budget request for FY2025 amounts to US$257.6bn, which is barely changed in cash terms from the previous year's US$255.8bn. Within this figure, operational readiness and personnel compensation have been accorded the highest priority. There has also been continued heavy investment in modernising shipyard infrastructure, including expanding the resilience of the stretched submarine industrial base. This has meant a real terms (i.e. adjusted for inflation) reduction in the money available for areas such as research and investment and warship procurement; the latter being reflected in a fall in planned purchases to just six battle force ships. This is the lowest figure since FY2008. Whilst procurement is anticipated to ramp up substantially in subsequent years of the Future Years Defense Program (FYDP), this seems likely to be contingent on a more favourable budgetary environment. In any event, long-standing plans to increase the US Navy's total size continue to be shifted to the right.

Although budgetary constraints are part of the picture, it has become evident that underperformance in the US shipbuilding sector is another big problem. In January 2024, Secretary of the Navy Carlos Del Toro directed a 45-day review of navy shipbuilding, '... to provide an assessment of national and local causes of shipbuilding challenges, as well as recommended actions for achieving a healthier US shipbuilding industrial base'. The results, revealed at the start of April, were far from encouraging. They revealed significant delays across a number of shipbuilding programmes being carried out across various yards. More specifically:

- Delivery of the lead *District of Columbia* (SSBN-826) strategic submarine was running 12–16 months behind schedule.
- Block IV *Virginia* (SSN-774) class attack submarine completion was delayed by about 36 months.
- Block V *Virginia* (SSN-774) class construction was around 24 months later than planned.
- The third *Ford* (CVN-78) class carrier *Enterprise* (CVN-80) was 18 to 26 months behind schedule.
- The lead *Constellation* (FFG-62) class frigate was expected to be about 36 months late.

Deliveries of the latest *Arleigh Burke* (DDG-51) class destroyer iterations, various amphibious ships and the *John Lewis* (T-AO-205) class oilers were also delayed, albeit being stable and aligning with current programme estimates. All-in-all, however, it has been suggested that, 'Projected delays of these lengths extending across this number of Navy shipbuilding programs at the same time amount to an unusual and arguably extraordinary situation in the post-World War II history of the Navy'.[3]

The reasons for the situation are multifaceted. Workforce and associated supply-chain challenges have constrained production at many yards and have been regarded as a problem for some time. This is reflected in the investment in shipbuilding infrastructure that has already been noted. However, the 45-day review revealed new areas of concern, not least limitations in the available number of warship designers. It is also important to note that some of the problems are of the US Navy's own making, with the case of the new *Constellation* class being a particularly egregious example. The programme started out with the aim of being a low-risk adaptation of the Italian variant of the FREMM frigate. However, an irresistible urge to adopt increasing numbers of US Navy-specific design changes meant that, as of late 2023, the final design was far from mature despite construction having already been underway for 16 months. The result is a predictable contribution to the delay referenced above, as well as unwelcome unplanned weight growth of more than 10 percent. A number of initiatives are now underway to address shipbuilding performance. It seems vital that they are successful if the US Navy is to rebuild its force structure towards its long-term goals.[4]

A photograph of the christening ceremony for the Flight IIA *Arleigh Burke* class destroyer *Harvey C. Barnum Jr.* (DDG-124) held at General Dynamics Bath Iron Works on 29 July 2023. Whilst past delays to US Navy destroyer construction are now broadly regarded as being under control, the overall performance of US shipbuilding is giving cause for concern. *(General Dynamics Bath Iron Works)*

Table 2.1.1: FLEET STRENGTHS IN THE AMERICAS – LARGER NAVIES (MID 2024)

COUNTRY	ARGENTINA	BRAZIL	CANADA	CHILE	COLOMBIA	ECUADOR	PERU	USA
Aircraft Carrier (CVN/CV)	–	–	–	–	–	–	–	11
Strategic Missile Submarine (SSBN)	–	–	–	–	–	–	–	14
Attack Submarine (SSN/SSGN)	–	–	–	–	–	–	–	54
Patrol Submarine (SSK)	–[1]	4	4	4	4	2	6	–
Fleet Escort (CG/DDG/FFG)	3	6	12	8	4	2	6	88[2]
Patrol Escort/Corvette (FFG/FSG/FS)	9	2	–	–	2	6	2	24
Missile Armed Attack Craft (PGG/PTG)	2	–	–	3	–	3	5	–
Mine Countermeasures Vessel (MCMV)	–	3	12	–	–	–	–	8
Major Amphibious Units (LHD/LPD/LPH/LSD)	–	2	–	1	–	–	1	32

Note:

1. Argentina's two remaining submarines are non-operational and unlikely to be returned to service. A number of other vessels are of uncertain operational status.
2. Includes one *Zumwalt* class destroyer that is not fully operational.

MAJOR NORTH AMERICAN NAVIES – CANADA

The Canadian government issued the results of its new defence policy review, *Our North, Strong and Free*, on 8 April 2024.[5] Building on the previous 2017 policy document *Strong, Secure, Engaged*, the review placed particular emphasis on bolstering the protection of Canada's sovereignty and broader interests in the Arctic. A rather modest additional increase of C$8.1bn (c. US$6bn) will be made to an already rising defence budget over the next five years, taking military spending to 1.76 percent of GDP by 2029–30. This remains short of the NATO target of two percent. The additional amount pledged over the next two decades is a more substantial C$73bn (c. US$55bn) but the back-loaded nature of the spending plan means that this is inevitably subject to more uncertainty. Sensibly, there is a focus on recruitment and retention in an attempt to rebuild regular and reserve numbers back to authorised levels.

Looking at future procurement, the defence review seemingly protects existing naval investment plans such as the new Canadian Surface Combatants (CSCs) whilst promising new capabilities such as an improved underwater surveillance capability. Further life extensions will be performed on *Halifax* class frigates and the interim at-sea replenishment capability provided by MV *Asterix* preserved. However, many potentially expensive future programmes appear to be categorised as unfunded options that will be subject to further exploration. From a Royal Canadian Navy perspective, the most important of these is the renewal and expansion of the submarine flotilla to provide a persistent deterrent for all three coasts. Whilst it seems that these will be under-ice capable, conventionally-powered boats, the possibility of acquiring nuclear-powered submarines cannot be entirely discounted given the inherent advantages of this type.

In the more immediate term, construction of the CSCs – derived from the British Type 26 frigate/Global Combat Ship – finally got underway at Irving Shipbuilding's Halifax yard on 28 June 2024 with the start of work on a production test module. This approach is similar to that previously adopted for production of the Royal Australian Navy's own Type 26-derived *Hunter* class frigates. The aim is that the initial module will be followed by the commencement of full rate production in 2025. The new ships will be classified as destroyers in Royal Canadian Navy service and be known as the 'River' class. The names of the initial batch of three will be *Fraser*, *Saint-Laurent* and *Mackenzie*. The project is currently estimated to cost as much as C$56bn to C$60bn (c. US$41bn to US$45bn) for a full 15-ship programme but independent estimates are higher. Essentially combining the Type 26 ship platform with a combat system that includes Lockheed Martin's Aegis combat management system and next generation AN/SPY-7 radar, the 'River' class will be more powerfully-equipped cousins to their British counterparts with a full load displacement in excess of 8,000 tonnes.

Irving Shipbuilding has been working on

An updated computer-generated graphic of the Canadian Future Surface Combatant, now known as the 'River' class destroyer. The design has undergone several changes in configuration since previous graphics were released, including deletion of the proposed CAMM surface-to-air missile system. *(Royal Canadian Navy)*

Table 2.1.2: CANADIAN NAVY: PRINCIPAL UNITS AS AT MID 2024

TYPE	CLASS	NUMBER	TONNAGE	DIMENSIONS	PROPULSION	CREW	DATE
Principal Surface Escorts							
Frigate – FFG	**HALIFAX**	12	4,800 tonnes	134m x 16m x 5m	CODOG, 29 knots	225	1992
Submarines							
Submarine – SSK	**VICTORIA** (UPHOLDER)	4	2,500 tonnes	70m x 8m x 6m	Diesel-electric, 20+ knots	50	1990

completing the previous *Harry de Wolf* class Arctic and Offshore Patrol Ship (AOPS) programme pending the start of 'River' class construction. The last year has seen the formal commissioning of the third and fourth vessels *Max Bernays* and *William Hall* on, respectively, 3 May and 16 May 2024. A fifth ship, *Frédérick Rolette*, was launched on 9 December 2023 whilst the keel of the sixth and final Royal Canadian Navy vessel, *Robert Hampton Gray*, was laid on 21 August 2023. Two variants of the class are also being built for the Canadian Coast Guard, with first steel cutting for the final vessel of the series taking place on the same day as work on the 'River' class test module commenced. It has been reported that the total cost of these final two ships has grown as much as C$2.1bn (c. US$1.5bn) amid ongoing criticism of the high expense associated with the implementation of Canada's National Shipbuilding Strategy (NSS).[6] Certainly, the reported amount does not bode well for future CSC costs. Meanwhile, the AOPS class is being increasingly widely deployed after initial crewing problems seem to have been addressed.

The west coast counterpart of AOPS and CSC construction under the NSS is the programme to complete two *Protecteur* class joint support ships at Seaspan's Vancouver Shipyard. The project – based on the German Navy's Type 702 *Berlin* class combat support ship – has been the subject of ongoing delays and cost increases. As of mid 2024, the launch of the lead ship was anticipated before the end of 2024. However, it seems questionable whether the already-postponed delivery date of 2025 will still be met. Seaspan point out that reinvigorating Canadian shipbuilding capacity after a long period of neglect has involved many challenges, not least the need to re-establish an indigenous supply chain. They argue that progress will be reflected in improved construction times for the second vessel – laid down in October 2023 – and other shipbuilding programmes.

A summary of existing Royal Canadian Navy strength is provided in Table 2.1.2.

MAJOR NORTH AMERICAN NAVIES – UNITED STATES

The US Navy retained 298 warships in its front-line 'battle force' as of mid-2024; a figure that was unchanged year-on-year. In broad terms, continued withdrawals of *Ticonderoga* (CG-47) class cruisers and older Littoral Combat Ships were counterbalanced by incremental growth in other battle force

The new Royal Canadian Navy Arctic and Offshore Patrol Ship *Margaret Brooke* pictured in somewhat sunnier climes than her primary intended theatre of operation during the course of the Operation CARIBBE deployment to the Caribbean in February 2024. Ships of the class are being more actively used as previous crewing problems have eased. *(Combat Camera Canada)*

Ships from the *Gerald R. Ford* (CVN-78) Carrier Strike Group and the *Bataan* (LHD-5) Amphibious Ready Group, together with the Hellenic Navy frigate *Navarinon*, sail in formation in the Mediterranean Sea on the last day of December 2023. The last year has brought greater clarity with respect to the US Navy's future force structure plans but the path to achieving them remains unclear against a backdrop of stagnating fleet numbers. *(US Navy)*

categories. Congressional action that prevented the premature retirement of additional Littoral Combat Ships and dock landing ships during FY 2024 meant that the fleet was a little larger than would otherwise have been the case. As further described below, the navy has now been persuaded to retain more Littoral Combat Ships in service than was previously planned. If this decision is maintained, fleet numbers will be somewhat higher in the early 2030s than once envisaged.

Publication of the navy's annual long-range plan for naval construction in March 2024 provided details of the eagerly-anticipated Battle Force Ship Assessment and Requirement Report (BFSAR).[7] This had been finalised in June 2023 and sets out the US Navy's targeted fleet structure in the new era of Distributed Maritime Operations (DMO). Table 2.1.3 compares this structure to previous US Navy plans, as well as current fleet composition. In overall terms, the 2023 BFSAR continues the direction of travel revealed in previous iterations. It sets out a broadly unchanged vision for the composition of the manned element of the fleet, albeit with a modest rebalancing from large to small surface combatants. However, the most noteworthy feature of the latest plan was a large increase in the number of uncrewed vehicles, both above and underneath the waves. Although the report was caveated with the warning that additional analysis would be required to determine future uncrewed vehicle inventory objectives, it is clear that such assets are playing a steadily increasing part in future US Navy operational concepts.

It is worth noting that, to date, the Biden Administration has not explicitly endorsed the goal set out in the latest BSFAR, nor any of the other force structure objectives. Moreover, given that the US Navy has been attempting to grow the fleet for a decade or more with very mixed success, it is hard not to view potential attainment of the current target with anything but a degree of scepticism. Indeed, the long-range shipbuilding plan itself acknowledges that achievement of the objective, 'assumes industry eliminates excess construction backlogs and produces future ships on time and within budget' and requires 'additional resources beyond the FYDP'. If this rather unlikely scenario is achieved, fleet size – but not exact composition – will reach the BSFAR objective around the early 2040s. An alternative scenario based on stable funding suggests the US Navy will struggle to grow beyond 345 battle force ships in the foreseeable future.

Looking at the shorter-term, planned US Navy procurement is set out in the revised FYDP for FY2025–2029 that is summarised in Table 2.1.4. This envisages the acquisition of a total of fifty-seven warships at a total cost of US$167.6bn over the next five years. Positively this represents an increase over the fifty-five ships costing US$146.4bn previously sought for FY2024–2028, which was itself more than the fifty-one ships for US$132.8bn planned for FY2023–2027. As previously noted, however, the immediate future is less encouraging. Only six ships are requested for the coming, FY2025, year. The most noteworthy decision is the reduction in *Virginia* (SSN-774) class attack submarine acquisition to just one boat. This is a pragmatic choice that reflects the need to reduce short-term pressure on the submarine industrial base to straighten out current delays and sustain an annual drumbeat of one strategic submarine and two attack submarines in the years ahead. Annual procurement of further *Columbia* (SSBN-826) class submarines does not commence until FY2026. However, the US$9.6bn allocated to complete funding of *Wisconsin* (SSBN-827), the second member of the class acquired in last year's budget, and support other elements of the programme, accounts for as much as a third of annual spending on warship construction. Total expenditure on the new strategic submarines will be nearly US$50bn over the five-year life of the FYDP in a further demonstration of the extent to which the project is skewing overall warship investment. The navy has also authorised investment of more than US$7bn to strengthen the submarine construction and maintenance enterprise over the past two years and looks set to spend an additional US$10bn during the FYDP.

Turning to surface ship acquisitions, the FY2025–2029 period sees *Arleigh Burke* (DDG-51) destroyer production maintained at two ships p.a.

Table 2.1.3: US NAVY FLEET STRUCTURE EVOLUTION

PLANNED FLEET STRUCTURE 'BATTLE FORCE' SHIPS	FSA 2016[1] (PRE-DMO)	BFSAR 2022[2] (POST-DMO)	BSFAR 2023[3] (MID 2023)	CURRENT[4] (MID 2024)
Strategic Submarines (SSBNs)	12	12	12	14
Attack Submarines (SSGNs/SSNs)	66	66	66	54
Aircraft Carriers (CVNs)	12	12	12	11
Large Surface Combatants (CGs/DDGs)	104	96	87	87
Small Surface Combatants (FFGs/FFs/MCMVs)	52	56	73	32
Large Amphibious Vessels (LHAs/LHDs/LPDs/LSDs)	38	31	31	32
Small Amphibious Vessels (Medium Landing Ship)	Nil	18	18	0
Auxiliary Vessels	71	82	82	66
Sub Total	**355**	**373**	**381**	**298**
Large Unmanned Surface & Sub-Surface Vessels	Not Stated	45[5]	134[5]	Nil
Total	**355+**	**418**	**515**	**298**

Notes:

1. Numbers based on the Force Structure Assessment (FSA) released in 2016. This was published before the development of the current Distributed Maritime Operations (DMO) concept.
2. Numbers based on the classified Battle Force Ship Assessment and Requirement (BFSAR) submitted to Congress in mid-2022 and summarised in the *Chief of Naval Operations Navigation Plan 2022*. The US Navy would hope to achieve this force design by 2045.
3. Based on details of the revised 2023 Battle Force Ship Assessment and Requirement published in the FY2024 Long-Range Shipbuilding Plan in March 2024.
4. Based on information contained in the Naval Vessels Register as of June 2024
5. Previous, secondary sources suggested a higher number of large uncrewed vessels in the BSFAR 2022. However, US Navy uncrewed vessel requirements are continuously evolving and the higher, c. 150 number previously reported may not provide a like-for-like comparison.

Procurement of *Constellation* class frigates alternates between one and two vessels each year in a so-called 'saw tooth pattern'. It is interesting to note that the cost of the former class has increased quite markedly and now averages over US$2.8bn for each unit. Meanwhile, the amphibious flotilla benefits from the resumption of LPD-17 Flight II amphibious transport dock production after a previous pause whilst force requirements were assessed as part of the BFSAR review process. FY2025 will also see the acquisition of the first LSM type medium landing ship that is intended to boost the ability of the US Marine Corps (USMC) to contribute to the DMO concept. The acquisition of a new, smaller T-AOL next-generation logistics ship – anticipated from FY2026 onwards – is also driven by the demands of the DMO philosophy. It is notable that each of these is now anticipated to cost over US$450m. This is triple the initial estimate.

Table 2.1.5 summarises the major components of current US Navy fleet strength as of mid-2024, with more detailed analysis of recent developments provided under the following category headings.

Aircraft Carriers: Construction of *John F. Kennedy* (CVN-79), the second *Ford* class carrier, is now in its

The *Virginia* class nuclear-powered attack submarine *Massachusetts* (SSN-798) pictured during the course of roll-out from HII Newport News Shipbuilding. The FY2025 Department of the Navy budget request proposes a temporary slowdown in orders for the class to help address a backlog of incomplete construction against a backdrop of severe pressure on the country's submarine industrial base. *(Huntington Ingalls Industries)*

Table 2.1.4: USN FY2025 FIVE-YEAR SHIPBUILDING PLAN (FY2025–FY2020)

SHIP TYPE	FY2024 Request	FY2024 Funded	FY2025 Request[1]	FY2026 Plan[1]	FY2027 Plan[1]	FY2028 Plan[1]	FY2029 Plan[1]	FY2025–29 Total FYDP[1]
Aircraft Carrier (CVN-78)	0	0	0 ($1,908)	0 ($3,188)	0 ($4,151)	0 ($4,643)	0 ($2,744)	**0 ($16,634)**
Strategic Submarine (SSBN-826)	1	1	0 ($9,557)	1 ($10,421)	1 ($10,235)	1 ($10,182)	1 ($9,143)	**4 ($49,538)**
Attack Submarine (SSN-774)	2	2	1 ($7,336)	2 ($9,360)	2 ($8,846)	2 ($8,477)	2 ($8,695)	**9 ($42,714)**
Destroyer (DDG-51)	2	2	2 ($6,451)	2 ($5,069)	2 ($5,219)	2 ($6,257)	2 ($5,394)	**10 ($28,390)**
Frigate (FFG-62)	2	2	1 ($1,170)	2 ($2,153)	1 ($1,173)	2 ($2,295)	1 ($1,146)	**8 ($7,937)**
Amphibious Assault Ship (LHA-6)	0	0	0 ($61)	0 ($500)	1 ($3,710)	0 ($0)	0 ($0)	**1 ($4,271)**
Amphibious Ship (LPD-17 F II)	0	0	1 ($1,562)	0 ($250)	1 ($1,798)	0 ($275)	1 ($1,894)	**3 ($5,779)**
Medium Landing Ship (LSM(X))	0	0	1 ($268)	1 ($200)	2 ($349)	2 ($305)	2 ($311)	**8 ($1,433)**
Replenishment Oiler (T-AO-205)	1	1	0 ($0)	2 ($1,657)	1 ($861)	2 ($1,711)	1 ($929)	**6 ($5,158)**
Light Replenishment Oiler (T-AOL(X))	0	0	0 ($0)	0 ($0)	1 ($453)	1 ($453)	1 ($453)	**3 ($1,359)**
Submarine Tender (AS(X))	1	0	0 ($0)	0 ($0)	1 ($1,113)	0 ($0)	1 ($1,559)	**2 ($2,672)**
Surveillance Ship (T-AGOS-25)	0	0	0 ($0)	1 ($425)	1 ($400)	1 ($436)	1 ($445)	**4 ($1,706)**
Total	**9**	**8**	**6 ($28,313)**	**11 ($33,223)**	**14 ($38,308)**	**13 ($35,034)**	**13 ($32,713)**	**57 ($167,591)**
Projected Battle Force			**287**	**283**	**280**	**286**	**291**	

Notes:

1. Figure in brackets relates to the dollar cost of the period's acquisitions in millions. Funding for some major units, such as aircraft carriers, is spread over the programme's life. This explains why funding is sometimes allocated in years when no procurement of a particular class is proposed.

final stages at the Newport News yard of Huntington Ingalls Industries (HII). She is expected to be delivered in July 2025, replacing *Nimitz* (CVN-68) in the fleet. The previously-noted delay to *Enterprise* (CVN-80) means that she will not now be completed until September 2029 at the earliest. As a result, the navy plans to squeeze an additional deployment out of *Dwight D. Eisenhower* (CVN-69) before she is finally decommissioned, an approach already implemented with respect to *Nimitz* herself. The extended nature of *Enterprise*'s construction risks, in turn, having a knock-on effect on the construction of *Doris Miller* (CVN-81). Accordingly, plans are being developed to start work on her in Newport News' No. 12 Dock before *Enterprise* is launched from the same facility.[8] The navy will have to decide in the next year or so whether to implement a two-carrier block buy contract for the next two vessels of the *Ford* class; the future CVN-82 and CVN-83. A similar arrangement for CVN-80 and CVN-81 is claimed to have saved between US$3bn and US$4bn. The latest shipbuilding plan has pushed the planned acquisition of CVN-82 from FY2028 to FY2030; a decision that could make it harder to maintain sufficient carriers in service several decades down the line.[9]

Surface Combatants: The US Navy's force of large combatants has declined over the past year. This essentially reflects the ongoing withdrawal of *Ticonderoga* class cruisers previously mentioned as Congressional opposition to their retirement has waned. The last 12 months have seen the departures of *Bunker Hill* (CG-53), *Mobile Bay* (CG-54), *San Jacinto* (CG-56) and *Lake Champlain* (CG-57), leaving just thirteen of the original twenty-seven ships in service. *Cowpens* (CG-63) and *Vicksburg* (CG-69) are also due for imminent retirement, having never completed modernisation work on which several hundred million dollars have been wasted. The remaining ships will be retired before the end of 2027, bringing the life of the class that introduced Aegis into the operational US Navy fleet to an end.

Previous construction delays mean that no new *Burke* class destroyers have actually been delivered over the last 12 months. However, *Jack H. Lucas* (DDG-125), the first Flight III variant equipped with the new AN/SPY-6 radar, was formally commissioned on 7 October 2023 after being delivered by HII's Ingalls yard the previous June.

Table 2.1.5: UNITED STATES NAVY: PRINCIPAL UNITS AS AT MID 2024

TYPE	CLASS	NUMBER	TONNAGE	DIMENSIONS	PROPULSION	CREW	DATE
Aircraft Carriers							
Aircraft Carrier – CVN	**FORD** (CVN-78)	1	100,000 tonnes+	333m x 41/78m x 12m	Nuclear, 30+ knots	4,600	2017
Aircraft Carrier – CVN	**NIMITZ** (CVN-68)	10	100,000 tonnes+	333m x 41/78m x 12m	Nuclear, 30+ knots	5,200	1975
Principal Surface Escorts							
Cruiser – CG	**TICONDEROGA** (CG-47)	13	9,900 tonnes	173m x 17m x 7m	COGAG, 30+ knots	365	1983
Destroyer – DDG	**ZUMWALT** (DDG-1000)	2[1]	15,800 tonnes	186m x 25m x 8m	IEP, 30+ knots	175	2016
Destroyer – DDG	**ARLEIGH BURKE** (DDG-51) – Flight III	1	9,700 tonnes	155m x 20m x 7m	COGAG, 30 knots	360	2023
Destroyer – DDG	**ARLEIGH BURKE** (DDG-51) – Flight II-A	44	9,400 tonnes	155m x 20m x 7m	COGAG, 30 knots	330	2000
Destroyer – DDG	**ARLEIGH BURKE** (DDG-51) – Flights I/II	28	8,900 tonnes	154m x 20m x 7m	COGAG, 30+ knots	305	1991
Littoral Combat Ship – FS	**FREEDOM** (LCS-1)	8	3,500 tonnes	115m x 17m x 4m	CODAG, 45+ knots	<50[2]	2008
Littoral Combat Ship – FS	**INDEPENDENCE** (LCS-2)	16	3,000 tonnes	127m x 32m x 5m	CODAG, 45+ knots	<50[2]	2010
Submarines							
Submarine – SSBN	**OHIO** (SSBN-726)	14	18,800 tonnes	171m x 13m x 12m	Nuclear, 20+ knots	155	1981
Submarine – SSGN	**OHIO** (SSGN-726)	4	18,800 tonnes	171m x 13m x 12m	Nuclear, 20+ knots	160	1981
Submarine – SSN	**VIRGINIA** (SSN-774)	23	8,000 tonnes	115m x 10m x 9m	Nuclear, 25+ knots	135	2004
Submarine – SSN	**SEAWOLF** (SSN-21)	3[3]	9,000 tonnes	108m x 12m x 11m	Nuclear, 25+ knots	140	1997
Submarine – SSN	**LOS ANGELES** (SSN-688)	24	7,000 tonnes	110m x 10m x 9m	Nuclear, 25+ knots	145	1976
Major Amphibious Units							
Amph. Assault Ship – LHD	**AMERICA** (LHA-6)	2	45,000 tonnes	257m x 32/42m x 9m	COGAG, 22+ knots	1,050	2014
Amph Assault Ship – LHD	**WASP** (LHD-1)	7[4]	41,000 tonnes	253m x 32/42m x 9m	Steam, 20+ knots	1,100	1989
Landing Platform Dock – LPD	**SAN ANTONIO** (LPD-17)	13	25,000 tonnes	209m x 32m x 7m	Diesel, 22+ knots	360	2005
Landing Ship Dock – LSD	**WHIDBEY ISLAND** (LSD-41)	10[5]	16,000 tonnes	186m x 26m x 6m	Diesel, 20 knots	420	1985

Notes:

1 Includes one ship commissioned but not included in the 'battle force' pending completion of combat systems installation.

2 Plus mission-related crew.

3 Third of class, SSN-23 is longer and heavier.

4 LHD-8 has many differences.

5 Includes four LSD-49 HARPERS FERRY variants.

General Dynamics Bath Iron Works, which shares *Burke* class construction with HII, is somewhat further behind completing its assigned ships but commenced sea trials for *John Basilone* (DDG-122) in March 2024. Current plans envisage DDG-51 construction being maintained into the 2030s prior to being replaced by the planned DDG(X). Meanwhile, work is underway at Ingalls on refitting the lead *Zumwalt* (DDG-1000) class destroyer with the hypersonic Conventional Prompt Strike (CPS) weapon system. *Michael Monsoor* (DDG-1001) will also receive CPS at Ingalls during a future modernisation period expected to begin in 2025 and her sister *Lyndon B. Johnson* (DDG-1002) arrived at Ingalls in January 2022 to complete combat systems activation.

The Littoral Combat Ship force saw the decommissioning of the *Freedom* (LCS-1) variants *Milwaukee* (LCS-5), *Detroit* (LCS-7), *Little Rock* (LCS-9) and *Sioux City* (LCS-11) between August and September 2023. The older *Fort Worth* (LCS-3) is one of the eight ships of the class that remain in service but is expected to be retired during the course of 2026. However, a further rethink about future deployment of the type means that there will be no further premature withdrawals for the time being. Instead, the surviving ships will be joined by the three remaining ships under construction to form a flotilla of ten *Freedom* class vessels dedicated to anti-surface warfare operations. The requirement for fifteen *Independence* (LCS-2) variants dedicated to mine countermeasures remains unchanged and, although Congress prevented the withdrawal of *Jackson* (LCS-6) and *Montgomery* (LCS-8) in FY2025, the navy hopes for a change of heart in the coming year. In the interim, the class has been increased by the delivery of *Kingsville* (LCS-36) in March 2024. The US Navy expects to receive *Pierre* (LCS-38), the final *Independence* variant, during the next year.

Although construction of the lead *Constellation* class frigate at Fincantieri Marinette Marine is badly delayed, progress to date was marked by a formal keel-laying ceremony on 12 April 2024. Options worth a little over US$1bn for the fifth and sixth members of the class – which are to be named *Hamilton* (FFG-66) and *Galvez* (FFG-67) – were exercised with Fincantieri in May 2024. Reports at the time of the contract award suggest that the new frigates now only have around 15 percent commonality with the FREMM 'parent' design; down from an initial figure of as much as 85 percent.

The *Ticonderoga* class cruiser *Vicksburg* (CG-69) is manoeuvred into a dry dock during a docking evolution at BAE Systems Shipyard in Norfolk, Virginia on 24 March 2020 in the course of a modernisation that was intended to extend her service life into the 2030s. A decision to decommission the ship during 2024 has meant that the modernisation work was never completed, resulting in the waste of several hundred million dollars. *(US Navy)*

The *Freedom* (LCS-1) variant Littoral Combat Ship *Marinette* (LSC-25) was the latest vessel of the type to join the operational fleet when she commissioned on 16 September 2023 at Menominee, Michigan. This photograph was taken on 6 November 2023 whilst she was transiting the St. Lawrence Seaway en route for her home base of Mayport, Florida. *(Marc Piché)*

Amphibious and Support Shipping: The inventory of large amphibious vessels has been bolstered by the 11 April 2024 delivery of the fabulously named *Richard M. McCool Jr.* (LPD-29), the thirteenth and final member of the *San Antonio* (LPD-17) Flight I class of amphibious transport docks. Her arrival takes the number of large amphibious warships to thirty-two, one more than the minimum threshold mandated by Congress. Like her immediate predecessor, *Fort Lauderdale* (LPD-28), the new vessel is a transitional ship incorporating some of the improvements in the Flight II iteration of the series. In addition, she is the first ship to incorporate the rotating AN/SPY-6(V)2 variant of the new SPY-6 radar family, which forms part of the new Enterprise Air Surveillance Radar (EASR) family.[10] Construction of the first two Flight II vessels is already underway at HII's Ingalls yard and a third, to be named *Philadelphia* (LPD-32), has been ordered. As previously noted, orders for additional vessels of the type will resume in FY2025.

Construction of large deck amphibious assault ships also continues at the HHI Ingalls shipyard. *Bougainville* (LHA-8), the first Flight I iteration of the *America* (LHA-6) class, was floated out on 30 September 2023. The keel of her sister, *Fallujah* (LHA-9), had been laid ten days previously. Construction of the next member of the class, *Helmand Province* (LHA-10), will commence in FY2027.

Whilst Congressional action has slowed premature withdrawals of further *Whidbey Island* (LSD-41) dock landing ships, many of the class are fast approaching the end of their notional 40-year service lives and are therefore likely to be retired in any event. There may be more resistance to the proposed withdrawal of four of the relatively new *Spearhead* (T-EPF-1) class expeditionary fast transports which were previously part of efforts to bolster overall amphibious assets by acquiring cheaper ships with commercial design origins to support second-line operations. Although the later ships of the 16-strong class are still under construction, the four oldest vessels have been put forward for withdrawal during FY2025 as being in excess of BSFAR requirements. The navy further argues that it, '… is challenged with maintaining crew manning and operator proficiency, and the class operational availability and material availability is below life-cycle projections'. In line with this, *Spearhead* and her sister *Choctaw County* (T-EPF-2) have already been assigned a reduced operating status. Nevertheless, the decision to retire relatively new ships from a class that is still being built stands alongside the similar process of Littoral Combat Ship withdrawals as evidence of poor management of limited resources.

Proposed FY2025 retirements also include the expeditionary transport dock *John Glenn* (T-ESD-2), another of the new ships acquired to reinforce the major amphibious warships. The concept of a floating amphibious transfer station is regarded as having been overtaken by a changing threat environment. In addition, the two ships completed to fulfil the role did not meet expectations. More positively, the *Lewis B. Puller* (ESB-3) expeditionary mobile base derived from the design has proved to be a success and four of the type have been delivered to date. A further two units are being built by General Dynamics NASSCO in San Diego. The first of these, *Robert E. Simanek* (ESB-7), was christened on 4 May 2024. Displacing as much as 90,000 tonnes in full load condition, these 239m long vessels are based on NASSCO's 'Alaska' class oil tanker design and are intended to act as a base for helicopters, troops and uncrewed systems in lower-threat areas.

Construction of support shipping remains dominated by the *John Lewis* (T-AO-205) fleet replenishment oiler programme, described further in Chapter 3.1. In addition to the next-generation logistics ships previously mentioned, other important projects include the new TAGOS-25 class of ocean surveil-

Two photographs of the last Flight I *San Antonio* (LPD-17) amphibious transport dock *Richard M. McCool Jr.* (LPD-29) undertaking trials in the Gulf of Mexico in January 2024. A 'transitional ship' paving the way for the new Flight II variant, LPD-29 was delivered on 11 April 2024. *(Huntington Ingalls Industries)*

lance ships and replacement AS(X) submarine tenders. The lead T-AGOS-25 was contracted with Austal USA in June 2023 and is currently at the design stage. Displacing a little over 9,000 tonnes with a length of 110m, the ship will be powered by an integrated electric propulsion system and be capable of reaching speeds of up to 22 knots. This makes the class much larger and faster than previous US Navy iterations of the type.[11] It seems, however, that the transition to production is taking longer than expected and exercise of one of a number of options for additional vessels has been deferred. Meanwhile, General Dynamics has emerged as the preferred supplier of the AS(X) tenders as other contenders have dropped out and is likely to be awarded a US$100m contract to develop the design. Again, however, actual production plans have been delayed and it is likely to be 2027 before the first construction contract is placed.

Hyman G. Rickover (SSN-795) – seen here in October 2023 during the course of her final sea trials from General Dynamics Electric Boat's shipyard in Groton, Connecticut – was the only boat of the class to be commissioned that year. Strenuous efforts are being made to increase production to, first, two and, then, 2.33 members of the class each year. *(General Dynamics Electric Boat)*

Submarines: Delivery of the new *Columbia* class strategic submarines has constantly been described as the US Navy's top priority programme. The programme encompasses twelve submarines that are set to become operational from the early 2030s onwards. It has always been appreciated that delivery of the lead boat in time for its first scheduled deterrent patrol in 2031 would pose a significant challenge and substantial effort has been devoted to managing this risk. Accordingly, the revelation that construction of *District of Colombia* is running between 12 and 16 months behind schedule is a major disappointment. It seems that significant causes of the delay are tardy delivery of the submarine's steam generator and a holdup in completing the bow dome, with completion of the former reportedly running around three years late.[12] The large amounts being spent on upgrading the submarine industrial base – including US$3.4bn of emergency supplemental funding requested in October 2023 – seems to be a belated recognition of the extent of the problem. Whilst they are likely to improve matters for later submarines in the series, there must be a concern that delays with *District of Colombia* will only worsen as the more complex integration stage progresses.

The delays impacting strategic submarine construction are reflected to an even greater extent with respect to the programme for *Virginia* nuclear-powered attack submarines.[13] These are jointly manufactured by HII Newport News and by General Dynamics Electric Boat (GDEB) at Groton in Connecticut under a post-Cold War era arrangement that was intended to sustain production at the rate of around one boat each year. The plan worked well until orders were increased to the rate of two p.a. from FY2011 to help compensate for the pending retirement of growing numbers of Cold War-built *Los Angeles* (SSN-688) class submarines. This, coupled with a substantial redesign focused on increasing weaponry loadout through insertion of the Virginia Payload Module (VPM) hull plug, was more than the industrial base could accommodate, particularly when *Colombia* class production was added into the mix. The end result has been a growing backlog of submarines that have been ordered but not built under the two boat p.a. 'drumbeat' given a current production rate of around 1.2 to 1.4 submarines each year. This has significant strategic consequences given that the current downward pressure on submarine numbers from *Los Angeles* retirements is in direct contrast to the imperative of increasing the submarine force identified by the BFSAR.

At the moment, the US Navy's submarine flotilla is just about holding its own. Indeed, overall submarine numbers have increased by one over the last year, with the retirement of *Key West* (SSN-722) in September 2023 counterbalanced by the deliveries of *Hyman G. Rickover* (SSN-795) from GDEB in August that year and of *New Jersey* (SSN-796) from HII Newport News in April 2024. Looking to the future, it is anticipated that the substantial investment in infrastructure and workforce development that is currently underway will – when combined with the temporary rebalancing of the programme by the reduced procurement envisaged for FY2025 – bring *Virginia* class production up to two submarines p.a. by 2028. This will subsequently increase to 2.33 boats each year to reduce the accumulated backlog and provide capacity for the transfer of submarines to Australia under the AUKUS agreement. In the meantime, efforts are being made to extend the lives of individual *Los Angeles* class submarines where this is possible to bridge the gap. However, this process can only be taken so far. As a result, non-strategic submarine numbers are likely to fall from the current fifty-four to below fifty before matters start to improve in the early 2030s.

Another problem faced by the US Navy submarine force – also being addressed by increased investment in infrastructure – relates to problems maintaining existing boats. The number of attack submarines either awaiting or in the course of depot maintenance increased from just over 20 percent of the force in FY2012 to 33 percent of the force in FY2023, dramatically reducing the number of vessels available for operations. This situation is, however, slowly starting to improve as money is invested in the four government-operated shipyards that carry out most of the maintenance. Notably, the number of submarines actually laid up awaiting work had fallen to a five-year low of just two as of FY2023 as space was created for boats to begin their required programmes of work.

Uncrewed Vessels: Whilst uncrewed vessels are clearly going to play an increasingly fundamental role in the future US Navy, it is probably fair to say that decisions in the types of vessel to build and how best to use them are still work in progress. Most attention has focused on efforts to develop a series of large uncrewed surface and underwater vehicles that will provide additional 'mass' as part of the DMO concept. More specifically, these comprise:

- A Large Unmanned Surface Vehicle (LUSV) aimed primarily at providing a greater, distributed missile capacity as part of a modular payload.
- A Medium Unmanned Surface Vehicle (MUSV) to increase intelligence, surveillance, reconnaissance and targeting capacity.
- An Extra-Large Unmanned Undersea Vehicle (XLUUV) to supplement the stretched force of crewed submarines in activities such as minelaying.

The navy has been testing a small number of prototype uncrewed surface vessels for a number of years but has yet to progress to series production. It seems that it is the LUSV concept that has reached the greatest maturity and, until recently, it was envisaged that orders for operational vessels would be placed from FY2025 onwards. However, it has become clear that further testing, evaluation and – particularly – design development is needed before the type is ready for production. Accordingly, the latest budget request pushed back planned orders by two years. The MUSV seems to be even further behind against a backdrop of questions over its continued relevance given the potential availability of less complex and costly alternatives. Accordingly, no orders for operational vessels are envisaged within the life of the current FYDP. However, a bespoke prototype – the first US Navy-ordered USV that is purpose built for autonomous operations from the keel up – was contracted from L3 Harris in July 2020. Named *Vanguard* (OUSV-3), she has been constructed by Austal USA, who launched her from their shipyard in Mobile Alabama in January 2024. On completion, she will join five other prototype USVs in the US Navy's Unmanned Surface Vessel Division One (USVDIV1). The contract with includes options for up to eight additional vessels but other options for further test ships are being explored.

The immediate future of XLUUV operation is tied to contracts with Boeing that were concluded in 2019 for the acquisition of five 'operationally relevant' vessels informed by the group's 'Echo Voyager' UUV. The agreements with Boeing for what has been designated as the 'Orca' XLUUV also encompassed an additional test and training asset. Delivery of the vessels has been considerably delayed. However, the initial test asset was handed over in December 2023 and the remaining five should be completed before the end of 2025. Current plans envisage ordering additional 'Orcas' at a rate of one each year from FY2026 onwards.

Operational Highlights: The usual snapshot of operations provided in the press briefing that accompanied the FY2025 Department of the Navy Presidential Budget request suggest that the US Navy's tempo of operations as of 7 March 2024 was broadly unchanged year-on-year. A total of 104 (105) out of a battle force of 292 (296) ships were deployed, representing an essentially unchanged ratio in the order of 35 percent. Some 57 or 20 percent of these ships were underway at the time

The second *Virginia* class submarine *Texas* (SSN-775) being flooded up at Portsmouth Naval Shipyard in February 2024 during a scheduled maintenance period. In addition to attempting to bolster the submarine construction base, the US Navy is also investing substantial sums to address a backlog of submarine maintenance. *(US Navy)*

participating in a total of eleven operations. Over 41,000 sailors and 33,000 marines were deployed.

One noteworthy feature of the information provided was the absence of the geographical distribution of ships that has accompanied previous reports. This nod to operational security might particularly reflect the increased pressure caused by the outbreak of hostilities between Hamas and Israel in the Middle East. The United States has been attempting to reduce the level of forces committed to the region in recent years in support of the 'Pivot to the Pacific' but the current situation has upset this strategy. The availability of sufficient carrier strike groups has long been one area of particular weakness. In mid-2024, it emerged that there would be a temporary gap in carrier coverage in the Western Pacific as a result of the diversion of the *Theodore Roosevelt* (CVN-71) group to maintain security in the Middle East at the same time that the forward-deployed *Ronald Reagan* (CVN-76) was scheduled to participate in the Hawaii-based RIMPAC 2024 exercises. *Reagan* herself is on the way home for a scheduled refit. She will be replaced by the newly overhauled *George Washington* (CVN-73) as the US Navy carrier based in Japan.[14]

The US Navy's broadly successful operations against Houthi rebel forces attacking shipping in the Red Sea are covered elsewhere. Another significant operation that has attracted less publicity has been the construction of a temporary causeway in Gaza to deliver seaborne aid directly into the territory, thereby helping alleviate the humanitarian crisis caused by Israeli actions against Hamas. Established in conjunction with the US Army, the pier has demonstrated an ability to deliver as much as 4,500 tonnes of supplies per week but has also seen its use significantly disrupted by periods of heavy weather. This may reflect lack of recent experience of maintaining such facilities in an operational environment, resulting in valuable lessons being learned with respect to amphibious resupply.

The development of uncrewed surface vessel operating concepts has been further refined by a five month-long deployment of USVDIV1's *Sea Hunter*, *Sea Hawk*, *Mariner* and *Ranger* to the Western Pacific between 7 August 2023 and 15 January 2024. The ships undertook visits to ports in Japan and Australia, participating in the Royal Australian Navy's Autonomous Warrior 2023 exercise in early November. A large part of the c. 46,000 nautical mile deployment was conducted in fully

The uncrewed surface vessels (USVs) *Mariner* (foreground) and *Ranger* pictured alongside the Japanese *Mogami* class frigate *Kumano* (FFM-2) in September 2023 in the course of a lengthy deployment of four US Navy prototype large USVs across the Pacific. Whilst extensive efforts are being made to refine design and operating concepts for a future generation of large US USVs, actual procurement of operational vessels is steadily shifting to the right. *(US Navy)*

The aircraft carrier *Ronald Reagan* (CVN-76) is seen arriving at Naval Base Guam on 19 June 2024. *Reagan* is being replaced as the US Navy's only forward-deployed carrier with the newly modernised *George Washington* (CVN-73). *(US Navy)*

autonomous mode, further demonstrating the stability of this technology. In May 2024, the US Navy stood up an additional uncrewed command – Unmanned Surface Vessel Squadron (USVRON) Three – at Naval Amphibious Base Coronado in California to oversee a fleet of smaller, 16ft unmanned surface vessels known as Global Autonomous Reconnaissance Craft (GARCs).

US Coast Guard: The US Coast Guard's fleet of patrol vessels (cutters) continues to be modernised under a programme that dates back two decades to 2004. Some elements of this have been successful and are now close to completion; others have been less so.

The largest vessels in the replacement programme are the 'Legend' or *Bertholf* (WMSL-750) class national security cutters, which have been built by HII Ingalls. It was intended that eight of these large, 4,500-tonne vessels would replace twelve *Hamilton* (WHEC-715) high endurance cutters but, in the end, eleven were actually ordered. The tenth of these – *Calhoun* (WMSL-759) – was commissioned on 20 April 2024 whilst the final vessel – *Friedman* (WMSL-760) – is still under construction.

At the other end of the scale, it was initially envisaged that fifty-eight 'Sentinel' or *Bernard C. Webber* (WPC-1101) fast response cutters would be bought to replace forty-nine 'Island' class patrol boats. The requirement has since been raised to seventy-one vessels; fifty-nine for use in home waters and six each to support missions in the Persian Gulf and the Indo-Pacific region.[15] Funding for sixty-nine of these has been approved so far, with money for the final two included in the Coast Guard's FY2025 budget request. Of these, fifty-seven had been delivered as of mid-2024. The fast response cutters are based on the Damen Stan Patrol 4708 design and displace c. 350 tonnes.

Acquisition of the 'Heritage' or *Argus* (WMSM-915) offshore patrol cutters that form the third leg of the cutter replacement programme has proved to be more problematic. It is intended that twenty-five of these should replace twenty-nine medium endurance cutters of various designs. The original contractor for the programme, Eastern Shipbuilding Group of Florida, has encountered significant difficulties delivering the four ships ordered from it. As a result, acquisition of subsequent vessels was subject to a new competition that ultimately saw Austal USA receive options to build the next eleven ships, one of which is now under firm contract. The much-delayed lead ship, which is only slightly smaller and less capable than the 'Legend' class, was finally christened and launched on 31 October 2023. However, it is unclear whether a revised delivery schedule targeting delivery before the end of 2024 will be met. The Coast Guard's FY2025 budget request seeks funding for the sixth ship.

The Coast Guard's plans to acquire new icebreakers have also encountered difficulties. Reflecting increasing concerns over Arctic security, the Coast Guard intends to replace its current operational fleet of one heavy and one medium polar icebreakers with between eight and nine new vessels. To date, contracts for two polar security cutters (with an outstanding option for a third) have been awarded to the former VT Halter Marine (now part of Bollinger Shipyards) but progress has been slow. When the deal was first struck in 2019, it was envisaged that the lead ship – *Polar Sentinel* (WMSP-21) – would be delivered in 2024. However, it was only in August 2023 that first steel cutting for initial test modules began against a backdrop of considerable problems in finalising the design. Current estimates suggest that the lead ship will not be delivered before 2028 and that the estimated cost of US$3.2bn for the three-ship programme is likely to be exceeded.

OTHER NORTH AND CENTRAL AMERICAN NAVIES

Whilst **Mexico** remains the only other navy of note in North and Central America, the programme of local construction of increasingly sophisticated patrol vessels that culminated with the delivery of the Damen Sigma 10514 *Benito Juárez* in 2020 was effectively put on ice with the advent of the current Obrador presidency in December 2018. Although Obrador will be succeeded by Claudia Sheinbaum in October 2024, their shared political background suggests that the navy will remain focused on internal security under her rule. As such, the significant progress made in developing a local naval construction industry may steadily dissipate.

Elsewhere in the Caribbean, the steady strengthening of constabulary maritime capabilities remains the order of the day. The latest country to complete naval modernisation is **Jamaica.** In May 2024 the Jamaica Defence Force Coast Guard took delivery of *Marcus Garvey*, the second of two Damen FCS 5009 patrol vessels ordered as part of a wider contract that also included the first FCS 5009 *Nanny of the Maroons* and two smaller Stan Patrol 4207 coastal patrol boats. When combined with two further Stan Patrol 4207 vessels ordered under an earlier contract and additional investment in coastal radar surveillance capabilities, the programme represents a substantial upgrade to the country's maritime security capacity.

Construction of smaller Metal Shark '85 Defiant' near costal patrol vessels (NCPVs) – based on the Damen Stan Patrol 2606 design – for maritime constabulary forces across the Caribbean and Central America also continues. To date, six of a planned total of up to thirteen of the vessels envisaged under a US$54m American military assistance programme have been delivered and the Louisiana-based builder launched a seventh on 6 February 2024. The company has been very active in the Caribbean and its surrounds, recently delivering the larger 115ft patrol vessel *Shahoud* to neighbouring **Guyana.**

MAJOR SOUTH AMERICAN NAVIES – BRAZIL

Recent naval developments in Brazil have been dominated by the advance of the country's submarine programme.[16] Construction of four French Naval Group-designed 'Scorpène' type boats under the giant PROSUB project is now seemingly making good progress after previous delays. *Humaitá*, the second submarine of the series, was commissioned at the Itaguaí naval base on 12 January 2024. The event was followed just over two months later on 27 March 2024 by the launch of *Tonelero*, the third member of the class. The ceremony was carried out in the presence of Brazilian President Luiz Inácio Lula da Silva and French President Emmanuel Macron in an indication of the strategic importance of the programme to both countries. The new submarine is expected to commence sea trials before the end of the year prior to delivery in 2025. *Angostura*, the fourth and final boat, remains under construction in the giant assembly hall at Itaguaí and is likely to be completed in 2026.

Progress with 'Scorpène' deliveries is allowing further withdrawals of the navy's veteran Type 209/1400 submarines. *Tapajó* was retired on 18 August 2023 and was quickly followed by her sister, *Tamoio*, on 14 September 2023. This leaves just the 35-year-old lead member of the class *Tupi* and the improved 2005-built *Tikuna* in service. These changes are highlighted in Table 2.1.6, which summarises the main components of Brazil's navy as of mid-2024. In addition to the changes high-

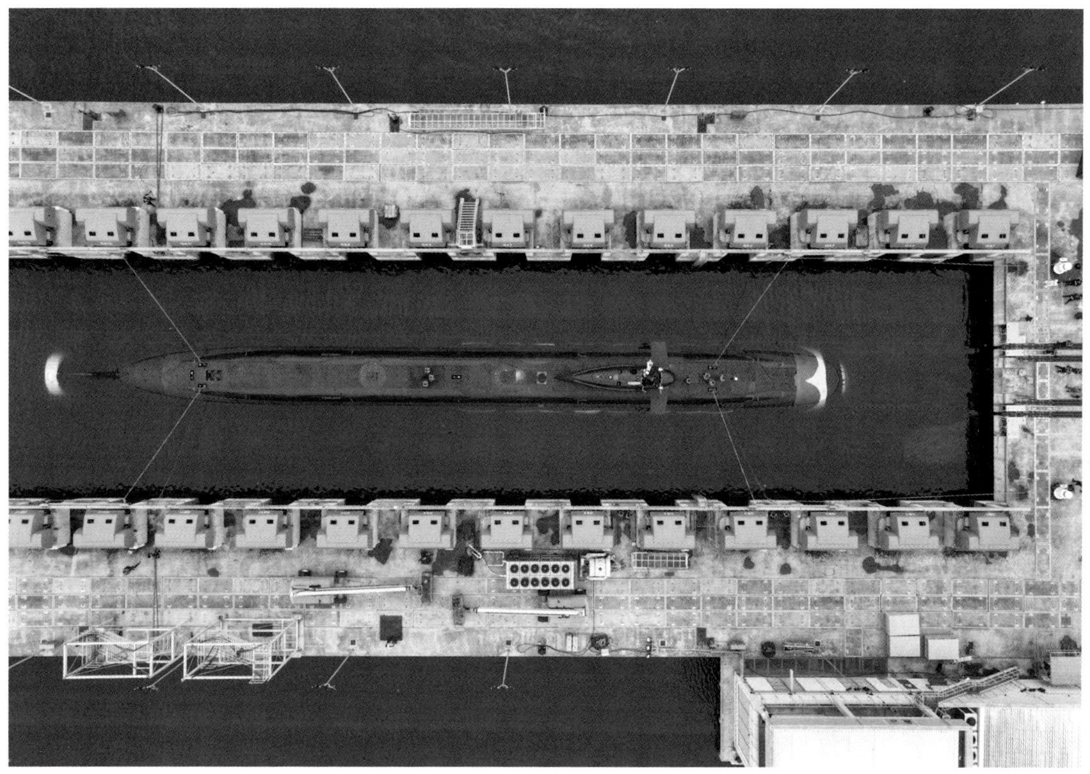

Tonelero – the third Brazilian Navy 'Scorpène' – was floated out at the Itaguaí naval base on 27 March 2024. Attention is now turning to the construction of Brazil's first nuclear-powered submarine. *(Naval Group)*

lighted, another significant departure in the course of the last year was the former US Navy *Newport* (LST-1179) class tank landing ship *Mattoso Maia*, previously *Cayuga* (LST-1186). Transferred to Brazil in 1994, she was finally retired on 31 October 2023.

Brazil's longer-term ambition is to deploy nuclear-powered submarines (SSNs) to protect its vast maritime interests in the Atlantic Ocean, sometimes referred to locally as the 'Blue Amazon'. These plans started to take tangible form over the last year with preliminary steel cutting work on test sections of the prototype SSN, which is to be named *Álvaro Alberto*. If all goes well, construction proper could commence in 2025 but it is likely to be a decade or more before she is fully operational.

The main construction programme for surface warships remains that for four new *Tamandaré* class MEKO type frigates from the thyssenkrupp Marine Systems (TKMS)/Embraer-controlled Águas Azuis consortium. The lead ship was rolled out of the assembly hall at the TKMS Estaleiro Brasil Sul in Itajaí in June 2024 prior to a planned August launch. Completion is anticipated in 2026 but this may prove to be optimistic. Construction of the second member of the class, *Jerônimo de Albuquerque*, is also underway. On 6 June 2024, her formal keel laying ceremony was held at Estaleiro Brasil Sul to mark a further stage towards the project's completion.

Another keel laying ceremony was held on 17 October 2023 at the Jurong Aracruz shipyard in Aracruz-Espirito Santo to mark progress with the new Antarctic support ship *Almirante Saldanha*. The 6,800-tonne ship is based on the Australian RV *Investigator* and is expected to enter service before the end of 2025.

OTHER SOUTH AMERICAN NAVIES

The most significant news from other South American navies comes from **Peru.**[17] The country launched an ambitious naval recapitalisation programme in 2022 that is eventually intended to encompass twenty-three vessels, including six multi-role frigates, three offshore patrol vessels and four submarines. In March 2024 it was announced that South Korea's Hyundai Heavy Industries (HHI) had

Table 2.1.6: BRAZILIAN NAVY: PRINCIPAL UNITS AS AT MID 2024

TYPE	CLASS	NUMBER	TONNAGE	DIMENSIONS	PROPULSION	CREW	DATE
Principal Surface Escorts							
Frigate – FFG	**GREENHALGH** (Batch I Type 22)	1	4,700 tonnes	131m x 15m x 4m	COGOG, 30 knots	270	1979
Frigate – FFG	**NITERÓI**	5	3,700 tonnes	129m x 14m x 4m	CODOG, 30 knots	220	1976
Corvette – FSG	**BARROSO**	1	2,400 tonnes	103m x 11m x 4m	CODOG, 30 knots	145	2008
Corvette – FSG	**INHAÚMA**	1	2,100 tonnes	96m x 11m x 4m	CODOG, 27 knots	120	1989
Submarines							
Submarine – SSK	**RIACHUELO** (Scorpène)	2	1,900 tonnes	71m x 6m x 6m	Diesel-electric, 20+ knots	35	2022
Submarine – SSK	**TIKUNA** (Type 209/1400 – modified)	1	1,600 tonnes	62m x 6m x 6m	Diesel-electric, 22 knots	40	2005
Submarine – SSK	**TUPI** (Type 209/1400)	1	1,500 tonnes	61m x 6m x 6m	Diesel-electric, 22+ knots	30	1989
Major Amphibious Units							
Helicopter Carrier – LPH	**ATLÂNTICO** (OCEAN)	1	22,500 tonnes	203m x 35m x 7m	Diesel, 18 knots	490	1998
Landing Ship Dock – LSD	**BAHIA** (FOUDRE)	1	12,000 tonnes	168m x 24m x 5m	Diesel, 20 knots	160	1998

been selected to partner local shipbuilder SIMA in the implementation of the first phase of this programme, which will involve the local assembly of the Korean company's designs. The c. US$460m initial contract encompasses one 3,400-tonne frigate, one 2,200-tonne offshore patrol vessel and two 1,400-tonne landing ship-like logistics support vessels. SIMA has previously worked with Korean industry on, inter alia, the *Pisco* class amphibious transport docks and *Rio Pativilca* so the selection of HHI over a number of European competitors is not a surprise. The Peruvian shipyard also remains heavily committed to a life extension programme encompassing the navy's four Type 209/1200 submarines. A major stage in this work was achieved on 27 December 2023 when SIMA's Callao yard returned *Chipana*, the first boat to go through the programme, to the water.

Neighbouring **Ecuador's** ASTINAVE continues to work towards completing the Fassmer MPV70 Mk III multi-role vessel ordered in 2020 whilst undertaking further refurbishments of *Esmeralda* Class corvettes. In April 2024, it was announced that South Korea was to transfer the recently-decommissioned lead 3,900-tonne *Tae Pyung Yang* class coast guard patrol vessel *KCG-3001* to the Ecuadorian Navy; a move that follows a previous transfer of two smaller patrol vessels. South Korea has been active in using such gifts to promote its naval export business. As such, it may well be that it is looking to expand its regional footprint to collaborate with ASTINAVE in due course.

Future production plans at **Colombia's** COTECMAR shipyard will be dominated by the selection of Damen's SIGMA 10514 design for the five frigates required to meet the needs of the navy's *Plataforma Estratégica de Superficie* (PES) programme. Preparations to commence construction of the first vessel in 2025 continue against the backdrop of reports suggesting the cost of the initial unit has increased to over US$500m as a result of inflation and equipment selection. This has resulted in some speculation that implementation of the contract may be delayed, or even that the programme may be renegotiated. There has, however, been better progress with another strand of Colombia's 'Naval Development Plan 2042' that envisages completion of four new indigenous offshore patrol vessels to a *Patrullero Océanico Colombiano* (POC) design. Work on *POC-93*, the first of these, started in March 2023 and has subsequently made rapid progress, with all hull blocks complete as of April 2024. The ship's launch is scheduled for mid-2025 prior to delivery early in the following year.

Naval developments in **Venezuela** have been dominated by the country's sabre rattling with respect to renewed territorial claims against neighbouring Guyana that are most likely intended to form a distraction from internal unrest. In December 2023, the country's armed forces embarked on a large exercise encompassing over fifteen vessels headed by three *Guaiquerí* oceanic patrol vessels in response to the arrival of the solitary British Royal Navy patrol vessel *Trent* on a goodwill visit to Guyana's capital. The cash-strapped navy has been otherwise focused on refurbishing existing vessels. It has also reportedly been taking delivery of missile-armed 'Peykaap III' interceptors from Iran in a development that probably owes more to political allegiances than naval requirements.

Uruguay's efforts to acquire new naval vessels reached a conclusion in December 2023 with the signature of a €82m (c. US$90m) contract with Spain's Cardama Shipyard for two new offshore patrol vessels, bringing a 20-year-long saga to a close. The decision has proved to be a controversial one given the Spanish company's lack of experience of constructing vessels of the type, reportedly driving the early retirement of the Uruguayan Chief of Naval Staff. With a main armament of a 30mm gun and facilities for helicopter operation, the 1,700-tonne vessels are optimised for constabulary missions and are likely less capable than the Chinese Type 056 corvettes that were the navy's original, but much more costly, choice. The navy has also received a further boost with the donation of a former South Korean *Chamsuri* class coastal patrol vessel to add to the previous transfer of former US Coast Guard 'Marine Protector' class cutters in 2022.

Although **Argentina** has plans to modernise its armed forces, things are likely to get worse for the navy before they get better. The first half of 2024 saw the final decommissioning of the MEKO 360 destroyer *Heroína* after a prolonged period of inactivity that had its origins in the seizure of a key propulsion component sent to the United Kingdom for repairs. Also leaving the fleet was the Type 42

The Chilean Navy has been seeing good progress with the construction of its new icebreaker, *Almirante Viel*, which is seen here shortly before her launch from ASMAR's Talcahuano shipyard on 22 December 2022. The new ship is expected to be commissioned in July 2024. *(Chilean Navy)*

destroyer *Hércules.* She was originally built at Barrow-in-Furness in the 1970s and was the last of the well-known class in service. Previously converted to a multi-role transport, she had also reportedly experienced a period of inactivity before being decommissioned on 24 June 2024. In addition to the entire submarine flotilla, a number of other surface warships are also believed to be inactive.

Current plans seem to be focused on the short-term acquisition of at least one second-hand *Ula* class submarine from Norway. This will be followed by a larger acquisition of new German Type 214 or French 'Scorpène' type boats. It is questionable whether the money will be found to fund these projects given past experience. Another plan involving the purchase of one of the soon to be decommissioned Italian *San Giorgio* class dock landing ships alongside Leonardo light helicopters seems to have better prospects of being realised.

Chile's impressive indigenous naval shipbuilding capacity has been demonstrated by ASMAR's construction of the VARD 9-203 type icebreaker *Almirante Viel* at the shipbuilder's Talcahuano yard. The vessel was launched in December 2022 and was very close to delivery as of mid-2024 after the commencement of sea trials on 18 April. The shipbuilder is working on a follow-on project for up to four amphibious transport docks that are also based on a VARD design. Firm orders for two of these ships have been placed to date, with the first to be delivered in 2027. In the longer term, ASMAR is likely to be involved in the local construction of replacement frigates for the increasingly elderly eight-strong flotilla of former Australian, British and Dutch vessels that are currently in service. However, there is a more pressing need to acquire a new pair of submarines given that the 1980s-era Type 209/1400 *Thomson* class boats have now entered their final operational cycles. Chile's newer pair of submarines form part of Naval Group's 'Scorpène' class. The acquisition of additional units of this type would therefore provide logistical support benefits.

Notes:

1. The Fiscal Responsibility Act is the most recent compromise agreement aimed at dealing with the ongoing US government deficit.

2. US Department of Defense FY2025 budget materials – including links to US department of the Navy documents can be found at: comptroller.defense.gov/Budget-Materials/Budget2025/. A noteworthy feature of the new budget was that it was announced before budget appropriations for the previous, FY2024, year had been passed into law. A deal on these was only hammered out towards the end of March, nearly six months after the fiscal year had begun. In the meantime, defence (and other government) activities were funded by continuing resolutions; essentially a short-term fix to provide time for a political consensus to emerge with all the inefficiencies this implies. The use of continuing resolutions in FY2024 was nothing new; indeed there has been a need to resort to them in all but four years in the period from FY1977 to date. However, the delay in the FY2024 appropriations was the longest for six years, perhaps reflecting the increasingly polarised nature of the US political system. The one percent uplift ignores FY2024 supplementary funding of US$58.3bn, much for Ukraine.

3. See the 30 May 2024 edition of Ronald O' Rourke's *Navy Force Structure and Shipbuilding Plans: Background and Issues for Congress RL32665* (Washington DC: Congressional Research Service, 2024), p. 12. This is one of numerous periodically updated reports by Mr O'Rourke, the Congressional Research Service's (CRS's) long-standing Specialist in Naval Affairs, which are referred to throughout this chapter. They can be accessed by searching the Congressional Research Service's website at crsreports.congress.gov or via the Federation of American Scientists' site at sgp.fas.org/crs.

4. The current problems with the *Constellation* class programme are discussed in the United States Government Accountability Office's (GOA's) report, *Navy Frigate: Unstable Design Has Stalled Construction and Compromised Delivery Schedules GAO-24-106546* (Washington DC: GAO, 2024) published on 29 May 2024 and readily available by searching the web.

5. See, *Our North, Strong and Free: A Renewed Vision for Canada*'s *Defence* (Ottawa: Department of National Defence, 2024) which is available by searching the web.

6. See David Pugliese, 'Cost of Canadian Coast Guard patrol ships jumps by $500 million in less than a year, MPs told' posted to the *Ottawa Citizen*'s site – ottawacitizen.com on 17 January 2024. Pugliese's work highlighting weaknesses in Canadian defence procurement decisions has made him something of a thorn in the side of Canada's defence establishment. This has clearly 'got under' at least one of his targets' skin. In August 2023, he was the subject of an unusual press release from Irving Shipbuilding criticising his alleged publication of, '… another inaccurate and misleading article about the National Shipbuilding Strategy (NSS) and the Halifax Shipyard' and concluding that, 'we trust that future articles will be handled with far more care and attention to the facts'.

7. See *Report to Congress on the Annual Long-Range Plan for Construction of Naval Vessels for Fiscal Year 2025* (Washington DC: Office of the Chief of Naval Operations, 2024). Much of this section is based on this report.

8. See Megan Eckstein, 'US Navy mulls timing of new double-carrier award amid Enterprise delay' posted to the *Defense News* site – defensenews.com – on 26 October 2023. Since her report was written, the US Navy has decided to push back CVN-82 acquisition to FY2030.

9. For a much more detailed analysis of the current status of the *Ford* class programme see another Ronald O'Rourke report, *Navy Ford (CVN-78) Class Aircraft Carrier Program: Background and Issues for Congress RS20643.*

10. The AN/SPY 6(V) radar series is explored in more detail in Chapter 4.2.

11. For further details of the new design see Zach Abdi, 'Austal USA Showcases T-AGOS 25 Model For The First Time' posted to the *Naval News* site – navalnews.com – on 11 January 2024.

12. See Ronald O' Rourke, *Navy Columbia (SSBN-826) Class Ballistic Missile Submarine Program: Background and Issues for Congress R41129.* Details of the factors behind the delays are described in pp. 8–9 of the 29 April 2024 version of this report.

13. See again Ronald O' Rourke, *Navy Virginia-Class Submarine Program and AUKUS Submarine (Pillar 1) Project: Background and Issues for Congress RL32418.*

14. See Dzirhan Mahadzi, 'Carrier USS Ronald Reagan Leaves Japan for the Last Time' posted to the USNI News site – news.usni.org – on 16 May 2024.

15. The increase in the requirement from fifty-eight to fifty-nine vessels reflects the need to replace *Benjamin Dailey* (WPC-1123), which was badly damaged in a shipyard fire on 10 December 2021 and subsequently scrapped as being beyond repair.

16. The *Poder Naval* site – naval.com.br – remains an essential source for detailed information on Brazilian Navy developments.

17. The Spanish-language *defensa.com* and its rival *infodefensa.com* remain invaluable sources of additional information on naval developments in Latin America.

2.2 REGIONAL REVIEW

ASIA AND THE PACIFIC

Author:
Conrad Waters

At 08.00 on Wednesday 1 May 2024, the People's Liberation Army Navy (PLAN) aircraft carrier *Fujian* departed China State Shipbuilding Corporation's Jiangnan Shipyard near Shanghai to commence her maiden sea trials. The Type 003 aircraft carrier – the third vessel in the PLAN's carrier programme after the Type 001 *Liaoning* and the Type 002 *Shandong* – differs from her predecessors in being fitted for catapult-assisted take-off but arrested recovery (CATOBAR) operation. She is equipped with three electromagnetic catapults for this purpose and improved naval aircraft are being developed to be launched from them. *Fujian* has an estimated length of 315m and a reported displacement of over 80,000 tonnes. This means that she ranks second only to the US Navy's *Ford* (CVN-78) class in size amongst the world's front-line warships.

Whilst *Fujian* undoubtedly cuts an impressive figure, her short-term impact is likely to be limited. The carrier's maiden voyage – a comparatively short eight days – will be followed by many more before she is finally accepted. Although her second period at sea, from 23 May to 11 June, followed on relatively quickly from the first, bringing her safely into service will be a complex process and require many hurdles to be overcome. As such, it is likely to be late 2025 or, possibly, sometime in 2026 before she is officially commissioned. Even then, it will take many more years of training and operational experience before the PLAN is able to emulate the capabilities of the US Navy's long-established carrier air wings. For the time being at least, *Fujian* represents a 'work in progress' rather than a completed tool of naval power.

On another level, however, the commencement of *Fujian*'s trials is representative of a further step in the PLAN's rapid and impressive transformation. Starting as a technologically backward coastal defence force at the end of the Cold War, the navy has achieved its current status as (primarily) an effective anti-access/area denial (A2/AD) arm of the Chinese military and is moving steadily towards the seeming ultimate objective of serving as a global tool of maritime power projection. In this regard, *Fujian* will undoubtedly be followed by additional, more powerful vessels. Indeed, it has been speculated that a Type 004 aircraft carrier – possibly equipped with nuclear propulsion – is at an early stage of construction. Given the PLAN's achievements in so many fields, there would likely be few who would wager against it achieving its ambition.

For many, a key question will be how the PLAN will ultimately utilise this capacity. Unfortunately, the omens are not entirely auspicious. In June 2024, the existing carrier *Shandong* was deployed in waters close to Luzon in the Philippines as a response to what Chinese government-friendly media described as, 'a deterrence against continuous Philippine provocations on Chinese islands and reefs in the South China Sea'.[1] The deployment followed a protracted campaign of harassment by the China Coast Guard against Philippine resupply missions to its outpost at the disputed Second Thomas Shoal that commenced in August 2023 and were ongoing as of mid-2024. The same month also saw a new China Coast Guard regulation enter into force that permits foreign nationals suspected of trespassing into the broadly defined 'waters under China's jurisdiction' to be detained for periods of up to 60 days. Many commentators have seen this as a further extension of Chinese 'grey zone' activities to enforce its controversial 'nine dash line' claim to much of the South China Sea.

It seems unlikely that China is seeking to provoke an all-out regional war. The importance of its maritime trade and the vulnerability of its sea lanes to interdiction would make this a reckless endeavour. A more likely intent is to achieve a slow but inexorable shift in the balance of power – notably by leveraging the advantage provided by its vast shipbuilding sector – to the extent that it is able to achieve its objectives by bullying any potential opponents into compliance. However, this approach is also seemingly fraught with hazard. It is forcing countries across the region to take sides in an increasingly polarised divide, whilst driving them to look to their own defences. It is this dynamic that is driving much of the naval procurement activity described in the remainder of this chapter. At the same time, the risk of miscalculation causing an unintended war cannot be discounted. This is, perhaps, the greater fear.

Table 2.2.1 provides a summary of the more significant regional fleets in Asia and the Pacific as of mid-2024.

The new Chinese aircraft carrier *Fujian* pictured on 8 May 2024 in the course of maiden sea trials from the China State Shipbuilding Corporation's Jiangnan Shipyard. Reportedly displacing over 80,000 tonnes and equipped with three electromagnetic catapults, she ranks second only to the US Navy's *Ford* (CVN-78) class in terms of warship size. *(China Military Online)*

Table 2.2.1: FLEET STRENGTHS IN ASIA AND THE PACIFIC – LARGER NAVIES (MID 2024)

COUNTRY	AUSTRALIA	CHINA[1]	INDONESIA	JAPAN	S KOREA	SINGAPORE	TAIWAN	THAILAND
Aircraft Carrier (CV)	–	2	–	2	–	–	–	–
Support/Helicopter Carrier (CVS/CVH)	–	–	–	2	–	–	–	1
Strategic Missile Submarine (SSBN)	–	6	–	–	–	–	–	–
Attack Submarine (SSN)	–	6	–	–	–	–	–	–
Patrol Submarine (SSK/SS)	6	50	4	22	21	4	4[4]	–
Fleet Escort (DDG/FFG)	10	100	7	42	28	6	26	8
Patrol Escort/Corvette (FFG/FSG/FS)	–	55	24	6	3	14	7	10
Missile Armed Attack Craft (PGG/PTG)	–	75	24[2]	6	18	–	c. 30	–
Mine Countermeasures Vessel (MCMV)	3	35	8	18	12	4	c. 6	5
Major Amphibious Units (LHD/LPD/LSD)	3	11	8[3]	3	2	4	2	2

Notes:
1: Chinese numbers approximate and exclude some obsolescent vessels.
2: Some additional Indonesian patrol gunboats are able to ship missiles.
3: Includes three vessels configured as hospital ships.
4: Taiwan's submarines are reported to have limited operational availability.

British Royal Navy and US Navy submarines are stepping up their visits to Australia as part of a phased pathway that will eventually see the Royal Australian Navy operate locally-built SSN-AUKUS submarines. This photograph shows sailors assigned to the *Los Angeles* class fast attack submarine *Springfield* (SSN-761), participating in a weapons handling exercise at the Royal Australian Navy's HMAS *Stirling* base on Garden Island off the coast of Perth in April 2022. From 2027, American and British submarines will be deployed to *Stirling* as part of Submarine Rotational Force-West. *(US Navy)*

MAJOR REGIONAL POWERS – AUSTRALIA

The way ahead for the future development of the Royal Australian Navy's (RAN's) underwater fleet was determined by the announcement of the trilateral AUKUS strategic partnership in September 2021 and the subsequent publication of the *AUKUS Nuclear-Powered Submarine Pathway* in March 2023.[2] The latter essentially established a phased approach to the RAN's operation of nuclear-powered attack submarines (SSNs). This process has already commenced with the embedding of Australian personnel in their two partners' submarine enterprises and an increase in the frequency of SSN visits to Australian ports. Later stages include the forward basing of American and British submarines to establish a rotational forward presence at the HMAS *Stirling* base in Western Australia prior to the RAN's acquisition of, first, American *Virginia* (SSN-774) and, subsequently, new SSN-AUKUS submarines. The latter type is based on the United Kingdom's next-generation SSNR design but will incorporate American submarine technologies. It will be built both in the United Kingdom and Australia, entering service with the Royal Navy from the late 2030s and being followed by the RAN boats early in the following decade.

With the pathway established, Australia has been moving quickly to implement the plan. Notably, an Australian Submarine Agency was established on 1 July 2023 to exercise management and oversight of the overall programme. AU$1.5bn (US$1bn) has been already approved for early priority works at HMAS *Stirling* to prepare for initial rotational deployments. Preliminary enabling works for the new Submarine Construction Yard at Osborne in South Australia that will eventually assemble Australia's members of the SSN-AUKUS class have also been authorised. In March 2024, it was announced that ASC Pty Ltd – builders of the RAN's existing *Collins* class patrol submarines – and BAE Systems will work in partnership to deliver Australia's new SSNs. The decision reflects BAE Systems' leadership of the SSN-AUKUS programme in the United Kingdom, as well as its existing presence in Osborne through the *Hunter* class frigate programme.

Australia has also made progress with revising the future structure of its surface flotilla with publication of its plans for an *Enhanced Lethality Surface Combatant Fleet* on 20 February 2024.[3] The new plan is based on an independent analysis of fleet structure that was commissioned in the aftermath of the country's 2023 strategic defence review. The decision to undertake this analysis reflected, inter alia, concerns that the then-planned fleet structure – focused on three existing *Hobart* class air defence destroyers, nine new *Hunter* class anti-submarine warfare (ASW) frigates and twelve *Arafura* class offshore patrol vessels (OPVs) – was no longer best suited to meet the RAN's needs in the light of the evolving strategic backdrop across the Indo-Pacific region. In overall terms, the resultant analysis concurred with this assessment, concluding that the current and planned surface combatant fleet was not appropriate for Australia's strategic environment. Accordingly, it offered a blueprint for a revised fleet structure offering greater capability in integrated air and missile defence, multi-domain trike and undersea warfare. The Australian government accepted virtually all the independent analysis's conclusions.

The revised surface fleet plan combines (1) a shift to a two-tier structure of major surface combatants that increases their overall numbers with (2) a reduction in the previously planned number of OPVs. The top tier of the fleet will now comprise three *Hobart* but only six *Hunter* class escorts. However, overall lethality will increase with the acquisition of six large optionally crewed surface vessels (LOSVs) each equipped with thirty-two vertical launch cells. Additionally, the new Tier Two component will add between seven and eleven frigates, all optimised for ASW. These are to be acquired as quickly as possible from a short list of 'exemplars' that encompasses the German MEKO A-200, Japanese *Mogami*, South Korean FFX and Spanish ALFA 3000 frigate designs. Meanwhile, the *Arafura* OPV class is regarded as '… an inefficient use of resources for civil maritime security operations [that] does not possess the survivability and self-defence systems to contribute to a surface combatant mission'. Accordingly, planned acquisition will be cut in half to encompass only the six already under construc-

Table 2.2.2: ROYAL AUSTRALIAN NAVY: PRINCIPAL UNITS AS AT MID 2024

TYPE	CLASS	NUMBER	TONNAGE	DIMENSIONS	PROPULSION	CREW	DATE
Principal Surface Escorts							
Frigate – FFG	**HOBART** (F-100)	3	6,300 tonnes	147m x 19m x 5m	CODOG, 28 knots	200	2017
Frigate – FFG	**ANZAC**	7	3,600 tonnes	118m x 15m x 4m	CODOG, 28 knots	175	1996
Submarines							
Submarine – SSK	**COLLINS**	6	3,400 tonnes	78m x 8m x 7m	Diesel-electric, 20 knots	45	1996
Major Amphibious Units							
Amph Assault Ship – LHD	**CANBERRA** (JUAN CARLOS I)	2	27,100 tonnes	231m x 32m x 7m	IEP, 21 knots	290	2014
Landing Ship Dock – LSD	**CHOULES** (LARGS BAY)	1	16,200 tonnes	176m x 26m x 6m	Diesel-electric, 18 knots	160	2006

tion, which will be assigned alternative roles. Constabulary missions will, instead, be performed by the smaller 'Evolved Cape' class patrol boats of both the Royal Australian Navy and Australian Border Force under a combined acquisition and sustainment model.

The new blueprint arguably has both positive and negative elements. If realised in full, it doubles the fleet of crewed and uncrewed surface combatants and increases total lethality by dint of the larger number of missiles carried. The new plans are also backed by AU$11.1bn (US$7.3bn) of additional investment over the next decade that will go a long way to addressing a previously predicted funding shortfall. Importantly, the plans aim to avoid the previous boom/bust cycle in Australian shipbuilding. Uncertainty over the often-criticised *Hunter* class's future is resolved, whilst continuity of surface warship construction at Osborne will likely be maintained by accelerating orders for the *Hobart* class's eventual replacement to compensate for the reduced frigate production run. Collaboration with the Royal Navy's future Type 83 destroyer programme seems possible in this regard. Similarly, curtailment of the *Arafura* class will ultimately be balanced by Tier Two frigate and LSOV assembly. However, it is not all good news. Notably, the planned TransCAP life-extension programme for the *Anzac* class is abandoned and the two earliest ships decommissioned in another example of the 'jam tomorrow, never today' philosophy that is seemingly a global rule of naval procurement. Perhaps most concerningly, the revised surface fleet structure plan follows the previous cancellation of the *Attack* submarine programme that resulted in AUKUS, becoming the second time within three years that Australia has upended a major element of its plans for the RAN's future.

Current RAN fleet composition is summarised in

The Australian government's 'Enhanced Lethality Surface Combatant Fleet' plan will see the early decommissioning of two *Anzac* class frigates. The top picture shows *Anzac* herself entering the HMAS *Stirling* base in Western Australia for the final time on 13 April 2024 prior to a formal decommissioning service the following month. The new plan also confirmed that the new *Hunter* class frigates (bottom) will be built in reduced numbers, with large USVs and a Tier Two component of up to eleven ASW-optimised frigates being ordered to increase overall combatant numbers. *(Australian Department of Defence/BAE Systems)*

Table 2.2.2. The decisions taken in the future surface fleet blueprint have already begun to take effect with the decommissioning of *Anzac* at a ceremony on 18 May 2024, reducing the fleet to just ten major combatants. More positively, 21 June 2024 saw the formal start of work on *Hunter* by BAE Systems at Osborne alongside confirmation that contracts for the construction of the first three frigates had been signed.[4] It will not be until 2034 that the lead ship, which is based on the Type 26/Global Combat Ship design, becomes operational. This is at least five years later than envisaged when BAE Systems' selection for the programme was first announced. The class's strike capability may well be increased through installation of Tomahawk cruise missiles following an August 2023 announcement that over 200 were to be acquired for use with the existing *Hobart* class.

The flotilla of smaller warships has also reduced with the withdrawals of the *Armidale* class patrol vessels *Larrakia* and *Maryborough* on 28 September 2023, followed by that of the lead *Huon* class mine countermeasures vessel (MCMV) on 30 May 2024. *Huon*'s retirement leaves just three of the once six-strong class in commission. Previous plans envisaged a variant of the *Arafura* design serving as a MCMV replacement and it seems possible that this might form the alternative role now sought for the truncated OPV class. However, delivery of the *Arafura* programme under Project SEA1180 Phase 1 is proving to be problematic, being officially listed as a 'project of concern' in October 2023. Whilst second-of-class, *Eyre*, was launched on 22 November 2023, the lead vessel had still not commenced sea trials by mid-2024 against a backdrop of reports that it had failed to meet certain civil safety standards. Better progress is being achieved with the 'Evolved Cape' class patrol boats that now effectively form both the *Armidale* and the *Arafura* class's 'replacements'. Six of the type are now in RAN service following the delivery of *Cape Pillar* in October 2023 and two additional units have been launched. In February 2024, an order for two further vessels was placed, thereby bringing the number of vessels ordered under what is officially known as Project SEA 1445 Phase 1 to ten.[5]

The Royal Australian Navy's 'Evolved Cape' class patrol boat *Cape Peron* pictured in December 2023. Two additional members of the class – which will form Australia's main constabulary force under the revised surface fleet structure plan – were ordered in February 2024. *(Australian Department of Defence)*

MAJOR REGIONAL POWERS – CHINA

China's PLAN remains numerically the largest in the world, with over 150 major surface combatants and more than 60 submarines in service as of mid-2024. US Department of Defense intelligence anticipates a further increase in these numbers over the coming decade, albeit not at the rate of expansion previously achieved.[6] Instead, the focus is likely to be on qualitative improvements, an approach that has already seen most of the PLAN's obsolescent Cold War era vessels pass into retirement. In line with this objective, the last year has seemingly seen something of a pause in the completion of new warships as current construction programmes transition to new designs, as well as improved iterations of existing classes. As such, the snapshot presented in Table 2.2.3 summarising major PLAN constituents shows little change from the previous year. This is, however, somewhat misleading as major changes – such as the pending arrival of the new carrier *Fujian* – are in the pipeline. These are more fully described in the assessment of major warship types that follows.

Aircraft Carriers and Amphibious Vessels: Whilst media attention has been focused on the commencement of *Fujian*'s sea trials, already described in the introduction, the PLAN has also been making progress with upgrading its flotilla of amphibious shipping. December 2023 saw the launch of *Jiangxi*, the fourth Type 075 'Yushen' class amphibious assault ship, from the Hudong-Zhonghua Shipbuilding yard in the heart of Shanghai. It had been nearly three years since the yard had launched the previous member of the class, a pause that might be explained by the phased transfer of shipbuilding activities to join the rival Jiangnan Shipyard on Changxingdao Island at the mouth of the River Yangtze.[7] In any event, it appears that she will be the final member of the class, with construction now transitioning to the first of an improved Type 076 'Yulan' variant that will reportedly be fitted with an electromagnetic catapult for launching UAVs.

Surface Combatants: PLAN surface warship construction continues to be dominated by three major classes. The 'high end' type remains the Type 055 'Renhai' destroyer class of around 12,000 tonnes displacement, which are primarily intended to work with the navy's new carrier strike groups. Construction is shared equally between the Jiangnan Shipyard and Dalian Shipbuilding Industry

The maiden voyage of the new Chinese PLAN Type 003 aircraft carrier *Fujian* has dominated headlines in 2024. However, there has been a temporary slowdown in the pace of new warship deliveries as production transitions to new programmes. *(China Military Online)*

Corporation (DSIC), which collectively delivered eight of the class from the start of 2020 to early 2023. They are now working on a second batch, which local observers speculate will incorporate lessons learned from previous ships of the type. Jiangnan launched *Jiaxing*, the first of this batch, in December 2023 and DSIC followed with *Baoding* in March 2024. At least two more of the ships are in the course of initial construction.

Jiangnan Shipyard and DSIC also continue to build the series of smaller Type 052D 'Luyang III' destroyers, having collectively delivered twenty-five of the class in two main variants between 2014 and 2022. The current programme of construction is reported to include another ten of the c. 7,500-tonne vessels, of which seven had been launched as of mid-2024. Their completion might allow withdrawal of some of the eclectic mix of destroyers equipped primarily with Russian technology that were commissioned in the early stages of the PLAN's modernisation.

China's third stream of surface warship construction has been focused on the Type 054A general purpose frigates. A total of forty of these were delivered to the PLAN over an extended 15-year period between 2008 and 2023 by Hudong-Zhonghua Shipbuilding and by the Huangpu Wenchong Shipbuilding at Guangzhou. Four others were built for the Pakistan Navy and a Type 818 variant remains in production for the China Coast Guard. However, recent reports confirm that PLAN construction has now transitioned to the Type 054B class. The lead vessel – reportedly named *Luohe* – was launched at Shanghai on 26 August 2023, subsequently commencing sea trials in January 2024. Initial photographs suggest that she is an enlarged evolution of the previous class, with a length of 150m and a displacement in the region of 6,000 tonnes. She is also noticeably stealthier than the Type 054A, incorporating features seen in the PLAN's larger destroyers.[8] Huangpu Wenchong Shipbuilding is also building at least one unit of the new class but it is possible that further orders may be delayed until trial results from the initial ships have been analysed.

Submarines: It is arguably in the field of underwater technology that the PLAN's progress has been the least rapid. This is particularly the case with respect to nuclear-powered submarines, where China's navy remains at a significant quantitative and qualitative disadvantage to its Western adversaries. Most recent estimates that the PLAN continues to field just six Type 094/Type 094A 'Jin' series strategic submarines and an equal number of Type 093/Type 093A 'Shang' class attack submarines, possibly supplemented by a handful of obsolete first-generation boats. Open source reports suggest that an additional pair of Type 093B 'Shang II' submarines were launched from the giant submarine construction complex at the Bohai Shipyard in Huludao between May 2022 and January 2023 but have yet to enter operational service. These are understood to be the first Chinese nuclear-powered submarines equipped with pump-jet propulsors.

Given that both the Type 093 and Type 094 designs are believed to have started to enter service nearly two decades ago, their rate of production stands in contrast to the rapid growth of the PLAN's surface fleet. It seems reasonable to speculate that China has not been entirely satisfied with what has been produced so far, particularly in the area of acoustic stealth.[9] However, the substantial investment made in shipyard infrastructure suggests that the situation may well change rapidly once the inevitable technical hurdles in producing satisfactory designs are overcome. This could see rapid production of the much-rumoured next-generation Type 095 and Type 096 submarines.

Meanwhile, conventional submarine production remains focused on the latest Type 039C of the 'Yuan' class, which incorporates an unusual stealth

Table 2.2.3: PEOPLE'S LIBERATION ARMY NAVY: PRINCIPAL UNITS AS AT MID 2024

TYPE	CLASS	NUMBER	TONNAGE	DIMENSIONS	PROPULSION	CREW	DATE
Aircraft Carriers							
Aircraft Carrier – CV	Type 001A (Modified Kuznetsov)	1	65,000 tonnes	315m x 35/75m x 10m	Steam, 32 knots	Unknown	2019
Aircraft Carrier – CV	Type 001 **LIAONING** (Kuznetsov)	1	60,000 tonnes	306m x 35/73m x 10m	Steam, 32 knots	Unknown	2012
Principal Surface Escorts							
Destroyer – DDG	Type 055 **NANCHANG** ('Renhai')	8	c. 12,000 tonnes	180m x 20m x 7m	COGAG, 30 knots	c.300	2019
Destroyer – DDG	Type 052D **KUNMING** ('Luyang III')	25	7,500 tonnes	156m x 17m x 6m	CODOG, 28 knots	280	2014
Destroyer – DDG	Type 051C **SHENYANG** ('Luzhou')	2	7,100 tonnes	155m x 17m x 6m	Steam, 29 knots	250	2006
Destroyer – DDG	Type 052C **LANZHOU** ('Luyang II')	6	7,000 tonnes	154m x 17m x 6m	CODOG, 28 knots	280	2005
Destroyer – DDG	Type 052B **GUANGZHOU** ('Luyang I')	2	6,500 tonnes	154m x 17m x 6m	CODOG, 29 knots	280	2004
Destroyer – DDG	Project 956E/EM **HANGZHOU** (Sovremenny)	4	8,000 tonnes	156m x 17m x 6m	Steam, 32 knots	300	1999
Destroyer – DDG	Type 051B **SHENZHEN** ('Luhai')	1	6,000 tonnes	154m x 16m x 6m	Steam, 31 knots	250	1998
Destroyer – DDG	Type 052 **HARBIN** ('Luhu')	2	4,800 tonnes	143m x 15m x 5m	CODOG, 31 knots	260	1994
Frigate – FFG	Type 054A **XUZHOU** ('Jiangkai II')	40	4,100 tonnes	132m x 15m x 5m	CODAD, 28 knots	190	2008
Frigate – FFG	Type 054 **MA'ANSHAN** ('Jiangkai I')	2	4,000 tonnes	132m x 15m x 5m	CODAD, 28 knots	190	2005
Frigate – FFG	Type 053 H3 **LIANYUNGANG** ('Jiangwei II')	8	2,500 tonnes	112m x 12m x 5m	CODAD, 27 knots	170	1992
Frigate – FSG	Type 056/056A **BENGBU** ('Jiangdao')	50[1]	1,500 tonnes	89m x 12m x 4m	CODAD, 28 knots	60	2013
Plus fewer than 5 remaining obsolescent frigates of the Type 053 H1G BEIHAI ('Jianghu V') class that remain active in second-line roles.							
Submarines							
Submarine – SSBN	Type 094/094A ('Jin')	c. 6	9,000 tonnes	133m x 11m x 8m	Nuclear, 20+ knots	Unknown	2008
Submarine – SSBN	Type 092 ('Xia')	1[2]	6,500 tonnes	120m x 10m x 8m	Nuclear, 22 knots	140	1987
Submarine – SSN	Type 093/093A ('Shang')	c. 6	6,000 tonnes	107m x 11m x 8m	Nuclear, 30 knots	100	2006
Submarine – SSN	Type 091 ('Han')	3[2]	5,500 tonnes	106m x 10m x 7m	Nuclear, 25 knots	75	1974
Submarine – SSK	Type 039A/039B/039C (Type 041 'Yuan')	c. 20+	2,500 tonnes	75m x 8m x 5m	AIP, 20+ knots	Unknown	2006
Submarine – SSK	Type 039/039G ('Song')	13	2,300 tonnes	75m x 8m x 5m	Diesel-electric, 22 knots	60	1999
Submarine – SSK	Project 636 ('Kilo')	10[3]	3,000 tonnes	73m x 10m x 7m	Diesel-electric, 20 knots	55	1997
Plus c. 10 obsolescent patrol submarines of the Type 035 ('Ming' Class), many in reserve. A Type 032 'Qing' trials submarine has also been commissioned for strategic missile trials.							
Major Amphibious Units							
Amph. Assault Ship – LHD	Type 075 HAINAN ('Yushen')	3	40,000 tonnes	237m x 36m x 8m	CODAD, 20+ knots	Unknown	2021
Landing Platform Dock – LPD	Type 071 KULUN SHAN ('Yuzhao')	8	25,000 tonnes	210m x 27m x 7m	CODAD, 20 knots	Unknown	2007

Notes:

1. The 22-strong Type 056 variant has been transferred to the Coast Guard after refit.
2. The operational status of these vessels is highly questionable.
3. It has been reported that the two older Project 877 EKM 'Kilos' have been decommissioned.

fin (US Navy sail). US Department of Defence estimates suggest that twenty-five or more of the series might be in service by 2025, with thirteen Type 039 'Song' and ten Project 636 'Kilo' class boats making up the balance of the forty-eight front-line submarines allocated across the PLAN's three fleets. The first member of the 'Yuan' class was delivered in 2006 and an entirely new design now seems overdue.

MAJOR REGIONAL POWERS – JAPAN

The Japan Self Defence Forces are currently at the start of a major period of investment following the publication of updated national security and defence strategies at the end of 2022. The new plans were reflected in the approval of a record c. US$56bn defence budget for FY2024–25 in December 2023, a figure which was around nine percent higher than the FY2023–24 out-turn. For the Japan Maritime Self Defence Force (JMSDF), the revised strategy will see particular emphasis on bolstering the capacity of the surface fleet. This will grow to encompass the four carrier-like DDH destroyers, two Aegis System Equipped Vessels (ASEVs), fifty other destroyers/frigates and twelve patrol vessels. This expansion will be accompanied by the acquisition of large numbers of long-range strike missiles, with the JMSDF initially seeking to deploy Tomahawk cruise missiles aboard its Aegis-equipped destroyers in similar fashion to the RAN's plans. A c. US$1.7bn agreement was concluded in January 2024 to purchase 400 of these weapons, which will start to enter service from 2025 onwards.

Further details of the two ASEVs were released over the course of the year. The ships replace previous plans for land-based, 'Aegis Ashore' ballistic missile defence (BMD) sites and are primarily intended to counter the threat posed by North Korea's missile programme. The first vessel will begin construction in the course of the coming year and both are likely to enter service in the course of 2028–9. The ships will be equipped with Lockheed Martin's AN/SPY-7 radar and will likely be fitted with as many as 128 vertical launch cells for SM-3 and SM-6 interceptors, Tomahawk cruise missiles and other missiles. With a length of 190m and a beam of 25m, the ASEVs will be cruiser-sized vessels displacing 12,000 tonnes in standard (light) condition, likely allowing them to replace the US Navy's *Zumwalt* (DDG-1000) class as the world's largest surface combatants. Propulsion will be provided by twin Rolls-Royce MT-30 gas turbines in a hybrid electro-mechanical configuration. According to FY2024–25 budget documents, unit cost is estimated at an eye-watering 395bn yen (c. US$2.5bn).

Jingei (SS-515) is the third li-on battery equipped member of the JMSDF's *Tagei* class. Built by Mitsubishi Heavy Industries at Kobe, she is seen here at the time of her delivery on 8 March 2024. Current JMSDF fleet structure plans involve maintaining the operational submarine flotilla at twenty-two modern boats (plus additional training and trials vessels) by maintaining a one submarine p.a. production 'drumbeat'. *(JMSDF)*

A summary of current surface fleet strength is provided in Table 2.2.4. The JMSDF continues to be bolstered by the arrival of *Mogami* (FFM-1) class frigates, which are joining the fleet at a rate of two ships per year. In line with this, the last year saw the delivery of *Yahagi* (FFM-5) on 21 May 2024, followed by that of *Agano* (FFM-6) on 20 June. Another six units of the twelve-strong class are under construction; unlike the earlier ships these will be equipped with a sixteen-cell Mk 41 vertical launch system (VLS) from build. The current defence budget marks the transition to a new FFM design that will be around 1,000 tonnes heavier than the 5,300-tonne *Mogami* and, inter alia, incorporate a greater VLS capacity. It is planned that the new class will also comprise twelve ships. The cost of the first two amounts to 174bn yen or 87bn yen (c. US$540m) per vessel.

The updated defence strategy maintained the targeted strength of the submarine flotilla at twenty-two boats, a level that was achieved in 2022. The operational force currently comprises two *Tagei* (SS-513) class submarines, twelve *Soryu* (SS-501) class submarines and eight *Oyashio* (SS-590) class boats. In addition, the lead *Tagei* class submarine was reclassified as a trials submarine when *Jingei* (SS-515) – the third member of the class – commissioned on 8 March 2024 and two further *Oyashio* class boats are used in a training capacity. The lead *Oyashio* submarine has previously decommissioned on 17 March 2023 after a total service life of 25 years in operational and training roles; reportedly the longest to date of any JMSDF submarine.[10] The latest defence budget includes funding for the eighth *Tagei* class submarine at a cost of 95bn yen (c. US$590m), maintaining a one unit p.a. 'drumbeat'.

Other new vessels included in the latest budget include the first of a new class of 14,500-tonne logistic support vessel at a cost of 83bn yen

(c. US$510m) and the sixth *Awaji* (MS-304) class mine countermeasures vessel for 26bn yen (c. US$160m). The latter acquisition suggests that the JMSDF remains committed to maintaining a force of dedicated mine warfare vessels despite a reduction in the overall size of the specialised mine countermeasures force as modular, multi-role vessels such as the *Mogami* class start to enter service.

MAJOR REGIONAL POWERS – SOUTH KOREA

A summary of Republic of Korean Navy strength is set out in Table 2.2.5. The changes to the table relate to long-established programmes, with the main addition to the surface fleet being the delivery of the eighth and final FFX-2 *Daegu* class frigate, *Chuncheon*, by Hyundai Heavy Industries (HHI) on 24 October 2023. Her arrival was counterbalanced by the withdrawal of the veteran *Po Hang* class frigates *Dacheon* and *Namwon* at the end of the year, leaving just three of the once-numerous series in South Korean Navy service. Meanwhile the underwater flotilla was bolstered by the arrival of the third KSS-3 *Dosan Ahn Chang-Ho* class submarine, *Shin Chae-Ho*, by HHI on 4 April 2024. This brings construction of the first batch of these boats to its conclusion. Work on all three units of the enlarged KSS-3 Batch 2 design is now underway at Hanwha Ocean, with orders for a final trio of KSS-Batch 3 units planned in due course.

Plans for future surface fleet construction have assumed a more solid form over the past year. The lead KDX-3 Batch 2, *Jeongjo the Great*, commenced sea trials from HHI's Ulsan shipyard in the autumn of 2023 and will be delivered before the end of 2024. Fabrication of the second member of the class commenced at HHI in July 2023 prior to formal keel-laying on 12 March 2024. A further vessel has been ordered. Alongside the existing trio of KDX-III Batch 1 *Sejong the Great* class destroyers, this will give the Republic of Korea Navy six large Aegis-equipped destroyers to form a key part of the 'Korean Air and Missile Defence' (KAMD) component of the so-called 'Three-Axis' deterrent. Standard SM-3 and SM-6 series missiles are being acquired to equip the ships for the ballistic missile defence role.

The remainder of the destroyer fleet currently comprises six KDX-2 and three KDX-1 destroyers, the former commissioning between 2003 and 2008 and the latter around the turn of the millennium. It appears that the KDX-2 vessels will ultimately be replaced by the new KDDX type, on which HHI completed basic design work at the end of 2023. The new ship will be equipped with indigenous South Korean sensors and weaponry and incorporate integrated electrical propulsion. Meanwhile, the KDX-1 ships will be replaced by a fourth batch of six FFX-4 frigates under a programme approved in April 2024. Their construction will follow on from

Table 2.2.4: JAPAN MARITIME SELF-DEFENCE FORCE: PRINCIPAL UNITS AS AT MID 2024

TYPE	CLASS	NUMBER[1]	TONNAGE	DIMENSIONS	PROPULSION	CREW	DATE
Support and Helicopter Carriers							
Aircraft Carrier – CV[2]	**IZUMO** (DDH-183)	2	27,000 tonnes	248m x 38m x 7m	COGAG, 30 knots	470	2015
Helicopter Carrier – CVH	**HYUGA** (DDH-181)	2	19,000 tonnes	197m x 33m x 7m	COGAG, 30 knots	340	2009
Principal Surface Escorts							
Destroyer – DDG	**MAYA** (DDG-179)	2	10,500 tonnes	170m x 21m x 6m	COGLAG, 30 knots	300	2020
Destroyer – DDG	**ATAGO** (DDG-177)	2	10,000 tonnes	165m x 21m x 6m	COGAG, 30 knots	300	2007
Destroyer – DDG	**KONGOU** (DDG-173)	4	9,500 tonnes	161m x 21m x 6m	COGAG, 30 knots	300	1993
Destroyer – DDG	**HATAKAZE** (DDG-171)	0 (2)	6,300 tonnes	150m x 16m x 5m	COGAG, 30 knots	260	1986
Destroyer – DDG	**ASAHI** (DD-119)	2	6,800 tonnes	151m x 18m x 5m	COGLAG, 30 knots	230	2017
Destroyer – DD	**AKIZUKI** (DD-115)	4	6,800 tonnes	151m x 18m x 5m	COGAG, 30 Knots	200	2012
Destroyer – DDG	**TAKANAMI** (DD-110)	5	6,300 tonnes	151m x 17m x 5m	COGAG, 30 knots	175	2003
Destroyer – DDG	**MURASAME** (DD-101)	9	6,200 tonnes	151m x 17m x 5m	COGAG, 30 knots	165	1996
Destroyer – DDG	**ASAGIRI** (DD-151)	8	4,900 tonnes	137m x 15m x 5m	COGAG, 30 knots	220	1988
Frigate – FFG	**MOGAMI** (FFM-1)	6	5,300 tonnes	133m x 16m x 5m	CODAG, 30+ knots	90	2022
Frigate – FFG	**ABUKUMA** (DE-229)	6	2,500 tonnes	109m x 13m x 4m	CODOG, 27 knots	120	1989
Submarines							
Submarine – SSK[3]	**TAGEI** (SS-513)	2[1]	4,300 tonnes	84m x 9m x 8m	Diesel-electric, 20+ knots	70	2022
Submarine – SSK	**SORYU** (SS-501)	12	4,200 tonnes	84m x 9m x 8m	AIP, 20+ knots[4]	65	2009
Submarine – SSK	**OYASHIO** (SS-590)	8[2]	4,000 tonnes	82m x 9m x 8m	Diesel-electric, 20+ knots	70	1998
Major Amphibious Units							
Landing Platform Dock – LPD	**OSUMI** (LST-4001)	3	14,000 tonnes	178m x 26m x 6m	Diesel, 22 knots	135	1998

Notes:

1. Figures in brackets refer to trials or training ships.
2. In the course of conversion to operate F-35B STOVL strike fighters.
3. The lead unit is now operated as a dedicated trials submarine.
4. The last two units of the class have their AIP plant replaced by lithium-ion batteries; an arrangement also adopted in the follow-on *Tagei* class

The Republic of Korea Navy completed deliveries of its first batch of three KSS-3 submarines in 2024 with the delivery of *Shin Chae-Ho* on 4 April 2024. In addition to their normal outfit of torpedoes, the class is equipped with six K-VLS vertical launch cells for the Hyunmoo 4-4 conventionally-armed ballistic missile. These photographs show *Shin Chae-Ho* (left) and her sister *Ahn Mu*, the second member of the class. *(Republic of Korea Defense Acquisition Program Administration)*

the six FFX-3 *Chungnam* class frigates, on which work is already underway. Both the KDDX and FFX-4 programmes are likely to be completed in the second half of the 2030s. At this time, the Republic of Korea Navy is likely to have around twelve large destroyers and twenty-four medium-sized frigates in commission.

A further notable development in the last 12 months has been the arrival of the navy's first three P-8A Poseidon maritime patrol aircraft on 19 June 2024. At that time, it was stated that the remaining trio were expected by the end of the month, completing a contract for six aircraft ordered in 2019. The new P-8As will provide a significant uplift in capacity over the elderly P-3C Orion aircraft that currently form the navy's principal airborne surveillance assets.

OTHER REGIONAL FLEETS

Brunei: The Royal Brunei Navy saw the completion of the transfer of two former Republic of Singapore

Table 2.2.5: REPUBLIC OF KOREA NAVY: PRINCIPAL UNITS AS AT MID 2024

TYPE	CLASS	NUMBER	TONNAGE	DIMENSIONS	PROPULSION	CREW	DATE
Principal Surface Escorts							
Destroyer – DDG	KDX-3 **SEJONG THE GREAT**	3	10,000 tonnes	166m x 21m x 6m	COGAG, 30 knots	300	2008
Destroyer – DDG	KDX-2 **CHUNGMUGONG YI SUN-SHIN**	6	5,500 tonnes	150m x 17m x 5m	CODOG, 30 knots	200	2003
Destroyer – DDG	KDX-1 **GWANGGAETO THE GREAT**	3	3,900 tonnes	135m x 14m x 4m	CODOG, 30 knots	170	1998
Frigate – FFG	FFX-2 **DAEGU**	8	3,600 tonnes	122m x 14m x 4m	CODLOG	140	2017
Frigate – FFG	FFX-1 **INCHEON**	6	3,000 tonnes	114m x 14m x 4m	CODOG, 30 knots	140	2013
Frigate – FFG	**ULSAN**	2	2,300 tonnes	102m x 12m x 4m	CODOG, 35 knots	150	1981
Corvette – FSG	**POHANG**	3	1,200 tonnes	88m x 10m x 3m	CODOG, 32 knots	95	1984
Submarines							
Submarine – SSK	KSS-3 **DOSAN AHN CHANG-HO**	3	3,800 tonnes	84m x 8m x 8m	AIP, 20+ knots	50	2021
Submarine – SSK	KSS-2 **SON WON-IL** (Type 214)	9	1,800 tonnes	65m x 6m x 6m	AIP, 20+ knots	30	2007
Submarine – SSK	KSS-1 **CHANG BOGO** (Type 209/1200)	9	1,300 tonnes	56m x 6m x 6m	Diesel-electric, 22 knots	35	1993
Major Amphibious Units							
Amph Assault Ship – LHD	LPX **DOKDO**	2[1]	18,900 tonnes	200m x 32m x 7m	Diesel, 22 knots	425	2007

Notes:
1. *Marado*, the second ship of the class, is built to a slightly different design.

Navy *Fearless* class patrol vessels gifted by their former owner with the handover of the new *Al-Faruq* at Changi Naval Base on 2 October 2023. Subsequently commissioned on 14 December 2023, the 500 tonne vessel joins her sister *As-Siddiq*, previously delivered in March 2023.

Indonesia: Indonesia continues to follow a two-tier fleet strategy. This involves a relatively small force of foreign-designed front-line warships being supplemented by numerous indigenous patrol vessels and other craft that help provide a naval presence across the archipelago's vast territorial waters. A growing economy has helped Indonesia steadily expand both fleet tiers in recent years. Moreover, many observers expect the rise of Defence Minister Prabowo Subianto as the country's president-elect in February 2024 to result in more money flowing into the armed forces' coffers. To some extent, however, the benefit of additional resources is being dissipated by the distribution of procurement contracts across a wide range of suppliers. This results in the acquisition of an eclectic range of equipment that is difficult to sustain. Two major naval contracts awarded in the first half of 2024 evidence a continuation of this questionable approach.

One of these contracts was announced on 2 April 2024. France's Naval Group reported that it had signed a contract with Indonesia five days previously that will see two 'Scorpène Evolved Full LiB' submarines assembled by PT PAL in Indonesia under a transfer of technology arrangement. The latest iteration of the well-established type that is already in service with, inter alia, neighbouring Malaysia, the new boats will be equipped with lithium-ion batteries. Naval Group claim that these allow a higher range of useful energy, a better indiscretion rate and a reduced charging time. The deal effectively replaces a previous agreement with South Korea's DSME (now Hanwha Ocean) to purchase a second trio of Type 209 *Nagapasa* class submarines to join the three that entered service between 2017 and 2021, complicating logistical support and training arrangements. Incredibly, however, Indonesia is also looking to acquire an 'interim submarine' type to provide an immediate boost to numbers as it looks to build its submarine flotilla to a total of twelve boats. Meanwhile, a US$100m contract including the supply of a British Submarine Manufacturing and Products SRV-F Mk3 rescue submersible and an Indonesian-built 'mothership' was agreed in September 2023.

The picture with respect to submarine acquisitions has also been reflected in the surface fleet. On 28 March 2024 – the same day the 'Scorpène' deal was signed – Italy's Fincantieri announced that it had agreed a €1.2bn (c. US$ 1.3bn) contract with the Indonesian Ministry of Defence for the supply of two frigate-like *Paolo Thaon di Revel* multirole offshore patrol vessels. The transaction is seemingly a replacement for a previous understanding based around the transfer of surplus Italian *Maestrale* class frigates and new FREMMs. The two vessels now contracted are being diverted from construction previously allocated to the Italian Navy, allowing a relatively rapid delivery planned for October 2024 and April 2025.[11] On arrival, the new ships will join a surface flotilla that already includes frigates and corvettes of British and Dutch origin, with South Korean and Anglo-Danish designed vessels on the way. Apparently not yet satisfied with this diverse force, the navy is now undertaking negotiations with France that could also see PT PAL undertake licensed construction of the FDI *Amiral Ronar'ch* design.

Current construction at Surabaya-based PT PAL, Indonesia's leading naval shipbuilding yard, is headed by two Babcock-designed 'Arrowhead 140' frigates under the *Merah Putih* (red and white) frigate programme. The keel of the first ship was laid in August 2023 and was followed by a first steel-cutting ceremony for her sister on 5 June 2024. It appears unlikely that the new ships will be operational before the end of the decade. As such, Indonesia is seeking cost-effective options to increase the number of its surface combatants in the interim. It seems that South Korea is willing to transfer up to three decommissioned *Po Hang* class corvettes as it attempts to build defence industrial ties. A US$35m budget to refurbish the first of these was reportedly agreed in mid-2024.

Shipyards around the country continue to be involved in the construction of new KCR missile-armed and PC patrol boats of various sizes. These include a new waterjet-propelled variant of the larger 60m KCR type, with local companies PT Tesco Indomaritim and PT Palindo Marine both reportedly working on examples of this variant. The latter yard has recently completed the fourth member of the equivalent but slower PC-60 *Dorang* class, delivering *Marlin* (PC-877) in September 2023.[12] Series production of the smaller PC-40 *Pari* class patrol vessel also continues, with around twenty of this 40m type now either completed or in the course of build. All these vessels tend to incorporate detailed

The veteran Indonesian frigate *Yos Sudarso*, originally a Dutch *Van Speijk* class variant of the British *Leander* type, seen in September 2023. Indonesia's modernisation of its small force of front-line surface combatants and submarines is resulting in the creation of an eclectic mix of vessels. *(Australian Department of Defence)*

changes dependent on builder, further adding to the diversity of Indonesia's fleet mix.

Malaysia: The Royal Malaysian Navy's longstanding '15 to 5 Transformation Plan' to reconfigure and simplify its fleet around five classes of warship totalling fifty-five major combatants remains a focal point of fleet planning. In practice, however, the passage of time is starting to unravel elements of the strategy as changes in both technology and the geopolitical backdrop start to intervene. Notably, in May 2024, a revised version of the plan – now referred to as the 'RMN Organisational Restructuring 2024' – revealed that the navy intended to add four mine countermeasures and two survey vessels to the planned force mix. This increases the targeted fleet size to fifty-seven surface vessels and four submarines. In practice, it seems unlikely that this structure will be achieved given the very slow progress made to date.

Another complication was added in June 2024 when it was confirmed that a variant of the Turkish 'Milgem' ('Ada') corvette design had been selected to meet the requirement for a second batch of littoral mission ships that form one of the core classes in the original RMN transformation plan. These c. 2,500-tonne ships will be much larger and more capable than the four 700-tonne *Keris* class patrol vessels delivered by China to form the first littoral mission ship batch. As such, they can hardly be considered as forming a homogenous class. The contract confirmed that the second batch will comprise three ships, which will all be constructed in Turkey and delivered before the end of 2027.

A major source of delay with Malaysia's naval modernisation has been the botched construction of an original six, now reduced to five, *Maharaja Lela* class 'Gowind' type frigates by Boustead Heavy Industries. The programme has now been restructured to allow work to recommence. The lead ship was subject to technical launch at the renamed Lumut Naval Shipyard on 23 May 2024. Her delivery is expected before the end of 2026; a schedule that may prove optimistic given the extent of past delays.[13]

New Zealand: As of mid-2024, the Royal New Zealand Navy (RNZN) was awaiting the announcement of an updated Defence Capability Plan (DCP) that will set the trajectory of future government investment in the New Zealand Defence Force. Its release will follow the publication of a trio of defence and security strategic documents – headed by *Secure Together*, an inaugural national security strategy – in August 2023 that acknowledged the need to revise the country's security posture in the light of a deteriorating international environment.[14] In September 2023, a request for information – entitled Maritime Fleet Market Research – sought input from industry on alternative fleet configurations, support arrangements and operating approaches to inform the DCP process. The RNZN currently operates nine ships in six classes, eight of which fall due for replacement by the mid-2030s. There is an acknowledgement that adoption of a simpler structure involving fewer separate warship classes, perhaps through greater use of modular equipment, might allow the creation of a more effective and cost-efficient fleet. In the meantime, the RNZN continues to work to resolve a crewing crisis that has seen both its offshore patrol vessels and one of the pair of surviving inshore patrol vessels laid up for lack of crews.

North Korea: The Korean People's Navy (KPN) has announced progress with two important programmes over the past year. Most significantly, 6 September 2023 saw the launch and naming of the first and, to date, only 'Sinpo-C' class submarine during a ceremony attended by President Kim Jong-un at the Sinpo South shipyard. The newly-launched *Hero Kim Kun Ok* is described by North Korea as a tactical nuclear attack submarine. It is widely considered to be a modified version of a Russian Project 633 'Romeo' class diesel-electric boat and has been reported as being under construction for a number of years. The new submarine incorporates an extended fin (sail) capable of housing four short-range ballistic and six cruise missiles, all potentially armed with nuclear warheads. This gives it a much higher capacity than the older 'Sinpo' class submarine *8.24 Yongung*, which has been the country's sole ballistic missile submarine (SSB) to date. North Korean media reports that the submarine-launching ceremony heralded the beginning of a new chapter for bolstering KPN naval power and that there were plans to convert other submarines into nuclear-armed vessels. Subsequently, in May 2024, satellite imagery suggested that work was underway on at least one additional 'Sinpo-C' class boat at the eponymous shipyard. In the longer term, North Korea would also like to acquire nuclear-powered submarines.[15]

Meanwhile, official news reports in August 2023 revealed the completion of a new light frigate that is commonly referred to as the first vessel of a new *Anmok* class. This appears to be one of a pair of new surface combatants previously reported as being under construction. In similar fashion to *Hero Kim Kun Ok*, the new warship is equipped with long-range cruise missiles, thereby potentially further distributing the Democratic People's Republic's nuclear strike capacity.

The Philippines: A comprehensive review of the Philippine Navy is set out in Chapter 2.2A.

Singapore: The Republic of Singapore Navy has continued to move forward with the renewal of its submarine flotilla over the past year. *Inimitable*, the fourth and final member of its new Type 218 *Invincible* class was subject to a formal launch ceremony at thyssenkrupp Marine Systems (TKMS) Kiel on 22 April 2024, bringing the programme closer to completion. Her delivery is scheduled for 2025. *Impeccable* became the first of the class to arrive in Singapore when she reached home waters aboard the transport ship *Rolldock Storm* in July 2023. However, neither she nor any other members of the class had been formally commissioned into naval service as of mid-2024 as an extensive programme of trials and training continued.

With the submarine programme drawing towards a close, Singapore is focusing on its next major project encompassing the construction of six Multi-Role Combat Vessels (MRCVs). These will replace the existing *Victory* class corvettes on a numerical like-for-like basis. Under a contract awarded in March 2023, Saab and Odense Maritime Technology are working under the auspices of Singapore's Defence Science and Technology Agency (DSTA) to develop the basic design.[16] Local company ST Engineering is responsible for detailed design and actual construction. Details have subsequently started to emerge about the new class, which are based on modular concepts and – at between 5,000 and 10,000 tonnes displacement – will be larger than Singapore's existing *Fearless* class frigates. The ships will incorporate an integrated propulsion system supplied by GE Vernova Power Conversion; the company previously responsible for systems used in the British Royal Navy's *Queen Elizabeth* class carriers and Type 45 destroyers. First steel cutting for the lead vessel took place on 8 March 2024, with delivery expected before the end of the decade.

The Republic of Singapore is coming close to completing the modernisation of its submarine flotilla with German-built Type 218 submarines. Here, *Inimitable*, the fourth and final member of the class is pictured at the time of her launch on 22 April 2024. *(thyssenkrupp Marine Systems)*

Whilst ST Engineering is heavily involved in the MRCV programme, it is German shipbuilder Fassmer that has been awarded the contract for another important surface vessel project. In November, the Singapore Ministry of Defence announced that it had been selected to supply four offshore patrol vessels based on the German Federal Police's *Potsdam* class. The new ships will replace the four re-rolled elderly *Fearless* class patrol vessels that now serve as the *Sentinel* class in Singapore's Maritime and Security Response Flotilla from 2028 onwards.

Taiwan: Whilst still in the shadow of mainland China's rapid naval expansion, Taiwan's Republic of China Navy (ROCN) is making further progress with implementing an asymmetrical maritime strategy that is primarily aimed at deterring any invasion across the Taiwan Strait. The most important element of this strategy is the renewal of its submarine flotilla under a programme that is ultimately intended to comprise eight new diesel-electric submarines. This would have potentially game-changing consequences for ROCN capacity given that its existing quartet of elderly boats is regarded as having limited operational value. Further details of the submarine's new design were revealed at an official naming ceremony for the lead boat that was conducted by Taiwan's then-President Tsai Ing-wen on 28 September 2023 at CSBC Corporation's Kaohsiung shipyard. Named *Hai Kung*, the new submarine is of modern appearance, with her aft control surfaces incorporating the increasingly popular cruciform configuration. She was subsequently floated out on 27 February 2024 and is currently in the course of performing harbour acceptance tests. All-in-all, she represents a remarkable political and technical accomplishment for the ROCN given the significant efforts mainland China has taken to deny Taiwan access to overseas submarine expertise.

Whilst it will still be some time before *Hai Kung* is operational, further members of the innovative *Tuo Chiang* class of stealthy, missile-armed catamaran corvettes continue to enter the fleet. A ceremony on 24 March 2024 saw the delivery of *An Chiang* and *Wan Chiang*. They are, respectively, the sixth and seventh members of the overall class and the final units of the first series production batch. Their arrival followed that of their sisters *Hsu Chiang* and *Wu Chiang* earlier in the year. A second series production batch of five vessels incorporating improved air defence weaponry is planned. A derivative has also been inducted into coast guard service.

Despite the primacy of the counter-invasion strategy, the ROCN is also considering how best to protect its sea lines of communication as its existing destroyers and frigates approach obsolescence. This has been one of the factors driving a programme for a new class of light frigate, which is being constructed in separate anti-submarine warfare (ASW) and anti-air warfare (AAW) configurations by CITIC Shipbuilding. The new ship is based on a design by America's Gibbs & Cox. It reportedly uses a combat management system derived from the Lockheed Martin CMS-330 found, inter alia, aboard the *Halifax* class frigates. Construction of the prototype AAW variant began in November 2023 and has subsequently been followed by the start of work on the lead ASW-configured ship in January 2024. A total of twelve of these vessels are eventually planned to replace legacy frigate types.

Thailand: The 'on/off' saga of the Royal Thai Navy's plans to create an underwater flotilla appeared to reach a conclusion in May 2024 when it was determined that the acquisition of a single S26T boat – an export variant of the PLAN's 'Yuan' class – would proceed. The deal hit the rocks when China failed to procure an export licence for the German MTU396 diesel engines intended to power the submarines. The proposed substitution of a Chinese-made CHD620 model proved unpalatable despite its specification for Pakistan's similar *Hangor* class. However, it appears that China has sweetened the US$390m deal with a number of concessions that are rumoured to include an anti-ship missile capacity. Current scheduling should allow the new submarine to enter service before the end of 2027, roughly a decade after the deal was first signed.

With negotiations on the submarine purchase seemingly satisfactorily concluded, the navy is turning its attention to acquire additional modern surface combatants. Four ships are ultimately envisaged to join the single *Bhumibol Adulyadej* class unit that was acquired from what was then DSME in 2019. At that time it was envisaged that more ships of the type would be built under a licence arrangement but it seems that the new requirement is being thrown open to international competition.

Vietnam: After undertaking a raft of acquisitions focused on Russian submarines and frigates in the previous decade, the pace of Vietnam People's Navy procurement has slowed. The only significant new arrival over the past year has been the former Indian Navy *Khukri* class corvette, *Kirpan.* Gifted to Vietnam as part of a wider programme of defence diplomacy, the ship was handed over at the end of July 2023 and has become Ship 16 in Vietnamese service. With supplies of further Russian equipment likely disrupted by the Russo-Ukrainian war, the way would seem to be open to alternative suppliers as Vietnam continues to cast a wary eye over Chinese expansion in the South China Sea.

Taiwan commissioned *An Chiang* and *Wan Chiang*, the latest members of the *Tuo Chiang* catamaran corvette class, at a ceremony held on 24 Match 2024. In this photograph, *An Chiang* is to the centre-right of the photo and the older *Ta Chiang* – second of the class – to the centre-left. Note the slightly different bridge arrangements of the two ships. *(Republic of China Navy)*

Notes:

1. For example, see Liu Xuanzun and Guo Yuandan, 'China's aircraft carrier Shandong spotted near Philippines amid tensions' posted to the *Global Times* site – gloabltimes.cn – on 30 June 2024.

2. *The AUKUS Nuclear-Powered Submarine Pathway: A Partnership for the Future* was published jointly by the three partner governments in March 2023. It can be readily accessed by searching the web.

3. See *Enhanced Lethality Surface Combatant Fleet: Independent Analysis of Navy's Surface Combatant Fleet* (Canberra: Australian Government, 2023). It and other related materials can currently be found at: defence.gov.au/about/reviews-inquiries/independent-analysis-navy-surface-combatant-fleet

4. Although 18 May marked the official start of production, it had been stated earlier that a number of previously constructed prototype blocks would also be used in *Hunter*'s assembly.

5. The RAN also operates two of the original 'Cape' class design under lease. The surface fleet review envisaged a total Australian fleet of twenty-five patrol vessels: six *Arafura* class OPVs and eight 'Evolved Capes' in the RAN, with a further eleven 'Evolved Capes; in the Australian Border Force (ABF). The new contract therefore suggests either a shift in the balance of this force between the RAN and ABF or some other change of plan.

6. The annual report *Military and Security Developments Involving the People's Republic of China* (Washington DC: US Department of Defense, 2023) includes regular updates of PLAN force development.

7. As noted in last year's *Seaforth World Naval Review*, Shanghai's main naval shipyards have been progressively transferred from the heart of the city to Changxingdao Island as part of a two decade-long plan to establish a colossal shipbuilding enterprise. An update on this process was provided by Matthew P. Funaiole, Brian Hart, Joseph S. Bermudez Jr., Jennifer Jun, and Samantha Lu in 'Tracking China's Naval Modernization at Key Shipyards' posted to the CSIS's *ChinaPower* project site – chinapower.csis.org – on 21 November 2023.

8. Further details of the Type 054B design are provided by Alex Luck in 'Chinese Navy Next Generation Frigate Starts Builder Trials' posted to the *Naval News* site – navalnews.com – on 18 January 2024.

9. An interesting insight into the history of the PLAN's submarine programmes is provided by Christopher P. Carlson and Howard Wang in *China Maritime Report No. 30: A Brief Technical History of PLAN Nuclear Submarines* (Rhode Island: China Maritime Studies Institute, US Naval War College, 2023), which is available on line at: digital-commons.usnwc.edu/cmsi-maritime-reports/30/

10. Last year's *Seaforth World Naval Review* failed to note *Oyashio*'s withdrawal.

11. The *Paolo Thaon di Revel* class is described in Chapter 3.2.

12. PT Palindo Marine, based on the western island of Batam, is one of the more active smaller yards involved in naval construction. It is also currently working in collaboration with Germany's Abeking & Rasmussen to build a new 105m hydrographic survey ship, on which work began in September 2023.

13. *Maharaja Lela* had previously been ceremonially launched on 24 August 2017 before the original construction programme collapsed, For more details of the technical launch, see Albert Lee, Malaysia's First Littoral Combat Ship Maharaja Lela Enters Water' posted to the *Naval News* site on 4 June 2024.

14. See *Secure Together: New Zealand's National Security Strategy 2023-2028* (Wellington: New Zealand Government, 2023) which is readily accessible by searching the web. The two other documents, both released by the New Zealand Ministry of Defence, were the *Defence Policy and Strategy Statement 2023* and *Future Force Design Principles 2023*.

15. For further detailed analysis on the submarine *Hero Kim Kun Ok*, see Vann H. Van Diepen, 'The Sleeper Has Awakened: Six Key Takeaways From the Rollout of North Korea's "Tactical Nuclear Attack Submarine"' posted to the Henry L. Stimson Center think tank's *38 North* project at 38north.org on 11 September 2023. A further post to the site by Jack Liu, Peter Makowsky and Iliana Ragnone on 8 May 2024 entitled, 'Sinpho South Shipyard: Indications of New Submarine Construction' brings the picture up to date.

16. Saab was previously involved in the basic design and supply of composite superstructures for Singapore's *Independence* class littoral mission vessels.

2.2A FLEET REVIEW

THE PHILIPPINE NAVY

Guardian of the Philippine Seas

Author:
Mrityunjoy Mazumdar

The archipelagic nation of the Philippines lies firmly in the cross hairs of an expansionist China by virtue of its location next to the disputed South China Sea. These resource-rich waters – often referred to as the West Philippine Sea by Filipinos – are rife with tensions between a number of countries possessing overlapping territorial and economic claims. However, it is China, in pursuit of its famous nine-dash line, which has been most eager to assert its dominance over the zone.[1] Always careful to operate within the confines of the 'grey zone', that is actions that fall short of war, China has nevertheless used a variety of methods and forces – notably the white-hulled vessels of its coast guard – to push the boundaries of what it can get away with. Clearly this stance has presented challenges to the Philippine Navy and other state agencies as the Philippines attempt to protect its own interpretation of the country's Exclusive Economic Zone (EEZ).

The Philippine Navy's latest frigate, *Antonia Luna*, proudly flies the Philippine National Flag from her main mast during an international exercise in the country's Exclusive Economic Zone in April 2024. The country's maritime interests are being increasingly challenged by China's 'grey zone' activities in the South China Sea, spurring on naval investment. *(Australian Department of Defence)*

THE MARITIME SECURITY ENVIRONMENT

The EEZ currently claimed by the Philippines is around 2.26 million square kilometres (874,000 square miles). It encompasses well over 7,000 islands (two-thirds uninhabited) and a coastline in excess of 36,000km (22,500 miles). Eleven of these islands falling within three major groups – Luzon in the north, the Visayas in the middle and Mindanao in the south – account for over 90 percent of the total land area. The waters of the EEZ encompass the South China Sea, Philippine Sea, Sulu Sea, Celebes Sea and the Luzon Strait; all famous for the many naval battles that took place there during the Second World War.

The archipelagic nature of the Philippines, with its many remote islands, leaves its waters vulnerable to both insurgency and criminal action. The seaborne threat from, in particular, Islamic militants has sometimes been a major issue, leading to security collaboration with neighbouring countries such as Indonesia. To this must be added the normal run of criminal activity at sea, including drug smuggling, piracy, human trafficking and illegal, unreported and unregulated fishing.

Turning to state actors, from Manila's perspective it is Beijing that is viewed as the primary external threat to maritime security and, as such, the major impetus for the current modernisation of the Philippine military. In contrast to his predecessor,

Rodrigo Duterte, the Philippines' current president, Ferdinand 'Bongbong' Romualdez Marcos Jr., has taken a firmer line against Chinese expansionism, strengthening diplomatic and security ties with like-minded countries such as Australia, Japan and the United States. From a practical perspective, confrontations at sea between the Philippines and China normally result in a war of words but the situation is fraught with the danger of a shooting war because of a possible miscalculation. There is also a perception by some that China's actions are becoming increasingly escalatory.[2] Whilst the Philippines benefits from a 1951 Mutual Defense Aid treaty with the United States that could be invoked in the case of conflict, some commentators question whether America's domestic politics would allow intervention in a dispute over what are essentially rocks and shoals in the South China Sea.

In line with this backdrop, the Philippine military has been steadily evolving from its traditional focus on ensuring the country's internal security to a more outward-looking defence strategy where the need to deal with external threats, in effect China, is assuming greater priority. Not surprisingly, the Philippine Navy has been in the forefront of this evolution, releasing an 'Active Archipelagic Defense Strategy' (AADS) in 2013 that has acted as a guide to subsequent naval modernisation. Essentially based on an asymmetric anti-access/area denial (A2/AD) approach, this strategy emphasises maritime situational awareness and collaboration between the navy, other branches of the armed forces and relevant government agencies. The latter is particularly relevant given the overlap between the Philippine Navy, the Philippine Coast Guard and agencies such as the Philippine National Police-Maritime Group and the Bureau of Fisheries and Aquatic Resources, potentially duplicating the use of scarce resources. Despite fluctuating political emphasis on the external threat, the AADS has proved influential, driving the release of the Philippine Marine Corps' Archipelagic Coastal Defense (ACD) concept of operations in 2021. Most significantly, the navy's approach has been reflected in the Philippine Department of National Defense's 'Comprehensive Archipelagic Defense Concept' (CADC) announced early in 2024. This has been described as representing a 'paradigm shift in the Philippines' defence strategy, confirming the trend of gradual reorientation from an internal to an external security focus'.[3]

HISTORIC DEVELOPMENT

The forerunner of the modern Philippine Navy was the Offshore Patrol (OSP). This small unit was established as a branch of the embryonic Philippine Army in February 1939 under the framework of the country's 1935 National Defense Act (which set out plans to create an independent Philippine military prior to planned independence from the United States). Initial plans envisaged this coastal protection force being equipped with British Thornycroft motor torpedo boats, a process that had only just commenced when the Second World War broke out. The OSP subsequently became part of the United States Army Forces in the Far East in the run-up to the Pacific War, seeing combat after Japan attacked the archipelago on 8 December 1941. The unit was reactivated after the Philippines' liberation in 1945, subsequently becoming a separate branch of the Philippine Armed Forces as the Philippine Naval Patrol (PNP) in October 1947 after the Philippines' independence on 4 July 1946. The PNP was renamed the Philippine Navy at the start of 1951.

The Philippine Navy has largely focused on internal security operations throughout its subsequent history, initially being equipped with an assortment of largely former US Navy minor combatants and auxiliaries for this purpose. A naval infantry force had been created in 1950, subsequently playing an active role in counterinsurgency operations. Despite its internal focus, navy landing craft did play a minor part transporting Philippine personnel to both the Korean and Vietnam wars. A welcome consequence of the end of the latter conflict in 1975 was the incorporation into the navy of large numbers of Republic of Vietnam Navy warships that had sought refuge in the Philippines after the then-South Vietnam's collapse.

Throughout the initial decades of its history, the Philippine Navy was overshadowed by the presence of significant elements of the US Pacific Fleet at the massive Subic Bay naval base in Luzon. This arguably further strengthened the emphasis the navy placed on internal security, as defence from external threats was essentially outsourced. Whilst the US Navy departed the facility in 1992 after the end of the Cold War, lack of funding in the aftermath of the 1997 Asian Financial Crisis and a temporary abatement of tensions with China meant that little in the way of adjustment could be achieved. It was only in 2021 that the last of the fleet's former US Navy Second World War-era combatants were retired.[4]

The now-retired Philippine Navy *Tomas Batilo* fast attack craft *Salvador Abcede* pictured during maritime security exercises with the Royal Australian Navy in October 2014. For much of its history, the Philippine Navy has prioritised internal security operations in coastal waters. *(Australian Department of Defence)*

The situation has started to improve over the last decade after the passing of the Revised AFP Modernization Act in December 2012, which was approved against a backdrop of further Chinese expansion into the South China Sea. The act provided for the upgrading of Philippine Armed Forces over three time periods or 'Horizons'; namely Horizon 1 (2013–17), Horizon 2 (2018–22) and Horizon 3 (2023–8). Whilst the plans first two phases have only been partially achieved, the programme has allowed the navy – in conjunction with the AADS concept referenced above – to make a start with the process of reconfiguration required to allow it to address external threats. Recently, early in 2024, the new Marcos Jr. regime has announced an enhanced 'Re-Horizon 3' initiative aimed at accelerating the process of military – and hence naval – modernisation.[5]

ROLES AND ORGANISATION

Today's Philippine Navy can be said to have three primary roles, viz:

- A military role in protecting the country's maritime interests and providing territorial defence.
- A diplomatic role participating in international defence and security engagements.
- A constabulary role providing maritime security and disaster response capabilities in conjunction with other appropriate agencies.

The navy currently has a little over 25,000 service personnel and around 1,100 civilian staff to support its operations. Dependent on source, it is believed that about 10,000 of the servicemen fall within the remit of the Philippine Marine Corps.

The Philippine Navy is headed by a Flag Officer-in-Command (FOIC), which is typically a 'three-star', Vice Admiral role. The current incumbent is Vice Admiral Toribio Adaci Jnr., who assumed office for a fixed, three-year term in November 2022. The FOIC reports to the Chief of Staff of the Armed Forces of the Philippines, who is in turn responsible to the Philippine President in his role as Commander-in-Chief. The FOIC exercises overall command from the naval headquarters Naval Station Jose V. Andrada in Manila. He is assisted by a Vice Commander (deputy commander), a Chief of Naval Staff (the navy's third highest-ranking officer) and various personal, co-ordinating and specialist staff. A Headquarters Support Group provides administrative, service support, and security.

The Philippine Navy has been acquiring new capabilities under a phased procurement programme spread over three 'Horizons'. This photograph shows *Davao del Sur*, one of two new amphibious transport docks that were commissioned in 2016–17, during training off Ternate, south of Manila. She forms part of the Philippine Fleet's Sealift Amphibious Force (SAF). *(US Navy)*

The navy's organisation employs a 'matrix' structure similar to that adopted by many large entities and which is subject to ongoing evolution. The accompanying structure chart attempts to replicate this on the basis of open source information as of mid-2024 but is subject to potential errors of interpretation.[6]

The core element of the Philippines' naval organisation is arguably formed by its two 'Type Commands'. These encompass (1) the Philippine Fleet and (2) the Philippine Marine Corps. Both are essentially organised in line with specific capability or unit types.

The Philippine Fleet: This can be regarded as the home of the navy's sailors and ships. The fleet is tasked with administering, preparing and managing designated units to assist the navy in fulfilling its objectives. It is currently commanded by Rear Admiral Renato David and organised into eight elements that comprise:

- **Offshore Combat Force (OCF):** Responsible for the navy's larger units.
- **Littoral Combat Force (LCF):** Responsible for smaller patrol vessels and attack craft.
- **Sealift Amphibious Force (SAF):** Responsible for sealift, amphibious and transport vessels.
- **Naval Air Wing (NAW)** Responsible for all crewed and uncrewed naval aircraft.
- **Fleet Support Group (FSG):** Responsible for support assets.
- **Fleet Training and Doctrines Centre (FTDC):** Responsible for overall education, training and doctrine development.
- **Submarine Group (SG):** Responsible for preparing for the future arrival of submarines in the fleet.
- **Mine Warfare Group:** Recently stood up to support the introduction of a mine countermeasures capability.

The Philippine Marine Corps (PMC): The PMC is

headed by the Commandant of the PMC (CPMC), currently Major General Arturo G. Roxas. He is assisted by a Deputy Commandant and a Chief of Marine Staff in a similar headquarters structure to that adopted by the Philippine Navy command. The headquarters is located at Fort Bonifacio in Taguig City east of Manila.

PMC combat forces encompass four Marine Brigades (Nos. 1 to 4 MBDE); each comprising three Marine Battalion Landing Teams (MBLT-1 to MBLT-12). There is also a Special Operations Force Reconnaissance Group. These are supplemented by a Combat Support Brigade – which includes armour and artillery elements – and various general support and sustainment forces. A relatively recent development is the formation of a PMC Coastal Defense Regiment whose primary task will be to operate BrahMos surface-to-surface missiles purchased from India. The PMC's force structure also includes three reserve Marine Brigades (Nos 7 to 9 MBDE) that would provide additional resources in time of crisis or war.

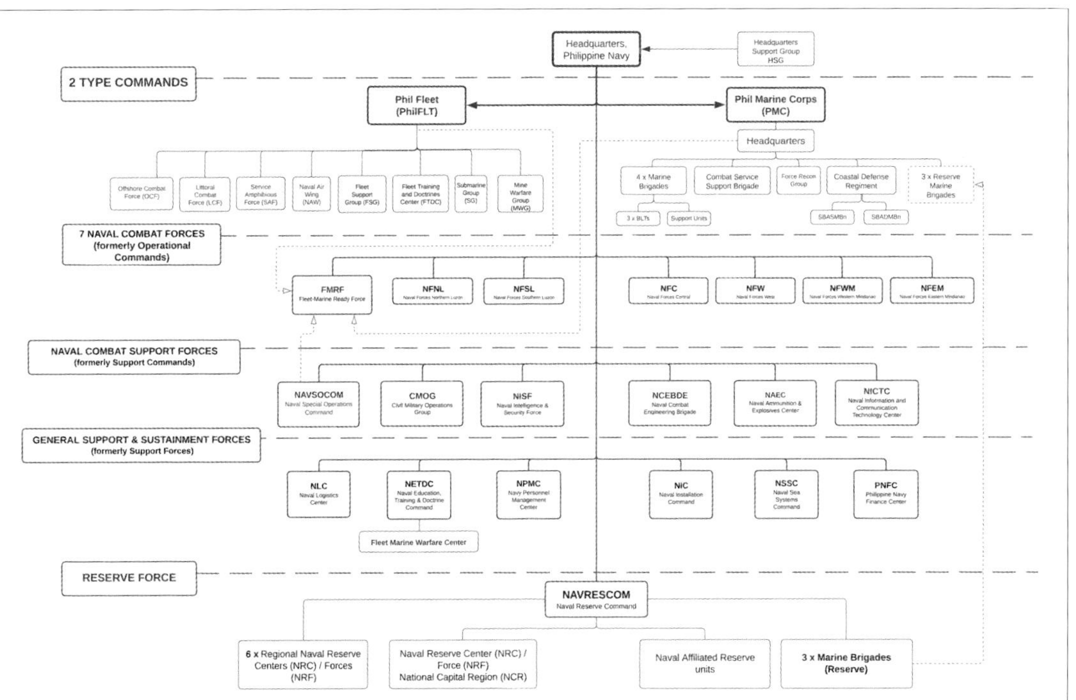

Operational and Support Commands: The other element of the Philippine Navy's organisational matrix is comprised of its Combat and Support Commands. Foremost amongst these are the seven Naval Combat Forces, previously known as the Operational Commands. Six of these – Naval Forces (NF) Northern Luzon, NF Southern Luzon, NF Central, NF West, NF Western Mindanao and NF Eastern Mindanao – are regional commands that are aligned with the Philippine Armed Forces' six geographical Unified Commands. Their focus appears to be largely on regional security. The seventh is the Fleet-Marine Ready Force (FMRF), which forms as the central operational fighting arm of both the navy and PMC.

The Naval Combat Force commands are supplemented by a number of Naval Combat Support Forces (previously Naval Support Commands) responsible for, inter alia, maritime domain awareness (MDA), naval intelligence, combat engineering and munitions supply. There is also a third tier of General Support and Sustainment Forces (previously Naval Support Units) encompassing areas such as logistics, education, training, personnel and finance.

Mention should also be made of the Naval Reserve Command, which is believed to be over 200,000 strong. It has eight units and associated

The Philippine Marine Corps (PMC), accounting for around a third of the navy's regular personnel, encompasses four active and three reserve Marine Brigades. This photograph shows PMC training underway in the western island of Palawan in August 2023. *(Australian Department of Defence)*

mobilisation centres that are organised on a regional basis in broadly similar fashion to the Naval Combat Forces/Unified Commands. It includes the reserve Marine Brigades referenced above, which are also regionally structured.

Bases: The focal point of Philippine Fleet activities is increasingly the Naval Operating Base-Subic (NOB-Subic) in eastern Luzon. It is here where most of the major warships tend to be based. However, many support and headquarters functions are located at Naval Base Heracleo Alano at Sangley Point in Cavite City and the adjacent Naval Station Pascual Ledesma (Cavite Naval Base) to the south of Manila. There are also smaller bases at San Vicente, Cagayan in the north of Luzon and at Lapu-Lapu City, Mactan near Cebu in the south of the Visayas. Over ten additional naval stations and several marine facilities are dotted around the country.

NAVAL VESSELS

A summary of current Philippine Navy strength is set out in Table 2.2A.1. In general terms, the various categories of warship coincide with the organisational split of the Philippine Fleet into the OCF, LCF and SAF structure previously described.

OFFSHORE COMBAT VESSELS

The navy currently operates nine warships with a significant capacity for offshore deployment following acquisitions of both new and second-hand vessels over the last decade. These comprise:

***Jose Rizal* Class Light Frigates:** The navy's most modern and capable warships are the two South Korean-built frigates *Jose Rizal* and *Antonio Luna*. Displacing c. 2,600 tonnes and having a length of 107.5m, the pair were built by Hyundai Heavy Industries (HHI) to the South Korean company's HDF-2600 design. The design was selected over a lower bid from India's Garden Reach Shipbuilders & Engineers (GRSE) based on the Project 28 *Kamorta* class corvette after a final competition phase that also included Daewoo Shipbuilding & Marine Engineering (DSME) and Navantia. The order with

Table 2.2A.1 PHILIPPINE NAVY FLEET COMPOSITION – MID 2024

PRINCIPAL UNITS

TYPE	CLASS	NUMBER	TONNAGE	DIMENSIONS	DATES[1]	CLASS[2]
Offshore Combat Vessels						
Frigate – FF	JOSE RIZAL (HDF-2600)	2	2,600 tonnes	108m x 14m x 4m	2020–1	*Jose Rizal* (FF-150), *Antonio Luna* (FF-151)
Corvette – FF	CONRADO YAP (PO HANG)	1	1,200 tonnes	88m x 10m x 3m	2019*	*Conrado Yap* (PS-30)
Patrol Ship – OPV	DEL PILLAR (HAMILTON)	3	3,300 tonnes	115m x 13m x 6m	2011–16*	*Gregorio del Pilar* (PS-15), *Ramon Alcaraz* (PS-16), *Andres Bonifacio* (PS-17)
Patrol Ship – OPV	JACINTO (PEACOCK)	3	700 tonnes	63m x 10m x 3m	1997*	*Emilio Jacinto* (PS-35), *Apolinario Mabini* (PS-36), *Artemio Ricarte* (PS-37)
Coastal Combat Vessels						
Patrol Ship – CPV	ALVAREZ (CYCLONE)	3	400 tonnes	55m x 8m x 2m	2004–23*	*General Mariano Alvarez* (PS-176), *Valentin Diaz* (PS-177), *Ladislao Diwa* (PS-178)
Fast Patrol Boat – F PB	ACERO ('Shaldag V')	6	95 tonnes	33m x 6m x 1m	2022–4	PG-901, PG-902, PG-903, PG-904, PG-906, PG-907
Patrol Boat – PB	JOSE ANDRADA ('Halter78')	22	55 tonnes	24m x 6m x 2m	1990–2000	PC-370 to PC-372, PC-374 to PC-381, PC-383 to PC-390, PC-392 to PC-393, PC 395
Patrol Boat – PB	'MPAC'	12	20 tonnes	15/17m x 5m x 2m	2009–19	BA-482 to BA-487, BA-489, BA-490 to BA-494
Other patrol vessels include two 65-tonne former US Coast Guard 'Point' Class cutters, two 45-tonne former US Navy 'Swiftboats' and four Chinese Type 966Y patrol craft						
Amphibious Ships						
Amph. Transport Dock – LPD	TARLAC (MAKASSAR)	2	11,500 tonnes	123m x 22m x 5m	2016–17	*Tarlac* (LD-601), *Davao del Sur* (LD-602)
Tank Landing Ship – LST	LST-542	1	4,200 tonnes	100m x 15m x 4m	1976*	*Benguet* (LS-507)
Tank Landing Ship – LST	LST-1	1	4,200 tonnes	100m x 15m x 4m	1976*	*Laguna* (LS-501)
Logistic Support Vessel – LSV	BACOLOD CITY (BESSON)	2	4,300 tonnes	83m x 18m x 4m	1993–4	*Bacolod City* (LS-550), *Dagupan City* (LS-551)
Landing Craft Heavy – LC	IVATAN (BALIKPAPAN)	5	500 tonnes	45m x 10m x 2m	2015–16*	*Waray* (LC-288), *Iwak* (LC-289), *Agta* (LC-290), *Ivatan* (LC-298), *Batak* (LC-290)
There are also six other large landing craft of various sizes and origins and around 40 smaller utility landing craft.						

Notes

1. Dates refer to induction of serving ships into the Philippine Navy. Ships marked with an asterisk were acquired second-hand and are often of considerable age.
2. Only names of ships displacing more than 100 tonnes are provided.
3. Auxiliaries include the research vessel *Gregorio Velasquez* (AGR-702), two smaller survey vessels and the presidential yacht *Ang Pangulo* (ACS-25). These are supplemented by three floating dry docks and various other harbour craft.

HHI was placed in October 2016 and later became subject to controversy after it transpired that much of the Thales equipment originally planned for the ships' electronics outfit had been substituted with items from Korean and other manufacturers. It seems that the navy had not been party to the approval of these changes, with the resulting fallout leading to the replacement of the then incumbent FOIC. Notwithstanding the controversy, HHI commenced construction of the two ships in May 2018. They were commissioned in July 2020 and March 2021, with some equipment fitted on a 'for but not with' basis.

The frigates are powered by a combined diesel and diesel (CODAD) propulsion system using four MTU-STX 12V1163-TB93 diesels. They can achieve a maximum speed of c. 25 knots and have a range of c. 4,500 nautical miles at 15 knots. Shipboard systems are controlled by a Servowatch integrated platform management system. The frigates have a core crew of 65 but can accommodate up to 110 personnel.

Sensors and combat systems have been broadly sourced, with Hanwha's Naval Shield Baseline 2 being specified as the core combat management system (CMS). The sensor outfit include Hensoldt's TRS-3D surveillance and Sharpeye navigation radars; a Leonardo NA-25X fire-control director; and Safran's Paseo electro-optical surveillance system. There is also a hull-mounted L3Harris Model 997 sonar set. The electronic warfare system includes Elisra NS9300A electronic support measures and Terma C-Guard DL-6T decoy launchers. Torpedo countermeasures are thought to be Naval Group Canto acoustic decoys.

Weaponry includes Leonardo's ubiquitous 76mm Oto gun in the forward position. This is supplemented by a 30mm Mk 44 Bushmaster cannon mounted in a Turkish Aselsan SMASH remotely-controlled weapon station (RCWS) atop the hangar. There are two twin midships-mounted LIG Nex1 C-Star surface-to-surface missile launchers and twin launchers to either side of the hangar for Simbad-RC short-range surface-to-air missiles. The anti-submarine warfare (ASW) suite includes a pair of SEA triple launchers firing Blue Shark lightweight torpedoes. There is also a flight deck and hangar for a single AW159 Wildcat helicopter that can operate in the ASW and anti-surface roles.

Fitted 'for but not with' equipment encompasses an eight-cell vertical launch system, a close-in weapons system and a Thales CAPTAS-2 towed-array sonar. Even without these systems, the frigates are still by far the most capable warfighting platforms in the Philippine Navy, giving the fleet its first-ever long-range anti-shipping capability and meaningful ASW potential. The two ships have been deployed actively in local waters and in international exercises since first delivered.

The frigate *Antonia Luna* departs Pearl Harbor in Hawaii in July 2022 prior to participating in the US Navy-sponsored RIMPAC 2022 exercises. She is one of two HDF-2600 light frigates ordered from HHI of South Korea in October 2016 and commissioned during 2020 and 2021. The C-Star surface-to-surface missile launchers seen fitted aft of the funnel represent a new capability for the expanding Philippine Navy Offshore Combat Force. *(US Navy)*

***Conrado Yap* Class Corvette:** South Korea gifted the decommissioned *Pohang* class corvette *Chungju* to the Philippines in support of its efforts to play a leading part in the navy's modernisation. The c. 1,200-tonne ship was first completed in 1987, being recommissioned into the Philippine Navy as *Conrado Yap* in August 2019. No significant modernisation of her combat systems – built around two 76mm Oto guns and two triple ASW torpedo tubes – was undertaken before transfer, although it is believed that the navy plans on upgrading her sensors and communications. Transfer of at least one more member of the class is anticipated in due course.

***Del Pilar* Class Patrol Ships:** Three elderly former US Coast Guard *Hamilton* (WHEC-715) class cutters are in service with the Philippine Navy as the *Del Pilar* class patrol frigates. The three ships – *Gregorio del Pillar*, *Ramon Alcaraz* and *Andres Bonifacio* – were recommissioned between 2011 and 2016 in the early phase of the navy's current modernisation. All were already over 40 years old at the time of their transfer. The navy initially classified these gun-armed vessels as frigates but they are now categorised as patrol ships. *Gregorio del Pilar* ran aground at the Hasa Hasa (Half-Moon) Shoal in the South China Sea on 29 August 2018 whilst conducting a maritime patrol. She subsequently re-entered service in September 2022 after repairs and upgrades funded by the United States.

The ships have been progressively modernised since entering Philippine Navy service, most notably with Saab's Sea Giraffe AMB surveillance radar.

Gregorio del Pilar – previously the lead US Coast Guard high endurance cutter *Hamilton* (WHEC-715) – is one of three of the class acquired by the Philippine Navy between 2011 and 2016. Originally completed in March 1967, her purchase nevertheless represented a noted improvement in the navy's ability to police its maritime interests. This photograph was taken in the Philippine EEZ in November 2023. *(Australian Department of Defence)*

Emilio Jacinto – formerly HMS *Peacock* – is one of three former Royal Navy patrol vessels transferred to the Philippine Navy in 1997 after their previous role as Hong Kong guard ships came to an end. She is seen here in the Sulu Sea to the south-west of the Philippines in March 2021. *(Australian Department of Defence)*

A further programme of upgrades is aimed at making the vessels more interoperable with the new vessels that are being acquired. Key elements include installation of Hanwha's Naval Shield Baseline 2 CMS and Elisra NS9300A electronic support measures equipment found aboard the *Jose Rizal* class frigates. The ships will also be equipped with ELAC's HUNTER 2.0 hull-mounted sonar. *Andres Bonifacio* has been the first member of the class to receive the upgrades, returning to operational service in the first half of 2024. Despite their age, these 3,300-tonne vessels are the largest ships in the Offshore Combat Force and look set to remain in service for several years to come.

***Jacinto* Class Patrol Ships:** Three of these former British Royal Navy *Peacock* class patrol vessels were acquired in 1997 after their previous role as Hong Kong patrol ships ended with the colony's return to China. Displacing some 700 tonnes and equipped with a 76mm Oto gun as their main armament, they have received progressive upgrades since their delivery.

LITTORAL COMBAT VESSELS

The Littoral Combat Force operates around fifty patrol vessels and interceptors of various sizes and capacity. The largest type in service comprises three c. 400-tonne former US Navy *Cyclone* (PC-1) class vessels. *General Mariano Alvarez* was acquired in 2004, with *Valentin Diaz* and *Ladislao Diwa* following in March 2023 as the class was finally being withdrawn from American service. The recent pair have a slightly different armament than the first ship.

The newest littoral assets are a series of Israeli *Acero* ('Shaldag Mk V') fast interdiction craft being acquired under a contract with Israel Shipyards that was concluded in early 2021. Displacing around 95 tonnes and capable of speeds of over 40 knots, the new vessels will replace the decommissioned *Tomas Batilo* class fast patrol boats that had originally been built as part of the South Korean PKM-200 class in the 1980s. To date, six vessels have been delivered in pairs between 2022 and 2024, with three additional hulls currently being assembled locally at the Naval Shipbuilding Center in Cavite. All vessels are armed with a 30mm Mk 44 Bushmaster cannon-equipped Rafael Typhoon RCWS and two Mini-Typhoon systems for heavy machine guns. In addition, all can be fitted with Rafael Spike NLOS short-range surface-to-surface missiles, with funding approved to equip four of the class so far.

The most numerous class of patrol ships in service are twenty-two *Jose Andrada* (Halter 78) coastal patrol boats commissioned over a decade between 1990 and 2000. Earlier members of the class were built in New Orleans but later ships were assembled locally in the Philippines. The vessels displace around 55 tonnes and carry a variety of close-range weapons. Also numerous are the twelve 20-tonne, Taiwanese-designed MPAC (Multi-Purpose Assault Craft) delivered in three variants from between 2009 and 2019. The first six (Mk I and Mk II) craft have bow ramps whilst the six Mk III variants are equipped with Spike ER missiles and a Mini Typhoon remote gun mount in its place. Amongst the handful of other vessels are four 12m Chinese Type 966Y patrol craft that were donated during the Duterte administration. Administratively, smaller

Valentin Diaz – formerly the US Navy's *Cyclone* class patrol boat *Monsoon* (PC-4) – was commissioned into the Philippine Navy in March 2023 when the type was withdrawn from US Navy service. Seen here in early 2024, she is now one of three of the class in Philippine service. *(Australian Department of Defence)*

patrol vessels are organised in Patrol Boat Divisions and Boat Attack Divisions whilst larger vessels appear to be stand-alone units.

SEALIFT AND AUXILIARY SHIPS

As previously indicated, the navy's amphibious vessels are operated by the Sealift Amphibious Force. By far the most capable amphibious warfare platforms currently in service are a pair of Indonesian-built *Tarlac* class amphibious transport docks – *Tarlac* and *Davao Del Sur* – that were commissioned in 2016 and 2017. Built by PT PAL in Indonesia to the *Makassar* class design, the class displaces some 11,500 tonnes and have a length of 123m, making them the largest ships in naval service. They are able to carry 500 troops plus trucks and armoured fighting vehicles and have a well deck capable of housing two 23m landing craft. There is a hangar for a single medium helicopter and the flight deck can handle two more. Armament is currently limited to positions for six heavy machine guns but the ships are fitted 'for but not with' positions for larger-calibre weapons.

In addition to fulfilling humanitarian assistance and disaster relief (HADR) roles, the design also has utility as an offshore command and control post capable of staging helicopter operations during counterinsurgency missions. *Tarlac* served in this role during the battle to recapture the city of Marawi in Mindanao from Islamic militants in 2017.[7] The success of the acquisition is reflected in a contract for two additional members of the class in June 2022. These will benefit from a number of modifications, including a taller well deck to embark missile-armed MPACs. Delivery is slated for 2025–6.

Four other large landing ships are in active service. They comprise the two Second World War-era tank landing ships (LSTs) *Laguna* and *Benguet* and two 1990s-built logistic support vessels *Bacolod City* and *Dagupan City*, which are variants of the US Army's *Besson* (LSV-1) design.[8] These larger vessels are complemented by eleven large landing craft, of which the five 500-tonne *Ivatan* (former Royal Australian Navy *Balikpapan*) class vessels acquired

This photograph of the *Tarlac* class amphibious transport dock *Davao Del Sur* was taken in July 2018 at the time of the RIMPAC 2018 exercise. The photograph shows the large flight deck for helicopter operations that is located immediately above the well deck. The positions for close-range armament are unoccupied as part of a 'fitted for but not with' approach. Two modified variants of the class are currently under construction in Indonesia. *(US Navy)*

between 2015 and 2016 are the most numerous. Also falling within this type is the locally-built *Tagbuana*, which entered service alongside the smaller indigenous *Manobo* in 2011. Displacing nearly 600 tonnes, *Tagbuana* holds the distinction of being the largest locally-built vessel in the Philippine Navy. The amphibious force is rounded off by around forty utility landing craft of largely US Navy origin.

There are a handful of larger auxiliaries, of which the most significant is probably the research vessel *Gregorio Velasquez.* Originally the USNS *Melville* (T-AGOR-14), she became the navy's first oceanographic research vessel when transferred in 2014. These are supplemented by the usual array of yard craft, including three floating dry docks and various tankers and tugs. Mention should also be made of the Japanese-built *Ang Pangulo*, which was supplied as part of war reparations and serves as the presidential yacht, as well as a transport and command ship.

NAVAL AVIATION

The current Naval Air Wing (NAW) started out as the Naval Air Section of the PNP. Subsequently changes in unit nomenclature included the Naval Air Unit (1960), Naval Air Group (1975) and finally the NAW in 2020. The NAW is headquartered at Sangley Point in Cavite City and appears to have four main subordinate groups, viz.

- **Naval Fixed Wing Air Group 30:** Comprising Light Utility Patrol Squadron 31 with around five Britten-Norman BN-2 Islander patrol aircraft and Maritime Patrol & Reconnaissance Squadron 32 with five Beechcraft C-90 King Air patrol aircraft.
- **Naval Helicopter Air Group 40:** Comprising Maritime Strike Helicopter Squadron 41 with four Leonardo AW109 multi-role helicopters and Anti-Submarine Helicopter Squadron 42 with two AW159 Wildcat sea control helicopters.
- **Naval Air Warfare Training and Doctrine Center 50:** Providing new and recurrent pilot training with Cessna fixed wing aircraft in Fixed Wing Training Squadron 53 and Robinson helicopters in Rotary-Wing Training Squadron 54.
- **Naval Aviation System Group 60:** Encompassing maintenance, logistics and support activities provided by a number of squadrons.

Bacolod City is one of two logistic support vessels derived from the US Army *Besson* class that joined the Philippine Nay in 1993–4. *(US Navy)*

Uncrewed Air Vehicles are operated by Maritime Unmanned Reconnaissance Squadron 71. This has Alpha and Bravo flights equipped with a total of eight Scan Eagle UAVs and four ground control stations.

COASTAL DEFENCE

Coastal defence is in the hands of the PMC's newly-formed missile defence regiment, which is tasked with bringing the navy's new BrahMos surface-to-surface missiles into service. The regiment comprises a Shore-Based Anti-Ship Missile Battalion and a Shore-Based Air-Defense Battalion, the latter serving to protect the BrahMos missile systems from aerial threats during operations. It is not clear that equipment has yet been selected for the air-defence unit.

The BrahMos missiles were ordered from India under a US$375m contract concluded in January 2022 in what was the first export order for the system. Initial deliveries commenced in April 2024. The agreement comprised the acquisition of three coastal missile batteries, each comprising three mobile missile launchers. It has been reported that work is well underway on a new base at Naval Station Leovigildo Gantioqui in Zambales, Western Luzon to house the new missiles and that other sites are under consideration. The base's location puts disputed areas of the South China Sea within the published, c. 300km range of the BrahMos export variant. The Philippine Army also plans to induct the system within the lifetime of the 'Re-Horizon 3' phase of the Philippine Armed Forces' modernisation programme.[9]

MARITIME DOMAIN AWARENESS

The Philippine Navy's Maritime Domain Awareness (MDA) system is known as the Philippine Navy Maritime Situational Awareness System (PNMSAS). It is administered by the Naval Information and Communication Technology Center (NICTC). Operational control lies with five Maritime Situational Awareness Centers at the regional level and the Maritime Research Information Center at Naval Headquarters, Manila at the national level. PNMSAS comprises a static network of around twenty-five littoral monitoring stations and around ten littoral monitoring detachments equipped with radar, AIS equipment and/or electro-optronic systems located in the various regional commands along with Intelligence Surveillance and

Reconnaissance (ISR) data provided by deployed ships, aircraft and PMC units.

The Philippine Coast Guard (PCG) runs a similar system of coastal surveillance systems. Since 2020, some twenty-one new radar stations, including eleven funded by Japan through its 'Official Security Assistance' grant aid, have been added to the PCG's existing network. These stations are largely in the Sulu and Celebes Seas to monitor seaborne criminal threats emanating from Malaysia and Indonesia.

Notionally, MDA data and analysis from the naval and coast guard networks – along with information from ten or so other government agencies operating in the maritime domain – are combined to provide a common picture under the framework of a National Maritime Council (previously the National Coast Watch Center). However, challenges remain with inter-agency competition and restrictive procedures. Accordingly, achieving a comprehensive and real-time understanding of the Philippines' extensive maritime zones is still work in progress.

The Philippine Navy operates a small force of largely 'utility type' maritime patrol aircraft and helicopters, such as this Leonardo AW109 Power. Five of this type were acquired to operate primarily from the *Del Pilar* and *Tarlac* classes but one has since been written off. *(US Navy)*

NAVAL SPECIAL OPERATIONS

Naval Special Operations Command (NAVSOCOM) is believed to have been created from the former Navy Special Operations Group and comprises several hundred personnel. It operates within the framework of the Armed Forces of the Philippines Special Operations Command (SOCOM) that was stood up in 2018 after the Marawi siege and comprises Special Forces from all branches of the military. As such, it appears to fall outside the normal Philippine Fleet organisations structure for administrative purposes.

NAVSOCOM is organised along similar lines to the US Navy Special Warfare Command with a SEAL Group, Naval Explosive Ordnance Disposal Group, a Naval Diving Group, a Special Boat Group (with Special Boat Teams), Combat Service Support Group and a Naval Special Operations Training and Doctrine Center. Combat elements are deployed to operational theatres as a Naval Special Operations Unit (NAVSOU). Each of these groups comprises a number of SEAL Platoons, as well as support units.

NAVSOCOM units are extensively deployed in counter-terrorism and internal security operations especially in the southern Philippines against Islamist militant groups operating in Mindanao and Sulu. NAVSOU teams are also deployed aboard PN patrol vessels and warships in maritime interdiction operations. The Command's capabilities are being further strengthened by partnerships with Special Forces units from friendly nations such as Australia and the United States.

The Marcos Jr. administration reassured NAVSOCOM at the time of the unit's 67th founding anniversary in November 2023 that it remains firm in its commitment to strengthen its capabilities through further investment under the Revised Armed Forces of the Philippines Modernisation Programme.

INTER-AGENCY COOPERATION

As noted earlier the Philippine Navy and PCG have overlapping roles in the domain of maritime security. Originally a branch of the navy, the PCG has been an armed service under the control of the Department of Transportation since 1998 but would be attached to the Department of National Defense in time of war. In the last decade or so, it has significantly expanded its capacity and capabilities, having recently received new patrol vessels from France and Japan. It currently operates over sixty patrol vessels and, mostly, smaller craft of various types, as well as numerous boats and RHIBs. There is also a small aviation arm with a handful of fixed-wing, rotary and uncrewed assets. Personnel numbers have been expanding rapidly and, at a reported 30,000, are somewhat larger than the regular navy.

The Philippine Navy carries out regular maritime interdiction and other maritime security operations with the PCG, other maritime agencies and other branches of the armed forces as part of efforts to improve interoperability. Notably, the navy and coast guard have worked together on resupply missions to the Filipino maritime outposts, such as *Sierra Madre*, in the South China Sea. The two forces also regularly engage with the US Navy and other foreign navies and coast guards in training and other activities.

FUTURE PLANS AND ACQUISITIONS

The Philippine Navy's overall development over the past two decades has been driven by a Strategic Sail

Plan 2020 first announced in late 2006 that set out a vision of creating a '…strong and credible Navy that our maritime nation can be proud of'. As part of the discussions that preceded the subsequent Revised AFP Modernization Act of December 2012, the navy aimed to give tangible form to this vision through its 'Philippine Fleet Desired Force Mix' acquisition plan. This included a 'wish list' of three submarines, six air-defence frigates, twelve anti-submarine corvettes, eighteen offshore patrol vessels and large number of smaller vessels. These requirements informed the naval elements of the three, five/six year 'Horizons' or procurement phases that were taken forward under the 15-year lifespan of the AFP Modernization Act. In practice, the navy's force structure objectives have fluctuated as time has progressed.[10] Additionally, the acquisitions achieved in the first two Horizon phases, covering the period up to 2022, have not been achieved in their entirety. Nevertheless, it is procurement contracts awarded under the 2018–22 'Horizon 2' phase that will drive the Philippine Navy's development forward over the next few years. These will result in the following major acquisitions:

***Malvar* Class Frigates:** A contract for these vessels – to be named *Miguel Malvar* and *Diego Silang* – was awarded to HHI in December 2021. Although initially referred to as corvettes, the HHI HDC-3100 design on which they are based is somewhat larger than the *Jose Rizal* class with a displacement of c. 3,200 tonnes and a length of 118m. Construction of the first hull commenced in May 2023 prior to an official launch ceremony on 18 June 2025. Press reports suggest the two ships will be delivered in 2025 and 2026 respectively. Equipment outfit and suppliers will be broadly similar to that found on the previous frigates although some equipment will be upgraded or improved. For example, the CMS is Hanwha's improved Naval Shield Baseline 4, the main radar is an Elta EL/M 2258 Alpha multifunction array, the electronic warfare system is also upgraded and there are sixteen VLS cells for what are believed to be VL-Mica surface-to-air missiles.

The lead *Miguel Malvar* class frigate – one of two ships ordered in December 2022 – is seen here at the time of her official 'launch' ceremony on 18 June 2024. The two frigates are essentially enlarged variants of the two HDF-2600 *Jose Rizal* class ships that are already in service. *(Hyundai Heavy Industries)*

HHI HDP-2200 Offshore Patrol Vessels: six of these 94m, 2,450-tonne offshore patrol vessels are also on order from HHI under a contract awarded in June 2022. Construction is expected to begin in the second half of 2024 for delivery in the 2026–8 time-frame. The vessels will share some equipment with the other HHI vessels but are expected to be entirely gun armed.

The HHI-built ships will be joined by the two modified *Tarlac* class amphibious transport docks and three remaining 'Shaldag V' fast interdiction craft that have already been described. Transfers of further second-hand South Korean Po Hang class corvettes, as well as of former US Coast Guard 'Island' and 'Marine Protector' class patrol boats are also on the cards within the short to medium term.

Longer-term developments will be directed by the new Marcos Jr.'s regime revised 'Re-Horizon 3' procurement plan agreed early in 2024. Whilst full details were not in the public domain as of mid-2024, this offers the prospect of an uplift in spending compared with previous Horizon phases. As a result, the next few years may see the realisation of the Philippine Navy's long-term ambition to deploy a submarine flotilla. Potential contenders for the eventual contract – which will most likely involve an initial pair of submarines – include Naval Group's 'Scorpène', Navantia's S-80 and a variant of the South Korean KSS-III. Beyond this core procurement objective, there is also likely to be further procurement of 'Shaldag' fast attack craft to enable the prospect of conducting swarm attacks in the littoral, with public statements suggesting as many as twenty-four of the type may eventually be operated. Improved MDA and the reconstitution of a mine countermeasures force are other likely priorities alongside continued modernisation of existing ships. The naval aviation arm is also expected to be reinforced with additional sea control helicopters to operate from the new surface combatants, transport helicopters for the PMC and the deployment of more sophisticated maritime patrol aircraft.

CONCLUSION

Over the last decade and a half the Philippine Navy – often derided as an antiquated coastal force equipped largely with 'museum ships' – has made

The *Jose Andrada* class patrol boat *Juan Magluyan* pictured in Philippine coastal waters in 2021. Although internal security is likely to remain an important Philippine Navy mission, planned investment will also provide the navy with a greatly enhanced capacity to deter external threats. *(Australian Department of Defence)*

meaningful progress with its modernisation efforts despite funding constraints. The advent of the current Marcos Jr. administration holds out the prospect of further progress. It has demonstrated greater willingness to push back against China's expansion in the South China Sea and supported the Comprehensive Archipelagic Defense Concept that provides the strategic framework to back this stance. Most significantly of all, the revised 'Re-Horizon 3' funding plans agreed early in 2024 hold out the promise of the substantial funding required to complete force modernisation. For the navy, the prospect of standing-up its own submarine flotilla would have a meaningful impact on its evolving A2/AD capacity.

Of course, the detailed contours of the 'Re-Horizon 3' programme and, more importantly, the actual release of funding to achieve the plan, remain an open question. However, there seems a reasonable prospect of the Philippine Navy achieving an increasingly modern, balanced force structure under which small numbers of submarines and surface combatants are supported by improved MDA through better surveillance, reconnaissance, and intelligence-gathering capabilities. In turn, this would give the navy far better capacity to work effectively with friendly regional navies. Whilst the future Philippine Navy will still be overshadowed by China's mighty PLAN, it will have become an increasingly credible deterrent against further encroachment on its maritime interests.

Notes

1. The nine-dash line, also sometimes referred to as the eleven-dash line, has been used to delineate China's claims to a large proportion of the South China Sea. In 2016, an arbitration tribunal constituted under the United Nations Convention on the Law of the Sea (UNCLOS) ruled that China had no legal basis to claim historic rights to the resources inside the line.

2. Most recently, in June 2024, several Chinese Coast Guard craft intercepted a Philippine Navy operation to resupply the grounded tank landing ship *Sierra Madre*, which acts as an outpost on the disputed Second Thomas Shoal. The incident resulted in injuries to several Filipino sailors, as well as the seizure and damage of equipment.

3. See further, Rej Cortez Torrecampo, 'A Paradigm Shift in the Philippines' Defense Strategy' posted to *The Diplomat* site – thediplomat.com – on 3 April 2024.

4. Two Second World War-era tank landing ships still remain in service.

5. More detail on recent and planned modernisation is provided in the subsequent 'Future Plans and Acquisitions' section.

6. At the time this chapter was written, the Philippine Navy's official website had not fully updated the details of its current organisational structure, leading to more than usual uncertainty.

7. The siege of Marawi – a city of over 200,000 people – took place between May and October 2017 after large areas had been seized by terrorists affiliated with the Islamic State. Over 1,000 people, most of them insurgents, died in the subsequent fighting that provides a clear indication of the ongoing internal security challenges faced by the Philippine state.

8. Another former LST, *Sierra Madre*, remains in commission and has been very much in the news as the focal point for clashes between Philippine and Chinese vessels on the Second Thomas Shoal. Originally commissioned as the US Navy *LST-542* class tank landing ship *LST 821* in November 1944, the ship was assigned the name *Harnett County* in 1955. She subsequently saw service as a floating logistical support base in the Vietnam War, being transferred to the then Republic of Vietnam Navy as *My Tho* in 1970. Escaping South Vietnam to Subic Bay after the country's collapse in 1975, she was incorporated into the Philippine Navy the following year, subsequently becoming *Sierra Madre*. The vessel was grounded on the Second Thomas Shoal in 1999 to act as an outpost to maintain the Philippines' claim to the area. The resupply of the PMC detachment maintained on the vessel has subsequently been subject to periodic harassment by Chinese vessels.

9. See Aaron-Matthew Lariosa, 'Philippines Builds First BrahMos Anti-Ship Missile Base Facing South China Sea' posted to the *Naval News* site – navalnews.com – on 14 June 2024.

10. The Strategic Sail Plan has also been updated, now being known as Sail Plan 2028.

2.3 REGIONAL REVIEW

Author:
Conrad Waters

THE INDIAN OCEAN AND AFRICA

On 19 October 2023 the US Navy destroyer *Carney* (DDG-64) carried out a series of interceptions of cruise missiles and drones that had been launched in the direction of Israel from Houthi rebel-controlled territory in Yemen. The engagement marked the start of a major escalation of what had previously been a proxy war between the Houthis' Iranian backers and a Saudi Arabian-led coalition for influence across the Middle East.[1] The initial interceptions were followed that November by a wider Houthi campaign to disrupt shipping transiting the Red Sea; a critical trade route between the European and Asia-Pacific economies. Whilst by no means the first attacks by rebel forces on ships in the region, the scope and intensity of the Houthi assault – that remained ongoing as of June 2024 – has already had significant consequences on a number of levels.

The initial Houthi attacks were ostensibly aimed at supporting the Hamas campaign against Israel that commenced with the massacres of 7 October 2023. Accordingly, the claimed targets of the initial attacks against shipping in the Red Sea and Bab al-Mandeb Strait were vessels with links to Israel. In practice, the affiliation of the ships that have been attacked has steadily expanded as the campaign has continued. Possibly because of targeting challenges, the offensive has been largely indiscriminate in any event. Whilst few attacks have been entirely successful – just two merchant ships had been sunk as of June 2024 – the disruptive effect has been disproportionate. Trade through the Suez Canal, which encompasses 30 percent of global container traffic, has been significantly curtailed. The diversion of shipping via southern Africa and increasing insurance costs have had a material but so far manageable impact on global supply chains.[2] Significantly, the vulnerability of the choke point to interdiction – already vividly demonstrated by the chaos that followed the 23 March 2021 grounding of the container ship *Ever Given* in the Suez Canal – has been confirmed.

The attacks brought a swift response from many countries whose shipping has been affected. This first saw the reinforcement of naval forces in the region to defend the shipping lanes. Subsequently, on 11 January 2024, this was followed by the first of a series of offensive strikes by American and British forces on Houthi weapon sites and supporting infrastructure. The achievements of this response can best be described as mixed. Even with the arrival of additional warships, the defending forces are stretched thinly over a wide area whilst countering relatively sophisticated attacks that have included both ballistic and cruise missiles as well as numerous drones. For example, a complex engagement in early January 2024 saw eighteen suicide drones, two cruise missiles and a single ballistic missile destroyed by a combination of American and British warships, as well as carrier-based aircraft.[3] Whilst these defensive actions have been generally successful, the mission is proving to be an extended one that draws, particularly, US Navy forces away from priorities in the Asia-Pacific region and elsewhere. It also seems unlikely, absent all-out escalation, that it will be possible to halt the attacks given a steady flow of replacement munitions from Iran.[4]

One other noteworthy feature of the Red Sea response has been the unwillingness of many of America's allies to be directly associated with Operation 'Prosperity Guardian', the US-led mission to ensure freedom of navigation across the region's sea lanes. Notably, France, Italy and Spain all failed to join the mission, with the first two navies subsequently becoming leading participants in the European Union's purely defensive Operation 'Aspides'. Whilst the actions of the various naval forces doubtless benefit from a degree of collaboration, the divided response seems unfortunate, not least given that 'Aspides' participants have only a limited pool of air-defence ships from which to draw.

The impact of the events in the Red Sea has extended to the neighbouring Gulf of Aden and into the western Indian Ocean. In addition to sporadic drone attacks, the crisis has been exploited by Somalia's pirates, who have seized the opportunity provided by re-routed shipping to resume their activities. The uptick in piracy has been met by an unprecedented response by the Indian Navy. It has deployed strong naval forces to the area as part of India's ambition to be a 'net provider of security' across the Indian Ocean region. Whilst India remains reluctant to be overtly drawn into the US 'security ecosystem', its steadily increasing capacity to promote regional stability will likely be welcomed by America and its allies given the steady deterioration in the overall global security situation.

The US Navy destroyer *Gravely* (DDG-107) launches Tomahawk land attack missiles against Houthi rebel military targets during January 2024 in response to attacks on shipping transiting the Red Sea. The so-called Red Sea crisis has vividly demonstrated the vulnerability of key shipping 'choke points' to interdiction and thinly-stretched Western naval resources. *(US Navy)*

Table 2.3.1: FLEET STRENGTHS IN THE INDIAN OCEAN, AFRICA AND THE MIDDLE EAST – LARGER NAVIES (MID 2024)

COUNTRY	ALGERIA	EGYPT	INDIA	IRAN	ISRAEL	PAKISTAN	SAUDI ARABIA	SOUTH AFRICA
Aircraft Carrier (CV)	–	–	2	–	–	–	–	–
Strategic Missile Submarine (SSBN)	-	-	1	–	–	–	–	–
Attack Submarine (SSN/SSGN)	–	–	–	–	–	–	–	–
Patrol Submarine (SSK/SS)	6	8	16	4	5	5	–	3
Fleet Escort (DDG/FFG)	2	16	24	-	-	10	12	4
Patrol Escort/Corvette (FFG/FSG/FS)	11	3	10	9	7	2	4	–
Missile Armed Attack Craft (PGG/PTG)	c. 12	c. 30	7	c. 30	8	10	9	1
Mine Countermeasures Vessel (MCMV)	3	c. 14	–	1	–	5	3	2
Major Amphibious (LPD)	1	2	1	–	–	–	–	–

Notes:

1 Algerian fast attack craft and Egyptian fast attack craft and mine countermeasures numbers approximate.

2 Iranian fleet numbers exclude large numbers of indigenously-built midget and coastal submarines, as well as numerous additional missile-armed patrol boats operated both by the Iranian Navy and Revolutionary Guard.

3 The South African attack craft and mine countermeasures vessels serve in patrol vessel roles. Not all the latter are operational.

INDIA

The Indian economy's rapid expansion over the past decade has supported substantial growth in the country's defence budget to the extent that it is now – at a provisional INR 6.22 trillion (c. US$ 75bn) for 2024–5 – the fourth largest in the world. However, personnel costs and pensions continue to account for a large share of the total, limiting the amount available for investment in new equipment. A hiatus in army recruitment during the Covid-19 pandemic and the introduction of the 'Agnipath' short-service model may improve the situation but there is still likely to be an imbalance between revenue and capital expenditure for the foreseeable future. The latest budget also fails to provide the usual distribution of capital spending between the three branches of the armed services, making it more difficult to analyse how well the Indian Navy – the smallest branch – is faring. However, a breakdown of the main modernisation headings suggest that purchases of aircraft and aero-engines – including those destined for naval aviation – is likely to take precedence over investment in the naval fleet in the immediate future.[5]

Indian defence modernisation is also being slowed by the impact of the Russo-Ukrainian War on the supplies of Russian-sourced equipment that have traditionally formed a significant portion of its defence imports. In addition to encouraging the further indigenisation of armament production under the *Atmanirbhar Bharat* ('self-reliant India') philosophy, it seems likely that Western producers may benefit. The Indian Navy has already inducted US-made Boeing P-8I Poseidon maritime patrol aircraft and Sikorsky MH-60R Seahawk sea control helicopters, whilst a large purchase of General Atomics MQ-9B uncrewed aerial vehicles (UAVs) is planned. In the meantime, the arrival of further Project 11356 *Talwar* class frigates from Russia's Yantar shipyard – once seen as a means of compensating for delayed domestic construction – is being pushed to the right. Accordingly, Table 2.3.2 highlighting current Indian Navy strength has seen little movement year-on-year. An analysis of major developments by warship category follows.

Aircraft Carriers and Major Amphibious Ships: The last year has seen the new indigenous carrier *Vikrant* receive post-delivery modifications whilst steadily progressing towards full operational service. There are increasing signs that India might order a second member of the class, a possibility discussed further in the review of world naval aviation contained in Chapter 4.1. Meanwhile, there has been little apparent progress with the proposed construction of four amphibious assault ships under a programme which was first initiated over a decade ago. A request for information for the new vessels was issued in August 2021 after a previous procurement competition was cancelled. Spanish shipbuilder Navantia's *Juan Carlos I* design is expected to be a leading contender for the project when it moves to the formal bidding stage, which could occur within the next year. Navantia has teamed with India's private sector Larsen and Toubro (L&T) to pursue the contract, which will likely see all four ships built locally to a foreign design.

Major Surface Combatants: There has been mixed progress with deliveries of major surface combatants over the last year. Positively, construction of the four Project 15B *Visakhapatnam* class destroyers is now drawing to a close at Mazagon Dock Shipbuilders Ltd (MDSL) in Mumbai. *Imphal*, the third ship of the class, was commissioned on 26 December 2023,

Table 2.3.2: INDIAN NAVY: PRINCIPAL UNITS AS AT MID 2024

TYPE	CLASS	NUMBER	TONNAGE	DIMENSIONS	PROPULSION	CREW	DATE
Aircraft Carriers							
Aircraft Carrier (CV)	**VIKRANT**	1	45,000 tonnes	263m x 62m x 9m	COGAG, 28 knots	1,650	2022
Aircraft Carrier (CV)	Project 1143.4 **VIKRAMADITYA** (KIEV)	1	45,000 tonnes	283m x 60m x 10m	Steam, 30 knots	1,600	1987
Principal Surface Escorts							
Destroyer – DDG	Project 15B **VISAKHAPATNAM**	3	7,400 tonnes	163m x 17m x 7m	COGAG, 30+ knots	300	2021
Destroyer – DDG	Project 15A **KOLKATA**	3	7,400 tonnes	163m x 17m x 7m	COGAG, 30+knots	330	2014
Destroyer – DDG	Project 15 **DELHI**	3	6,700 tonnes	163m x 17m x 7m	COGAG, 32 knots	350	1997
Destroyer – DDG	Project 61 ME **RAJPUT** ('Kashin')	3	5,000 tonnes	147m x 16m x 5m	COGAG, 35 knots	320	1980
Frigate – FFG	Project 17 **SHIVALIK**	3	6,200 tonnes	143m x 17m x 5m	CODOG, 30 knots	265	2010
Frigate – FFG	Project 11356 **TALWAR**	6	4,000 tonnes	125m x 15m x 5m	COGAG, 30 knots	180	2003
Frigate – FFG	Project 16A **BRAHMAPUTRA**	3	4,000 tonnes	127m x 15m x 5m	Steam, 30 knots	350	2000
Corvette – FSG	Project 28 **KAMORTA**	4	3,400 tonnes	109m x 13m x 4m	Diesel, 25 knots	195	2014
Corvette – FSG	Project 25A **KORA**	4	1,400 tonnes	91m x 11m x 5m	Diesel, 25 knots	125	1998
Corvette – FSG	Project 25 **KHUKRI**	2	1,400 tonnes	91m x 11m x 5m	Diesel, 25 knots	110	1989
Submarines							
Submarine – SSBN	**ARIHANT**	1	7,500+ tonnes	112m x 11m x 10m	Nuclear, 25+ knots	100	2016
Submarine – SSK	Project 75 **KALVARI** ('Scorpène)	5	1,800 tonnes	68m x 6m x 6m	Diesel-electric, 20 knots	45	2017
Submarine – SSK	Project 877 EKM **SINDHUGHOSH** ('Kilo')	7	3,000 tonnes	73m x 10m x 7m	Diesel-electric, 17 knots	55	1986
Submarine – SSK	**SHISHUMAR** (Type 209/1500)	4	1,900 tonnes	64m x 7m x 6m	Diesel-electric, 22 knots	40	1986
Major Amphibious Units							
Landing Platform Dock – LPD	**JALASHWA** (AUSTIN)	1	17,000 tonnes	173m x 26/30m x 7m	Steam, 21 knots	405	1971

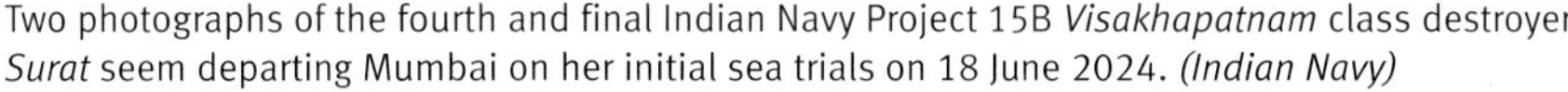

Two photographs of the fourth and final Indian Navy Project 15B *Visakhapatnam* class destroyer *Surat* seem departing Mumbai on her initial sea trials on 18 June 2024. *(Indian Navy)*

whilst her sister *Surat* commenced sea trials on 18 June 2024.[6] A larger Next Generation Destroyer – sometimes referred to as Project 18 – has been under consideration for some time, with procurement of up to eight vessels in two batches seemingly envisaged. However, it is likely to be some years yet before the project is formally launched.

Progress with completing the seven smaller Project 17A *Nilgiri* class frigates is less advanced despite previous hopes of significantly improved build times as a result of the increased use of modular building techniques in the design. Four of the vessels are also being built by MDSL, which launched *Mahendragiri* – its final vessel – on 1 September 2023. Completion of the other three members of the class has been assigned to Kolkata's Garden Reach Shipbuilders & Engineers Ltd (GRSE), which launched *Vindhyagiri* – their final vessel – 15 days earlier on 17 August. As of May 2024, MDSL anticipated delivering the lead ship by the end of March 2025, which may prove to be optimistic. Current Indian Navy plans envisage follow-on orders for up to eight of an improved Type 17B variant.[7]

Tushil, the first of the new batch of four Project 11356 frigates referred to above, commenced sea trials from Yantar at Kaliningrad in March 2024.

Vindhyagiri, the third and final member of the Project 17A *Nilgiri* class frigates being built by Kolkata's GRSE – and sixth member of the seven-strong class overall – pictured at the time of her launch on 17 August 2023. Construction of the class is currently running behind schedule. *(Indian Navy)*

She will likely be delivered before the end of the year and may be followed by a sister, *Tamala*, in 2025. The final pair of the batch are being built under licence at Goa Shipyard Ltd (GSL), which held keel-laying ceremonies for both ships in 2021. Neither had been launched as of mid-2024, suggesting their completion will be several years in the future.

Delays to new construction may have influenced the extent of the mid-life modernisations planned for the Project 16A *Brahmaputra* class frigates, which trace their design origins to the British Royal Navy's *Leander* class of the 1960s. The ships' steam turbine plants are to be replaced by diesels under a programme that could extend their remaining service lives from 10 years to as many as 20. *Beas*, the last ship of the class to be completed, has reportedly already entered Cochin Shipyard Ltd (CSL) to commence the upgrade. She will be followed by her two sisters if the modernisation proves successful.

Smaller Surface Combatants: The most significant programme for Indian Navy smaller combatants currently underway is that for sixteen Anti-Submarine Warfare Shallow Water Craft (ASW-SWC). Ordered in April 2019, their construction is split equally between CSL and GRSE, which are each building variants to their own design. GRSE has made better progress in delivering its part of the contract, part of which has been sublet to L&T's Kattupalli shipyard. Six of their eight ships had been launched as of mid-2024, with delivery of the lead ship, *Arnala*, expected before the end of the year. CSL's construction programme is less advanced following delays in the supply of equipment but the first three of its vessels – *Mahe*, *Malwan* and *Mangrol* – were launched in a combined ceremony at Kochi on 30 November 2023. Both variants displace under 1,000 tonnes and, as their designation suggests, they are optimised for anti-submarine operations in the littoral.

The new ships will serve alongside six larger, c. 2,500-tonne Next Generation Missile Vessels, which will be capable of 35 knots on combined diesel and gas (CODAG) propulsion and operate in the anti-surface warfare role. CSL was awarded the contract for their construction in March 2023 but, although numerous long-lead items have been procured, work had yet to start as of mid-2024. Further advanced are eleven Next Generation Offshore Patrol Vessels that were ordered from GRSE (four ships) and GSL (seven ships) on the same day as the new missile vessels. GRSE cut steel for its first two ships on 24 February 2024, with GSL starting work on its first pair the following month. MDSL is also working on new offshore patrol vessels, having been contracted for six ships for the Indian Coast Guard on 20 December 2023. Plans for Next Generation Corvettes and new mine countermeasures vessels remain at the planning stage.

The Indian Navy is commissioning increasing numbers of sophisticated specialist vessels. This photograph shows *Sandhayak*, the first of four new large survey vessels ordered from GRSE. *(Government of India)*

Auxiliary Vessels: A significant development occurred on 25 August 2023 with the long-awaited order for five 45,000-tonne fleet support vessels from Hindustan Shipyard Ltd (HSL) at a reported cost of INR 190bn (c. US$2.3bn). The ships were originally to be built to a design provided by Turkey's TAIS but local press reports suggest that the Turkish company has been dropped from the deal for political reasons. Work on the lead ship began in April 2024 and is expected to be delivered during 2027. Meanwhile, deliveries of a new series of survey vessels has already commenced with the completion of *Sandhayak* by GRSE in December 2023. Subsequently commissioned on 3 February 2024, the new 3,000-tonne vessel will be followed by three sisters before the end of 2025.

Submarines: A number of news reports in mid-2024 suggested that India's second strategic submarine – the c. 6,000-tonne *Arighat* – will be officially commissioned before the end of 2024 after completing an extended period of trials. Launched in November 2017, she is an improved variant of the earlier *Arihant*, which commissioned in August 2016. Two additional strategic submarines of enlarged design are at various stages of completion at the Navy Ship Building Centre (SBC) in Vishakhapatnam.

Conventional submarine numbers remained fixed at sixteen boats during the last year. *Vagsheer*, the sixth and last *Kalvari* ('Scorpène) class submarine, commenced sea trials from MDSL in May 2023 but had not been delivered as of mid-2024. In July 2023, plans to acquire an additional three members of the class were announced during an official visit by India's President Modi to France. The deal, which has yet to be finalised, will see this new batch equipped with an indigenous air-independent propulsion (AIP) system developed by India's Defence Research and Development Organisation (DRDO). If successfully concluded, the order will provide a bridge to the considerably delayed follow-on programme for six Project 75(I) submarines. Consortia comprising MDSL in alliance with Germany's thyssenkrupp Marine Systems (TKMS) and L&T in partnership with Navantia are vying for the deal, with their proposals currently subject to technical evaluation.

OTHER INDIAN OCEAN NAVIES

Bangladesh: The Bangladesh Navy achieved a further milestone in its long-term modernisation plans with the commissioning of the Sher-e-Bangla naval base at Kalapara in the south-west of Bangladesh on 13 July 2023. Extending over an area of some 700 acres, the facility has been under construction since 2013 and will reportedly encompass naval aviation and port facilities once it is fully complete. Its commissioning follows the official inauguration of the navy's first submarine base at Cox's Bazar in the east of the country earlier in 2023.

The opening of the new naval base was accompanied by the entry into service of four indigenously-built utility landing craft and the first four of a second batch of five *Padma* class inshore patrol vessels. The 350-tonne vessels were ordered from the state-owned Khulna Shipyard in May 2019 and follow on from five older members of the class delivered in 2013. Seven variants have also been delivered to the Bangladesh Coast Guard. Having previously modernised its small force of surface combatants – comprising seven frigates and six corvettes – with a mixture of new and second-hand ships between 2010 and 2020, there has been something of a pause in further major acquisitions as the new vessels are assimilated. However, there are medium-term plans to build a new class of frigates at Chittagong Dry Dock to a modern, Western design.

Bangladesh's navy has been reinforced by considerable numbers of new and second-hand warships in recent years. This photograph shows the frigate *Somudra Avijan,* formerly the US Coast Guard high endurance cutter *Rush* (WHEC-723), on exercises with the new Chinese-built Type 056 corvette *Prottoy* on exercises in December 2021. *(US Navy)*

Myanmar: The Myanmar Navy has been following a similar trajectory to its Bangladeshi counterpart in recent years. The acquisition of submarines from India and China has been accompanied by an ambitious programme of indigenous construction of increasingly sophisticated surface combatants. However, there has been no news of notable developments over the past year. This may reflect the impact of Myanmar's increasingly bitter civil war on military priorities, with the ruling military junta facing an uphill struggle to counter multiple insurgencies.

Pakistan: The Pakistan Navy's modernisation programme continued to gain traction throughout 2023–4. The most significant development was the launch of the lead *Hangor* class submarine by Wuchang Shipbuilding in China on 26 April 2024. Eight of these submarines – an export variant of the People's Liberation Army Navy's Type 039B/Type 041 'Yuan' class – were ordered under a deal announced in 2015 but subsequent realisation of the project has been slow. Four of the eight boats are being assembled at Karachi Shipyard & Engineering Works (KSEW), which held a formal keel-laying ceremony for its second unit in February 2024. Whilst the project is unlikely to be realised until the end of the decade, the new submarines will provide Pakistan with, in conjunction with its three modernised 'Agosta 90B' type boats, a potent asymmetrical counterweight to the dominant Indian Navy.

The 'Agosta 90B' modernisation is being completed by Turkish industry, with which Pakistan is forming an increasingly close relationship. Another sign of this partnership is the construction of four *Babur* class light frigates, which is being split between Istanbul Naval Shipyard and KSEW. The lead ship was commissioned into the Pakistan Navy at a ceremony at Istanbul on 23 September 2023, subsequently departing for home waters in June 2024. With a length of 109m and a full load displacement approaching 3,000 tonnes, the Pakistani ships are larger than the Turkish 'Milgem' type on which they are based and their armament includes twelve VLS cells for the extended-range variant of the MBDA CAMM surface-to-air missile. All the remaining members of the class are now in the water following the launch of *Tariq* – the second KSEW unit – on 2 August 2023 and it is currently envisaged deliveries will be completed before the end of 2025. The design of a larger *Jinnah* variant remains under development.

The Pakistan Navy is also taking deliveries of upgraded offshore patrol vessels built to the Dutch Damen shipbuilding group's designs. Having received two OPV1900 *Yarmook* class vessels in 2020, it is now awaiting a further pair of larger ships being constructed to the Damen OPV2600 design. The first of these was launched from Damen's shipyard at Galati in Romania on 12 September 2023, taking the name *Hunain.* She was later followed by her sister, *Yamama,* in February 2024. Although precise details have still to be released, the pair will benefit from a heavier armament – that seems likely to include CAMM – than the initial ships. All four ships are referred to as corvettes in Pakistan Navy service.

AFRICAN NAVIES

South Africa continues the protracted implementation of its naval modernisation plans against the backdrop of the country's continued economic troubles. October 2023 saw the delivery of *King Shaka Zulu*, the second of three Damen Stan Patrol 6211 inshore patrol vessels being built under Project Biro, by Damen Shipyards Cape Town. The third and as-yet unnamed final vessel should commence sea trials in September 2023, bringing the programme closer to its conclusion somewhat earlier than had once been envisaged. Less positively, delays continue to impact the completion of *Nelson Mandela*, the hydrographic survey ship being built under the contemporaneous Project Hotel by Sandock Austral Shipyards. As of mid-2024 her construction continued with a revised delivery date yet to be set. The South African Navy hopes to launch a project to replace the veteran replenishment ship *Drakensberg* – which will reach her 40th birthday in 2027 – once current programmes are concluded. However, it is far from clear how this will be afforded given a significant lack of resources for defence investment.[8]

An overhead view of *King Shaka Zulu*, the second of three Damen Stan Patrol 6211 inshore patrol vessels built by Damen Shipyards Capetown for the South African Navy, pictured in the course of sea trials in June 2023. She was delivered in October that year. *(Damen)*

In contrast with South Africa, naval modernisation in many Sub-Saharan African countries is now progressing at a relatively rapid pace after a protracted period when the maritime domain was largely ignored. A case in point is **Angola**, which has been undertaking an ongoing programme of upgrades to its navy over the last decade. Notably, July 2023 saw the formal inauguration of the upgraded Soyo naval base in the far north of the country as part of steps to improve the security of the country's offshore energy resources. The base, which is now the largest in the country, was expanded under a €270m (US$290m) contract with Portugal's Mota-Engil Group that was awarded in 2019. The navy is also close to concluding deliveries of a range of naval vessels from the Privinvest shipbuilding group. The most recent arrival is *ND15* – the first of a pair of 70m tank landing ships – built by the company's Constructions Mécaniques de Normandie (CMN) subsidiary. A contract for an even more ambitious project involving the acquisition of three advanced BR71 Mk II corvettes derived from the CMN *Baynunah* class design was agreed with Abu Dhabi Ship Building (ADSB) in February 2023.

Angola's naval investment reflects increasing recognition across the continent of both the value of offshore assets and also of the need to protect them. Another important beneficiary has been **Nigeria's** navy, which has recently seen a sustained period of investment after a period of prolonged neglect. The most significant project currently underway is for two 76m offshore patrol vessels contracted with Turkey's Dearsan in November 2021. The first of these ships was launched at Istanbul on 26 October 2023, with her sister following on 19 April 2024. Dearsan has also subsequently agreed contracts to modernise the Nigerian Navy's sole frigate – the veteran German-built MEKO 360 *Aradu* – and supply a single 57m *Tuzla* class coastal patrol vessel in another sign of the Turkish naval construction sector's growing influence in international markets.

Further to the north along Africa's western coast, **Senegal** has completed deliveries of the three OPV 58S patrol vessels ordered under a contract with France's Piriou in November 2019. *Cayor*, the final vessel of the trio, was handed over at Piriou's Concarneau yard in Brittany on 16 April 2024, six months after the delivery of the second of the class, *Niani*, on 14 November 2023. The 600-tonne, 62m long vessels are heavily armed for ships of their type. Armament includes a 76mm gun, Marte surface-to-surface and Mistral SIMBAD-RC surface-to-air missiles, which are all controlled by a Naval Group Polaris combat management system.

The northern coast of Africa saw significant naval procurement during the first two decades of the current Millennium but recent activity has been far more muted. Whilst it is difficult to draw any definitive conclusions, it seems possible that the pause in **Algeria's** once-active naval modernisation might have been impacted by the Russo-Ukrainian War, with rumoured plans for new submarine acquisition delayed. The Algerian Navy currently operates two early Project 877 and four later Project 636 Russian 'Kilo' class submarines and the initial pair are now likely approaching the end of their service lives. Meanwhile, the core of the surface fleet was modernised by the receipt of German (two MEKO A200 AN) and Chinese (three *Adhafer* class) frigates between 2015 and 2018, suggesting immediate requirements for major surface combatants have been met. However, the three Russian Project 1234 'Nanuchka' class fast attack craft that form part of the second tier of combatants are now well past their fortieth birthdays. As such, acquisitions of further Chinese Type 056 corvettes similar to the single *El Moutassadi* that was delivered in 2023 may be agreed to maintain fleet numbers.

Neighbouring **Egypt's** major programme of modernisation and expansion also seems close to running its course after significant acquisitions in recent years. December 2023 saw the delivery of *Al Qadeer*, the third of four MEKO A200 EN frigates ordered from Germany's TKMS in 2018. The German shipbuilder noted the speed with which the new ship had been completed; first steel cutting had occurred in the autumn of 2020, with technical launch in April 2022. The fourth and final vessel, *Al Jabbar*, is being assembled at Alexandria Shipyard in Egypt. She was launched on 4 December 2023 and is expected to be delivered during 2025.

MIDDLE EASTERN NAVIES

A number of important naval programmes in the Middle East are also drawing to a close. Notably, **Saudi Arabia's** contract with Spanish shipbuilder Navantia to acquire five 'Avante 2200' *Al Jubail* class corvettes reached its conclusion on 7 March 2024 when the project's final ship, *Unayzah*, was commissioned at the King Faisal naval base in Jeddah. Like her sister *Jazan* – delivered in December 2023 – she is significant for having been transported from Navantia's shipyards in the Bay of Cadiz whilst still in an incomplete state. This allowed final outfitting and combat management system integration to take place in Jeddah under a transfer-of-technology agreement with Saudi Arabian Military Industries (SAMI). Navantia has formed a joint venture with SAMI in Saudi Arabia to improve the country's naval integration and support facilities in line with the country's Saudi Vision 2030. The intention is that the new enterprise will be involved in further naval projects involving the two countries.

Construction of the four Multi-Mission Surface Combatants (MMSCs) that form the other leg of Saudi naval modernisation is less advanced as builder Fincantieri Marinette Marine struggles to retain workers whilst transitioning from Littoral Combat Ship to *Constellation* (FFG-62) class frigate production. The lead ship – a derivative of the *Freedom* (LCS-1) class design and believed to have been allocated the name *Saud* – remained under assembly as of mid-2024 prior to a planned launch later in the year. She will reportedly be the first vessel to be lowered into the water by the yard's new shiplift, which will replace the sideways dynamic launches used to date.[9]

Qatar's major project of naval expansion is also now close to fruition. *Al Fulk*, the hybrid air defence amphibious transport dock that forms the last of seven warships ordered from Fincantieri under a project first announced in 2016, commenced sea

Cayor – pictured here in March 2024 – is the final member of a class of three heavily-armed offshore patrol vessels recently delivered by France's Piriou to Senegal. *(Bruno Huriet)*

Germany's thyssenkrupp Marine Systems is in the course of completing a class of four MEKO A200 EN frigates for Egypt. This photograph shows *Al Qadeer*, the third member of the class, at the time of her delivery in December 2023. *(TKMS)*

trials from Fincantieri's Muggiano yard in May 2024. The c. 9,000 tonne vessel is derived from the Italian Navy's *San Giorgio* design and similar to the Algerian *Kalaat Beni Abbes* that Fincantieri delivered in 2014. In conjunction with two eight-cell Sylver A50 missile launchers for Aster surface-to-air missiles, a combination of Leonardo's Kronos multi-function and long-range surveillance radars gives the new ship a powerful air defence capability. Fincantieri is now reportedly seeking further lucrative naval contracts with Qatar, including the potential sale of a logistic support vessel similar to the Italian *Vulcano.*[10]

The **United Arab Emirates** has also been inducting new capabilities in the form of the two 'Gowind' light frigates ordered from France's Naval Group in 2019. The delivery of *Bani Yas* took place at the group's Lorient facility on 21 October 2023 and was followed by that of her sister, *Al Emarat*, on 27 June 2024. The contract with Naval Group included an option to build two additional vessels in the UAE. However, this seems unlikely to be exercised given local ADSB's focus on the indigenous 'Falaj 3' offshore patrol vessel programme. Whilst this project is being realised with support from Singapore's ST Engineering, ADSB's future development seems likely to be driven by an alliance with Fincantieri. In February 2024, the Italian group announced the 'Maestral' joint venture with ADSB's parent EDGE Group 'to capitalise on global opportunities for the design and manufacture of advanced naval vessels'. The new entity's first contract is a €400m (c. US$430m) order for ten 51m patrol vessels for the UAE coast guard, which will be based on Italy's *Saettia* class.

Fear of **Iran** continues to be one of the major drivers of naval developments in the Middle East. In addition to continuing sporadic harassment of international shipping, the navy is seemingly seeking to expand beyond its traditional anti-access/area-denial (A2/AD) role to increase its presence across the world's oceans. Notably, a flotilla comprising the frigate *Dena* and the logistic support vessel *Makran* completed the Islamic Republic of Iran Navy's first global circumnavigation between September 2022 and May 2023. From a procurement perspective, the most notable recent arrival has been that of the frigate *Deylaman*, which was commissioned into Iran's Northern Fleet in the inland Caspian Sea on 27 November 2023. She is the fifth member of the indigenous 'Moudge' class, derivatives of Iran's British Vosper Thornycroft-designed *Alvand* class originally delivered in the early 1970s. She replaces her sister *Damavand*, which became a total loss after grounding at the entrance to the port of Bandar-e Anzali in January 2018.

Whilst recent events in **Israel** have been dominated by the land war with Hamas in the Gaza Strip, there have been several notable naval developments in the last year. All four of the SA'AR 6 corvettes that were constructed by TKMS in Germany but outfitted by Israel Shipyards in Haifa have now entered service after completion of extensive trials. In late 2023, the

Bani Yas, the first of two 'Gowind' corvettes built by Naval Group for the United Arab Emirates, pictured in the course of sea trials in July 2023. *(Naval Group)*

lead ship – *Magen* – was deployed to the Red Sea in response to the deteriorating security situation in the region. Here she carried out the first operational use of her C-Dome air defence system in April 2024 when she shot down a drone approaching the port of Eilat. The Israeli Navy has also played a significant role in the blockade of Gaza and protecting the country's offshore energy infrastructure.

Israel has also been taking delivery of other new vessels, including the first of a quartet of 'Shaldag Mk V' interceptors from Israel Shipyards and two 2,500-tonne landing craft – *Nahshon* and *Komemiyut* – from Bollinger Shipyards' Pascagoula yard (formerly VT Halter Marine) in the United States. The latter ships are reportedly based on the US Army's *General Frank S. Besson* class logistics support vessels and restore a capacity last used in the 1990s. However, the most significant event is probably the launch of *Drakon*, the third and final member of the second batch of *Dolphin* class boats, in August 2023. Photographs confirm that she has been built with a large, extended fin that has supposedly been incorporated into her revised design to provide the capability to house vertically-launched missiles. News reports suggest that her sea trials are likely to commence in mid-2024, suggesting her long-awaited delivery is imminent.

The Israeli Navy corvette *Eilat* (foreground) and fast attack craft *Hetz* seen operating in the Red Sea in early 2022. The Israeli Navy has subsequently played an important but little-reported role in the conflict with Hamas. *(US Navy)*

Notes:

1. Yemen has been the location of a civil war between the internationally-recognised Presidential Leadership Council and the rebel Houthi movement – now headed by their Supreme Political Council – since 2014. The two sides have been supported by, respectively, a Saudi-led coalition and Iran in a reflection of the split between the Sunni and Shia Islamic religions. Neither side has gained a decisive advantage in the war, which has led to the Houthis controlling an extensive area of the eastern Red Sea coast.

2. An analysis of the early impact of the shipping crisis was provided by investment bank J P Morgan's global research team in 'What are the impacts of the Red Sea shipping crisis?' posted to the jpmorgan.com site on 8 February 2024.

3. The destroyers involved in the engagement were the US Navy's *Gravely* (DDG 107), *Laboon* (DDG-58) and *Mason* (DDG-87) and the British *Dragon*. F/A-18E/F Super Hornet strike fighters from *Dwight D. Eisenhower* (CVN-69) also assisted in repelling the attack. The action was just one of many defensive actions that have taken place in the Red Sea since October 2023, with French, German and Italian warships also successfully downing drones and missiles.

4. An interesting assessment of the difficulties faced in ending the Houthi campaign was provided by the K2 Integrity consultancy's Bilal Sabbagh in an article, 'Why Houthi Attacks in the Red Sea Are Likely to Persist: They're Popular' posted to the *Maritime Executive* site – maritime-executive.com – on 24 March 2024. As noted in Norman Friedman's chapter on 'Post-Cold War Naval Evolution' in section four of this annual, the need to counter cumulatively numerous attacks also raises challenges in replenishing finite shipboard supplies of air defence missiles.

5. As always, a detailed review of the Indian defence budget is provided by the *Observer Research Foundation's* Laxman K Behera. See 'Examining India's Interim Defence Budget 2024-25' posted to their orfonline.org website on 26 February 2024.

6. The Project 15A and Project 15B designs were described by Mrityunjoy Mazumdar in the 2024 edition of *Seaforth World Naval Review*. In the event, it seems that *Surat*'s delivery will be faster than anticipated.

7. A good indication of the current status of India's major warship programmes is provided in the transcripts of the quarterly investor presentations held by GRSE and MDSL, which both have minority shareholdings traded on the local BSE and NSE stock exchanges. These can be found on the two shipbuilders' websites.

8. More details of the progress of South Africa's naval modernisation programmes can be found on the *defenceWeb* site – defenceweb.co.za – which remains an excellent source of news on naval developments across the African continent.

9. See Chris Cavas, 'First Look: Fincantieri Marine Group Production Includes US Navy's Frigate, LCS and Saudi Combatants' posted to the *Naval News* site – navalnews.com – on 2 February 2024.

10. See Luca Peruzzi, 'DIMDEX 2024 – Fincantieri's training, support and shipbuilding opportunities in Qatar' posted to *the European Defence Review On-Line* site – edrmagazine.eu – on 26 March 2024.

2.4 REGIONAL REVIEW

Author:
Conrad Waters

EUROPE AND RUSSIA

On 5 April 2024, Norway became the latest European country to adjust its defence strategy to the deteriorating security climate with the publication of its quadrennial Long-term Defence Plan for the period through to 2036.[1] Heralded by the Norwegian government as 'a historic plan', the new document largely lived up to this description by heralding an additional Norwegian Kr.600bn (c. US$56bn) of defence spending over the next 12 years. Having hit the NATO target of spending two percent of national income (GDP) on defence in 2024, this figure will steadily rise to almost 2.7 percent by 2030. Although this increased investment is spread across all branches of the armed forces, the new plan has a strong maritime element. This partly reflects the government's awareness that 'Norway is a maritime nation with a strong maritime legacy'. In terms of money, strengthening the Royal Norwegian Navy is the largest investment within the long-term plan.

In specific terms, the navy will benefit from a package of procurement that is headed by a minimum of five new frigates equipped with anti-submarine helicopters to replace its remaining four *Fridtjof Nansen* class vessels. This programme is being pursued with some urgency, with shipyards in several allied NATO countries already eagerly eyeing up a large and potentially lucrative contract. The existing programme to acquire Type 212CD submarines from Germany will be increased from four to five boats (with an option for a sixth). Additionally, much of the rest of the navy's and coast guard's inventory of other vessels will be replaced by ten large and eighteen smaller vessels of standardised designs. These will be equipped with a range of modular weapons and sensors in a further demonstration of the extent to which navies are seeking to adopt ongoing improvements in such technology to streamline procurement and enhance operating efficiency.

On a broader level, the new Norwegian strategy has much to recommend it as a pragmatic response to the recognition of the '… need to spend more on and pay more attention to defence and preparedness' as the security environment deteriorates. In this regard, the plan stands in welcome contrast to other recent defence updates, such as the Canadian defence policy review that was published just three days later.[2] The Canadian document has similarities to the Norwegian plan in its recognition of the changed global backdrop, as well as a shared recognition of the growing strategic importance of both countries' 'Far North'. Regrettably, however, it does much less in the immediate term to provide the financial resources to reflect this conclusion. As a result, Canada's strategy contains many important elements, notably renewal and expansion of its submarine flotilla, that remain unfunded options subject to further analysis.

Other welcome elements of Norway's Long-term Defence Plan include its emphasis on improving situational awareness; the priority afforded to rebuilding weapons stocks; and a pledge to increase the defence establishment's depth by recruiting (particularly) additional reservists. There is a recognition that desire to increase personnel numbers will need to be supported by innovation in recruitment and retention methods, as well as a strengthening of the Norwegian armed forces' educational institutions. Perhaps most significant from a 'navalist's' perspective is the Norwegian government's appreciation that the country's geographical position necessitates prioritisation of a maritime strategy despite many defence strategists' inevitable focus on the largely land-based aspects of the current Russo-Ukrainian War.

Meanwhile, Thursday 7 March 2024 saw another significant development in Scandinavia's security architecture through the formal accession of Sweden to the NATO alliance. Sweden becomes the security partnership's 32nd member, following on from Finland's arrival on 4 April 2023. The two countries' membership marks the culmination of a steady growth in collaboration with alliance countries in the security field that was given impetus by the outbreak of the Ukraine conflict. In addition to transforming the maritime balance of power across the Baltic, their arrival likely holds out the prospect of a further strengthening of cooperation in defence procurement, including in the naval sphere. One tangible example of this emerged in September 2023 with the announcement of a strategic partnership between Sweden's Saab and the United Kingdom's Babcock International. Subsequently, in May 2024, it emerged that the British company was to support Saab in the design development of the Swedish Navy's new *Luleå* class surface combatant. The agreement is likely just one of many opportunities that will open as the two new members become more firmly embedded in the alliance.

Norway's lead *Fridtjof Nansen* class frigate is seen against the backdrop of the Goliat oilfield in the Barents Sea in December 2023. The four remaining vessels of the *Nansen* class will be replaced by at least five new 'blue water' frigates as part of a major programme of investment in the Royal Norwegian Navy. *(Catharina Molland Dale/Norwegian Armed Forces)*

TABLE 2.4.1: FLEET STRENGTHS IN WESTERN EUROPE – LARGER NAVIES (MID 2024)

COUNTRY	FRANCE	GERMANY	GREECE	ITALY	NETHERLANDS	SPAIN	TURKEY	UK
Aircraft Carrier (CVN/CV)	1	–	–	1	–	–	–	2
Support/Helicopter Carrier (CVS/CVH)	–	–	–	1	–	–	–	–
Strategic Missile Submarine (SSBN)	4	–	–	–	–	–	–	4
Attack Submarine (SSN)	5	–	–	–	–	–	–	6
Patrol Submarine (SSK)	–	6	10[2]	8	3	2	12	–
Fleet Escort (DDG/FFG)	15	11	13[2]	17	6	11	17	15
Patrol Escort/Corvette (FFG/FSG/FS)	11	5	–	–	–	–	9	–
Missile Armed Attack Craft (PGG/PTG)	–	–	16	–	–	–	18	–
Mine Countermeasures Vessel (MCMV)	11	8[1]	3	10	4	6	11	7
Major Amphibious (LHD/LPD/LPH/LSD)	3	–	–	3	2[3]	3	1	5

Notes:

1 Two further units used as support vessels and two as recruitment platforms.

2 Headline figures overstate the actual position, as some old units are of doubtful operational status.

3 Also one joint support ship with amphibious capabilities.

MAJOR REGIONAL POWERS – FRANCE

The receipt of French parliamentary approval for the *Loi de Programmation Militaire* 2024–2030 (LPM 2024–30) on 13 July 2023 has established the likely structure and funding for the French armed forces until the end of the decade.[3] The act provides a headline spending figure of €413bn (c. US$445bn) for the seven-year period; some 40 percent more than the budget allocated in the previous LPM 2019–25. Despite the extent of the increase – and a view that the navy has fared relatively well out of the agreement – the available money is essentially adequate to fund current naval programmes rather than allowing any significant expansion. This reflects the large investment required in, for example, replacing the country's quartet of strategic submarines, as well as the aircraft carrier *Charles de Gaulle*. In essence, therefore, the coming years will see the *Marine Nationale* achieve qualitative but not quantitative enhancement.

Table 2.4.2, summarising the French Navy's major units as of mid-2024, provides a starting point for examining the changes that will occur over coming years. The table reflects the replacement of the existing *Rubis* class nuclear-powered attack submarines with the new *Suffren* class, described further in Chapter 3.3. The remaining elderly A-69 *D'Estienne d'Orves* class corvettes, now re-rolled as patrol vessels, are also being retired as replacements finally start to appear on the horizon. Further detail is provided under the major category headings that follow.

Aircraft Carriers: France's sole aircraft carrier, *Charles de Gaulle*, returned to front-line service early in 2024 after completion of a mid-cycle docking at Toulon. She is due to be replaced in 2038 with the new *porte-avions de nouvelle génération* (PANG), on which design definition work continues. Current plans envisage the PANG's subsequent design and construction phase being launched by early 2026, with assembly taking place at Chantiers de l'Atlantique in Saint-Nazaire. However, the first long-lead items – for the nuclear propulsion system – have already been ordered under contracts announced in April 2024. The LPM provides for studies into the acquisition of a second aircraft carrier in time for a final decision in 2028. However, the financial commitment to operating a second carrier and its supporting infrastructure would be formidable.

Submarines: On 20 March 2024, a ceremony to mark initial steel cutting for the first third-generation French strategic submarine (SNLE 3G) took place at Naval Group's shipyard in Cherbourg. Launched in February 2021, the programme aims to replace France's existing four *Le Triomphant* class boats on a like-for-like basis from 2035 onwards. France has also begun tests of the M51.3 iteration of its M51 submarine-launched ballistic missile, conducting a successful land-based firing on 18 November 2023. The new weapon reportedly has an improved third stage to increase both range and survivability against anti-missile defences. It is expected to enter operational service onboard the *Le Triomphant* class in the second half of the current decade before equipping the new SNLE 3G boats as they are delivered.

The flotilla of nuclear-powered attack submarines benefitted from the entry into active service of *Duguay-Trouin* – the second member of the *Suffren* class – on 4 April 2024. Her arrival counterbalances the retirement of the third *Rubis* class submarine *Casabianca* in September 2023, leaving just three of the type in service.

Major Surface Combatants: Deliveries of new French surface warships are currently subject to a pause following the entry into operational service of the final FREMM type frigate, *Lorraine*, in November 2023. Frigate production is now transitioning to the new *frégate de défense et d'intervention* (FDI) but there will be a gap before these arrive in numbers. Construction of *Amiral Ronar'ch*, the lead ship of this new class, is well advanced at Naval Group's Lorient shipyard. She will commence sea

TABLE 2.4.2: FRENCH NAVY: PRINCIPAL UNITS AS AT MID 2024

TYPE	CLASS	NUMBER	TONNAGE	DIMENSIONS	PROPULSION	CREW	DATE
Aircraft Carriers							
Aircraft Carrier – CVN	**CHARLES DE GAULLE**	1	42,000 tonnes	262m x 33/64m x 9m	Nuclear, 27 knots	1,950	2001
Principal Surface Escorts							
Frigate – FFG	**AQUITAINE** (FREMM)	8[1]	6,000 tonnes	142m x 20m x 5m	CODLOG, 27 knots	110	2012
Frigate – FFG	**FORBIN** ('Horizon')	2	7,100 tonnes	153m x 20m x 5m	CODOG, 29+ knots	195	2008
Frigate – FFG	**LA FAYETTE**	5	3,600 tonnes	125m x 15m x 5m	CODAD, 25 knots	150	1996
Frigate – FSG	**FLORÉAL**	6	3,000 tonnes	94m x 14m x 4m	CODAD, 20 knots	90	1992
Frigate – FS[2]	**D'ESTIENNE D'ORVES** (A-69)	5	1,300 tonnes	80m x 10m x 3m	Diesel, 24 knots	90	1976
Submarines							
Submarine – SSBN	**LE TRIOMPHANT**	4	14,400 tonnes	138m x 13m x 11m	Nuclear, 25 knots	110	1997
Submarine – SSN	**SUFFREN**	2	5,300 tonnes	100m x 9m x 7m	Nuclear, 25+knots	65	2020
Submarine – SSN	**RUBIS**	3	2,700 tonnes	74m x 8m x 6m	Nuclear, 25+ knots	70	1983
Major Amphibious Units							
Amph Assault Ship – LHD	**MISTRAL**	3	21,500 tonnes	199m x 32m x 6m	Diesel-electric, 19 knots	160	2006

Note:

1 Includes two slightly-modified *Alsace* variants.

2 Now officially reclassified as offshore patrol vessels.

Two photographs of the first FDI type frigate *Amiral Ronar'ch* under tow on the River Scorff in Lorient in May 2024 as harbour acceptance trials continued. The new frigate is expected to commence sea trials in the second half of 2024. *(Naval Group)*

trials in 2024, suggesting a 2025 delivery date is achievable. However, there will then be a hiatus in deliveries of further units to the French Navy due to the priority being given to completing the export order for the Hellenic Navy's *Kimon* class variant. Accordingly, *Amiral Louzeau* – the second French ship – will be the fifth of the class to enter production, pushing her completion back towards the end of the decade. Naval Group had previously been awarded a contract to modernise three of the five existing *La Fayette* class frigates to maintain the front-line force of surface combatants at fifteen units. However, the delay may put this target in jeopardy. Modernisation of *Aconit*, the third and final member of the *La Fayette* class to go through the life extension and upgrade programme, was completed at the end of 2023.

In July 2023, a much more ambitious and costly mid-life modernisation of the navy's 'Horizon' class air defence destroyers was announced. The €1.5bn (c. US$1.6bn) upgrade includes the two French and two Italian members of the class. It is being undertaken by the Naviris joint venture between Naval Group and Fincantieri in collaboration with the Eurosam partnership of MBDA France, MBDA Italia and Thales. The work includes an improved command and control system, as well as Leonardo's Kronos Grand Naval and Thales' SMART-L MM/N active electronically-scanned array radars. Significantly, the upgrade will include integration of the Aster Block 1 NT surface-to-air missile. This will provide a better capability against medium-range ballistic missiles.

Minor Warships and Auxiliaries: An important element of French naval modernisation moved forward on 17 November 2023 with the order of an initial batch of seven *patrouilleurs hauturiers* (PHs) – previously referred to as *patrouilleurs océaniques* – to undertake offshore patrol duties from the navy's Metropolitan bases in Brest, Cherbourg and Toulon. The cost of the €900m (c. US$975m) programme is split between Naval Group (project manager and supplier of the combat management system); Thales (supplier of the class's surveillance equipment); and a temporary consortium comprising the CMN, Piriou and Socarenam shipyards (that will build the ships). Displacing around 2,400 tonnes, the new offshore patrol vessels will have a range of 6,000 nautical miles and a maximum speed in excess of 20 knots. They will be equipped with Naval Group's SETIS command and control technology and a wide range of sensors including Thales' Bluewatcher hull-mounted sonar. This reflects the fact that 'delousing' France's strategic submarines during departure from their base near Brest is one of their mission requirements. The ships are capable of supporting a light helicopter or drones but are otherwise lightly armed. Construction of the first ship, named *Trolley de Prévaux* after an admiral who was executed in 1944 for his work supporting the French Resistance, has already commenced at Piriou's yard at Concarneau. Three additional vessels – taking the class to ten ships overall – are planned beyond the lifespan of the current LPM.

Construction of the six smaller *patrouilleurs outre-mer* (POMs) that form the PHs' counterparts in Overseas France is making steady progress.[4] *Teriieroo a Teriierooiterai*, second member of the class, arrived

In November 2023, the French government placed an initial order for seven *patrouilleurs hauturiers* from a consortium of French shipyards. The new vessels will be based in Metropolitan France but have sufficient size and endurance for long-distance operations. The first vessel is already under construction and should be delivered by the end of 2026. *(Naval Group)*

at the port of Papeete in Tahiti on 23 May 2024 to take up her duties. Sister-ship *Auguste Techer* was launched at Socarenam's Saint-Malo yard in December 2023 and is currently being outfitted at Boulogne. If all goes well, the remaining three members of the class should all be delivered before the end of 2025.

Jacques Chevallier, the first of four new replenishment vessels – *bâtiments ravitailleurs de force* (BRFs) – was officially accepted at Toulon in July 2023 after the completion of initial trials but has yet to enter the operational fleet. The second member of the class, *Jacques Stosskopf*, is expected to be launched at Saint-Nazaire in the second half of 2024. Work is also underway on the third unit, *Émile Bertin*. Progress with the project has paved the way for decommissioning the previous-generation *Durance* class replenishment oiler *Marne* in October 2023, leaving only *Somme* from that class in service. Other decommissionings during the last year included the 'Tripartite' class mine countermeasures vessel *Orion*. The fleet's remaining conventional minehunters will be steadily withdrawn as the navy transitions to autonomous solutions deployed, inter alia, from bespoke 'motherships'. In August 2023, France signed a memorandum of understanding with Belgium and the Netherlands that is expected to result in the use of their rMCM mothership design as the basis for France's own *bâtiment de guerre des mines* (BDGM) project.

Operationally the French Navy has been heavily involved in the effort to protect shipping transiting the Black Sea, playing a leading role in the European Union's 'Aspides' operation. As of mid-2024, the FREMM type frigates *Languedoc*, *Alsace* and *Lorraine* as well as the 'Horizon' type destroyer *Forbin* had all seen operational service in the Red Sea. Notably, on 21 March 2024, *Alsace* proved the capabilities of the enhanced French FREMM air-defence variant when she destroyed a salvo of three ballistic missiles that were targeting her and her accompanying shipping. This was reportedly the first time that the Aster missile system had been used to engage a ballistic missile threat.

MAJOR REGIONAL POWERS – ITALY

Italy's *Marina Militare* has also been an active participant in Operation 'Aspides', conducting a number of successful engagements against drone attacks. Its leading role is further evidence of the growing importance of an expanding navy that, in many aspects, has achieved quantitative – if not quite qualitative – equivalence with its British and French counterparts.[5] A summary of its current major units is provided in Table 2.4.3. Further analysis of specific warship types follows.

Aircraft Carriers and Amphibious Ships: The amphibious assault ship *Trieste* had still to be commissioned in mid-2024. A prolonged period of trials and crew training commenced as long ago as August 2021, suggesting that the process has not been entirely straightforward. Recent reports suggest that she will enter service before the end of 2024, replacing the veteran aircraft carrier *Giuseppe Garibaldi* and – most likely – the dock landing ship *San Giorgio*. The other two dock landing ships will likely be replaced before the end of the decade by a pair of larger dock landing ships that are currently being designed as part of the navy's LXD programme.

Surface Combatants and Patrol Vessels: The Italian Navy continues to build two classes of major surface warship. One is the multi-mission FREMM type that originated as a Franco-Italian project but which has produced ships of significantly different appearance. Fincantieri are close to completing the Italian Navy's ninth and tenth members of the class following their predecessors' transfer to Egypt in 2020 as part of a major armaments deal. The ships combine the characteristics of the previous separate anti-submarine warfare (ASW) and general purpose variants in a single hull. The most advanced of the pair, *Spartaco Schergat*, was launched from Riva Trigoso in November 2023 and is currently on sea trials. She was followed by a sister, *Emilio Bianchi*, on 24 May 2024. Both ships will be delivered before the end of 2025. Current Italian Navy plans envisage future production of a FREMM EVO (evolved) variant benefitting from technological advances that have occurred since *Carlo Bergamini* – the lead Italian FREMM – was delivered in 2013.

The other line of surface combatant production is represented by the *Paolo Thaon di Revel* class PPA-type multi-mission patrol vessels, which are now

Table 2.4.3: ITALIAN NAVY: PRINCIPAL UNITS AS AT MID 2024

TYPE	CLASS	NUMBER	TONNAGE	DIMENSIONS	PROPULSION	CREW	DATE
Aircraft Carriers							
Aircraft Carrier – CV	CAVOUR	1	28,100 tonnes	244m x 30/39m x 9m	COGAG, 29 knots	800	2008
Aircraft Carrier – CVS	GIUSEPPE GARIBALDI[1]	1	13,900 tonnes	180m x 23/31m x 7m	COGAG, 30 knots	825	1985
Principal Surface Escorts							
Frigate – FFG	CARLO BERGAMINI (FREMM)[2]	8	6,700 tonnes	144m x 20m x 5m	CODLOG, 27 knots	145	2013
Frigate – FFG	ANDREA DORIA ('Horizon')	2	7,100 tonnes	153m x 20m x 5m	CODOG, 29+ knots	190	2007
Destroyer – DDG	DE LA PENNE	2	5,400 tonnes	148m x 16m x 5m	CODOG, 31 knots	375	1993
Frigate – FFG	MAESTRALE	2	3,100 tonnes	123m x 13m x 4m	CODOG, 30+ knots	225	1982
Frigate – FFG/FF[3]	PAOLO THAON DI REVEL	3	6,250 tonnes[3]	143m x 17m x 5m	CODAGOL, 32+ knots	[3]	2022
Submarines							
Submarine – SSK	TODARO (Type 212A)	4	1,800 tonnes	56m x 7m x 6m	AIP, 20+ knots	30	2006
Submarine – SSK	PELOSI (Improved SAURO)	4	1,700 tonnes	64m x 7m x 6m	Diesel-electric, 20 knots	50	1988
Major Amphibious Units							
Landing Platform Dock – LPD	SAN GIORGIO	3	8,000 tonnes	133m x 21m x 5m	Diesel, 20 knots	165	1987

Note:
1 Now operates largely as a LPH. To be replaced by *Trieste* before the end of 2024.
2 Class includes *Bergamini* (GP) and *Fasan* (ASW) variants.
3. Varies dependent on armament configuration.

increasingly referred to as multi-mission combat vessels and are really frigates in all but name. Seven of these ships have been ordered with different levels of equipment, of which three have now been delivered following the arrival of *Raimondo Montecuccoli* in September 2023. However, two of the class were sold to Indonesia in March 2024 and replacements will be required. Further detail on the class is provided in Chapter 3.2.

The PPA class was originally envisaged as encompassing at least ten vessels but plans have subsequently changed. Instead, three smaller 2,300-tonne offshore patrol vessels (OPVs) were ordered under a €925m (c. US$1bn) on 31 July 2023 under a contract which includes options for a further three units. The new ships will take the place of some of the existing patrol forces operating from Augusta, Cagliari and Messina. Italy's remaining patrol vessels will be replaced by the planned European Patrol Corvette (EPC), now also referred to as the Modular and Multirole Patrol Corvette (MMPC). A two-year contract for preliminary design studies valued at €87m (c. US$95m) was let to Naviris joint venture and Navantia in October 2023. If all goes to plan, the new design will also replace the *Floréal* class patrol frigates in the *Marine Nationale* and existing Spanish Navy OPVs. Denmark, Greece and Norway are also potential participants in the project.

Fincantieri launched *Emilio Bianchi*, the Italian Navy's tenth and final FREMM, from its Riva Trigoso shipyard on 25 May 2024. The seventh PPA multi-role combat ship *Domenico Millelire* can be seen in the background. *(Fincantieri)*

Atlante, the Italian Navy's second *Vulcano* class, pictured being readied for launch at the Castellammare di Stabia shipyard near Naples on 18 May 2024. The French Navy's *Jacques Chevallier* BRFs are a variant of this design. *(Fincantieri)*

Italy also has well-advanced plans for a pair of anti-air warfare destroyers to replace the elderly *Durand de la Penne* class. It is possible that orders for the vessels – that are likely to cost around €2.5bn (US$2.7bn) – will be placed within the next 12 months.

Submarines: Current Italian Navy submarine production is focused on the Type 212NFS (Near Future Submarine) variant of the existing Type 212A design. An option for the fourth unit of the class valued at €500m (US$540m) was exercised on 28 June 2024, the same day work on the third boat began. The announcement also noted an engineering change agreement encompassing delivery of lithium-based batteries in replacement of traditional lead-acid battery energy storage. Deliveries of the new submarines are likely to commence around the end of the decade, replacing the existing quartet of *Pelosi* (improved *Sauro*) class boats. In the medium term the Italian Navy is seeking to increase its submarine flotilla to ten units by transitioning production to a Type 212NFS EVO type.

Minor Warships and Auxiliaries: Italy's construction of front-line combatants is supplemented by extensive production of minor warships and auxiliaries. Foremost amongst these is the second *Vulcano* class logistic support ship *Atlante*, which was launched from Fincantieri's Castellamare di Stabia yard on 18 May 2024. Recent plans suggest that planned orders for the type will be increased from three to four. Another significant vessel now in production is a new 'NIOM' hydro-oceanographic ship to replace the existing *Magnaghi.* The as-yet unnamed vessel will displace over 6,000 tonnes and is equipped to operate in both Mediterranean and Arctic environments. Her keel was laid at Riva Trigoso on 6 May 2024.

Other new orders over the past year include four 33m cadet training vessels and an initial pair of lighthouse tenders of modular design that can be used for diving support or even minelaying. In contrast to many other navies, new dedicated mine countermeasures vessels are also planned. Both coastal and oceanic types are envisaged to replace the existing *Lerici/Gaeta* classes, with an order for six of the former type possible within the next year.

MAJOR REGIONAL POWERS – RUSSIA

The continuation of the Russo-Ukrainian War has made the already difficult analysis of Russian Navy developments all the more tricky due to increasing limitations on both the amount and credibility of open source information. In overall terms, the naval aspects of the war have been one of the more unsatisfactory elements of a generally lacklustre Russian performance. Practically, the Black Sea Fleet has continued to suffer relatively high levels of attrition of amphibious vessels and smaller combatants to a mixture of Ukrainian drone and missile attack. Losses of the latter raise questions over the utility of the numerous 'green water' corvette-like missile boats that have formed a significant part of total Russian construction in recent years but which appear to suffer from limited survivability in a high threat environment. An overview of the broader lessons that can be learned from the war to date is contained in Chapter 1.2. Meanwhile, Table 2.4.4 estimates current Russian fleet strength, with further analysis following below.

Submarines: The modernisation of the country's underwater assets continues to be a high priority for the Russian Armed Forces and, consequently, is the area where most success is being achieved. Current procurement has three main strands, with the top priority being accorded to the Project 955/955A 'Borey/Borey A' class strategic submarines. December 2023 saw the commissioning of *Imperator Aleksandr III*, the fourth Project 955A boat and seventh member of the class overall, at the Sevmash yard in Severodvinsk. The ceremonial launch of *Knyaz Pozharskiy* took place at the same facility on 4 February 2024. Another two members of the class are under construction and, according to Russian news agency Tass, a further pair will be laid down before the end of 2024. This will take the 'Borey' series to twelve submarines, spilt evenly between the Northern and Pacific Fleets, and likely allow the remaining Project 667BDRM 'Delta IV' boats to be retired.

Construction of Project 855M 'Yasen M' class nuclear-powered attack submarines continues in parallel with the strategic submarines at Sevmash. Accordingly, *Krasnoyarsk* – third of the modified series and the fourth Project 855 'Yasen' ('Severodvinsk') type boat overall – was commissioned alongside *Imperator Aleksandr III* on 11 December 2023. *Arkhangelsk*, next of the series, was launched on 29 November 2023 and is likely to enter service around the end of 2024. It seems likely that further members of the class will follow at roughly annual intervals, with a total of eight of the Project 855M variant likely to be in service by the end of the decade. As no further members of the class have been laid down since 2020, there will then be a pause and – potentially – a transition to a new variant. The balance of the nuclear-powered attack submarine force is comprised largely of Project 949A 'Oscar II' and Project 971 series 'Akula' class boats laid down in the late Soviet era. It is difficult to ascertain the status of all these units but, possibly, over fifteen are either operational or under active refit.

Construction of latest-variant Project 636.3 ('Improved Kilo) class patrol submarines continues at the Admiralty Shipyards at Saint Petersburg. Production is being maintained at around one unit each year, essentially replacing life-expired members of the original class. However, one of the new type – *Rostov-na-Donu* – was heavily damaged on 13 September 2023 by hits from two Ukrainian Storm Shadow/SCALP EG cruise missiles whilst docked at Sevastopol and may not be repairable. Meanwhile, January 2024 saw acceptance of *Kronstadt*, the first series-produced member of the Project 677 'Lada' class to be completed. She replaces the prototype unit *Sankt Petersburg*, which was decommissioned early in 2024 after over a decade of disappointing performance.

Aircraft Carriers and Amphibious Warships: As of mid-2024, the sole Russian Project 1143.5 aircraft carrier, *Admiral Kuznetsov*, remained under refit, nearly seven years after work commenced. Latest open-source reports suggest that she may be in a position to commence post-refit trials before the end of 2024 but the date has been pushed back many times in the past. It has even been speculated that she will never return to service.

As previously mentioned, Russian amphibious forces are suffering heavy losses in the war against Ukraine. Known losses during the last year include the Project 775 ('Ropucha') class large landing ships *Novocherkassk*, which was destroyed in a missile strike on 26 December 2023, and *Tsezar Kunikov*, which sank after a drone attack on 14 February 2024. Several other vessels have reportedly been damaged, some potentially beyond repair. With little progress reported with either the pair of Project 23900 *Ivan Rogov* class amphibious assault ships being built in the Crimea or the two improved Project 11711 *Ivan Gren* class landing ships under construction in the somewhat safer waters of the Baltic, the capability of the navy's amphibious flotilla has been materially degraded.

TABLE 2.4.4: RUSSIAN NAVY: SELECTED PRINCIPAL UNITS AS AT MID 2024

TYPE	CLASS	NUMBER[1]	TONNAGE	DIMENSIONS	PROPULSION	CREW	DATE
Aircraft carriers							
Aircraft Carrier – CV	Project 1143.5 **KUZNETSOV**	1	60,000 tonnes	306m x 35/73m x 10m	Steam, 32 knots	2,600	1991
Principal Surface Escorts							
Battlecruiser – BCGN	Project 1144.2 **KIROV**	2	25,000 tonnes	252m x 29m x 9m	CONAS, 32 knots	740	1980
Cruiser – CG	Project 1164 **MOSKVA** ('Slava')	2	12,500 tonnes	186m x 21m x 8m	COGAG, 32 knots	530	1982
Destroyer – DDG	Project 956/956A **SOVREMENNY**	c. 2	8,000 tonnes	156m x 17m x 6m	Steam, 32 knots	300	1980
Destroyer – DDG	Project 1155.1 **CHABANENKO** ('Udaloy II')	1	9,000 tonnes	163m x 19m x 6m	COGAG, 29 knots	250	1999
Destroyer – DDG	Project 1155 **UDALOY**	c. 7	8.500 tonnes	163m x 19m x 6m	COGAG, 30 knots	300	1980
Frigate – FFG	Project 22350 **GORSHKOV**	3	5,500 tonnes	135m x 16m x 5m	CODAG, 30 knots	210	2018
Frigate – FFG	Project 11366M **GRIGOROVICH**	3	4,000 tonnes	125m x 15m x 4m	COGAG, 30 knots	200	2016
Frigate – FFG	Project 1154 **NEUSTRASHIMY**	2	4,400 tonnes	139m x 16m x 6m	COGAG, 30 knots	210	1993
Frigate – FFG	Project 1135 **BDITELNNY** ('Krivak I/II')	c. 2	3,700 tonnes	123m x 14m x 5m	COGAG, 32 knots	180	1970
Frigate – FFG	Project 20385 **GREMYASHCHIY**	1	2,500 tonnes	106m x 11m x 5m	CODAD, 27 knots	100	2020
Frigate – FFG	Project 20380 **STERGUSHCHIY**	9	2,200 tonnes	105m x 11m x 4m	CODAD, 27 knots	100	2008
Frigate – FFG	Project 11611 **TATARSTAN** ('Gepard')	2	2,000 tonnes	102m x 13m x 4m	CODOG, 27 knots	100	2002
Submarines							
Submarine – SSBN	Project 95/955A **YURY DOLGORUKY** ('Borey')	7	20,000+ tonnes	170m x 13m x 10m	Nuclear, 25+ knots	110	2010
Submarine – SSBN	Project 677BDRM **VERKHOTURYE** ('Delta IV')	5[2]	18,000 tonnes	167m x 12m x 9m	Nuclear, 24 knots	130	1985
Submarine – SSGN	Project 855/855M **SEVERODVINSK** ('Yasen')	4	13,500+ tonnes	120m x 14m x 9m	Nuclear, 30+ knots	90	2013
Submarine – SSGN	Project 949A ('Oscar II')	c. 7	17,500 tonnes	154m x 8m x 9m	Nuclear, 30+ knots	100	1986
Submarine – SSN	Project 971 ('Akula I/II')	c. 10	9,500 tonnes	110m x 14m x 10m	Nuclear, 30+ knots	60	1986
Submarine – SSK	Project 677 **KRONSTADT** ('Lada')	1	2,700 tonnes	72m x 7m x 7m	Diesel-electric, 21 knots	40	2024
Submarine – SSK	Project 636.3 (Improved 'Kilo')	10	3,200 tonnes	73m x 10m x 7m	Diesel-electric, 20 knots	55	2014
Submarine – SSK	Project 877 ('Kilo')	c. 10	3,000 tonnes	73m x 10m x 7m	Diesel-electric, 20 knots	55	1981

Notes:

1. Table only includes main types and focuses on operational units and/or ships believed to be under active modernisation or refit.
2. One additional unit is being used in an experimental role.

Admiral Golokov, the Russian Navy's third *Admiral Gorshkov* class frigate, became the most significant addition to Russia's surface fleet in recent years when she was commissioned on 25 December 2023. This picture was taken whilst she was still fitting out at Severnaya Verf in Saint Petersburg in May 2021. *(Russian Ministry of Defence – Mil.ru)*

The nuclear-powered battle cruiser *Pyotr Velikiy* remains Russia's largest surface combatant pending the delayed return of her modernised sister, *Admiral Nakhimov*, to the fleet in 2026. This photograph was taken in March 2022 whilst the ship was being shadowed in international waters by the Norwegian Coast Guard. *(KV Nordkapp/Norwegian Armed Forces)*

Surface Combatants: Deliveries of new surface warships to the Russian Navy remain painfully slow. The most significant arrival over the last year was the third Project 22350 *Admiral Gorshkov* class frigate, *Admiral Golokov*, which was commissioned on Christmas Day 2023. Seven other members of the class are either under construction by or on order from Saint Petersburg's Severnaya Verf but none of these had reached the launch stage as of mid-2024.

Numbers of Project 20380 *Steregushchiy* class light frigates have also increased by one with the delivery of *Rezkiy* from the Amur Shipbuilding Plant in Russia's Far East in September 2023. This takes total deliveries to nine units in the 16 years since the lead ship was commissioned in February 2008. Three more members of the class are being built at Severnaya Verf and the Amur Shipyard but future construction is likely to be focused on the improved Project 20385 *Gremyashchiy* variant, just one of which has been delivered to date. The second member of the class, *Provornyy*, was badly damaged in a fire at Severnaya Verf in December 2021 that destroyed her composite superstructure but the rebuilt ship was relaunched in June 2024. Four further vessels are under construction at the Amur plant and more may be ordered given dissatisfaction with the cost of the sole Project 20386 class frigate *Derzkiy*. Laid down in 2016, this prototype remains under construction.

There has been mixed progress with delivering the smaller corvette-like missile boats that the Russian Navy has increasingly ordered to make up fleet numbers. Positively, production of the twelve Project 21631 'Buyan M' missile boats is nearly complete. *Naro-Fominsk*, the eleventh ship, was commissioned in December 2023 and *Stavropol*, the final unit, launched in June 2024. However, production of the 18-strong Project 22800 'Karakurt' class remains slow and has also been disrupted by the war against Ukraine. Notably, *Askold* was severely damaged by a missile strike whilst still under construction at the Crimean Zaliv Shipbuilding Yard in November 2023. *Tsiklon*, one of the four of the class to be delivered to date, has also reportedly been destroyed as a result of a missile strike which hit her whilst berthed at Sevastopol in May 2024.

The slow progress with delivering new surface combatants means that Soviet-era warships continue to form a significant element of the fleet despite increasing difficulties maintaining these elderly ships in service. Ongoing delays to completing the refit of the Project 1144.2 nuclear-powered battlecruiser *Admiral Nakhimov* at Sevmash, which has now been pushed back to 2026, are indicative of the extent of the problem. The cost and time taken to complete the work suggest that a similar upgrade planned for sister ship *Pyotr Velikiy* is increasingly unlikely to proceed.

Minor Warships and Auxiliaries: Russian yards continue to progress a large number of projects for minor warships and auxiliaries. Whilst many have seemingly been less disrupted by the current war, the conflict is challenging the wisdom of some previous procurement priorities. A case in point is the destruction of the Project 22160 *Vasily Bykov* class patrol vessel, *Sergey Kotov.* She was sunk in an attack by 'Magura V5' sea drones on 5 March 2024, less than two years after being delivered. The class's modular configuration had previously been criticised for leaving the ships under-armed when operating in higher-threat environments; a claim seemingly proved by subsequent events.

Beyond the immediate influence of the Ukraine war, the growing importance of the Arctic continues to have a significant impact on Russian procurement. On 28 June 2024, the lead Project 23550 'universal patrol ship' – in essence an armed icebreaker – *Ivan Papanin* commenced initial sea trials from the Admiralty Shipyards. One of four ships, two of which are being built for the Russian Border Guard, she is noteworthy for being designed with a modular layout that allows the installation of 'Kalibr' and 'Uran' surface-to-surface missiles. Whilst all eyes are currently concentrated on the Black Sea, it may be that it is the Arctic to which attention will next turn.

MAJOR REGIONAL POWERS – SPAIN

Table 2.4.5 summarises the current status of the Spanish fleet. The most significant development has undoubtedly been the arrival of the lead S-80 class submarine, *Isaac Peral.* She was delivered by Navantia's Cartagena shipyard on 30 November 2023, marking a major step towards the completion of a once-troubled project.[6] Her three sister boats remain under various stages of construction at Cartagena, with the Spanish Navy hoping for additional orders to rebuild their underwater flotilla to six submarines. Meanwhile, *Isaac Peral*'s arrival has paved the way for the withdrawal of the Agosta (S-70) class submarine *Tramontana* on 16 February 2024. This leaves just *Galerna* from the original quartet in service.

The surface counterparts of the S-80 class are the five new F-110 frigates, also known as the *Bonifaz* class. A formal keel-laying ceremony for the lead ship was held at Ferrol on 9 August 2023, whilst assembly of the second member of the class, *Roger de Lauria*, commenced on 16 December 2023. Valued at some €4.8bn (c. US$5.2bn), the programme is reportedly well on track to commence deliveries from 2028 onwards, replacing the six elderly *Santa María* (FFG-7) frigates. Again, the navy hopes to secure additional F-110 orders in due course to, at least, maintain fleet numbers. Displacing around 6,100 tonnes, the new frigates are equipped with the AN/SPY-7 radar also used, inter alia, in the Canadian 'River' class and Japanese Aegis System Equipped Vessels. Aboard the Spanish ships, the radar is linked to an indigenous Navantia Sistemas SCOMBA combat management system via the new Lockheed Martin International Aegis Fire Control Loop.

A computer-generated image of the Spanish Navy's F-110 *Bonifaz* class frigate design. The ship used the Lockheed Martin AN/SPY-7 multifunction radar, which is linked to the ship's indigenous SCOMBA combat management system by the US group's International Aegis Fire Control Loop. *(Lockheed Martin)*

Table 2.4.5: SPANISH NAVY: PRINCIPAL UNITS AS AT MID 2024

TYPE	CLASS	NUMBER	TONNAGE	DIMENSIONS	PROPULSION	CREW	DATE
Principal Surface Escorts							
Frigate – FFG	**ÁLVARO DE BAZÁN** (F-100)	5	6,300 tonnes	147m x 19m x 5m	CODOG, 28 knots	200	2002
Frigate – FFG	**SANTA MARÍA** (FFG-7)	6	4,100 tonnes	138m x 14m x 5m	COGAG, 30 knots	225	1986
Submarines							
Submarine – SSK	**ISAAC PERAL** (S-80)	1	3,000 tonnes	81m x 12m x 6m	DE and AIP, 19+ knots	35	2023
Submarine – SSK	**GALERNA** (S-70/AGOSTA)	1	1,800 tonnes	68m x 7m x 6m	Diesel-electric, 21 knots	45	1983
Major Amphibious Units							
Amph Assault Ship – LHD	**JUAN CARLOS I**	1	27,100 tonnes	231m x 32m x 7m	IEP, 21 knots	245	2010
Landing Platform Dock – LPD	**GALICIA**	2	13,000 tonnes	160m x 25m x 6m	Diesel, 20 knots	185	1998

A steadily improving financial environment is also permitting progress with the renewal of second-line vessels. In December 2023, Navantia received a €157m (c. US$170m) contract for the construction of two coastal hydrographic vessels to replace existing units. Displacing around 900 tonnes and with a length of 47m, the new ships will be built at the group's yards in the Bay of Cadiz. Acquisitions of second-hand vessels have also seen the arrival of a second logistic support vessel, *El Camino Español*, to support the existing *Ysabel* in meeting the army's transport requirements, as well as a new salvage tug, *Carrnota*. A new coastal patrol boat, *Isla Pinto*, has been delivered to support surveillance operations off the North African enclave of Melilla. More significant acquisitions on the way include two additional BAM type patrol vessels and, ultimately, new corvettes under the European MMPC project.

The Type 23 frigate *Argyll* pictured in the Frigate Refit Complex at Devonport. In May 2024, it was announced that a costly post-life extension refit had been abandoned against a backdrop of personnel shortages. *(Babcock International)*

MAJOR REGIONAL POWERS – UNITED KINGDOM

The British Royal Navy remains under considerable overstretch to meet commitments across the globe. In particular, events in the Middle East have added another set of missions to a fleet that is already, inter alia, split between supporting the response to a worsening security situation in Europe whilst attempting to adjust a politically-driven shift in emphasis towards Asia and the Pacific. A long-awaited Defence Command Paper (DCP 23) – *Defence's response to a more contested and volatile world* – was published on 18 July 2023.[7] Its ostensible aim was to provide information on the capabilities the British armed forces would need to deal with the ever-changing environment. Unfortunately, DCP 2023 was long on words but short on tangible detail, only rarely allowing the occasional hard fact to penetrate a haze of vagueness and ambiguity. In any event, an increasingly likely change of British government in July 2024 will result in a wholesale reconsideration of defence strategy, most probably reprioritising the NATO mission.

In the interim, the Royal Navy has continued to experience what will hopefully be a temporary reduction in capability but which might turn out to be a further period of 'managed decline'. Foremost amongst a number of problems is a resurgent personnel crisis after a period when the balance between recruitment and retention seemed to be in better control. This has seemingly resulted in the premature retirement of a number of warships and auxiliaries, combined with the long-term laying up of others. The situation is being exacerbated by poor availability across many parts of the fleet due to the elderly nature of many ships; an inadequate track record of investment in support infrastructure; and delays in delivering new warships to the fleet. Current fleet strength is summarised in Table 2.4.6, with more detailed observations following.[8]

Aircraft Carriers and Amphibious Ships: The lead *Queen Elizabeth* class carrier has been undergoing repairs and maintenance at Rosyth since March 2024 after the identification of corrosion in one of her shaft lines. Her position as 'ready' carrier was taken by her sister *Prince of Wales*, demonstrating the wisdom of maintaining both ships in the fleet. Meanwhile, neither of the *Albion* class amphibious assault ships is operational. *Albion* entered 'reduced readiness' in July 2023 and there are seemingly insufficient sailors available to crew the newly refitted *Bulwark*. The new multi-role support ship (MRSS) programme, which will replace existing amphibious shipping, entered the initial concept development phase in May 2024. Up to six ships are eventually envisaged to replace the *Albion* and 'Bay' classes plus the veteran Royal Fleet Auxiliary (RFA) *Argus* on a numerical like-for-like basis.

Surface Combatants: The Royal Navy's flotilla of major surface combatants has fallen to a new low of fifteen ships following an announcement in May 2024 that the Type 23 frigates *Argyll* and *Westminster* were to be retired. *Argyll* was close to completing a costly post-life extension refit at Babcock's Devonport yard and seems to be another victim of the current crewing crisis. The withdrawals takes the remaining number of British Type 23s to just nine at a time when delivery of the first of the replacement Type 26 and Type 31 frigates is still some way off. As of mid-2024, *Glasgow* – the lead Type 26 – was in the course of final outfitting on the Clyde but *Venturer* – the first Type 31 – had yet to be launched. The delivery of both these classes is more fully described in Chapter 4.3. Some respite will be provided by steadily improving availability of Type 45 destroyers. *Dauntless* proved the value of the

Table 2.4.6: BRITISH ROYAL NAVY: PRINCIPAL UNITS AS AT MID 2024

TYPE	CLASS	NUMBER	TONNAGE	DIMENSIONS	PROPULSION	CREW	DATE
Aircraft Carriers							
Aircraft Carrier – CV	QUEEN ELIZABETH	2	65,000 tonnes	284m x 73m x 11m	IEP, 26 knots+	1,600	2017
Principal Surface Escorts							
Destroyer – DDG	DARING (Type 45)	6	7,500 tonnes	152m x 21m x 5m	IEP, 30 knots	190	2008
Frigate – FFG	NORFOLK (Type 23)	9	4,900 tonnes	133m x 16m x 5m	CODLAG, 30 knots	185	1990
Submarines							
Submarine – SSBN	VANGUARD	4	16,000 tonnes	150m x 13m x 12m	Nuclear, 25+ knots	135	1993
Submarine – SSN	ASTUTE	5	7,800 tonnes	93m x 11m x 10m	Nuclear, 30+ knots	100	2010
Submarine – SSN	TRAFALGAR	1	5,200 tonnes	85m x 10m x 10m	Nuclear, 30+ knots	130	1983
Major Amphibious Units							
Landing Platform Dock – LPD	ALBION	2[1]	18,500 tonnes	176m x 29m x 7m	IEP, 18 knots	325	2003
Landing Ship Dock – LSD (A)	LARGS BAY	3	16,200 tonnes	176m x 26m x 6m	Diesel-electric, 18 knots	60	2006

Notes:

1. Both currently at extended states of readiness.

power improvement project (PIP) propulsion upgrade programme during a Caribbean deployment in 2023. *Daring* and *Dragon* are also reportedly close to returning to sea having completed the enhancement.

Submarines: The operational strength of the Royal Navy's underwater flotilla is also at a low ebb. Press reports have speculated that there have been times during the past year when none of the fleet's nuclear powered attack submarines have been at sea. The situation is, however, on an improving trajectory. *Anson*, the fifth *Astute* class nuclear-powered attack submarine, was reportedly ready to enter the operational cycle as of mid-2024 following completion of trials and working-up after her delivery the previous year. *Agamemnon*, the sixth boat, was ceremonially christened on 22 April 2024 and is expected to be launched before the year's end. Large amounts are being spent in improved support and maintenance arrangements at Devonport and Faslane to increase the availability of the submarines that are already in service.

Investment in the next-generation Anglo-Australian SSN-AUKUS submarines is also stepping up. The Royal Navy members of the class are expected to enter service from the late 2030s and, as noted in the Introduction to this book, significant investment is being made in industrial infrastructure to support their construction. The expansion of these facilities is being underwritten by £4bn (c. US$5bn) of contracts signed with BAE Systems, Rolls-Royce and Babcock International on 1 October 2023 to start a five-year 'Detailed Design and Long Lead Items' (D2L2) project phase. This will encompass 'the design, prototyping and purchase of main long lead components for the first UK submarines', including early fabrication work on the first boat. The end of D2L2 will then be followed by the implementation of a new contract

The strategic submarine *Victorious* arrived at Devonport in May 2023 to commence a delayed deep maintenance period. This will extend her life into the 2030s, after which she will be replaced by one of the new *Dreadnought* class. *(Babcock International)*

phase from October 2028 that will progress final construction of the first submarines. As of mid-2024, no firm decision had been taken on the number of British SSN-AUKUS boats that will be required.

Work also continues at pace on the new *Dreadnought* class strategic submarines that need to enter service in the 2030s to maintain the British nuclear deterrent. In the interim, *Vanguard* has returned to the operational fleet after completion of her long-delayed refit and refuelling at Devonport, allowing her sister *Victorious* to enter the maintenance cycle. At the end of January 2024, a test firing of a Trident submarine ballistic missile carried out from *Vanguard* as part of post-refit trials ended unsuccessfully. This represented the second consecutive failure for a British Trident launch. Whilst the British Ministry of Defence downplayed the significance of the incident as an 'event specific' anomaly, the effect on the credibility of the United Kingdom's deterrent posture is inevitably of concern.

Minor Warships and Auxiliaries: The last year has seen a further rundown of the Royal Navy's traditional mine countermeasures force as part of the transition to an autonomous future. Notably, the withdrawal of the *Sandown* class minehunters *Pembroke* and *Penzance* leaves just *Bangor* from a once 13-strong type in front-line service to supplement the six older but larger 'Hunt' class vessels. The new RFA, *Stirling Castle*, is being used to explore how best the new uncrewed technology might be supported. Initial trials seem to suggest that acquisition of a trio of bespoke vessels similar to the Belgo-Dutch rMCM motherships is the preferred way forward.

Another auxiliary, *Proteus*, has been acquired to act as a multi-role ocean surveillance ship. Formerly the offshore support vessel *MV Topaz Tangaroa*, she entered service in October 2023 and will be tasked with guarding critical undersea infrastructure such as communications cables. A purpose-built vessel may follow in due course. Meanwhile, the crewing crisis is impacting the RFA service particularly hard. The multi-role replenishment ship *Fort Victoria* and the new replenishment tanker *Tiderace* had both joined the fast fleet tankers *Wave Knight* and *Wave Ruler* in extended readiness for lack of crews as of mid-2024.

The British Royal Fleet Auxiliary's multi-role ocean surveillance ship *Proteus* formally entered service in October 2023. She is seen here departing Portsmouth in the course of that month. *(Derek Fox)*

MID-SIZED REGIONAL FLEETS

Germany: The *Deutsche Marine* is moving forward with implementing the 'Vision 2035+' fleet structure plan that was announced in March 2023.[9] This envisages a large and more capable fleet centred on fifteen large frigates, six to nine smaller corvettes and six to nine submarines that will be bolstered by significant numbers of uncrewed vessels. A notable feature of the planned structure is the consistent use of a multiple of three for all force elements. This reflects the calculation that each deployable vessel needs the support of two additional units undergoing training or maintenance.

The navy's flagship programme is that for the new F126 *Niedersachsen* frigate class, previously known as the MKS-180. Four of these ships were ordered from Damen in June 2020. They will be constructed in sections at various German yards before being outfitted at NVL's Blohm & Voss facility in Hamburg. First steel cutting for the lead ship took place at the NVL Peene shipyard in Wolgast on 5 December 2023 and was followed by a keel-laying ceremony on 3 June 2024. Delivery is planned for mid-2028; a target which looks ambitious given recent delays with other German Navy construction. With a length of 167m and a displacement of c. 10,500 tonnes, the F126 frigates are the largest combatants to be built by Germany since the Second World War. Programme cost was originally estimated at c. €5.5bn (c. US$6bn) for the first four ships, with an additional €500m located for mission modules and other project requirements. However, inflation has subsequently added a further €320m to this total. In June 2024, €3.1bn (c. US$3.5) more was allocated to exercise an option for two more ships in line with the planned 'Vision 2035+' fleet structure. The plan ultimately envisages the frigates serving alongside a new class of six F127 air defence ships and three of the existing F124 *Baden-Württemberg* stabilisation frigates to achieve the targeted number of fifteen ships.[10]

The large frigates will be supplemented by between six and nine of the smaller K130 *Braunschweig* class corvettes. Five of these are already in service, whilst a second batch of five improved *Köln* class variants was ordered in 2017. Although *Karlsruhe*, the third of these, was christened in an almost complete state in May 2024, the whole programme has been badly delayed by problems with integrating their combat management systems. If all goes well, deliveries may commence over the next year. The 'Vision 2035+' requirement will likely be met by ordering further vessels of the improved type, with the original batch potentially transferred to friendly fleets.

The modernisation of the German Navy's submarine flotilla is currently focused on the new Type 212CD design that has been ordered in conjunction with Norway. Production started on the first of four Norwegian units in September 2023. However, work on the two German boats that have been ordered to date has yet to begin.

There has been mixed progress with the delivery of smaller warships and auxiliaries. In December 2023, a German Federal Audit Office report revealed that the cost of recapitalising Germany's mine countermeasures vessel force with eleven new 'high end' vessels capable of global deployment in contested environments had increased from €2.8bn to €6bn between 2014 and 2018. This ultimately resulted in the project's collapse and a requirement to implement life-extensions for existing, already elderly vessels. More positively, the programme for new, Type 424 signals intelligence ships has moved to the production stage after signature of a design and construction contract with NVL in July 2023. The following month saw work commence on the first of a pair of new Type 707 replenishment oilers at Neptun Werft in Rostock. The contract is also being managed by NVL but is being implemented in association with Meyer Group, owners of the Rostock yard.

Greece: Hellenic Navy modernisation efforts are currently focused on Naval Group's construction of FDI type frigates at Lorient under a contract concluded in March 2022. The French Navy has reassigned production slots for their own FDIs to Greece to meet a challenging delivery schedule. Under this arrangement, *Kimon*, the lead Greek ship and second member of the class overall, was ceremonially launched on 4 October 2023. Keel laying for *Nearchos* and *Formion*, respectively the second and third units of the three-ship programme, has also taken place. The Hellenic Navy also has an option for a fourth member of the class that has yet to be exercised.

Other elements of Hellenic Navy fleet modernisation encompass three to four smaller corvettes, for which Fincantieri and Naval Group have been shortlisted, and life-extensions for the MEKO 200HN *Hydra* class frigates. Decisions on both programmes

The new German F126 *Niedersachsen* class frigates, displacing around 10,500 tonnes, will be the navy's largest surface combatants since the end of the Second World War, Although designed by Dutch Damen, they will be built in German yards and show a marked similarity to previous Deutsche Marine designs, including the use of twin superstructure blocks to assist survivability. *(Damen)*

The lead Hellenic Navy *Kimon* class FDI type frigate pictured at the time of her technical launch at Lorient on 28 September 2023. A formal launch ceremony was subsequently held on 4 October that year. *(Naval Group)*

remain pending. The navy has also reportedly held discussions with the United States over acquisition of retired *Freedom* (LCS-1) class Littoral Combat Ships, as well as longer-term involvement in the *Constitution* (FFG-62) class frigate programme. Both these plans seem speculative given that the way forward for higher priority projects have yet to be determined. The navy's patrol forces are, however, benefitting from the transfer of former US Coast Guard 'Island' class patrol cutters. The four ships delivered under the deal are being upgraded by Salamis Shipyards before beginning their new period of service.

The Netherlands and Belgium: A long-awaited decision on the future of the Royal Netherlands Navy was announced on 15 March 2024 when it was revealed that Naval Group's diesel-electric 'Blacksword' variant of its 'Barracuda' family had been provisionally selected to replace the existing four *Walrus* class boats on a numerical like-for-like basis. Naval Group's selection followed a fiercely-fought completion in which designs from Germany's tkMS (Type 212CD E) and Saab (C718) had also been shortlisted. It is envisaged that Dutch industry will play a leading role in the project's delivery. Notably, the Netherlands' Royal IHC is participating as a strategic partner in Naval Group's bid. The first pair of the quartet of new *Orka* class submarines is to be delivered within ten years of signature of the contract. However, the lead member of the *Walrus* class has already been withdrawn from service, retiring on 12 October 2023 to provide spares for her remaining sisters.[11]

The Royal Netherlands Navy is also embarking on two other national projects. One is for four new frigates to replace the existing LCFs of the *De Zeven Provinciën* class, which are currently undergoing a life-extension programme as their replacements take shape.[12] It was originally intended to acquire the quartet of new ships under a joint programme with Germany. However, this ambition has foundered due to Germany's preference for American, as opposed to Dutch, electronics to equip what will be their F127 type. The new Dutch frigates are required from 2034, suggesting a more than usual sense of urgency will be necessary if the timetable is to be met. The other project, for six LPX amphibious transport ships, is due to commence deliveries even earlier, in 2032. However, this programme involves ships of less complexity. It was hoped that they might be delivered as an Anglo-Dutch project but, again, national requirements have seemingly proved incompatible. Interestingly, the new ships will replace both the *Rotterdam* class amphibious transport docks and *Holland* class patrol vessels. It will be interesting to see how the capabilities of the two types will be merged.

A computer-generated image of the ASWF frigate design that Damen has been contracted to build for the Royal Netherlands Navy and Belgian Naval Component. The ships will be fitted with Thales' Above Water Warfare System (AWWS) fire-control cluster and sensor suite, which – inter alia – integrates the APAR Block 2 X-band and the SM400 Block 2 S-band radars whose arrays can be seen in the image. *(Damen)*

Belgo-Dutch naval collaboration was cemented on 29 June 2023 with the signature of a contract with Damen for the delivery of two pairs of 'ASWF' anti-submarine warfare frigates for the respective navies. A series of equipment selection announcements for the c. 6,400-tonne ships has followed over the past year but actual construction is not scheduled to begin until 2025. In the interim, work continues on the other major collaborative project between the two navies involving the supply of six mine countermeasures motherships and associated drones to each fleet under the rMCM programme. Delivery of the project was entrusted to Belgium Naval & Robotics, a consortium comprising French companies Naval Group and Exail, under a €1.9bn (c. US$2.1bn) contract signed in 2019. This envisaged delivery of the first, Belgian unit – named *Oostende* – by the end of 2024; a schedule that is reportedly running around eight months late. The Dutch Navy's first ship – named *Vlissingen* – was launched on 19 October 2023 and is reportedly about six months late. The second pair is also slightly behind schedule but the remaining ships should be delivered on time to meet the programme's originally planned close-out in mid-2030. Withdrawals of remaining legacy 'Tripartite' class minehunters have already commenced as part of the transition to the new ships.

Turkey: The Turkish Navy passed another milestone on 19 January 2024 with the commissioning of the lead 'I' or *Istanbul* class frigate, the first indigenous vessel of this type. She is a stretched variant of the four original 'Ada' class corvettes that were delivered under the first phase of the 'Milgem' national ship programme between 2011 and 2019. In January 2023, a contract for three additional ships was allocated to a consortium comprising the publicly-owned defence technology company STM and TAIS; itself a partnership of the leading Turkish shipyards Anadolu, Sedef and Sefine. Keel-laying ceremonies have subsequently been held at Anadolu Shipyard (ADIK) on 15 November 2023 and Sedef on 20 May 2024 for, respectively, *İzmir* and *İzmit*, the second and third ships. In January 2024, the acquisition of a further four units was announced, bringing the total class to eight vessels. The decision probably reflected a desire to maintain production whilst the design of the long-delayed TF2000 air defence destroyer is completed. This process will be influenced by the results of the mid-life modernisation of the MEKO 200TN *Barbaros* class frigates with indigenous equipment. *Oruçreis*, the first member of the class to complete the upgrade, commenced post-refit trials in November 2023.

Underneath the waves, progress continues towards delivering the six Type 214 'Reis' class submarines. These were originally contracted with Germany's tkMS as long ago as 2009 and are being constructed at Gölcük Naval Shipyard. In June 2024, the third member of the class – *Murat Reis* – was rolled out of the construction hall to be prepared for launch from the yard's floating dock. Meanwhile, lead boat *Piri Reis*'s trials programme – which commenced in December 2022 – is taking longer than expected. However, her acceptance is reported as being imminent.

Turkey's increasingly successful naval industry is involved in a wide range of other projects to meet both national and export requirements. Other notable events in the last year included the deliveries of the large fast fleet oiler *Derya* and smaller replenishment vessel *Üsteomen Arif Ekmekçi* – second member of the class – at the same ceremony that saw *Istanbul* inducted into the fleet. The two prototype 'Hisar' class offshore patrol vessels *Akhisar* and *Koçhisar*, also 'Ada' class corvette derivatives, were launched at a joint ceremony at Istanbul Naval Shipyard on 23 September 2023. Looking to the future, the Turkish Navy has also embarked on the preliminary design phase of an indigenous aircraft carrier that has an indicative displacement of c. 60,000 tonnes and will potentially be operated in short take-off and barrier arrested recovery (STOBAR) mode. If progressed, the project will be a truly national endeavour that will probably be decades in its realisation.[13]

The third Turkish Navy Type 214 submarine, *Murat Reis*, in the course of being rolled-out of the Gölcük Naval Shipyard in June 2024 prior to launch. *(Turkish Armed Forces)*

OTHER REGIONAL FLEETS

Black Sea and Mediterranean: The continuation of the war with Russia and Turkey's closure of the Dardanelles and Bosphorus to warships under the terms of the 1936 Montreux Convention means that **Ukraine's** navy is unlikely to experience significant change until the conflict is over. It has already commissioned the former British Royal Navy *Sandown* class minehunters *Chernihiv* and *Cherkasy*, previously *Grimsby* and *Shoreham*, in a ceremony on 2 July 2023. However, they will likely remain in British waters until the straits are reopened. Additional mine countermeasures vessels have been pledged by other NATO countries and will likely be much in demand given reports of significant mining activity in the Black Sea. Another prospective addition is the pair of 'Ada' class corvettes ordered from Turkey before the war began. *Hetman Ivan Mazepa*, the first of these, commenced sea trials in May 2024. The keel of the second ship, *Hetman Ivan Vyhovskyi*, was laid on 18 August 2023.

Modernisation of **Romania's** navy has essentially stalled with the failure of the contract first agreed with Naval Group to supply four new 'Gowind' type corvettes and modernise existing ships. The agreement, reportedly valued at US$1.3bn, was cancelled in August 2023 after the French shipbuilder and local partner Santierul Naval Constanta (SNC) seemingly failed to agree terms for completing the deal. The navy's modernisation efforts now seem to be focused on participation in the European Patrol Corvette (EPC) programme. In practice, this kicks the can on a procurement decision several years down the road. Mine countermeasures capability is, however, being reinforced in similar fashion to Ukraine's by the transfer of the former Royal Navy *Sandown* class minehunters. *Sublocotenent Ion Ghiculescu*, formerly *Blyth*, was officially taken over in September 2023. She subsequently arrived in Constanta in December after receiving permission to transit the Turkish straits. She is to be followed by *Pembroke*, which will reportedly take the name *Căpitan Constantin Dumitrescu*.

Bulgaria is seemingly making better progress modernising its small force of front-line naval combatants. On 4 August 2023, the MTG Dolphin yard at Varna launched *Hrabri*, the lead ship of two corvette-like multipurpose modular patrol vessels based on NVL's OPV-90 design. The shipyard noted at the time that the building process for the vessel was on schedule, with her delivery due at the end of 2025.

Elsewhere in the Mediterranean there have been few developments of note amongst the region's smaller navies. **Croatia** does, however, continue to make progress with construction of its new *Omiš* class patrol boats. The lead vessel of this c. 250-tonne class was delivered at the end of 2018 and four further units are on order. The first of these additional vessels was reportedly close to launch as of mid-2024 and may be delivered by the year's end.

The Atlantic and Northern Europe: Moving north towards colder climates, **Ireland's** ongoing naval crewing crisis has seen the number of sailors serving in the Irish Naval Service decline from 936 in 2019 to 722 in 2024. However, significant efforts to improve pay and conditions are seemingly starting to have an effect and the situation is stabilising. At the moment, just two of the service's six offshore patrol vessels are fully operational, with another on standby. They should soon be joined by the two 'Lake' class inshore patrol vessels acquired from New Zealand. The pair are expected to enter service in the second half of 2024 after completing modifications and crew training. In April 2024, it was announced that the ships would take the names *Aoibhinn* and *Gobnait.* This resumes the past practice of naming Irish vessels after female mythological and historical personages.[14]

A full review of **Portugal's** navy is contained in the following Chapter 2.4A.

In the Baltic, **Finland** marked a major milestone in the delayed implementation of its Squadron 2020 project when a keel-laying ceremony was held at the Rauma Marine Constructions (RMC) yard on 11 April 2024 for the first of four *Pohjanmaa* class multi role corvettes. It had previously taken a long time to finalise the design of the new ship, for which first steel cutting commenced in October 2023. Construction is taking place in a covered ship hall built to support the project, a move explained by RMC as being partly driven by security considerations. Previous statements suggest that sea trials of the lead vessel should commence in 2026 and that all four ships should be delivered by the end of 2029. This is a demanding schedule given previous programme delays.

Another country marking the start of work on a major programme of surface naval combatant construction over the past year was **Poland.** On 16 August 2023 a first steel-cutting ceremony was held at the PGZ Naval Shipyard in Gdynia for *Wicher*; the first of three Arrowhead 140 type frigates being built under licence from the United Kingdom's Babcock International. The ship's keel-laying subsequently followed on 31 January 2024. It is intended that she will be launched in 2026. The Polish Navy is also benefitting from construction of a second batch of three 'Kormoran II' minehunters following the delivery of an initial trio by Remontowa Shipbuilding between 2017 and 2023. *Jaskółka*, the first ship being built under the new contract, was launched on 26 June 2024. Work on her sister, *Rybitwa*, is also underway. However, the main naval beneficiary of the rapid expansion of Poland's defence spending is likely to be the long-delayed programme for new submarines. A request for information for the so-called 'Orka' submarines released in mid-2024 brought a predictably strong response. Notably, South Korean companies have joined European competitors in pitching proposals.

A computer-generated graphic of the Polish Arrowhead 140-based *Miecnik* frigate. The design, which has evolved since this image was released in 2022, has similarities with the British Type 31 frigate but is equipped with a more comprehensive outfit of weapons and sensors in line with the Polish Navy's requirements. *(Babcock International)*

The future trajectory of **Denmark's** naval modernisation will be determined by the conclusion of a new Danish Defence Agreement 2024–2033 in mid-2023.[15] This allocated c. Danish kr.155bn (c. US$16.8bn) – a figure subsequently raised – for investments in strengthening Danish defence and security as part of a plan to spend two percent of GDP on defence no later than 2030. Implementation of the new spending plan will be subject to a series of phased 'partial agreements'. To date, these have included new naval air defence missiles and anti-submarine warfare equipment. Later stages are likely to encompass more significant spending on warship construction, probably commencing with a replacement for the four *Thetis* class light frigates. The requirement for increased spending on naval modernisation has been highlighted by the experience of the frigate *Iver Huitfeldt* during operations in the Red Sea. Notably significant equipment malfunctions that included a software issue with the combat management system and early detonation of proximity-fuze rounds in the course of an ultimately successful engagement with Houthi drones on 9 March 2024 forced the ship's early withdrawal from operations. The fallout included the relief of Denmark's then Chief of Defence, General Flemming Lentfer, for allegedly failing to keep politicians abreast of the problems.

Future naval developments in **Norway** will be governed by the 2024 Long-term Defence Plan described in this chapter's introduction. **Sweden** is also in the course of updating its defence planning. The Swedish parliamentary defence committee submitted its proposals for the 2026–30 period in April 2024. These support procurement of the four planned *Luleå* class surface combatants – previously referred to as the 'Visby Generation 2' corvettes – as a high priority. In addition to the modernisation of the five existing *Visby* class corvettes, which are being equipped with CAMM surface-to-air missiles, it is suggested that the possibility of further expanding the surface fleet with additional vessels derived from an existing design should be examined. Construction of a new class of submarines to replace the *Gotland* class will be required to maintain a flotilla of five boats once the A-26 Blekinge class is delivered. The potential acquisition of a sixth submarine is also regarded as a matter for further consideration. In the interim, the Swedish Navy continues to benefit from incremental strengthening of its capabilities under previous plans. Notably, delayed delivery of the surveillance vessel *Artemis* took place on 15 December 2023. Subsequently, in June 2024, Saab received a Swedish kr.400m (c. US$37.5m) order for ten of the latest CB-90 NG variant interceptors. These will replace older vessels that have been gifted to Ukraine.

The Swedish Navy is to receive a new batch of the latest CB-90 NG combat boat variant to replace older units gifted to Ukraine. *(Saab)*

Notes:

1. See *The Norwegian Defence Pledge: Long-term Defence Plan 2025–2036* (Oslo: Norwegian Ministry of Defence, 2024) and readily accessible by searching the web.

2. The naval aspects of Canada's defence review are described more fully in Chapter 2.1.

3. A detailed overview of the LPM is provided by Jean François Auran in 'Examining the French Military Programming Act 2024–2030' posted to the *European Security & Defence* site – euro-sd.com – on 30 January 2024.

4. The POMs are more fully described by Bruno Huriet in his chapter, 'Auguste Bénébig: First of France's New Patrouilleurs Outre-Mer' published in *Seaforth World Naval Review 2024* (Barnsley, Seaforth Publishing, 2023), pp. 104–19.

5. Articles posted by the long-established Italian naval correspondent Luca Peruzzi to the *Naval News* site navalnews.com – remain a valuable source of information on the fleet's development.

6. The class was reviewed by the editor in 'S-80 Class: Demonstrating the Benefits of Perseverance', *Seaforth World Naval Review 2024* (Barnsley, Seaforth Publishing, 2023), pp. 137–51.

7. See, *Defence's response to a more contested and volatile world CP901* (London: Ministry of Defence, 2023), which is readily available by searching the web.

8. The article, 'A year in review – The Royal Navy in 2023' posted to the *Navy Lookout* site – navylookout.com – on 31 December 2023 provides a good overview of the navy's status at that time. More broadly, the site's regularly posted articles on a wide range of current Royal Navy developments are an excellent source of in-depth analysis.

9. *Das Zielbild für die Marine ab 2035* (Rostock: Inspector of the Navy, 2023). It can be found by searching the German Armed Force's website: bundeswehr.de

10. In the meantime, the navy's existing surface warships have been tested by the deployment of the F123 *Sachsen* class frigate *Hessen* to the Red Sea as part of Operation 'Aspides'. Whilst generally successful, a technical weapons control glitch saw the 'failure' of a Standard SM-2 engagement against a misidentified MQ-9 Reaper drone.

11. Jaime Karremann's Marineschepen website – marineschepen.nl – remains a valuable source of more detailed analysis on Dutch and Belgian naval programmes.

12. For further details of the LCF modernisation, see Richard Scott, 'Keep on Keeping on: Dutch LCF Modernisation' posted to the *European Security & Defence* site on 21 May 2024.

13. For further detail on the Turkish Navy's proposed aircraft carrier see Tayfun Ozberk's 'New Details About Turkiye's Future Aircraft Carrier' posted to the *Naval News* site on 25 April 2024. More broadly, Devrim Yaylali's site (formerly the *Bosphorus Naval News* blog) – devrim yaylali.com – remains a leading English language source for Turkish Navy developments.

14. See the Irish Government's press release, 'Tánaiste and Minister for Defence, Micheál Martin TD names the two Naval Service Inshore Patrol Vessels (IPVs)' posted to gov.ie on 5 April 2024.

15. Details of the Danish Defence Agreement 2024–33 can be found on the Danish Ministry of Defence website.

2.4A FLEET REVIEW

THE PORTUGUESE NAVY

Serving the Country for over 700 Years

Author:
Jean François Auran

On 12 December 2017, the Portuguese Navy (*Marinha Portuguesa*) celebrated its 700th anniversary. Its first known naval battle took place even earlier, during the reign of King Alfonso I in 1170, when a Portuguese fleet defeated a Muslim armada off Cape Espichel. At the forefront of navigation techniques, the navy first contributed to the creation of the Portuguese Empire and, then, to its defence. It took part in the First World War alongside the Allies. Between 1961 and 1975, the navy played an active role in the colonial wars in Angola, Guinea, Mozambique and Portuguese India that ultimately saw Portugal withdraw from its imperial possessions. During this time, the *aviso* (sloop) *Afonso de Albuquerque* was lost in action against the Indian Navy at Mormugao on 18 December 1961 in the course of India's annexation of Goa. After the empire's independence, the Portuguese Navy refocused towards Europe and the vast, 1,727 million square-kilometre Portuguese Exclusive Economic Zone (EEZ), which includes the waters that surround the overseas autonomous regions of the Azores and Madeira. Today, the Portuguese Navy plays a critical role supporting both NATO and European Union operations.

A photograph of the Portuguese Navy's MEKO 200PN frigate *Corte-Real* dating to November 2017. Today's Portuguese Navy plays a critical role supporting NATO and EU missions but many of its assets are facing obsolescence; all three of the MEKO 200PN *Vasco da Gama* class are over 30 years old. *(US Navy)*

COMMAND STRUCTURE AND STRENGTH

The Chief of Staff of the Navy (CEMA) is the commander of the Portuguese Navy and the National Maritime Authority of Portugal.[1] The current CEMA is Admiral Henrique Eduardo Passaláqua de Gouveia e Melo. He is supported by the Vice Chief of Staff of the Navy (VCEMA), who also has specific responsibility for directing the Portuguese Navy's General Staff. The Navy General Staff (EMA) is essentially a multi-disciplinary body tasked with assisting the navy's overall decision-making process.

CEMA commands a variety of operational, administrative and support functions, including four directorates (*superintendências*) encompassing personnel, materiel, financial and information disciplines. Operational direction of the Portuguese Navy is exercised by the Naval Command (ComNav). This is responsible for five geographical Maritime Zone Commands (CZMs) – three in continental Portugal and one each in the Azores and Madeira – as well as the fleet's ships, marine infantry and naval divers.

The navy's flotilla of warships and other operational assets is effectively organised on an administrative and logistical support basis, being subdivided by category into a number of squadrons encompassing surface, submarine, support, and aviation elements. Portugal's famous Marine Corps (*Fuzileiros*) – often claimed to be the country's oldest permanent military force – forms a separate part of Naval Command, providing a versatile amphibious force with the combat capacity to project power from sea to land.[2] Other important functions are performed by the Naval Tactics and Analysis Centre (CITAN) and the Navy Operational Experimentation Centre (CEOM). The former plans and conducts operational unit training, evaluation, and preparation whilst the latter is focused on the development of new maritime technologies, including unmanned naval systems and other emerging and disruptive technologies.

The current strength of the Portuguese Navy is believed to be approximately 7,000 personnel, around 1,300 lower than the authorised headcount. Local media reports that – in common with many other navies – the fleet's headcount has been subject to significant attrition in recent years, inevitably putting its operational effectiveness into question.

CURRENT MISSIONS

Acting under the general direction of the Chief of Staff of the Portuguese Armed Forces, the Portuguese Navy's fundamental mission is to work in collaboration with the country's other military branches to promote and safeguard Portugal's interests, particularly at and via the sea. Most obviously, this includes the maritime defence of the country and its islands, the protection of their territorial waters, and the security of the broader EEZ. In line with overall defence strategy, the navy's permanent forces are orientated towards surveillance, patrol and inspection operations in support of this objective of ensuring the country's maritime sovereignty. In addition, the navy can deploy an immediate reaction force to provide a national response to a crisis or catastrophe, such as a requirement to conduct an evacuation of its citizens from an area of conflict. A third requirement is the ability to generate modular forces to deploy in support of Portugal's collective and international defence responsibilities, most notably within the context of its NATO, European Union and United Nations obligations.[3]

The navy also has an important secondary role in supporting coastguard functions within the framework of Portugal's National Maritime Authority

Portugal's famous Marine Corps (*Fuzileiros*) – often claimed to be the country's oldest permanent military force – provide the Portuguese Navy with a niche amphibious capability that helps both to support the national requirement of sustaining a sovereign reaction force and also to contribute to collective defence arrangements. These photographs show the *Fuzileiros* conducting exercises with US and NATO partners. *(US Navy)*

This photograph of the Portuguese Navy submarine *Tridente* was taken in May 2021 whilst she was departing Lisbon to participate in NATO Exercise Steadfast Defender 2021 in support of the country's collective defence responsibilities. *Tridente* is one of two Type 214 submarines ordered from Germany's HDW in 2004. She entered service in 2010. *(US Navy)*

The Portuguese Navy's two former Dutch *Bartolomeu Dias* class frigates are at the heart of its combat capability and both have recently received significant mid-life modernisations in the Netherlands. This striking overhead photograph of *D. Francisco de Almeida* was taken in August 2019 before her upgrade period commenced. *(US Navy)*

(AMN) system. This essentially gives the CEMA the additional responsibility of coordinating a wide range of coastguard-related activities conducted by non-naval entities within the paramilitary and civil sphere. Central to the operation of this system are the General Directorate of the Maritime Authority (DGM) and the Maritime Police. Together they provide the means of ensuring the control and safety of navigation through such services as the Directorate of Lighthouses, preserving and protecting natural resources, and preventing and combatting crime. The DGM also currently encompasses twenty-eight harbourmasters' offices. In addition to their own assets, the AMN system ensures that the DGM and Maritime Police have ready access to naval resources should the situation so require.

The Portuguese Navy's day-to-day operations are heavily influenced by the need to patrol its vast economic zone within the Portugal-Azores-Madeira triangle. Inevitably, the *Marinha* plays an important role in the fight against the narcotics trade. This was demonstrated by two significant drug seizures that took place within the space of two months in February and March 2023, during which hauls of – respectively – eight and three tonnes were seized. A sign of more recent international developments is the need to escort Russian vessels through Portuguese areas of maritime interest. For example, in November 2023, the patrol vessel *Setúbal* monitored the activities of the scientific research vessel *Akademik Ioffe*, which is owned by the Institute of Oceanography of the Russian Federation. The same month saw the frigate *Corte-Real* oversee the transit of its counterpart *Admiral Grigorovich* through mainland Portugal's EEZ.

FLEET COMPOSITION: A PROVEN OCEANIC CAPABILITY

The Portuguese fleet, although relatively compact, holds all the capabilities necessary for modern naval combat.[4] Current fleet structure is set out in Table 2.4A.1 whilst the main force components are further described below.

Submarines: Portugal is not new to submarine operations, having been using submersibles for over 100 years. The current *Tridente* class is comprised of two boats: *Tridente* (S160) and *Arpão* (S161). Both are Type 214 submarines equipped with air-independent propulsion that were ordered from the

INTERNATIONAL COOPERATION

An important part of Portugal's current defence strategy is focused on collective defence through participation in international alliances and partnerships. The Portuguese Navy is actively involved in supporting this strategy, most notably through NATO and the European Union.

The Portuguese Navy has been an active participant in NATO and other international missions. This photograph shows the frigate *Corte-Real* operating with the Danish frigate *Esbern Snare* and two Swedish *Visby* class corvettes off the Norwegian coast. *(Marius Vågenes Villanger/Norwegian Armed Forces)*

NATO: As a founding member of the alliance, Portugal has always played a committed role within NATO, first hosting the IBERLANT Command from the late 1960s. Since 2012, the Naval Striking and Support Forces NATO Command has been headquartered in Oeiras west of Lisbon. It is headed by a US Navy Vice-Admiral – who also acts as the US Navy Sixth Fleet Commander – and supported by a total of fifteen NATO members.

Portuguese warships have also participated in NATO's permanent maritime forces, as well as in 'ad hoc' deployments and exercises, for many years. For example, the frigate *Corte-Real* has been integrated within Standing NATO Maritime Group One (SNMG1) on several occasions in recent years, acting as the group's flagship during the height of the Covid-19 Pandemic. Another Portuguese warship with substantial recent NATO experience is the submarine *Arpão*, which deployed in support of NATO's Operation 'Sea Guardian' maritime security mission in the Mediterranean for periods during both 2022 and 2023 as part of Portugal's ongoing commitment to the alliance's endeavour. Subsequently, in April 2024, the submarine departed Lisbon for colder climates as part of NATO's Operation 'Brilliant Shield', becoming the country's first submarine to operate under the Arctic ice sheet in the process. The same month saw the frigate *Bartolomeu Dias* integrate within the French Navy's *Charles de Gaulle* carrier strike group as part of the *Marine Nationale*'s 'Ákila' mission. The deployment saw the French carrier group placed under NATO operational control for the first time during the Neptune Strike 24.1 exercise.

The navy's commitment to NATO is also demonstrated by its organisation of the annual NATO REPMUS (Robotic Experimentation and Prototyping using Maritime Uncrewed Systems) trials focused on the use of unmanned vehicles. The serials bring together personnel from alliance and partner navies, as well as industry and research, to explore the use of drones for the benefit of naval operations.

European Union: The European Union's steady expansion into defence-related activities has added another dimension to the Portuguese Navy's international focus. Notably, Portugal has actively participated in the EUNAVFOR 'Atalanta' anti-piracy operation since its start. In December 2023, Commodore Rogério Paulo Figueira Martins de Brito took command of the operation's 45th rotation.

The Portuguese Navy is also a participant in collective security activities with selected European partners. Alongside France, Italy and Spain it is a member of EUROMARFOR, a non-permanent naval force activated two or three times each year for training or operational deployment. Command is rotated between the participants every two years. The Portuguese Navy has also deployed warships in support of the '5+5' (Western Mediterranean Forum) initiative, which includes five EU nations and the five Arab Maghreb states.

Other Partnerships: The Portuguese Navy is also active in other defence and maritime partnerships. One of these is Operation 'Mar Aberto' (Open Sea), which aims to foster cooperation with the Community of Portuguese Language Countries (CPLP).[1] Enhancing the maritime security of Portuguese-speaking countries in the Gulf of Guinea has become a logical area of focus given the prevalence of criminal activities such as piracy in this region. The patrol ship *Zaire* was deployed for a five-year mission to São Tome and Principe from January 2018 to July 2023, with a crew comprising both Portuguese and Sao Tomean members. This mission aimed to develop local capabilities in the Gulf of Guinea. During this period, *Zaire* conducted nineteen search and rescue operations, thirty-one joint inspection actions, thirteen maritime security actions in the context of piracy, and participated in several international exercises. In May 2023, the patrol boat *Centauro* arrived to take over the mission.

1. The Community of Portuguese Language Countries (CPLP) was created on 17 July 1996, at the Lisbon Constitutive Summit. It comprises Angola, Brazil, Cape Verde, Guinea-Bissau, Equatorial Guinea, Mozambique, Portugal, São Tome and Principe, and Timor-Leste.

German company Howaldtswerke-Deutsche Werft GmbH (HDW) in 2004.[5] They have a length of 67.7m, a beam of 6.3m, a draught of 6.7m and a submerged displacement of 2,020 tonnes. Their official maximum speed is in excess of 10 knots on the surface and 20 knots submerged, with a maximum cruising range on the surface of 12,000 nautical miles. They have a total crew of thirty-three and space for up to ten additional personnel. The class is fitted with 533mm tubes equipped with Black Shark heavyweight torpedoes developed by the Italian company WASS. In 2023, *Arpão* became the first Portuguese submarine to cross the Equator as part of a deployment that took her as far as Rio de Janeiro and Capetown.

Frigates: The navy's spearhead is made up of its five frigates. The two most modern are the pair of 3,300-tonne *Bartolomeu Dias* class frigates: *Bartolomeu Dias* (F333) and *D. Francisco de Almeida* (F334). Part of the eight-strong *Karel Doorman* or 'M' class originally built for the Royal Netherlands Navy at the then Koninklijke Schelde Groep yard in Vlissingen between 1985 and 1995, they were transferred to the Portuguese Navy in 2009 and 2010. The Portuguese vessels have recently completed a major mid-life upgrade to extend their lives to 2035. The modernisation is based on – but less extensive than – that previously applied to Dutch and Belgian members of the class. Armament includes a 76mm OTO main gun of the 'Compact' type, sixteen Mk 48 vertical launchers for RIM-7 series NATO Sea Sparrow surface-to-air missiles, two quad Mk 141 launchers for RGM-84 series Harpoon surface-to-surface missiles, and two twin Mk 32 launchers for Mk 46 lightweight 324mm torpedoes.

The other three frigates – *Vasco da Gama* (F330), *Álvares Cabral* (F331) and *Corte-Real* (F332) – form the MEKO 200PN *Vasco da Gama* class and have been in service since delivery from Germany in the early 1990s. They are also in the course of modernisation to extend their lives until 2035, although the progress of the upgrades has been slow. The c. €120m (c. US$130m) programme is being undertaken in Portugal at the Alfeite Arsenal and envisages upgrading two ships to allow continued front-line operation (with a strong emphasis on the anti-submarine warfare mission). A more limited life-extension programme for the third frigate will see it optimised for the maritime security role, including the deployment of amphibious detachments. These ships will already be more than 35 years old by the time their modernisation is completed.

Patrol Vessels: The Portuguese Navy historically used elderly corvettes originally designed for colonial service for oceanic constabulary missions and two of these vessels still remain in service. These remaining ships are the 1971 vintage *António Enes* (F471) of the *João Coutinho* class and the slightly

Table 2.4A.1: PORTUGUESE NAVY: PRINCIPAL UNITS AS OF MID 2024

TYPE	CLASS	NO.	TONNAGE	DIMENSIONS	PROPULSION	COUNTRY	DATE[1]
Submarines (2)							
Submarine – SSK	Type 214 (U-209PN)/**TRIDENTE**	2	2,000 tonnes	68m x 6m x 7m	Diesel-electric & AIP, 20 knots	Germany	2010
Frigates (5)							
Frigate – FFG	**KAREL DOORMAN/BARTOLOMEU DIAS**	2	3,300 tonnes	122m x 14m x 6m	CODOG, 29 knots	Netherlands	2009
Frigate – FFG	MEKO 200PN/**VASCO DA GAMA**	3	3,200 tonnes	116m x 14m x 6m	CODOG, 32 knots	Germany	1991
Corvettes (2)							
Corvette – FF	**BAPTISTA DE ANDRADE**	1	1,400 tonnes	85m x 10m x 3m	Diesel, 23 knots	Spain	1975
Corvette – FF	**JOÃO COUTINHO**	1	1,400 tonnes	85m x 10m x 3m	Diesel, 22 knots	Spain	1971
Offshore Patrol Vessels (4)							
Patrol Vessel – OPV	**VIANA DO CASTELO** (NPO1S/NPO2S)	4	1,900 tonnes	83m x 13m x 4m	Diesel, 21 knots	Portugal	2011
Coastal Patrol Vessels (4)							
Patrol Vessel – CPV	**FLYVEFISKEN/TEJO**	3[2]	350 tonnes	54m x 9m x 3m	Diesel, 20 knots	Denmark	2016
Patrol Vessel – CPV	**CACINE**	1	300 tonnes	48m x 8m x 2m	Diesel, 20 knots	Portugal	1971
Patrol Boats (10)							
Patrol Boat – PB	**CENTAURO**	4	100 tonnes	27m x 6m x 3m	Diesel, 26 knots	Portugal	2000
Patrol Boat – PB	**ARGOS**	5	100 tonnes	27m x 6m x 3m	Diesel, 26 knots	Portugal	1991
Patrol Boat – PB	**RIO MINHO**	1	70 tonnes	22m x 6m x 1m	Diesel, 9 knots	Portugal	1991
Hydrographic Ships (4)							
Survey Ship – AGS	**STALWART/D. CARLOS I**	2	2,300 tonnes	68m x 13m x 6m	Diesel-electric, 10 knots	United States	1996
Survey Ship – AGS	**ANDRÓMEDA**	2	250 tonnes	31m x 8m x 3m	Diesel, 12 knots	Portugal	1987

Notes

1. Date refers to induction of the oldest remaining ship of the class into the Portuguese Navy.
2. There are plans to activate a fourth ship of this class and a further vessel is being held as a source of spares.
3, There are also two sailing ships and two yachts as well as various harbour craft.

INFRASTRUCTURE

Located on the south bank of the Tagus River Estuary in the former Royal Estate of Alfeite, Lisbon Naval Base (BNL) is the focal point of the Portuguese Navy's logistical support infrastructure and by far its most important naval facility. It is one of a number of naval facilities co-located within the Alfeite area, including the School of Naval Technology and the base of the *Fuzileiros* (Marines).

Alfeite Arsenal: The origins of the current naval base can be traced to commencement of construction on the Alfeite Arsenal in 1928 as part of a project to consolidate naval facilities within the Lisbon area financed by German reparations payable under the terms of the Treaty of Versailles. Since 2009, the Arsenal do Alfeite, SA has been legally separated from the rest of the base infrastructure, becoming a publicly-owned company under the supervision of the Portuguese Ministry of National Defence. It specialises in shipbuilding and the maintenance and repair of ships, weapons systems, and military and security equipment throughout their operational lives.

The Naval Academy: The current Naval School was founded in 1782 under the name of the *Academia Real dos Guardas Marinhas* (the Royal Academy of the Portuguese Marine Guards), located in Terreiro do Paço, Lisbon. In 1845, the academy changed its name to the Naval School. The school remained at Terreiro do Paço in Lisbon until 1936, when it moved to Alfeite. At the time of writing, the school has 227 students, including 32 female and 17 foreign trainees. Training takes place over four years, corresponding to the annual graduation of around 50 students.

Lisbon Naval Base – located on the south side of the Tagus Estuary – is the Portuguese Navy's main logistical support facility and the focal point for a number of adjacent naval facilities. The top photographs show the submarine *Arpão*, second member of the *Tridente* class docked at the base in January 2020; the decommissioned fleet support tanker *Bérrio* – formerly RFA *Blue Rover* – is moored further along the quay. The bottom photograph, taken on the same date, shows the two frigates of the *Bartolomeu Dias* class in the foreground and the *Vasco da Gama* class frigate *Corte-Real* (behind) moored at the base. *(Jean François Auran)*

Joao Roby is the last survivor of four *Baptista de Andrade* class corvettes built for the Portuguese Navy by Bazán (now Navantia) in Spain in the 1970s. Originally intended to help police Portugal's overseas colonies, she is now focused towards undertaking oceanic constabulary missions in the Portugal-Azores-Madeira triangle. *(Portuguese Navy)*

younger *João Roby* (F487) from the *Baptista de Andrade* class, which was delivered in March 1975. Both these corvettes will soon be replaced after considerable delay.

The future of ocean constabulary operations is represented by the *Viana do Castelo* class of offshore patrol vessels (OPVs), of which four are currently in service. The class was built in two batches and is the result of the NPO 2000 project, which launched in the early 2000s. The four ships – *Viana do Castelo*, *Figueira da Foz*, *Sines* and *Setúbal* (respectively P360 to P363) – are primarily used for operations in the North Atlantic Ocean. These OPVs have a length of 83m, a beam of 12.9m and a draft of 3.8m and displace 1,850 tonnes. Each vessel has a crew of forty-two and incorporates space for additional personnel. Of mono-hull design, they are lightly armed but have a platform for helicopter operations and are being progressively upgraded to operate a range of modular systems. Interestingly, they have a minelaying capability. Together, these give them the capacity to conduct a broader range of missions than a typical OPV; for example, *Viana do Castelo* was integrated into Standing NATO Mine Countermeasures Group 2 (SNMCMG2) in 2022.

In addition to its OPVs, the Portuguese Navy has also acquired five second-hand c. 350-tonne former Royal Danish Navy *Flyvefisken* class patrol ships under a deal first announced in 2014. Their previous modular armament has not been acquired and they will be used in the constabulary role. Three of these five ships have been returned to operational service as the *Tejo* class after spending many years laid up in Denmark, with at least one of the remainder allocated as a source of spare parts. The task of returning the vessels to operational service has seemingly not been straightforward and, in March 2023, the crew of one – *Mondego* (P592) – refused to deploy on a mission due to safety concerns. *Zaire* (P1146) – the sole remaining ship of the once-numerous *Cacine* class – completes the roster of small patrol ships. There are, however, also two classes of smaller, coastal patrol boats designed locally at the Alfeite Arsenal that are used for patrol, search and rescue, and fishery protection duties. The five boats of the *Argos* class entered service in 1991, being joined by the four modified *Centauro* class units from 2000 onwards. The two types of boat differ largely in respect of their armament and the construction materials used. All displace less than 100 tonnes and have a core crew of just eight.

The Portuguese Navy also operates four hydrographic and research vessels, four sailing ships and yachts of various displacements, as well as the usual array of patrol and yard craft. The fleet has been without a replenishment capacity since the support tanker *Bérrio* (A5210) was decommissioned in 2020.

Aviation Assets: The Portuguese Navy's Helicopter Squadron was formed in 1993 and has been located at the Montijo Air Base since its creation. It operates five Super Lynx Mk 95 helicopters; three being newly-constructed and two being former British Royal Navy HAS 3 aircraft. The squadron was declared operational in 1995 and has since participated in a number of significant international deployments. The helicopters are fitted with Bendix RDR 1500 surveillance radar and can be equipped with Mk 46 lightweight torpedoes and door-mounted machine guns. A modernisation contract signed in 2016 will extend their operational lives in to the 2030s. It is based on the use of AW159 Wildcat technology and includes a new glass cockpit with integrated display units, a tactical processor, improvements to the avionics suite, and a new electrically-powered rescue hoist. LHTEC CTS800-4N engines will replace the original power plant. Redeliveries commenced in mid-2021. The helicopters are typically embarked in the frigates. A usual detachment comprises the helicopter, two pilots, a sensor operator and a rescue swimmer along with a maintenance detachment of nine.

Fixed-wing naval aviation remains under the control of the Portuguese Air Force, which operates both P3-C Orion and C-295 Persuader maritime patrol aircraft. In common with navies worldwide, the Portuguese Navy is steadily inducting increasing numbers of unmanned aerial vehicles (UAVs) into its inventory.

THE FUTURE FLEET

After years of under-investment, the Portuguese Navy is embarking on a major recapitalisation effort that encompasses several new warship classes.

In addition to its front-line warships and patrol vessels, the Portuguese Navy operates a number of specialised auxiliaries. This is the hydrographic survey vessel *Almirante Gago Coutinho*. The ship's scientific equipment includes multi-beam sounding systems, which allow hydrographic surveys to be carried out at depths of up to 11,000m. *(Portuguese Navy)*

The current Military Programming Law (LPM) for the period through to 2034 that was approved in July 2023 allocated €5.6bn (c. US$ 6bn) to new investment across the Portuguese armed forces, including funding for OPV, multi-role support ship and refuelling tanker projects. Even more positively, a number of these programmes have already been contracted.

Prominent amongst the new naval projects is the multi-functional naval platform *D. João II*; an innovative and 'disruptive' vessel that accords well with the Portuguese Navy's strategic vision. A contract for the new ship was signed with the Dutch Damen group in November 2023 on the back of funding of €94.5m from the European Union's Recovery and Resilience Plan and a further €37.5m from the Portuguese government. Displacing some 7,000 tonnes and with an overall length of 107m, the vessel has a 94m-long flight deck that can support the operation of a wide range of UAVs, as well as Portuguese Navy Lynx and Air Force AW101 helicopters. There is a hangar for the maintenance and preparation of drones, positions for up to twelve TEU containers and additional space for vehicles and other cargo.[6] A ramp at the stern will assist the operation of unmanned surface and unmanned underwater vehicles. The latter will include the Portuguese ROV *Luso*, which is capable of diving to depths of 6,000m. Whilst core crew is limited to just forty-eight, there are additional cabins for specialist crew and austere accommodation that could be used, for example, in humanitarian operations or by Special Forces. Construction is expected to begin before the end of 2024, with delivery expected in 2026.

The following month – on 29 December 2023 – Portugal signed a €300m (c. US$330m) contract with local shipbuilder West Sea Estaleiros Navais for the procurement of six modified units of the *Viana do Castelo* OPV class. The new vessels of this third

The Portuguese Navy operates five Super Lynx Mk 95 helicopters, which are based and maintained at the Montijo Air Base, which is located south of Lisbon. *(Jean François Auran)*

In November 2023, Portugal signed a contract with the Dutch Damen group for the construction of the multifunctional support platform *D. João II*. According to the Portuguese Navy, the new 'drone carrier' will be a multi-role, innovative, and environmentally-friendly naval platform. *(Damen)*

series (NPO3S) will have similar dimensions to the existing ships but will include a range of enhancements – such as electronic support measures (ESM) system and Link 16/22 communications – to give them greater military utility, as well as to equip them to operate the new generation of unmanned and modular systems more effectively. Whilst unlikely ever to be considered credible front-line combatants, with a bit of imagination the class could be regarded as providing a useful second-line frigate force. Delivery of the new vessels is expected between 2027 and 2030. The first two are to be named *Funchal* and *Aveiro*.

The navy is also working on replacements for its smaller patrol craft, which are all regarded as being at or close to the end of their useful lives. The project for the new coastal patrol vessels is still at the early design stage and is being carried out in conjunction with Lisbon-based Vera Navis Ship Design (VNSD). The design team also includes the participation of MAURIC and Stadt Towing Tank As. Preliminary images suggest another disruptive concept that

The *Viana do Castelo* class OPV *Setúbal* was delivered in December 2018, formally entering service on 30 March 2019. A €300m order for six additional vessels of the type – which will be built to a modified design – was placed in December 2023. The new ships will be equipped with additional equipment aimed at giving them greater military utility. *(Portuguese Navy)*

incorporates a trimaran hull form with a platform and hangar to support drone operations at the stern.

The recent LPM also envisages the acquisition of a new replenishment capability to replace the withdrawn *Bérrio*. The CEMA has also outlined a need for two more submarines in the medium term.[6]

Table 2.4A.2: PORTUGUESE NAVY: FUTURE CONSTRUCTION PROGRAMMES

MULTIFUNCTIONAL NAVAL PLATFORM

Displacement:	7,000 tonnes
Dimensions:	107m x 20m x 5m
Propulsion:	Diesel-electric, 17 knots
Number/Cost:	One vessel/€132m
Scheduled Delivery:	2026

OFFSHORE PATROL VESSEL (NPO3S)

Displacement:	1,900 tonnes
Dimensions:	83m x 13m x 5m
Propulsion:	Diesel-electric, 20 knots plus
Number/Cost:	Six vessels/€300m
Scheduled Delivery:	2027 onwards

COASTAL PATROL VESSEL

[Note all details speculative]

Displacement:	375 tonnes
Dimensions:	44m x 14m x 3m
Propulsion:	Not known, c. 18 knots
Number/Cost:	Up to eight vessels/to be determined
Scheduled Delivery:	To be determined

The current Military Programming Law also envisages the acquisition of two new replenishment tankers to replace the withdrawn *Bérrio*.

CONCLUSION

Today's Portuguese Navy is at a crossroads. It plays an important international role supporting national, NATO and European objectives and has become an essential partner in improving the maritime security situation in the Gulf of Guinea. In 2023 its ships covered nearly 250,000 nautical miles, corresponding to more than eleven circumnavigations of the globe. At the same time, it has suffered from limited investment in the post-Cold War era and many of its ships are now somewhat long in the tooth. Recent events impacting other navies in the Red Sea show the potential consequences of such neglect in operational terms. Positively, the Portuguese Navy is now in the process of implementing an innovative modernisation plan that sets it on the right track for the future. This plan will need to be concluded in full if the Portuguese Navy is to maintain its current relevance to its international partners.

Notes

1. The National Maritime Authority is tasked with performing Portugal's coastguard functions. See further under the 'Current Missions' section.

2. The *Fuzileiros* have their main base at the Portuguese Navy's Alfeite facility in Lisbon, whilst their training school is close by at Vale do Zebro. Their force structure includes combat, force protection and Special Forces units, as well as supporting assets. In addition to light weapons, they are equipped with anti-tank weapons and mortars of various calibres.

3. The three primary elements of Portugal's defence strategy resulted from the now somewhat dated 'Defence 2020' reforms approved in 2013. They reflected the low likelihood of a state-based threat to Portugal's territorial integrity but the risk posed by terrorists and other non-state actors in the global environment of the time. The vulnerability of the Portugal-Azores-Madeira 'strategic triangle' to any spillover of unrest in potentially unstable African nations was likely a significant consideration.

4. Portuguese Navy warships carry the prefix NRP (*Navio da República Portuguesa*). The prefix UAM (*Unidade Auxiliar da Marinha*) is used for ships that are not classified as warships.

5. HDW is now part of thyssenkrupp Marine Systems (TKMS). The submarines are sometimes referred to as Type 209 (PN) boats as this was the basis of the original HDW proposal.

6. In an interview given to the online news site *Naval News* – navalnews.com – at the DIMDEX 2024 exhibition the CEMA outlined a vision of a fleet focused on the multi-functional naval platform, the new patrol vessel design and submarines. However, it may well be that this statement was made with respect to current and imminently planned warship procurement rather than the navy's overall structure.

3.1 SIGNIFICANT SHIPS

JOHN LEWIS (T-AO-205) CLASS OILERS

Author:
Sidney E. Dean

Modernising US Navy Fleet Support Capabilities

On 26 July 2022 the United States Navy (USN) took possession of the first vessel of the *John Lewis* (T-AO-205) class of fleet replenishment oilers. The new ships are currently replacing the ships of the *Henry J. Kaiser* (T-AO-187) class in the US Navy's Combat Logistics Force. This chapter looks at the origins of the T-AO-205 programme and describes the design and equipment of the resulting ships.

THE COMBAT LOGISTICS FORCE

The US Navy's Combat Logistics Force (CLF) operates various types of underway replenishment (UNREP) vessels, including dry cargo & ammunition ships, as well as fleet oilers. The primary function of fleet oilers is to resupply ship's fuel and aviation fuel to warships – including aircraft carriers – while at sea. Additionally they carry and transfer smaller amounts of lubricants, potable water, fresh and frozen foods, spare parts and dry goods; however, they do not carry cargoes of ammunition. Oilers maximise fleet mobility, especially during combat and crisis operations.[1] By eliminating the combat vessels' need to resupply in port, the oilers permit prolonged uninterrupted operations at sea. In addition to saving time, this keeps the warships largely independent of local ports' willingness to grant access, and prevents enemy forces from targeting ships as they enter or leave port.

Like all CLF vessels, the *John Lewis* class oilers are operated by the Military Sealift Command (MSC). Crews are composed of civilian merchant mariners (CIVMARS) employed by the MSC rather than

Left and right: The lead *John Lewis* (T-AO-205) class fleet replenishment oiler pictured departing San Diego in the course of builders' sea trials in February 2022. Twenty of these new vessels are planned to replace existing oilers and to expand the replenishment capacity of an increasingly distributed US Navy fleet. *(General Dynamics NASSCO)*

military personnel. As non-combatant vessels, their names are preceded by USNS (United States Naval Ship) rather than USS (United States Ship). Fleet oiler hull numbers are preceded by T-AO (Transport-Auxiliary Oiler). All ships of the T-AO-205 class are to be named in honour of United States citizens who made significant contributions to civil and human rights.[2]

PROJECT DEVELOPMENT

The programme to construct *John Lewis* class oilers essentially arose as a result of the need to replace the preceding *Henry J. Kaiser* class. The *Kaiser* class oilers entered service between 1986 and 1996, and are fast approaching the end of their forecast 35-year service lives. One unit was decommissioned in 2022, with another seven proposed for decommissioning by 2029.[3] At the same time, the US Navy's increasing operational tempo, encompassing extended deployments in potential or actual conflict zones, requires an expanded capability to support warships at sea. The increase in coalition and multinational fleet operations is also increasing demand for resupply at sea. The fleet oilers will support not only US Navy vessels, but also ships from allied and partner fleets.

Initial planning for a successor to the *Kaiser* class began as the Future Fleet Replenishment Ship or T-AO(X) programme. An analysis of alternatives by the Center for Naval Analyses completed in 2011 reviewed several potential T-AO(X) designs and made recommendations regarding ship capacities and the number of ships required to meet demand. The following year, in May 2012, a so-called USN 'Gateway 2' review approved production of a capability development document (CDD) and initially recommended a class of seventeen oilers that would be based on a new design but with capabilities broadly similar to the *Kaiser* class. The recommended threshold capabilities were formally accepted in October 2012 at the 'Gateway 3' review. An acquisition decision memorandum was subsequently signed by the Undersecretary of Defense for Acquisitions, Technology & Logistics on 5 April, 2013.

A Naval Sea Systems Command (NAVSEA) solicitation for trade-off industry studies led to three fixed-price contracts being awarded to General Dynamics/National Steel and Shipbuilding Company (GD/NASSCO), Huntington Ingalls Industries (HII), and VT Halter Marine in July 2013. The ten-month awards provided competing studies that explored affordable design concepts for the next-generation oiler and aided NAVSEA in devising system specifications ahead of the next solicitation.

Following submission of the trade-off industry studies, the US Department of Defense announced in July 2014 that it had waived a competitive prototyping requirement for the T-AO(X) programme; this decision was intended to speed development and fielding of the new ships while saving up to US$1.35bn in extra expenses for prototype construction and evaluation. The decision was justified by the fact that the design programme was non-developmental and low-risk, incorporating no new technology. In June 2015, the USN issued a request for proposals (RfP) for design and construction of the first six vessels to GD/NASSCO and HII, with VT Halter Marine being excluded from consideration at this stage.

NASSCO's concept was ultimately selected and a design and production contract for the first six ships of the class awarded as a block-buy contract on 30 June 2016. Under this arrangement, a firm contract with a headline value of US$640.2m was placed for the first ship and additional options agreed for ships 2–6 and various other support services that could take the total contract value to US$3.16bn. It was hoped to achieve an additional saving of US$45m per ship over the normal savings associated with series-built ships for units two to six by eschewing the standard annual contracting method. At this point the programme was officially re-designated from T-AO(X) to T-AO-205. Planned class numbers were subsequently increased to twenty vessels in line with emerging US Navy requirements.[4]

Construction of the *John Lewis* class has been allocated to the General Dynamics NASSCO shipyard at San Diego, which has a long track record of constructing other auxiliary vessels for the US Navy's Military Sealift Command. This picture shows the final hull section of the third *John Lewis* class oiler – *Earl Warren* (TA-O-207) – being lifted into place in April 2022. *(General Dynamics NASSCO)*

ACQUISITION PLANS AND COSTS

Through to Fiscal Year 2024 (FY2024) the United States Congress has authorised procurement of ten of the twenty planned oilers. This includes two additional vessels which were added to the initial contract in May 2018 and the ninth ship, T-AO-213, which was contracted in May 2023. Contract award for the tenth unit was delayed due to the late passage of the FY2024 budget, which was not approved until March 2024; however, the

Table 3.1.1: *JOHN LEWIS* (T-AO-205) FLEET REPLENISHMENT OILERS: CLASS LIST

NAME	PROGRAMME	ORDERED	LAID DOWN	LAUNCHED[2]	DELIVERED	CONTRACT PRICE[3]	CEILING[3]
John Lewis (T-AO-205)	FY2016	30 June 2016	13 May 2019	12 January 2021	26 July 2022	US$640m	US$713m
Harvey Milk (T-AO-206)	FY2018	28 March 2018[1]	3 September 2020	6 November 2021	11 July 2023	US$480m	US$535m
Earl Warren (T-AO-207)	FY2019	27 December 2018[1]	30 April 2022	28 October 2022	7 May 2024	US$466m	US$519m
Robert F. Kennedy (T-AO-208)	FY2019	27 December 2018[1]	5 December 2022	28 October 2023	[2025]	US$463m	US$516m
Lucy Stone (T-AO-209)	FY2020	12 March 2020[1]	8 August 2023	[2024]	[2026]	US$473m	US$526m
Sojourner Truth (T-AO-210)	FY2020	12 March 2020[1]	N/a	N/a	N/a	US$479m	US$534m
Thurgood Marshall (T-AO-211)	FY2022	4 August 2022	N/a	N/a	N/a	US$680m	US$729m
Ruth Bader Ginsburg (T-AO-212)	FY2022	4 August 2022	N/a	N/a	N/a	US$690m	US$740m
Harriet Tubman (T-AO-213)	FY2023	19 May 2023	N/a	N/a	N/a	US$736m	Not known

Notes

1. Options for T-AO-206 to T-AO-210 were agreed under the original 30 June 2016 block-buy contract. Ordered dates refer to the subsequent award of full funding contracts for these ships.
2. The christening dates for T-AO-205 (17 July 2021) and T-AO-207 (21 January 2023) were later than their technical launch dates.
3. The contract price relates to the originally agreed 'headline' target price for the ship and the price ceiling the maximum price payable to the contractor. Refer to the text for more detail. These figures are subject to minor variation after the contract award.
4. Procurement of the as-yet-unnamed T-AO-214 was authorised in FY2024. A further ten ships are planned.

formal procurement contract is expected by the end of FY2024 (30 September 2024).

The US Navy's FY2025 Presidential Budget Request does not call for any new T-AO-205 procurement in that year, but does project procurement of the 11th and 12th units of the class in FY2026, with four additional ships planned for authorisation through to 2029. Overall the Navy has alternated between ordering one, two or no oilers in any given year, a strategy dictated by the need to balance oiler acquisition with the overall shipbuilding plan and budget. The procurement schedule for the 2016–2024 timeframe, by year, can be visualised as 1–0–1–2–2–0–2–1–1. For the five year 2025–2029 timeframe the Navy's annual procurement plan is 0–2–1–2–1.[5]

As is often the case with naval projects, project construction costs have increased over initial estimates. The US Government Accountability Office reported in June 2023 that T-AO-205 hit its ceiling price of US$715.8m when finally delivered in 2022 and that cost overruns for the first four ships amounted to US$274m.[6] This unwelcome development is due in part to construction challenges and delays discussed further below. Cybersecurity modifications that were added to the contract in August 2022, cost growth in government-furnished equipment (GFE) for the ships, and general increases in materiel prices also contributed to these overruns. Some of these inflationary pressures are likely to continue into the future. The most recent USN estimate for six ships – the 11th to 16th units of the programme – expected to be procured in the FY2025-29 timeframe equates to a unit cost of US$859.6m. This is an increase of 54 percent over the average unit cost of US$556.9m of the four units planned for procurement in the FY2021–FY2025 period at the time of the FY2021 USN budget submission.

CONSTRUCTION AND DELIVERY

A summary of order information and key construction dates relating to the *John Lewis* class is provided in Table 3.1.1, with further detail set out in the description that follows:

First of Class: Construction of all members of the T-AO 205 class is conducted at the GD/NASSCO shipyard in San Diego, California. First steel for lead vessel, USNS *John Lewis*, was cut on 20 September 2018. The keel-laying ceremony took place on 13 May 2019, and was attended by Congressman Lewis. The ship was launched on 12 January 2021. After completion of outfitting, initial sea trials began in February 2022. T-AO 205 was formally handed over to the USN on 26 July 2022 following completion of acceptance trials with the Navy's Board of Inspection and Survey. This marked the ship's official in-service date.

When the initial production contract was awarded in 2016, the USN expected delivery of the first of class vessel in August 2020; by the time of keel laying that target had been moved to November 2020. Actual delivery in July 2022 was therefore 20 months later than the amended target date. Several factors contributed to the setback. These include a July 2018 flooding incident at the shipyard (which rendered a graving dock temporarily inoperable and required yard-wide rescheduling of ship construction); late delivery of outfitting materials including main engines; a need to repair or rework parts of the ship before it was deemed ready for delivery; and a significant labour shortage due to both structural issues and the temporary effects of the Covid-19 crisis.

John Lewis's delivery was followed by an approximate year-long post-delivery test and trials period, which commenced on 6 October 2022. Initial Operational Test and Evaluation (IOT&E) and Live Fire Test & Evaluation (LFT&E) began in FY 2023 while the ship was still completing these post-delivery trials. During the IOT&E phase, *John Lewis* was used to validate the operational capability of the entire T-AO-205 class.

The January 2024 report from DOD's Director, Operational Test and Evaluation (DOT&E), which covers events of the preceding year 2023, delivered a mixed review of progress with the IOT&E programme to date. According to the report, testing was incomplete due to unavailability of some ship types that the T-AO 205 class is designed to replenish; as a result the USN was able to demonstrate only eight of twenty-three replenishment 'events' called for in the operational test design. The

John Lewis (T-AO-205) commenced sea trials in February 2022 after a construction programme that was delayed by labour shortages and materiel supply problems, as well as a significant flooding incident at the NASSCO shipyard. Delivered in July that year, she then embarked on a lengthy period of post-delivery and operational trials that was expected to result in the declaration of initial operational capability around mid-2024. (General Dynamics NASSCO)

John Lewis's trials programme has included the performance of replenishment at sea evolutions with a wide range of US Navy warship types. Here the Littoral Combat Ship *Canberra* (LCS-30) breaks away from the replenishment oiler after completing refuelling. (US Navy)

ability to deliver fuel and cargo to the CVN-68, CG-47, DDG-51, DDG-1000 and LCS-2 classes was demonstrated successfully, as was the ability to deliver and receive fuel from another combat logistics ship. Notably absent through the end of 2023 were tests to validate the ability to resupply amphibious warships of any type. The DOT&E report also noted that the USN had yet to demonstrate simultaneous operation of five connected replenishment stations or to conduct operationally-relevant vertical replenishment of dry cargo. Other factors which were tested in FY2023 included the ability to operate in a cyber-contested environment, acoustic and underwater electromagnetic trials, as well as physical damage control and survivability (the last mentioned as part of Total Ship Survivability Trials, or TSST).[7]

According to the T-AO-205 programme office at the MSC, final contractual trials for *John Lewis* took place in August 2023. During these trials, seven tests were not completed satisfactorily and a number of identified build deficiencies had yet to be remedied. This caused DOT&E to state that the ship was not ready for fleet introduction. All the deficiencies noted were corrected during a 'post shakedown availability' period for the vessel, which began on 2 November 2023. During this five-month maintenance and rectification period – the first for T-AO-205 – the ship also received several systems improvements and post-delivery upgrades. As of May 2024, MSC expected the outstanding tests – which related to the main propulsion and communications systems – to be concluded before the end of June. At this point, DOT&E was expected to recommend declaration of the ship's initial operational capability (IOC).[8]

Follow-on Vessels: The delays affecting T-AO 205 have had a trickle-down effect, so that construction of the entire class continues to run behind schedule. The current status of subsequent vessels procured in 2016 as part of the initial tranche is:

- *Harvey Milk* (T-AO-206): Christened in November 2021, delivered 11 July 2023.
- *Earl Warren* (T-AO-207): Christened in January 2023 and delivered on 7 May 2024.
- *Robert F. Kennedy* (T-AO-208): Christened in October of 2023.
- *Lucy Stone* (T-AO-209) and *Sojourner Truth* (T-AO-210): Under construction.

The actual or anticipated delivery dates of T-AO 206 through T-AO 208 were respectively seven, four and twelve months behind the original plan as of March 2024. Looking forward, the USN's FY2024 budget documents forecast T-AO-209 through to T-AO-17 to have seven to 20-month delivery delays. In addition to the throughput effect from the lag in building the first-of-class, the setbacks are primarily due to late delivery of materials and major components, as well as ongoing labour shortages. Regarding components, the greatest single issue has centred on timely delivery of the main reduction gear (MRG). A decision to relocate production of the MRG from Europe to the United States resulted in unexpected challenges bringing manufacturing back up to speed. In the case of T-AO-208, the MRG was actually damaged during production, significantly disrupting the ship's construction. Regarding the workforce, American shipyards are currently plagued by retention problems as experienced personnel retire. Industry – including GD/NASSCO – is having difficulty recruiting an adequate number of replacements, most of whom must be put through several years of training before they become fully qualified.

DESIGN AND CAPABILITIES

The capability profile of the new T-AO-205 class oilers largely matches those of the preceding *Kaiser* class. In particular, the *John Lewis* class design relies largely on existing rather than new or developmental technologies. This decision was taken to preclude the delays and setbacks which have plagued some development programmes based on unproven technologies. In contrast to some other recent USN

Robert F. Kennedy (T-AO-208) pictured at the time of her launch on 28 October 2023. She will be the fourth of the *John Lewis* class to enter service when delivered in 2025. Five further ships are under construction or on contract and procurement of the tenth vessel has also been authorised. Ten further ships are likely to be approved, extending production into the mid-2030s. *(General Dynamics NASSCO)*

warships, the design was largely (95 percent) completed before construction of the lead ship began. Requirements for modular open systems architecture (MOSA) were incorporated into the design program to ensure the capability for future technology upgrades.

Platform Design: While the *John Lewis* class is equipped with modern machinery and electronic systems, the general design concept retains many aspects of the *Kaiser* class, which will ease transition for crew members switching between ship types. Construction of the lead vessel consumed 18,575 tonnes of steel. Each hull is constructed in a modular fashion. Approximately 200 large, prefabricated sections or 'blocks' are outfitted with equipment, piping, wiring and other essential elements and then assembled to form the hull and superstructure of the vessel. While considerable interior and exterior outfitting is still required after completion of the hull, this approach saves time and effort over older techniques which required completion of the bare hull before piping or wires could be installed.

The new ships are longer and have a greater displacement than the previous oiler class. The hull is 227.3m long overall with a 32.2m beam and a 10.2m draft; the length between perpendiculars is 216.4m. The displacement is 22,173 tonnes (light ship) and 49,850 tonnes at full load. Further design particulars are provided in Table 3.1.2.

Unlike the *Kaiser* class, twelve of which are single-hull vessels, all *John Lewis* class ships will be double hulled in accordance with construction standards for modern commercial oil tankers. The new oilers also have strengthened cargo and ballast tanks. This will significantly reduce the risk of environmental damage in an event where the outer hull is punctured. The ships conform to American Bureau of Shipping (ABS) standards, specifically the ABS Steel Vessel Rules 2015. The oilers also conform with MARPOL Annex I pollution mitigation requirements.

Congress has mandated that, at the latest beginning with the seventh ship of the class, the following components must be manufactured in the United States:

Table 3.1.2.

JOHN LEWIS (T-AO-205) PRINCIPAL PARTICULARS

Building Information:	
Laid Down:	13 May 2019[1] Launched: 12 January 2021 Delivered: 26 July 2022
Builders:	General Dynamics NASSCO, San Diego, California
Dimensions:	
Displacement:	49,850 tonnes full load displacement. Light displacement is c. 22,000 tonnes.
Overall Hull Dimensions:	227.3m x 32.2m x 10.2m. Length between perpendiculars is 216.4m.
Equipment:	
Armament:	Fitted with positions for 9 x heavy machine guns. Space and weight reserved for Phalanx CIWS or SeaRAM.
Aircraft:	Flight deck for 1 x heavy helicopter.
Countermeasures:	AN/SLQ-25A Nixie torpedo countermeasures. Fitted for systems include Anti-Torpedo Torpedo Defense System (ATTDS).
Sensors:	Raytheon Anschütz Synapsis navigation/surface surveillance radars.
Communications:	USN communications suite including satellite communications.
Cargo Capacity:	162,000 barrels of oil. 200 tonnes of potable water. Dry stores capacity of 1,576m^3 and chill/refrigerated capacity of c. 1,362m^3.[2]
RAS & Handling Equipment:	5 x fuel at sea (FAS) stations: 3 x port and 2 x starboard. 2 x replenishment at sea (RAS) stations: 1 x port and 1 x starboard. Stern refuelling position. Fuel and stores receiving capability. 2 x telescopic cranes.
Propulsion Systems:	
Machinery:	Diesel. 2 x 14.4MW Fairbanks Morse MAN 12V 48/60 CR diesels with PTO/PTI capacity driving twin shafts via reduction gearing.
Speed:	Sustained speed of 20 knots at 85% MCR. Endurance in excess of 6,000 nautical miles at 20 knots.
Other Details:	
Complement:	c. 95 core crew. Accommodation for a total of 125 personnel.
Class:	20 ships planned, of which 10 had been authorised as of mid-2024.

Notes

1. First steel cut on 20 September 2018
2. Official sources differ on chill/refrigerated stores capacity.

- Auxiliary equipment (including pumps) for shipboard services.
- Propulsion equipment (including engines, reduction gear and propellers).
- Shipboard cranes and spreaders for shipboard cranes.
- Anchor chains.

Propulsion and Power: The T-AO-205 class oilers can reach a top speed of 20 knots and have an endurance in excess of 6,000 nautical miles without refuelling; fuel consumption for this range is not to exceed 14,000 barrels. The main propulsion system consists of two 14.4 MW (19,000bhp) Fairbanks Morse MAN 12V 48/60 CR four-stroke diesel engines with a power take-off/power take-in (PTO/PTI) capability. The diesels power two controllable-pitch propellers via reduction gearing and twin shafts. The engines' common rail fuel injection system incorporates an advanced control system enabling consistent delivery of precise amounts of fuel, thereby improving engine performance and fuel efficiency while reducing engine noise. The engines' exhaust after-treatment system limits emissions, reflecting the USN's desire to enhance environmental protection standards where possible.

Power for the ship's electrical distribution system is provided by three Bergen B32:40L8A diesel generator sets, which each provide 3.84MW of power. This is supplemented by a total of 5.3MW (two x 2.65MW) from the power take-off mode referred to above.

Survivability and Self-Defence: As mentioned previously, the TA-O-205 class is constructed to ABS (American Bureau of Shipping) commercial standards. In addition, there is compliance with USN OPNAVINST 9070.1 on survivability for USN surface vessels. In effect, the class's survivability equates to the US Navy's Level 1 requirement – the lowest of three levels – in a reflection of the ships' non-combatant roles. Crew safety is, however, a particularly important emphasis. Personal Protective Equipment (PPE) is carried for a minimum of 125 personnel. This includes standard safety equipment,

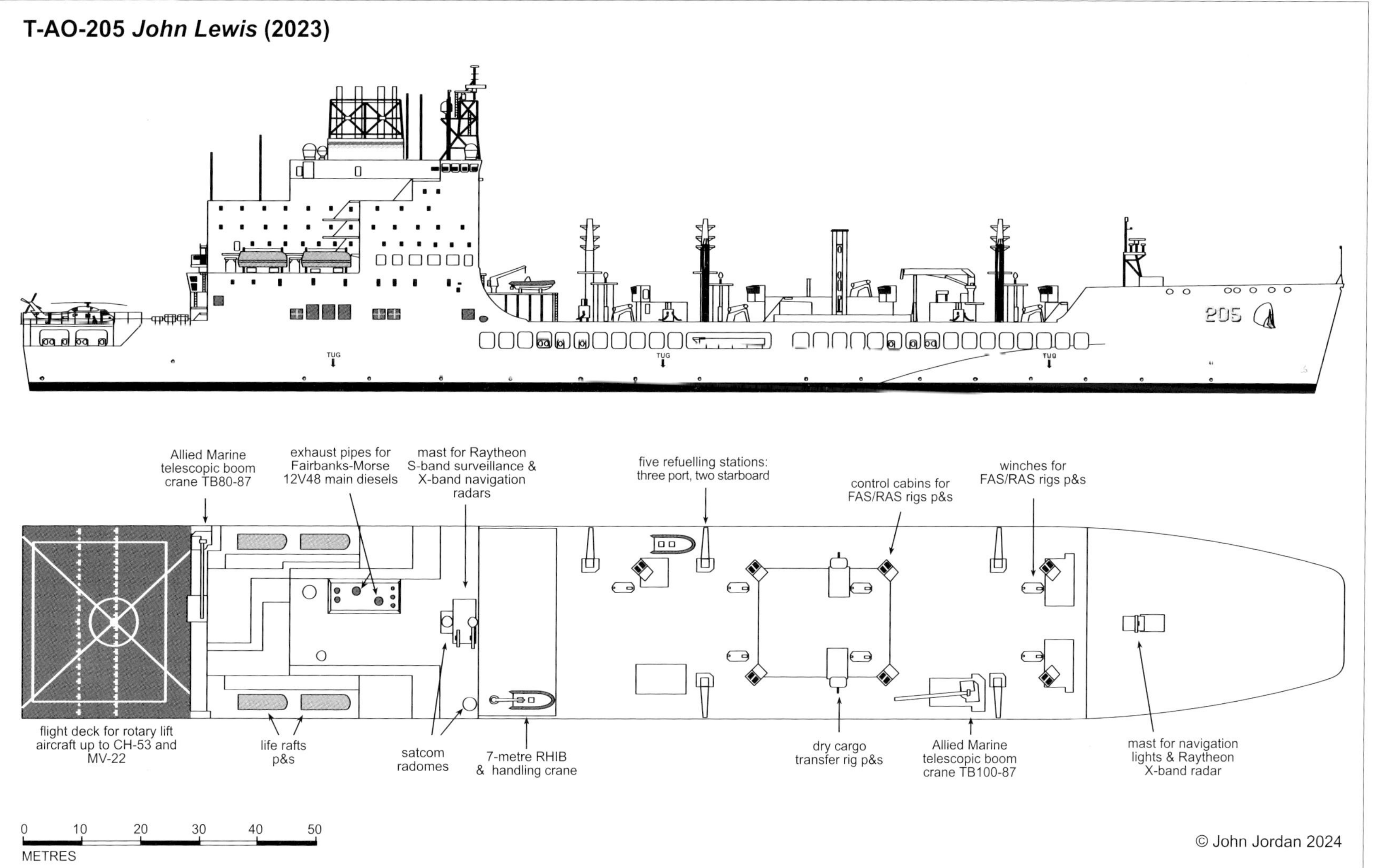

© John Jordan 2024

as well as Chemical, Biological and Radiological PPE. Fully-enclosed lifeboats as well as life rafts will be carried for the entire 125-person complement. For search and rescue operations, personnel transfers or to assist ship visits, the oilers carry two ready-to-deploy, 7m Ribcraft RHIB fast boats. They are suspended from Vestdavit PLRH-5000 davits, which incorporate motion compensation and other safety features to permit handling in high sea states. One boat is carried to starboard immediately before the superstructure, while the second is located just abaft of the port-side No. 2 FAS (fuel at sea) rig.

The standard self-defence suite for the T-AO-205 class includes the AN/SLQ-25A Nixie torpedo countermeasures system as well as the Advanced Degaussing System (Anti-Mine) for reducing the ship's magnetic signature. Additionally, the ships are designed to carry defensive weapon capabilities. However, these are not carried as standard equipment; rather, they will be mounted as operational requirements and the threat environment dictate.

The ships have space for Navy Expeditionary Combat Command Expeditionary Security Teams (ESTs) which will embark with crew-served weapons (.50in calibre machine guns) to provide limited self-defence against a small boat attack. Nine permanent mounts for the EST's crew served weapons are distributed around the ship; secure storage for the teams' weapons and ammunition is also provided. Additionally, the class has space, weight, power and cooling (SWAP-C) margins for future installation of either the Phalanx close-in weapon system (CIWS) or the SeaRAM (Rolling Airframe Missile) for defence against missile attack, as well as the Anti-Torpedo Torpedo Defense System (ATTDS).

Given the increasingly contested environment in which fleet oilers will be expected to operate, there has been ongoing discussion about enhancing the self-defence suite of the *John Lewis* class. A 2016

These photographs taken during the construction of *Earl Warren* (T-AO-207) provide a number of insights into her class's design. These include the use of a bulbous bow and the incorporation of bilge keels to improve stability. Additionally, her stern reveals a twin skeg arrangement, with two shaft-lines and twin rudders assisting manoeuvrability and reliability during potentially hazardous replenishment operations. Structurally, the class is constructed to ABS commercial standards in line with their essentially non-combatant role. However, there is provision for an extensive self-defence capability, albeit largely on a 'fitted for but not with' basis. *(General Dynamics NASSCO)*

USN report concluded that, even after the installation of a CIWS or ATTDS, the new oilers will only have a limited capability to defeat a submarine-launched torpedo attack and no capability to defeat a missile attack. The report found that operations in contested environments will require both air and surface escorts. To date no decisions have been made regarding an upgrade or enhancement of the self-defence suite. The fact that extra defensive weaponry would likely increase unit costs by several tens of millions of US$ remains an important consideration.

Sensors and Communications: The *John Lewis* class oilers are equipped with Raytheon Anschütz Synapsis radars (operating in X-band and S-band frequencies). These sensors are suitable for both maritime surveillance and navigation. Several satellite communications radomes are distributed across the top of the superstructure as part of a comprehensive communications suite.

Replenishment Capacity and Capabilities: Despite the new ships' larger dimensions, the T-AO 205 class's capacity of 162,000 barrels of aviation and diesel fuel is actually somewhat smaller than the 180,000-barrel capacity of the *Kaiser* class as first designed. Conversely, the *John Lewis* class' dry stores capacity of 1,576m³ exceeds that of the older vessels. The T-AO 205 series' freeze/chill capacity for fresh foods is 1,362m³ and their potable water capacity is 200 metric tonnes. The freeze, chill and dry goods storage holds are arranged to allow direct forklift access. This accelerates the transfer rate for unit-load cargo pallets.[9]

Like the *Kaiser* class, the *John Lewis* class oilers can service up to two vessels simultaneously. Replenishment procedures will remain unchanged from the previous ships but will become more efficient thanks to more modern technology. The T-AO-205 class is equipped with ten main cargo centrifugal pumps with a 3,000 gallons-per-minute capacity to enable the efficient transfer of liquid cargo to receiving vessels. The ships have five fuel at sea (FAS) stations (three portside, two starboard) equipped with hoses and probes, and two replenishment at sea (RAS) stations for transferring dry goods, provisions, spare parts and personnel. The portside FAS are equipped with double probes and a 2.5in span line, while the starboard FAS stations have single probes and the 2.5in span line. Unlike the *Kaiser* class, the *John Lewis* class is also equipped with one astern fuel delivery station which enables the oiler to dispense fuel to vessels from the aft section. Additionally the ships have three receiving stations on the starboard side which enable them to refill depleted cargo tanks by taking on fuels from other oilers. In the same vein, the RAS stations can receive cargo and personnel at sea from other vessels.

Two views of replenishment gear aboard *John Lewis* (T-AO-205) and *Harvey Milk* (T-AO-206). Each ship has five FAS positions – three to port and two to starboard – as well as two RAS positions for solid stores. The telescopic Allied Marine crane, one of two aboard, provides an additional means of handling heavy cargo. *(General Dynamics NASSCO)*

Automation and Electronic Control Systems: According to *John Lewis*'s first captain, Kevin Farrin, the vessel's cargo fuel pumps and piping systems have the highest delivery rate in the US Navy's fleet.

This is largely due to enhanced electronic control systems which increase the cargo delivery and transfer rate between ships, while reducing crew workload and enhancing safety.[10] While the RAS and FAS stations themselves do not represent new technology, they have been upgraded with the newly developed Electronic-Standard Tensioned Replenishment Along-side Method (E-STREAM) system. E-STREAM was developed by engineers at the Naval Surface Warfare Center's Port Hueneme Division in cooperation with D&K Engineering of San Diego, which builds the system. *John Lewis* is the first oiler to receive E-STREAM.

The system consists of two elements. The control station combines an operator console and an automated computing system to calculate optimal payloads and transfer rates, while the deck section energises and controls winches and other machinery using variable frequency drive technology. Sensors supervise the travel of the load between ships, enabling the system to automatically bring the load to a smooth stop at its destination. For solid cargo transfer, the electronic control system enables up to twice the transfer speed for lighter loads; alternatively it permits safe delivery of heavier loads than are possible without automation. The iteration of E-STREAM installed on the *John Lewis* class is also suitable for fuel and other liquid transfers. Safety features for fuel transfers include a vapour control system (VCS) to eliminate overpressure and vacuum hazards, prevent critical overheating of the piping system, and eliminate liquid condensate carrying over to the receiving vessel and potentially contaminating the fuel. The automated computing system also calculates optimal transfer rates and shutdown time to speed delivery without risking mechanical damage to the receiving vessel or overfill and spillage of fuel.

E-STREAM promises to shorten the time needed for an average UNREP operation. In addition to improving efficiency, this enhances force protection by permitting receiving ships and oilers to break away sooner from the vulnerable refuelling configuration. Transfers can also be conducted under less favourable environmental conditions, increasing flexibility and the availability of fuel and supplies.

Cargo Cranes: In addition to the RAS and FAS stations, a single Allied Marine Systems TB100-87 telescopic boom crane is located on the forward portion of the deck for loading and unloading heavy cargo. A second AMS telescopic boom crane (Model TB80-87) is located aft of the 'castle', on the port side. These cranes have a safe working load between 5,000kg and 10,000kg depending on boom extension.

VERTREP Capability: The T-AO-205 class oilers do not carry assigned aircraft, but have a landing platform capable of accommodating various USN and US Marine Corps vertical lift aircraft (H-1, H-53, H-60 and MV-22 series), as well as MSC-operated commercial logistics helicopters. This enables helicopters to take on internal or external loads for the vertical replenishment (VERTREP) of receiving warships. The aircraft can also refuel aboard the oiler. The helicopter refuelling system and auxiliary power services integral to the *John Lewis* class are new to fleet oilers and will provide greater flexibility during VERTREP operations. Operational testing to establish shipboard helicopter launch and recovery parameters and to certify the *John Lewis* class flight deck for aviation operations was successfully completed in late 2022.

Accommodation and Crew: The T-AO-205 class has a standard complement of 95 CIVMARS, but accommodation for 125 personnel. Accommodation areas are more spacious and comfortable than on the *Kaiser* class. They are mixed-gender compliant. According to GD/NASSCO, the permanent crew is expected to consist of twenty-four personnel licensed with Merchant Mariner credentials issued by the US Coast Guard; seventeen Chief Petty Officers (CPO) in positions of supervisory and technical responsibility, and circa fifty-four certified but unlicensed merchant mariners.

IN SERVICE

Since delivery in July 2022, *John Lewis* has regularly deployed at sea to conduct mission-relevant refuelling and resupply operations with a variety of vessels as part of the readiness validation process. These deployments have taken place, for the most part, in the eastern Pacific (as far west as Hawaii), reflecting the ship's homeporting at San Diego.

On 12 December 2022, *John Lewis* received a distress call while transiting between Hawaii and California. The crew changed course to begin a search operation for a recreational sailor who had been adrift without a sail or propulsion for six days, and located the damaged boat some 250 miles south-west of San Diego. Unable to lower a rescue boat due to sustained 25-knot winds, the ship's crew manoeuvred alongside the sailboat, enabling the single occupant to board the oiler via the pilot's

Accommodation standards aboard the *John Lewis* class show improvements over previous oilers and are configured for mixed-gender crewing. This photograph shows the spacious dining hall aboard *Harvey Milk* (T-AO-206). *(General Dynamics NASSCO)*

ladder. The marooned sailor received first aid in the ship's medical bay, and remained on board for the return voyage to San Diego.

Harvey Milk, the second ship of the class to enter service, has now completed her transit to her assigned homeport in Norfolk, Virginia and should begin operational deployments in 2025. The third unit, *Earl Warren*, completed sea trials in March 2024 and was delivered at San Diego on 7 May of that year. As of mid-2024 the USN had not announced a formal target date for delivery of the next ship, *Robert F. Kennedy*. If the timeline of *Harvey Milk* and *Earl Warren* can be taken as an approximate guideline, then *Kennedy* is likely to be delivered around mid-2025.

According to NASSCO President David Carver, the shipbuilder may be able to accelerate fleet replenishment oiler production in the near future. The San Diego shipyard is currently constructing the final two units of the *Lewis B. Puller* (ESB-3) class expeditionary sea bases; based on the construction schedules of the previous units, the final ESB could be delivered in early 2027, freeing up space and personnel for other work. While the firm is also pursuing new contracts for other ships, Carver suggested that a so-called saw tooth pattern – in which the shipyard alternates building one and two vessels per year – would be a viable way to speed delivery of the oilers. During a February 2024 interview with *Defense News*, Carver stated that NASSCO was 'really starting to hit its stride' with regard to the T-AO-205 class, learning lessons with the construction of each hull. Physical capacity is also being improved through expansion of the block assembly line. Completed in December 2023, this expansion will permit the shipyard to build one additional component block per week. Cumulatively over 50 weeks this extra capacity would equate to constructing an additional quarter-ship per year. In Carver's assessment, this would permit the shipyard to maintain a saw tooth construction schedule for the T-AO 205 class while simultaneously beginning work on an unrelated new class of ships.[11]

Such a saw tooth approach would match the USN's acquisition plan for the 2026–2029 time-frame, as previously described above, taking total procurement for the new fleet oilers to sixteen of the twenty planned units. Future procurement is more speculative but if, say, a decision was made to procure one fleet oiler each year after 2029, then the final unit would be acquired on FY2033. If there were no significant new construction delays or other interruptions, delivery of the 20th *John Lewis* class fleet oiler, with the hull number T-AO-224, could be expected circa 2036–2037. Full operational capability of the class would be declared at that point. The vessels are designed with a 35-year service life. The first-in-class is expected to be decommissioned around 2055, with the last vessels of the unit serving into the early 2070s.

Notes

1. According to the USN, fleet replenishment oilers on overseas deployment normally have a capacity to operate five underway replenishment stations. However, some fleet oilers assigned closer to US waters are crewed to operate with up to three underway replenishment stations to reduce costs.

2. The first-in-class ship *John Lewis* (T-AO-205) honours Congressman John Robert Lewis (1940–2020), a prominent campaigner against racial segregation who was elected to the House of Representatives in 1987. The then Secretary of the Navy, Ray Mabus, announced the name selection in January 2016, making the ship one of the few USN vessels to be named after a living person.

3. Eighteen T-AO-187 oilers were originally ordered but two were cancelled before completion. A further vessel was sold to Chile in 2019.

4. It seems that the original requirement for seventeen T-AO(X)s was based on replacing the fifteen members of the *Kaiser* class and the USN's two active *Supply* (T-AOE-206) fast combat support ships on a numerical like-for like-basis. However, evolving operational requirements driven by thinking such as the Distributed Maritime Operations (DMO) concept is expanding the need for replenishment vessel numbers. Notably, combatant vessels are likely to operate singly or in smaller dispersed groups, requiring simultaneous resupply in a variety of locations. To further support DMO, the USN is acquiring thirteen light replenishment oilers (T-AOLs) to augment the *John Lewis* class. The T-AOLs will be smaller and cheaper than the T-AO-205 class. Procurement is set to begin in 2027.

5. See Ronald O'Rourke, *Navy John Lewis (TAO-205) Class Oiler Shipbuilding Program: Background and Issues for Congress R43546* (Washington DC: Congressional Research Service, 2024). The details are contained on page 6 of the version of the report issued on 26 March 2024.

6. These figures are quoted in US Government Accountability Office Report *GAO-23-106059*, pp. 161–2 (Washington DC: GAO, 2023). The report can currently be accessed at: www.gao.gov/assets/gao-23-106059.pdf. The ceiling price is the maximum price payable by the US government under the fixed-price-incentive type contract agreed with NASSCO. This arrangement also specifies a lower, headline target contract price that the contractor is incentivised to achieve through an adjustable profit mechanism. Other useful sources of cost information are the Ronald O' Rourke report referenced in note 5 and *Selected Acquisition Report (SAR) T-AO 205 John Lewis Class Fleet Replenishment Oiler (T-AO 205 Class)* (Washington DC: US Department of Defense, 2023). Due to the use of varying accounting conventions, it can be difficult to reconcile the various figures quoted.

7. See *Director, Operational Test & Evaluation, FY2023 Annual Report* (Washington DC: Office of the Director, Operational Test & Evaluation, 2024), pp. 244–5. This can be found at: https://www.dote.osd.mil/Annual-Reports/2023-Annual-Report/

8. Information regarding defect correction and completion of final key events was provided to the author by the MSC in May 2024.

9. The T-AO-205 class's design requirement was based around a capacity of 156,000 barrels but this was slightly exceeded. *Kaiser* class vessels completed with double hulls have a reduced capacity of 159,000 barrels of fuel. Official US Navy documents differ in stated dry cargo capacity. For example, Naval Sea Systems Command state that there are 1,530m³ of dry stores capacity and as much as 1,646m³ of freeze/chill capacity.

10. Captain Farrin's comments were reported by Jennifer Hunt and Bill Mesta in a MSC press release, 'USNS John Lewis-class Fleet Replenishment Oilers: Honoring our Nation's Heroes While Ushering in the Future of Naval Logistics' dated 5 December 2022.

11. See Megan Eckstein, 'NASSCO readying for one program's end, downturn in repair workload' posted to the *Defense News* website – www.defensenews.com – on 27 February 2024.

12. The author wishes to thank Mr. Paul Hugill, Fleet Oiler (T-AO) Program Manager at the Military Sealift Command, for generously taking time to provide detailed information regarding the *John Lewis* class. Thanks also go to Ms Jennifer F. Hunt of the MSC public affairs office for her support, which ensured that this article reflects the most recent project status as of mid-2024.

P430

3.2 SIGNIFICANT SHIPS

PAOLO THAON DI REVEL CLASS PPAs

Author:
Conrad Waters

The Italian Navy's New Multi-Purpose Frigates

The Italian Navy's growing ranks of major surface combatants are currently being bolstered by deliveries of two distinct frigate classes. Ten multi-mission FREMM frigates – commissioned from May 2013 onwards under a joint programme with France – are now being supplemented by seven ships of the new *Paolo Thaon di Revel* class. Although officially classified as *pattugliatori polivalenti d'altura* (PPAs) or multi-role offshore patrol vessels, *Paolo Thaon di Revel* and her sisters are essentially multi-purpose combat ships in all but name. Fundamentally, the FREMM design was driven by a requirement to undertake 'high end' anti-submarine operations, with particular implications in areas such as silencing.[1] In comparison, the PPA is configured as a flexible vessel that is equally well suited for performing a broad range of warfighting and constabulary roles.

In common with all major Italian warships, the PPAs are being built by the shipbuilding giant Fincantieri, which has formed a temporary consortium with aerospace and defence conglomerate Leonardo (formerly Finmeccanica) to deliver the programme. The new frigates are typified by the increasingly popular modular approach to warship design. Under this, dedicated mission zones are used to house containerised equipment that is optimised for specific operations. Another important design feature is the use of a high level of automation – notably an ingenious bridge arrangement known as a 'naval cockpit' – to reduce the overall crewing requirement. The PPAs also incorporate an adaptable propulsion system that can be configured to support a wide variety of mission objectives. In combination with an innovative hull form, this allows a high maximum speed of over 32 knots to be achieved.

This chapter explores the origins and features of a cutting-edge and unusual warship class that is attracting interest far beyond Italy's shores.

Left: *Paolo Thaon di Revel*, the lead Italian Navy PPA, cuts through the waters of the Mediterranean during the course of sea trials. She was initially delivered in the PPA 'Light' configuration, which omits some equipment incorporated in the type's 'Full' design. Although officially classified as multi-role offshore patrol vessels, the PPAs are multi-purpose combat ships in all but name. *(Fincantieri)*

PROGRAMME ORIGINS

The origins of the PPA project are linked closely with the approval of the Italian *Programma Navale per la tutela della capacità marittima della Difesa* (the Naval Programme for the Protection of Maritime Defence Capability); commonly referred to as the 'Naval Law' of 2014. Promoted by Italy's then Chief of Naval Staff, Admiral Giuseppe De Giorgi, the programme was essentially targeted at combatting the block obsolescence of a major part of the Italian fleet through approval of a multi-year (2014–2034) plan of naval construction and subsequent sustainment. Authorised at a time when tensions with Russia had not reached their current intensity, a major element of the programme was the incorporation of an intrinsic dual-use capacity – facilitating deployment in support of both military and humanitarian support operations – in the new vessels. Other important considerations were achieving efficiencies in ongoing crewing and support costs, as well as enhancing the competitiveness of Italy's naval construction sector.

As ultimately implemented, the €5.4bn (c. US$5.9bn) programme has encompassed the construction of eleven naval vessels.[2] These comprise:

- One LHD type amphibious assault ship (€1.17bn).
- Seven PPAs in various configurations (€3.84bn).
- One AOR type logistic support ship (€0.37bn).
- Two multi-role fast craft for Special Forces operations (€0.04bn).

Forming the most significant component of the new construction authorised under the Naval Law, the

Construction of the PPAs was funded by the so-called Naval Law of 2014, which provided over €5bn to modernise the Italian Navy. This photograph shows the fourth PPA – and first to be completed in 'Full' configuration – *Giovanni delle Bande Nere* fitting out alongside the amphibious assault ship *Trieste* at Muggiano near La Spezia in April 2022. *Trieste* was another of the ships funded by the Naval Law. *(Lorenz Amiet)*

PPA was initially conceived as a 'one size fits all' replacement for several Italian Navy warship classes ranging from destroyers to patrol vessels in dimensions and capability. This required the new ships to be capable of an equally broad range of mission profiles under various conditions. Fincantieri summarise these as:

1. During Peacetime

- Performance of presence missions in support of national and international obligations.
- Constabulary operations to protect maritime trade and resources whilst combatting illegal activity.
- Provision of humanitarian assistance in line with the dual-use concept.
- Support for international naval collaboration with allied and friendly states.

2. During Times of Crisis

- Pre-positioning to support an immediate crisis response.
- Assistance for operations in the littoral, including by Special Forces.
- Evacuation of military and civilian personnel from crisis areas.
- Undertaking maritime interdiction and blockade.
- Protection of national and allied maritime trade and resources.

3. During Wartime

- Sea control in anti-surface warfare (ASuW) and anti-submarine warfare (ASW) scenarios.
- Surveillance and control of air space in anti-air warfare (AAW) scenarios.
- Support of amphibious operations, for example through provision of naval gunfire support.

The Naval Law envisaged the construction of as many as ten PPAs in support of these missions.

This picture of *Paolo Thaon di Revel* (foreground) operating alongside the ASW-configured Italian FREMM *Carlo Margottini* in October 2023 provides a good illustration of the different overall design characteristics of the Italian Navy's two current frigate types. The PPA is designed to perform a wide range of missions during times of peace, crisis and all-out war, being initially conceived as a 'one size fits all' replacement for several previous warship classes. A requirement for high speeds means that the class has finer lines than the somewhat slower FREMM. *(Italian Navy)*

Table 3.2.1: *PAOLO THAON DI REVEL* PPAS: CLASS LIST

NAME	PENNANT	VARIANT[1]	STEEL CUT	LAID DOWN	LAUNCHED[2]	DELIVERED	SHIPYARD
Paolo Thaon di Revel	P430	'Light'	13 February 2017	9 May 2017	15 June 2019	18 March 2022	Muggiano
Francesco Morosini	P431	'Light'	3 October 2017	16 February 2018	22 May 2020	22 October 2022	Riva Trigoso/Muggiano
Raimondo Montecuccoli	P432	'Light Plus'	31 May 2018	8 November 2018	13 March 2021	27 September 2023	Riva Trigoso/Muggiano
Giovanni delle Bande Nere	P434	'Full'	14 March 2019	28 August 2019	12 February 2022	[2024]	Riva Trigoso/Muggiano
Marcantonio Colonna	P433	'Light Plus'	25 June 2020	3 September 2020	26 November 2022	–[3]	Riva Trigoso/Muggiano
Ruggiero di Lauria	P435	'Light Plus'	7 April 2021	20 October 2021	6 October 2023	–[3]	Muggiano
Domenico Millelire	P436	'Full'	8 March 2022	17 May 2022	[2024]	[2026]	Riva Trigoso/Muggiano

Notes
1. As first built.
2. This date normally refers to the date of the naming ceremony but occasionally to the technical launch.
3. Sold to Indonesia under a contract announced in March 2024. Replacement vessels planned.

However, the available funding limited firm orders to just six vessels when a contract was placed through the European joint armament programme management agency OCCAR with the Fincantieri/Finmeccanica consortium on 5 May 2015. The agreement also encompassed options for the additional four PPAs, one of which was exercised in November that year. The other three options have not been taken up, with the Italian Navy prioritising other construction programmes.

DESIGN AND CONSTRUCTION

The feasibility studies for the PPA project were conducted by a joint team encompassing members drawn from both the Italian Navy and industry. During this phase, which was concluded in 2014, high-level requirements and associated technical solutions were defined so as to allow Fincantieri to produce a conceptual design that could be used as the basis for subsequent contract negotiations. An important driver of the PPA design was the Italian Navy requirement for a maximum speed of 32 knots. This had significant implications both for the ship's hull form – which has a higher length to breadth ratio than the preceding FREMM – and its innovative propulsion system.[3] It was also important to exercise close control of overall weight, as reflected in a decision to utilise light alloys for the ship's superstructure.

Contract award in 2015 was followed by the production of, first, functional and, then, detailed designs by Fincantieri. This process was accompanied by two major design reviews; a preliminary review (system design review) concluded in mid-2016 and a final review (critical design review) held the following year. Physical construction work commenced on 13 February 2017 when a first steel-cutting ceremony for the lead ship was held at Fincantieri's shipyard at Muggiano near La Spezia. This was followed by formal keel laying on 9 May that year and a launching ceremony on 15 June 2019. 'Godmother' at the event was Irene Imperiali, granddaughter of the ship's namesake, Admiral Paolo Thaon di Revel.[4] Sea trials subsequently commenced on 12 November 2019 but the advent of the Covid-19 pandemic forced the originally planned delivery date of May 2021 to be postponed. *Paolo Thaon di Revel* was ultimately handed over to the Italian Navy at Muggiano on 18 March 2022; a day after completion of the final official acceptance review by representatives from OCCAR, the Italian authorities and industry. Details of this and subsequent deliveries are set out in Table 3.2.1.

Production of all seven PPAs has taken place at Fincantieri's shipyards at Muggiano and Riva Trigoso in Liguria, northern Italy. The group's Naval Vessels Division runs these facilities as an integrated unit in view of their complementary capabilities. The c. 173,000m² Riva Trigoso site is optimised for fabrication and assembly. It is equipped with a 174m x 60m slipway that can support the simultaneous assembly of up to three frigate-sized vessels and has recently received c. €20m (c. US$22) of investment in improved fabrication facilities.[5] On reaching an advanced stage of completion, ships are rolled onto the barge *Atlante I* for transportation to Muggiano, where they are 'launched' in the shipyard's floating dock. As well as building submarines and smaller vessels, the c. 150,000m² Muggiano yard is the focal point for final outfitting and setting-to-work activi-

PPAs are built at Fincantieri's integrated naval shipyards at Riva Trigoso and Muggiano in Liguria. Most of, but not all, the class were assembled at Riva Trigoso before being transferred by barge to Muggiano for final outfitting and setting-to-work. This photograph shows the seventh and final PPA – *Domenico Millelire* – in the later stages of construction at Riva Trigoso on 15 May 2024. Weather conditions on the day confirm that the Mediterranean is not always sunny! *(Conrad Waters)*

The third PPA, the 'Light Plus' configured *Raimondo Montecuccoli,* pictured fitting out at Muggiano in early 2022. The Qatari Emiri Navy corvette *Sumaysimah* can be seen immediately ahead. Muggiano's c. 1,200m of quayside and access to a floating dock make the facility well suited for final outfitting and commissioning activities, although it is also able to construct and assemble warships. *(Lorenz Amiet)*

This photograph of the sixth PPA, *Ruggiero di Lauria*, was taken shortly before her launch at Muggiano in October 2022. It provides a clear view of the PPA's unusual bow, which is optimised for hydrodynamic efficiency at high speeds. Whilst most of the PPAs were launched from Riva Trigoso, both *Ruggiero di Lauria* and the class's lead ship, *Paolo Thaon di Revel*, were constructed in their entirety at Muggiano in order to balance out workloads between the two sites. *(Fincantieri)*

ties. It benefits from c. 1,200m of quayside and access to the floating dock as required. Close to the naval base at La Spezia, the yard also hosts offices and staff supporting Italian Navy pre-commissioning activities, facilitating crew familiarisation and training. Taken together, the integrated yards employ over 5,000 workers when sub-contractors are taken into account.

Fincantieri notes that division of work between the yards provides additional advantages, such as ready access to the network of specialised sub-contractors that exist in the two localities. For example, Muggiano is situated within the so-called 'Nautical Mile' that is home to a number of renowned maritime companies, helping to sustain a highly-skilled ecosystem of outfitting companies and workers. It is also possible to use the two shipyards to balance out fluctuations in activity. Notably, Muggiano's fabrication and assembly capacity was used to construct PPA 1 (*Paolo Thaon di Revel*) and PPA 6 (*Ruggiero di Lauria*) in their entirety due to heavy workload at the Riva Trigoso site.[6]

Funding considerations meant that the seven PPAs were ordered in three different configurations, each encompassing steadily increasing combat capacity. Under this 'fitted for but not with' approach, all members of the class share a common platform design and combat system architecture but those in less-capable configurations lack certain items of equipment. The three configurations are known as:

- **'Light'**: The basic variant, based around an all-gun armament and fitted with the X (NATO I/J)-band arrays from the dual-band 'Kronos' radar. This variant also lacks certain countermeasures. PPA 1 and PPA 2 were completed to this configuration.
- **'Light Plus'**: An enhanced configuration encompassing Sylver vertical launch system (VLS) cells for Aster surface-to-air missiles. In this iteration, C (NATO G/H)-band arrays are installed instead

Two pictures of *Paolo Thaon di Revel* taken during sea trials. Funding constraints meant that the PPAs have initially been built in three 'Light', 'Light Plus' and 'Full' variants incorporating progressively higher equipment configurations. *Paolo Thaon di Revel* and the second ship, *Francesco Morosini*, were both completed as 'Light' variants lacking, inter alia, a missile armament and a number of sensors. *(Fincantieri)*

of the X-band arrays of the 'Light' variants and a radar electronic countermeasures (RECM) jammer capability provided. PPA 3, PPA 5 and PPA 6 were ordered as 'Light Plus' configured ships.

- **'Full':** The fully-equipped variant, including both C and X-band radar arrays, decoy launchers and active towed array sonar. There are also enhancements to the infrared tracking system. PPA 4 and PPA 7 are the two PPAs initially built in 'Full' configuration.

All PPAs can also be equipped with additional equipment, such as ASW torpedo tubes and the latest iteration of the 'Teseo' surface-to-surface missile system.[7]

The common design of all three PPA iterations means that reconfiguration to a higher specification is an easy task, essentially involving installation of the missing equipment. Current Italian Navy plans envisage the upgrade of the first two PPAs to 'Full' configuration, a task that is likely to be undertaken in conjunction with the vessels' scheduled six month maintenance periods. Ultimately, it seems probable that all the Italian Navy PPAs will be configured as 'Full' variants if funding permits.

DESIGN DESCRIPTION

A PPA has a full-load displacement of c. 6,350 tonnes in 'Full' configuration. The corresponding displacement for a 'Light' variant is around 120 tonnes less, the difference being accounted for by the reduced amount of equipment. All ships have an overall length of 143m (133m between perpendiculars) and a maximum beam of 16.5m. The draught of a 'Full' variant at full load is in the order of 5m, increasing to a maximum of 7.9m at the propellers. Further details of *Paolo Thaon di Revel* as completed in 'Light' configuration are provided in Table 3.2.2 whilst Table 3.2.3 sets out the comparable informa-

Table 3.2.2.

PAOLO THAON DI REVEL (PPA 'LIGHT') PRINCIPAL PARTICULARS

Building Information:	
Fabrication Commenced:	13 February 2017 Launched: 15 June 2019 Delivered: 18 March 2022
Builders:	Fincantieri SpA at its shipyard at Muggiano in Liguria.
Dimensions:	
Displacement:	c. 6,200 tonnes full load displacement.
Overall Hull Dimensions:	143.0m x 16.5m x 5.0m (7.9m maximum). Length between perpendiculars is 133.0m.
Weapons Systems:	
Missiles:	Nil. Space and weight reserved for: [2 x Sylver A50 8-cell VLS modules for a total of 16 Aster 15 or Aster 30 surface-to-air missiles.] [4 x twin launchers for Teseo Mk2/E surface-to-surface missiles.]
Guns:	1 x 127mm OTO main gun. 1 x 76mm OTO Sovraponte gun. 2 x 25mm OTO remote weapons stations. Light machine guns.
Torpedoes:	Nil. [Space and weight reserved for 2 x triple 324mm anti-submarine torpedo tubes for Eurotorp MU-90 torpedoes.]
Aircraft:	2 x SH-90 or 1 x EH-101 helicopters. Provision for UAV operation.
Modular Facilities:	Two modular zones (amidships and aft) with space and handling facilities for containerised equipment.
Countermeasures:	Elettronica integrated RESM and CESM EW suite. [Space and weight reserved for 2 x RECM jammers and 2 x ODLS-20 decoy launchers. Provision for torpedo-defence system.]
Principal Sensors:	Kronos Starfire AESA radar with 4 x fixed arrays. [Provision to expand to Kronos Dual Band with 4 x additional Kronos Quad arrays.] 2 x navigation radars. 1 x NA30 S Mk2 fire-control system. IRST system. [Provision for towed-array sonar.]
Combat System:	SADOC 4 (Athena Mk 2) combat management system. Integrated communications system includes Links 16 and 22.
Propulsion Systems:	
Machinery:	CODAGOL. 1 x GE LM2500+G4 gas turbine rated at 32MW and 2 x MTU 20V 8000 M91L diesels rated at 10MW each. 2 x GE electric motors rated at 1.35MW each powered by 4 x MAN 12V175D diesel generators rated at 1.6MW each via the ship's electrical distribution system. 2 x shafts. 1 x tunnel thruster rated at 0.6MW.
Speed and Range:	Designed maximum speed 32 knots in CODAG mode. Range is 5,000 nautical miles at 15 knots.
Other Details:	
Complement:	Accommodation provided for c. 180 personnel. Core crew is c. 135.
Class:	Seven PPAs including two – *Paolo Thaon di Revel* (P430) and *Francesco Morosini* (P431) – initially completed in 'Light' configuration.

tion for *Giovanni delle Bande Nere,* the lead 'Full' variant ship.

Structure and General Arrangement: The PPAs are built with a steel hull and an aluminium alloy superstructure. As mentioned previously, the decision to utilise an alloy superstructure was driven by weight considerations, helping to achieve the class's high design speed whilst also assisting stability. Interestingly, a key reference for the PPAs' hull form was the commercial high-speed ferry *Gotlandia II* (now *Golden Princess*), which was completed at Riva Trigoso and Muggiano during 2005–2006. This ferry was built with an innovative twin-shaped wave piercing bow that extends the length of the ship at the waterline and is optimised for hydrodynamic efficiency at high speeds. This form was adopted in the PPAs as another step towards meeting the required 32-knot speed. Other noteworthy features of the hull design include the use of twin stabilisers (located in the forward propulsion room) and bilge keels as a contribution towards roll-reduction, particularly at low speeds. The ability to sustain operations in adverse weather conditions was another important design requirement. The ships are equipped with twin rudders.

A PPA's main deck (No. 1 deck) runs from the upwardly-sloping forecastle to the helicopter deck at the aft of the ship. The deck below (No. 2 deck) is the damage control ('safety') deck. It encompasses two passageways to port and starboard that run for the most of the ship's length at this level and which therefore form the main 'below decks' access routes. Moving downwards, there are two further (No. 3 and No. 4 deck) levels before reaching the hold. The hull is sub-divided into fourteen watertight sections by thirteen transverse bulkheads that extend from the keel to the No. 2 damage control deck (and as far as No. 1 deck forward and aft). In general terms,

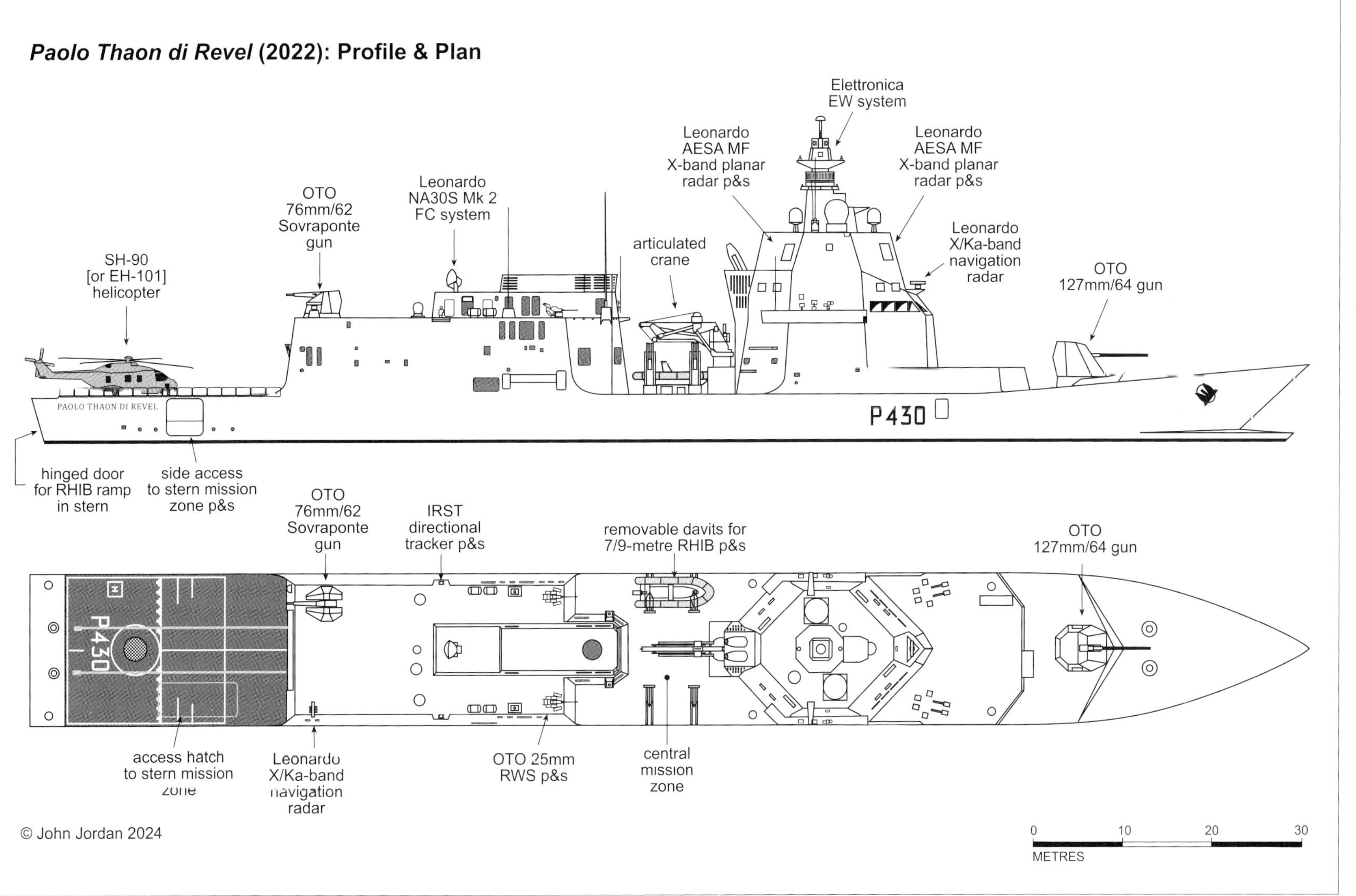

© John Jordan 2024

A fin stabiliser awaiting installation in the final PPA, *Domenico Millelire*. The PPA design incorporates a relatively slender hull form to assist in achieving a high maximum speed and the incorporation of bilge keels and twin fin stabilisers assists ship stability. *(Conrad Waters)*

This view of *Francesco Morosini* provides a good indication of the PPA design's overall layout. The design has two superstructure blocks divided by a central modular mission zone for containerised equipment. These two blocks essentially demarcate the split of the two main damage controls zones that are incorporated to assist survivability. There is also a second mission zone located under the large flight deck at the aft of the ship. *(Italian Navy)*

these bulkheads are not pierced below the damage control deck, with compartments only accessible vertically below this level.[8] In line with relevant Italian Navy standards, a PPA can remain afloat with three adjacent sections flooded across its entire displacement range.

Above the main deck, a PPA's decks are numbered from 01 deck upwards. There are two main superstructure blocks; that forward having five deck levels and the one aft three. The bridge and combat information centre are located on 03 deck of the forward block. There is a main vertical access staircase – reminiscent of a similar arrangement in the Italian FREMMS – that runs upwards from the damage control deck level to 03 deck aft of the command spaces.

Survivability: A PPA has two main damage control zones effectively demarcated by the forward and aft superstructure blocks. Each is equipped with one of the two main switchboards, ensuring a degree of redundancy within the electrical distribution network, which is based on the ring main principle. The platform control room (machinery control room) located on the damage control deck (No. 2 deck) would be a focal point for damage control operations in any emergency and is supplemented by a secondary control room in line with the redundancy principle.

There is a single citadel to protect the ship's crew when operating in a nuclear, biological and chemical (NBC) contaminated environment. This encompasses the main command and control centres – including the bridge and platform control room – as well as the main accommodation and living spaces.

A PPA adopts a somewhat different approach to passive survivability than the FREMMs. The superstructure's alloy construction has essentially prevented the use of traditional steel armour. Instead, there is extensive use of fire-resistant (class A60) materials and limited areas – such as the bridge and some magazine spaces – are equipped with Kevlar-type protection to provide security against light weapons and splinters. Similarly, the operator positions in the bridge cockpit (see further below) and some other key areas of the ship benefit from enhanced shock resistance to safeguard their continued operation in a warfighting environment.

Propulsion and Power Generation System: A PPA's propulsion system is located in four compartments that extend upwards to below the level of the damage control deck in the centre part of the ship. The arrangement is designed to allow propulsion to be maintained after the flooding of two adjacent compartments and power generation to continue even if three adjacent machinery spaces are under water.

Optimised for flexibility and efficiency, a PPA's CODAGOL propulsion train incorporates a relatively traditional combined diesel and gas (CODAG) arrangement that can be supplemented by the use of electric propulsion motors for low speed operation. The various prime movers are connected to twin shaft-lines using featherable controllable, five-bladed pitch propellers and can be used in a wide range of configurations depending on specific operational conditions. The main propulsion plant comprises two Rolls-Royce MTU 20V 8000 M91L diesels each rated at 10MW and a single GE LM2500+G4 gas turbine, which produces 32MW of power. Each power unit can be used individually or in combination via cross-connected reduction gearing. For example, a PPA can cruise at 18 knots on a single diesel engine but requires both main diesels and the gas turbine to be connected to achieve the class's 32-knot maximum design speed. Endurance is 5,000 nautical miles at 15 knots.

Design of the electric propulsion system was contracted to GE Power Conversion (now part of GE Vernova). It encompasses electrical MV3000 drives and motors that are linked to the class's electrical distribution system. This is, in turn, supplied by the four 1.6MW MAN 12V175D diesel generators.[9] The two motors are connected to their respective shaft-lines by auxiliary reduction gears. Each motor has an output of 1.35MW and, in combination, can propel the ship to a maximum speed of 10 knots. The motors are reversible (hybrid) machines that can also be used to generate electrical power when the main propulsion system is being used. This enhances the flexibility and redundancy inherent in the power generation system and extends the life and maintenance cycles of the primary diesel generators. PPAs are also equipped with a tunnel thruster forward to assist manoeuvrability in confined conditions.

Italian Navy personnel working on the forecastle of an unidentified PPA. Although the PPA design adopts a generally stealthy appearance, the presence of capstans and bollards on the open deck suggests that maximising radar stealth was not a key design objective. *(Italian Navy)*

Raimondo Montecuccoli pictured at high speed in late 2023 during the Mare Aperto 2023-2 exercises. The PPAs utilise a flexible CODAGOL propulsion arrangement that can propel the class up to speeds of 32 knots. *(Italian Navy)*

The propulsion plant and 690 V/60 Hz AC electrical distribution network are controlled by an integrated platform management system (IPMS) in what is now a ubiquitous arrangement in modern warship design. Allowing platform data to be accessed and managed remotely from relevant consoles, it utilises a fully redundant data network. Centralised monitoring and control is normally conducted from the main platform control room. This is typically manned by a crew of three – assigned, respectively, to propulsion, electrical distribution, and auxiliaries/ship safety – whose work is assisted by large bulkhead-mounted displays and multi-screen consoles. There is also a position for a platform control room supervisor. It is worth noting that the IPMS benefits from a considerable degree of automation. For example, it can automatically determine which elements of the propulsion system to bring online to, say, optimise fuel consumption or minimise exhaust gas emissions.

Command and Control: A cutting-edge feature of the PPA design is its so-called 'naval cockpit' that has been introduced with the class. This provides a position from which two operators – a 'pilot' and 'co-pilot' – can access an integrated console linked to a PPA's separate platform management and combat management system (CMS) networks in order to perform a wide-range of navigation, platform control and weapon command functions. Benefitting from a considerable level of automation, the cockpit minimises the level of crewing required to conduct normal navigation functions whilst facilitating a rapid response to unexpected threats.

The cockpit is located in the foremost part of the bridge to provide operators with an optimal field of view for both navigation and combat duties. Its overall layout is not dissimilar to that found in the cockpit of a large modern aircraft. The two pilots seated in the cockpit are essentially assigned officer of the watch (OOW) and principal warfare officer (PWO) roles, with the former being responsible for

Table 3.2.3.

GIOVANNI DELLE BANDE NERE (PPA 'FULL') PRINCIPAL PARTICULARS

Building Information:	
Fabrication Commenced:	14 March 2019 Launched: 12 February 2022 Delivered: Scheduled for 2024
Builders:	Fincantieri SpA at its shipyards at Riva Trigoso and Muggiano in Liguria.
Dimensions:	
Displacement:	c. 6,350 tonnes full load displacement.
Overall Hull Dimensions:	143.0m x 16.5m x 5.0m (7.9m maximum). Length between perpendiculars is 133.0m.
Weapons Systems:	
Missiles:	2 x Sylver A50 8-cell VLS modules for a total of 16 Aster 15 or Aster 30 surface-to-air missiles. [Space and weight reserved for 4 x twin launchers for Teseo Mk2/E surface-to-surface missiles.]
Guns:	1 x 127mm OTO main gun. 1 x 76mm OTO Sovraponte gun. 2 x 25mm OTO remote weapons stations. Light machine guns.
Torpedoes:	Nil. [Space and weight reserved for 2 x triple 324mm anti-submarine torpedo tubes for Eurotorp MU-90 torpedoes.]
Aircraft:	2 x SH-90 or 1 x EH-101 helicopters. Provision for UAV operation.
Modular Facilities:	Two modular zones (amidships and aft) with space and handling facilities for containerised equipment.
Countermeasures:	Elettronica integrated RESM and CESM EW suite. 2 x RECM jammers and 2 x ODLS-20 decoyer launchers. Provision for torpedo defence system.
Principal Sensors:	Kronos Dual Band AESA radar with 4 x fixed arrays in C-band and 4 x fixed arrays in X-band. 2 x navigation radars. 1 x NA30 S Mk2 fire-control system. DSS IRST system. Leonardo lightweight towed array sonar.
Combat System:	SADOC 4 (Athena Mk 2) combat management system. Integrated communications system includes Links 16 and 22.
Propulsion Systems:	
Machinery:	CODAGOL. 1 x GE LM2500+G4 gas turbine rated at 32MW and 2 x MTU 20V 8000 M91L diesels rated at 10MW each. 2 x GE electric motors rated at 1.35MW each powered by 4 x Isotta Fraschini 6V170C2Me diesel generators rated at 1.6MW each via the ship's electrical distribution system. 2 x shafts. 1 x tunnel thruster rated at 0.6MW.
Speed and Range:	Designed maximum speed 32 knots in CODAG mode. Range is 5,000 nautical miles at 15 knots.
Other Details:	
Complement:	Accommodation provided for c. 180 personnel. Core crew is c. 170.
Class:	Seven PPAs including two – *Giovanni delle Bande Nere* (P434) and *Domenico Millelire* (P436) – initially completed in 'Full' configuration.

navigation and platform management and the latter for control of sensors and weapons systems. A commanding officer's console located immediately aft of and slightly higher (20cm) than the cockpit allows the ship's commander to access platform and combat management system data, access communication systems and control the pilots' work (for example, by authorising or prohibiting the use of weapons).

The cockpit represents a new way of working for the Italian Navy, a fact reflected by the maintenance of some traditional features until the new arrangement takes hold. Notably, a traditional helmsman's position has been retained, providing a degree of redundancy for key navigational operations. The bridge also has positions for four CMS operators, providing something of an intermediate step between the limited combat management functions that can be carried out in the cockpit and the full capacity provided by the main combat information centre (CIC) located immediately aft of the bridge.[10]

In line with the operating concept introduced with the naval cockpit, a PPA's CIC would typically be manned in higher-threat situations. Its layout is based on two main rows of CMS consoles that run transversely across the width of the ship. They face a large, wall-mounted mission screen on the compartment's forward bulkhead that extends for much of the ship's breadth and on which multiple images can be displayed so as to enhance situational awareness. There are additional CMS consoles running parallel with the ship's sides, as well as a large tactical display table towards the compartment's rear.[11] A backup CIC position is also provided in line with the principal of redundancy inherent throughout the PPA design concept.

The combat management system is the latest Mk 4 evolution of the family of SADOC command systems found aboard previous Italian warships, such as the preceding FREMMS. The system is also commonly referred to as Athena Mk 2 in line with its export designation. Ergonomically, the main

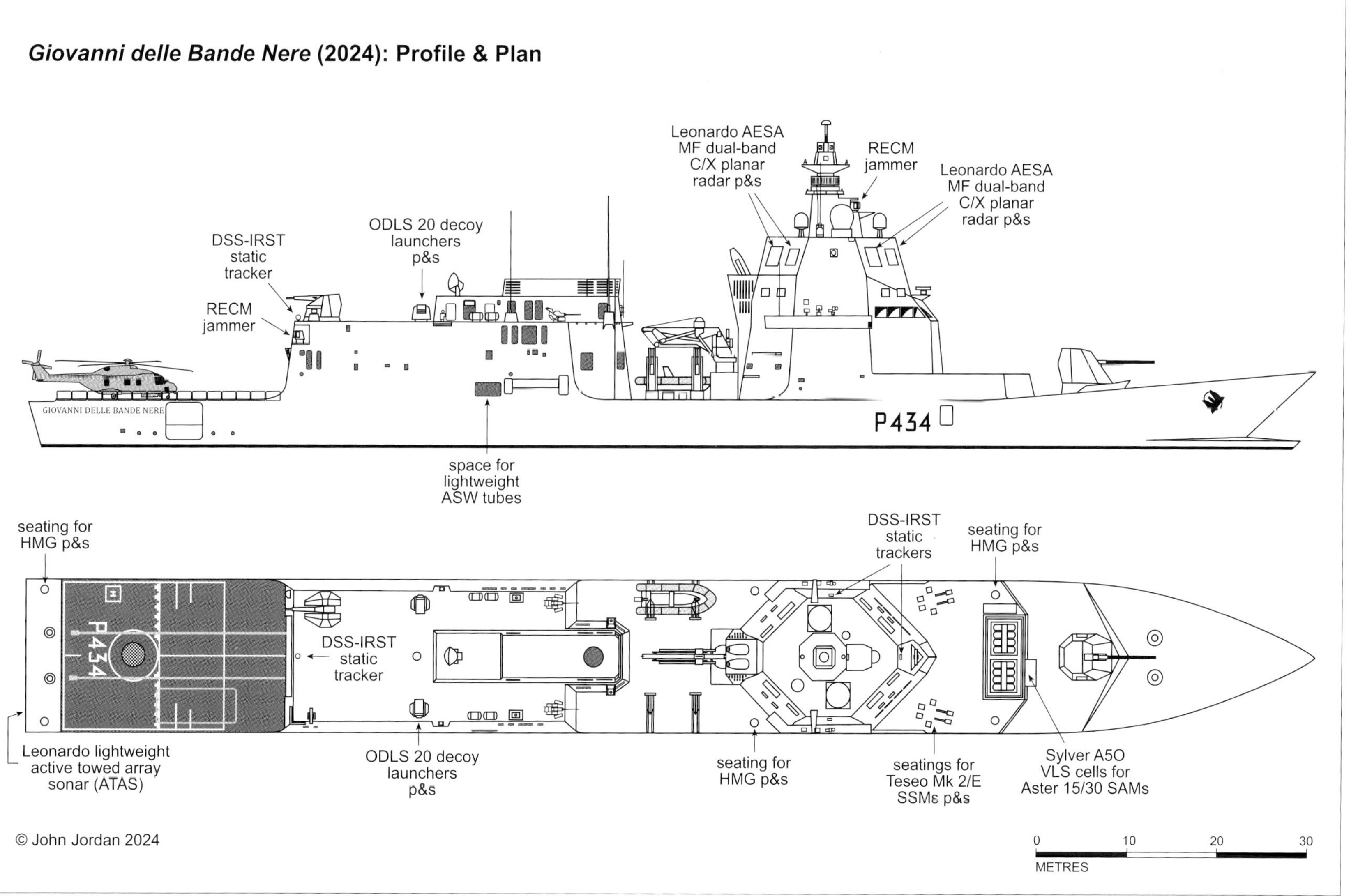

Two views of the bridge arrangement aboard a PPA. The innovative 'naval cockpit' located at the bridge's forward extremity allows a wide range of key navigation, ship control and weapon command functions to be performed by just two crew members. There is a command position immediately behind the cockpit, with a more traditional helmsman's station and a total of four combat management system consoles (only two can be seen) further aft. *(Italian Navy)*

A PPA's combat information centre is located immediate aft of the bridge. It incorporates a large bulkhead-mounted screen for visual displays and rows of consoles for the ship's SADOC Mk 4 combat management system. Each has a single, multifunction touch screen that can be reconfigured according to operator assignment. *(Italian Navy)*

visual difference from earlier iterations of the system is the substitution of a large single, multifunction touch screen – that can be quickly configured for a specific operator's role – for each of the consoles in place of the smaller, multiple screens used previously. In common with most modern combat management systems, SADOC's hardware and software are based on commercial-off-the-shelf (COTS) technology and it utilises an 'open' system architecture to facilitate integration of new sensors and weapons throughout a ship's life.

Command and control functions also benefit from an integrated communications suite that incorporates a comprehensive range of traditional radio and satellite communications. These support multiple tactical data links, including NATO Link 11 and Link 16 capability.

Sensors and Weapons: The outfit of sensors and weapons installed in the PPAs shows considerable variation in light of the decision to complete the class in different 'Light', 'Light Plus' and 'Full' configurations. As a result, only the ships designated as 'Full' variants will realise the full general-purpose potential inherent in the PPA design. This is particularly evident with respect to the class's Leonardo-produced 'Kronos' radar system, which is the design's principal sensor.

Sensors: As installed in the 'Full' PPAs, the multi-function Kronos radar system is fitted in its Kronos Dual Band iteration. This integrates two sets of active electronically-scanned array (AESA) radars operating in different radar frequencies: four C-band arrays (marketed as 'Kronos Quad') and four X-band arrays (marketed as 'Kronos StarFire').[12] The concept utilises a common system manager – the system's 'brain' – to combine the strengths of both sets of arrays under the philosophy that the combined 'whole' will be able to achieve a better performance than that possible from its individual components. In simplified terms, the lower frequency C-band arrays provide the PPA's long-range surveillance and air defence capability whilst the higher frequency X-band arrays provide greater resolution over shorter distances to enhance, for example, surface surveillance or close-range air defence. The system is reportedly capable of supporting engagements against the emerging generation of threats, such as tactical ballistic missiles. It is fully integrated with the class's Leonardo-supplied identification friend or foe (IFF) equipment and the Elettronica (now ELT) sourced electronic warfare suite.

The omission of air defence missiles from the 'Light' PPAs has meant that the longer-range potential of the C-band arrays could sensibly be dispensed with in ships built to this configuration. As such, they are only equipped with the shorter-ranged X-band radar. In contrast, the 'Light Plus' PPAs are fitted with Kronos C-band arrays for surveillance and surface-to-air missile guidance but lack the X-band radar. This is arguably a more questionable decision given the likely impact on overall system performance.

All PPAs are fitted with the NA30 S Mk2 fire-control system, which combines radar and optronic sensors for fire-control purposes. Located atop the hangar superstructure, it is the primary control system for the class's gun armament. The Kronos radars can act as a supplementary backup in this role. Also common to all ships are two dual-band

A view of *Paolo Thaon di Revel's* forward superstructure taken in March 2022, just after she had been delivered. Equipment for her Elettronica-integrated CESM and RESM electronic warfare suite is at the top of the masthead, with an IFF ring located immediately below. A number of communications radomes are located atop the bridge structure, with two of the four X-band 'Kronos StarFire' Multifunction arrays on the forward bridge sides. A Leonardo dual X/Ka-band navigation radar is positioned on a platform above the bridge's 'naval cockpit'. The main OTO 127mm gun on the forecastle utilises automated loading and can fire Vulcano extended-range ammunition. *(Italian Navy)*

Leonardo navigation radars, which operate in the X and Ka bands.

The Elettronica-supplied electronic warfare suite is managed by an electronic warfare management unit that integrates its various components. All PPAs are equipped with communications electronic support measures (CESM) and radar electronic support measures (RESM) sub-systems whilst the 'Light Plus' and 'Plus' variants are also fitted with radar electronic countermeasures (RECM) jammers. One of these is installed on the forward face of the mast on the bridge superstructure and the other at the starboard end of the hangar. Countermeasures aboard the PPAs completed in 'Full' configuration are supplemented by Leonardo ODLS-20 decoy launchers, which are fitted to the port and starboard sides of the hangar roof.

Leonardo's Distributed Static Staring-InfraRed Search and Tracking System (DSS-IRST) complements the PPAs' other surveillance systems. In complete configuration, it comprises a network of four stabilised, static (non-rotating) search head units to detect potential targets and three additional stabilised directional head units for target investigation. DSS-IRST can be used to provide information on a range of traditional and asymmetric threats, becoming a principal source of situational awareness when a ship is operating under radar silence. 'Full' PPAs are equipped with the complete system, whilst other variants have received a reduced version comprising just two directional units.

The PPAs are not equipped with hull-mounted sonar. However, they still have the capacity to undertake submarine detection, most notably by provision for the installation of Leonardo's new lightweight ATAS active towed-array sonar. This will equip the 'Full' PPAs, with the other variants being fitted for but not with the system.

Missile Systems: Missile systems are only fitted to PPAs completed in 'Light Plus' and 'Full' configurations. These variants are equipped with sixteen vertical launch system (VLS) cells for surface-to-air missiles in the form of two Naval Group A50 Sylver octuple modules. The VLS cells can house the full family of MBDA Aster 15 medium-range (in excess of 30km) and Aster 30 long-range (in excess of 120km) surface-to-air missiles that are, amongst others, widely used across the French, Italian and British navies. This will include the future Aster 30 Block 1 NT variant, which will provide the class with the ability to intercept short and medium-range tactical ballistic missiles. Equipped with active radar homing, Aster missiles are guided via data updates by the Kronos multi-function radar until the onboard sensor takes over in the final stages of an engagement.

PPAs also have space and weight reserved for the latest Mk 2/E iteration of MBDA's Teseo/Otomat family of surface-to-surface missiles, which is capable of engaging surface warships and land-based targets. Expected to enter service during the second half of the decade, the missile can travel in excess of 350km at a high subsonic speed in sea-skimming mode and benefits from high terminal manoeuvrability. It seems likely that these missiles will first be installed aboard 'Full' configuration PPAs.

Guns and Torpedoes: Gun armament is common across all PPAs. The main gun is an OTO 127mm/64 lightweight mounting that is located forward and which is equipped with automatic ammunition handling. In addition to standard munitions, it is capable of firing the 'Vulcano' family of extended-range ammunition, allowing targets to be engaged at ranges of up to 100km. The mounting would be particularly valuable as a means of providing gun fire support during amphibious operations. The 127mm gun is supplemented by an OTO 76mm/62 'Sovraponte' ('above deck') mounting. Located to starboard atop the aft end of the hangar, this incorporates significant weight savings over previous iterations of the Oto Melara 76mm series. In conjunction with the 'Strales' guidance system and DART guided munitions, it provides a potent inner-layer defence capacity against both missiles and asymmetric threats. The mounting can also fire a wide range of other ammunition types.

In addition to its larger guns, a PPA is also equipped with two OTO remote weapons stations fitted with 25mm guns for close-range defence. There are also positions for up to six heavy machine guns. Non-lethal equipment includes Leonardo's MASS long-range acoustic device (LRAD).

Provision is also made for installation of triple 324mm tubes for lightweight ASW torpedoes in positions located to the port and starboard sides of the aft superstructure block.

Aircraft: Aircraft facilities are common across all PPAs and form, inter alia, an important part of the ASW component of the class's general-purpose capability. The aft of the ship is dominated by a large flight deck and hangar for helicopter operations, which are also supported by a fully automated moving and handling system. The facilities can sustain the embarkation of one AW101 (designated EH-101 in Italian Navy service) or two NFH90 (SH-90) helicopters. The hangar is sufficiently high to allow a complete range of maintenance operations to be conducted on both helicopter types up to and including the removal of the main rotor-head. This evolution is supported by the installation of a two-tonne capacity roof mounted crane.

The class is also designed to be able to handle the future generation of unmanned aerial vehicles (UAVs).

Modular Areas: Modularity is a key element of the PPA design, with a capacity to handle significant amounts of (largely) containerised equipment an important element supporting the class's dual-use design requirement. Accordingly, the PPAs are equipped with two positions or zones for modular mission equipment, one located amidships at main deck level and one under the helicopter deck at the stern. The modular approach allows a wide range of operations to be performed without impacting other ship systems or reducing operational availability. In addition to supporting dual use operations such as humanitarian aid and disaster response (HADR) missions, the mission zones can be used, for example, in conjunction with unmanned vehicle or Special Forces operations. They also provide a ready means of expanding class capabilities in the future.

The central modular area located amidships is sized to host up to eight ISO 1C (20ft) containers with a maximum weight of 80 tonnes. Dependent on the number of containers required, embarkation requires removal of one or both of the 10-tonne capacity davits fitted to port and starboard that are usually fitted to launch and recover RHIBs of up to 11m in length. The containers can be handled from harbours not having their own handling facilities by means of a 20-tonne (at 14m) capacity crane located on the ship's centreline. The midships access area is also equipped with a lift for handling up to two pallets of stores that runs downwards to the damage control deck level.

The stern mission zone is capable of housing five ISO 1C containers (or other equipment). Access to the zone is via a hatch in the flight deck, from the

This photograph of *Paolo Thaon di Revel's* stern depicts a SH-90 (NFH90 series) helicopter operating from the ship's large flight deck, as well as the openings for the stern ramp and 'fitted for but not with' active towed-array sonar and torpedo defence system. There is a second dual X/Ka-band radar to the starboard end of the hangar roof, with a non-deck-penetrating OTO 76mm 'Sovraponte' mounting to port. Also evident are the NA30 S Mk2 fire-control system aft the funnel and the port 25mm remote weapons station. A platform for one of the two directional units for the IRST system is located between the 76mm and 25mm mountings. *(Italian Navy)*

stern ramp or by means of two large openings in the ship's sides. There is no provision for autonomous loading of containers, which would normally be carried out through the flight deck opening with the assistance of shore-side cranes. However, equipment can be moved within the mission zone by means of a roof-mounted 10-tonne crane.

The Italian Navy has already developed three specialised facilities for use on the PPAs and other similarly equipped ships on the basis of the containerised approach. These encompass accommodation (for thirty-two personnel), hospital and electrical power distribution modules. Accommodation and hospital modules are based on joining five ISO 1C containers together. Additional modules, including one for pollution control, are under development. The PPAs' aft mission zone is equipped with all the necessary connections to allow different containerised configurations operate in a 'plug and play' mode.

The location of the ship's stern ramp immediately aft of the stern reconfigurable modular area also facilitates the use of this zone to support small boat operations. These can be stowed in the mission area prior to launch from the ramp via the sliding water-tight door that divides the two compartments. In similar fashion, the zone's side openings facilitate the deployment and recovery of surface and underwater drones.

Crew Facilities: PPAs are provided with accommodation for a total of around 180 personnel, which is more than sufficient to house the entire complement

This interior view of a PPA hangar shows its ability to embark and maintain two SH-90 sized helicopters. The hangar roof is sufficiently high to allow onboard replacement of the main rotor head of any of the helicopter types likely to be embarked in the class. *(Italian Navy)*

of a fully-manned PPA in 'Full' configuration. As mentioned above, the possibility of installing additional containerised accommodation for particular mission requirements is an important benefit of the class's modular design approach. Accommodation for commissioned officers and petty officers is based on established Italian Navy standards, being similar to that found aboard the FREMMs (typically single-berth cabins for officers and two-berth cabins for non-commissioned officers). Accommodation for ratings is provided to a more austere level, being focused on three berthing areas equipped with multiple bunks, with a total capacity for sixty-two crewmembers.

INTO SERVICE

As of mid-2024, the first three PPAs have been accepted into Italian Navy service and delivery of a fourth – the first 'Full' variant, *Giovanni delle Bande Nere* – is imminent. The operational ships have already been very active. Notably, the lead ship, *Paolo Thaon di Revel*, departed Italy for the Middle East in August 2022 to participate in the EMASoH (European Maritime Awareness in the Strait of Hormuz) Operation AGENOR maritime security mission. Her sister, *Francesco Morosini*, subsequently participated in the mission during 2023 in the course of a five-month deployment that took her to the Far East as part of a naval diplomacy and marketing deployment. In late April 2024, PPA 3 – *Raimondo Montecuccoli* – also departed for the Far East via the Atlantic Ocean and Panama Canal on a similar 'flag waving' voyage. In addition to conducting various port calls in support of the Italian maritime sector, she is also scheduled to participate in the RIMPAC 2024 exercises.

Future deliveries of PPAs to the Italian Navy will slow due to the announcement of the first export contract for the class by Fincantieri on 28 March 2024. The €1.18bn (c. US$1.3bn) deal with Indonesia will see PPAs 5 and 6 – the 'Light Plus' configured *Marcantonio Colonna* and *Ruggiero di Lauria* – re-allocated to the Indonesian Navy to

These photographs show a RHIB being transferred from a PPA's aft modular mission zone to the ship's stern ramp through the sliding watertight bulkhead that splits the two compartments and then being launched through the ship's stern door. The mission zone is sized to handle modular containerised equipment, as evidenced by the container to starboard in the top photo. *(Italian Navy)*

Paolo Thaon di Revel seen at sea in April 2022, soon after her acceptance by the Italian Navy. She departed Italy for the Middle East later that year to participate in the Operation AGENOR maritime security mission in the Strait of Hormuz. *(Italian Navy)*

The PPAs have already been widely deployed across the world since first entering service in March 2022. In late April 2024, *Raimondo Montecuccoli* – pictured here in late 2023 – became the second member of the class to depart on a lengthy mission to the Far East. *(Italian Navy)*

meet an urgent requirement for new ships. The contract followed on from *Francesco Morosini*'s visit to Indonesia in July 2023 as part of her Far Eastern deployment. At this stage it is not entirely clear whether – and, if so, to what extent – the two vessels will be upgraded to 'Full' configuration as part of the contract. The Italian Navy currently envisages purchasing two additional ships in 'Light Plus' configuration to make good the transfers.

The final PPA from the current order – PPA 7 *Domenico Millelire* – is currently at an advanced stage of construction at the Riva Trigoso yard. She

Giovanni delle Bande Nere in the course of fitting-out in 2022. Whilst she will enter service before the end of 2024, future deliveries of PPAs to the Italian Navy will slow due to sale of the fifth and sixth members of the class to Indonesia. *(Lorenz Amiet)*

will be launched in mid-2024 with anticipated delivery by the end of 2026.

ASSESSMENT

The *Paolo Thaon di Revel* class PPAs represent a state-of-the-art general-purpose frigate design that is far removed from their original patrol vessel categorisation. Equipped with a wide range of cutting-edge equipment supplied largely by Italian industry, they are front-line combatants that gain additional flexibility from the modular features that are inherent within the design. Like all general-purpose warships, they are not without their compromises. The Italian Navy's traditional quest for speed has seemingly driven design choices – such as the use of an alloy superstructure and a complex propulsion train – that might not find universal favour. However, Fincantieri's design team has undoubtedly produced an innovative ship that provides a level of capability absent from many of its competitors.[13]

From an Italian Navy perspective, the arrival of the PPAs is significant on a number of levels. The navy has wanted to expand its reach beyond its Mediterranean backyard for a number of years and the class provides an optimal way to achieve this ambition. The design's modular flexibility is ideally suited for extended deployments, as evidenced by the global tasking mandated for those vessels that have already been delivered. It seems likely that the PPAs will play an ongoing role sustaining the Italian Navy's international presence. Moreover, the class is also being used to introduce features and equipment that will play an important part in driving forward future navy capability and practices. The PPAs' naval cockpit and modular zones – as well as equipment such as the Kronos AESA radars – are already being adopted for future classes. Finally, it is worth noting that the PPAs will only gain further significance if the navy's hopes of upgrading all the class to 'Full' configuration are realised.

From an international sales perspective, the PPA offers an attractive level of capability to fleets with pockets that are sufficiently deep to afford its relatively large price tag. The range of missions it is able to perform across scenarios of varying intensity appears to be a particular strength. The recent Indonesian contract represents the early fruit of Fincantieri's marketing efforts. It would not be surprising if further export contracts were to follow.

Notes

1. A description of the Italian FREMM variants is contained in the editor's 'Italian FREMMs: Carlo Bergamini (General-Purpose) and Virginio Fasan (Anti-Submarine) Frigates', *Seaforth World Naval Review 2015* (Barnsley: Seaforth Publishing, 2014), pp 88–107. Although the FREMMs were purposely designed as multi-mission frigates that could be optimised for different roles, the fact that all ships shared broadly similar hulls and propulsion systems meant that acoustic stealth for silent ASW operations was a common design-driver across all variants. Two of the ten original Italian FREMMS were sold to Egypt late in their construction process and replacements are currently being completed. In addition, there are plans for at least two of an evolved FREMM EVO design.

2. These figures are drawn from the Italian Court of Audit (*Corte dei conti*) report n. 19/2019/G of 23 December 2019 on *Il Programma Navale per la tutela della capacità marittima della Difesa*. This is currently available by searching the web.

3. The Italian FREMMS have an overall length to beam ratio of 7.3:1 whereas the ratio for the PPAs is a comparatively slender 8.7:1.

4. Grand Admiral Paolo Thaon di Revel (1859–1948) was an Italian naval officer and politician. He was Italy's Chief of Naval Staff for much of the First World War and acted as President of the Senate between 1943 and 1944 following the collapse of the previous fascist regime.

5. Riva Trigoso also houses Fincantieri's specialised Mechanical Components Division, which produces equipment such as fin stabilisers, rudders and propellers using autonomous manufacturing techniques.

6. The Naval Vessels Division also has access to other Fincantieri group sites should circumstances require, having recently assembled large naval vessels at its facilities at Castellammare di Stabia in the Bay of Naples and Palermo in Sicily.

7. The torpedo tubes will likely be fitted after delivery from stocks released by the retirement of older warships.

8. The aftermost bulkhead incorporates a sliding watertight arrangement between the main deck and No 3 deck between the double-decked aft mission bay and the stern ramp. This allows rigid hull inflatable boats (RHIBs) stowed in the mission zone to be transferred to the ramp for launch.

9. From PPA 4 onwards, the MAN generators have been replaced by 16V170C2Me gensets produced by Fincantieri's Isotta Fraschini subsidiary.

10. Leonardo, who played a lead role in the design of the cockpit concept, point out that the new arrangement still produces significant crewing efficiencies in its current form. They note that a previous Italian Navy frigate would require a minimum command crew of 11–12 personnel; the commander, two to three helmsmen, a communications officer and seven CMS operators. The current PPA configuration reduces this to seven people – the commander, pilot, co-pilot and four CMS operators. See '"In flight" with PPAs: the advanced technology of the PPAs' (Pattugliatori Polivalenti di Altura) naval cockpit' posted to Leonardo's website on 13 October 2022.

11. The PPA 'Light' variants are fitted for but not with four CMS consoles that are typically assigned to the air defence system installed in the two other configurations.

12. In general terms, higher-frequency radars produce a sharper beam for a given antenna size but have a shorter range.

13. The PPA makes an interesting comparator with Germany's F125 class 'stabilisation' frigates, which share a number of similar design aims and are both well suited for international deployment. However, the PPA benefits from a much greater ability to participate in high-intensity missions and seems to be a much more flexible vessel overall. Further details of the German ship are provided in the author's '*Baden-Württemberg* class: Germany's F125 type stabilisation frigates', *Seaforth World Naval Review 2018* (Barnsley: Seaforth Publishing, 2017), pp 116–31.

14. This chapter has been based on contemporary Italian Navy, Fincantieri and Leonardo documentation supplemented by appropriate press releases and reports. This has been supplemented by the opportunity provided to the author to visit PPA 7 *Domenico Millelire* at Riva Trigoso and ask detailed questions to the key members of Fincantieri's staff. The author would particularly like to thank the following Fincantieri personnel for their considerable assistance:

- **Renato Gastaldo**, Vice President Production, Riva Trigoso Shipyard
- **Micaela Longo**, Group Strategic Communication, Media Relations
- **Fabio Rinaldi**, Sales Regional Manager, Europe and Israel, Naval Vessels Division
- **Simone Serpagli**, Vice President Project Manager PPA

3.3 SIGNIFICANT SHIPS

SUFFREN CLASS SUBMARINES

Upholding French Interests from beneath the Waves

Author:
Bruno Huriet

On 12 July 2019, *Suffren* – the first of the *Marine Nationale*'s new class of nuclear-powered attack submarines – was officially unveiled at Naval Group's shipyard at Cherbourg in Normandy by President Emmanuel Macron. Speaking just before the unveiling, the then French Chief of Naval Staff, Admiral Christophe Prazuck, summed up the new submarine's missions. He said, '*Suffren* is a hunter. This is not a boat that goes into hiding; it is a boat that is built for combat. *Suffren* will take over the missions of the *Rubis* class submarines, namely:

- Ensuring the safety of our strategic submarines.
- Acting as "bodyguard" for the aircraft carrier *Charles de Gaulle*, patrolling the sea hundreds of miles ahead.
- Serving as an intelligence agent near crisis zones, utilising sensors to assess the situation ashore.'

He continued, 'We have added two missions:

- Acting as a sniper, hitting targets inland, hundreds of kilometres away, using cruise missiles.
- Functioning as a Special Forces operative, delivering commando teams to conduct intelligence and offensive operations on a much larger scale than before.'

Suffren was launched shortly after the official unveiling ceremony, subsequently embarking on a long period of tests and trials. Delivered on 6 November 2020, she completed a long endurance cruise before being admitted into active service on 3 June 2022.[1]

FRENCH NAVY SUBMARINES

Suffren is the 108th submarine built at Cherbourg. The site was once a naval arsenal and is now one of Naval Group's major shipyards, specialising in submarine design and construction.[2] *Morse* – the first submarine built at the facility – was launched in 1899. The boat has been followed by numerous conventional submarines up to and including the current generation of 'Scorpène'-type export designs. In 1967, there was a further significant development when President Charles de Gaulle launched *Le Redoutable*, the first French nuclear-powered submarine. Equipped with sixteen missiles carrying nuclear warheads, her class became a core component of French deterrence. In total, Cherbourg designed and built sixteen nuclear-powered submarines before *Suffren*, viz.:

- Six *Le Redoutable* class strategic submarines (SSBNs); active from 1971 to 2008. This type is designated as a *sous-marin nucléaire lanceur d'engins* (SNLE) in French terminology.
- Six *Rubis* class nuclear-powered attack submarines (SSNs), which entered service between 1983 and 1993. This type is known as a *sous-marin nucléaire d'attaque* (SNA) in French service. Three of the class currently remain active.
- Four *Le Triomphant* class strategic submarines, placed into service between 1997 and 2010.

After *Le Redoutable* entered active service, the submarine forces of the French Navy gradually became totally nuclear-powered, the last of the four conventional units of the *Agosta* type being decommissioned in 2001. Accordingly, the current fleet includes four SSBNs of the *Le Triomphant* type and the three remaining *Rubis* class SSNs.[3] The latter class is being steadily replaced by the new *Suffren* class boats, of which *Suffren* herself and *Duguay-Trouin* are already in service.

With a length of some 73.6m and displacing only 2,670 tonnes in submerged condition, the *Rubis* class are considered to be the smallest SSNs in the world. They are powered by a K48 reactor (generating 48MW of thermal power), which supplies steam to two turbo-alternators that feed electricity to a main propulsion motor. They are equipped with four 533mm torpedo tubes for launching up to fourteen heavy torpedoes (or a mix of torpedoes and SM-39 Exocet anti-ship missiles).

The *Rubis* class submarines have benefitted from

Left: The lead *Suffren* class submarine pictured off Brest on 13 July 2020 in the course of her initial sea trials. She had previously being unveiled to the public at a ceremony at Naval Group's Cherbourg shipyard, where all French nuclear-powered submarines have been built. *(Bernard Prézelin)*

Two photographs of the *Rubis* class nuclear-powered attack submarine *Saphir* taken off Toulon in September 2013. The *Suffren* class are direct replacements for the *Rubis* class, whose service lives had to be extended due to delays to the replacement programme in the cash-restricted post-Cold War era. *Saphir*, the second *Rubis* class submarine to be completed, was the first of the series to be decommissioned when she was withdrawn from service in June 2019. Her forward section was subsequently used to replace that of her fire-damaged sister, *Perle*. *(Bernard Prézelin)*

ongoing modernisation since first entering service over three decades ago.[4] When first designed, the primary mission of these 'submarine hunters' was to ensure the safety of France's strategic submarines as they departed their home base at L'île Longue, near Brest. It is considered vital that France's deterrent is not compromised by a foreign submarine waiting close to the coast to track a SSBN before it 'disappears' into the deep ocean. As noted by Admiral Prazuck, naval force protection and – increasingly – intelligence gathering and Special Forces operations have also been important requirements. Due to the submarines' small size, their crews of seventy are known to face fairly spartan living conditions.

PROGRAMME ORIGINS

In similar fashion to other leading navies, the *Marine Nationale* starts to consider requirements for the next series of combat units as soon as an existing programme reaches its conclusion. This consideration needs, inter alia, to explore the threats the navy will face in the next 20 or 40 years and ask which systems will need to be developed as a result. In line with this process, a series of preparatory design studies was carried out in the course of the 1990s to pave the way for the development of an eventual *Rubis* class replacement that was then known as the *sous-marin d'attaque future* (SMAF).[5] Subsequently, in 1998 the French Defence Procurement Agency – the *Direction générale de l'armement* (DGA) – and the French Navy commenced the next, feasibility phase of SSN design work under a project that came to be known as the 'Barracuda' programme. These studies were, in turn, followed by a project definition phase completed between 2001 and 2006.[6]

The *Rubis* class had been designed during the 1970s for the Cold War. Given the changed post-Cold War environment, the requirements for the new generation of SSN inevitably evolved. It was considered that the French Navy would need to be able to act faster and further across a broader spectrum of missions. Design considerations therefore focused on providing greater autonomy and improved maintainability/redundancy. Support for new missions such as the provision of a land attack capability and an enhanced capacity to deploy Special Forces also featured prominently. Technologies developed for the contemporary *Le Triomphant* class, notably in the field of acoustic discretion and combat systems, were also to be incorporated into the new programme.

In common with many other countries, the end of the Cold War caused numerous French armament programmes to 'slide'. France's new SSNs were no exception. Delay after delay meant that the first of the new submarines was only ordered on 22 December 2006, with first steel cutting taking place the following year. One consequence of these delays was a need to extend the life of the existing *Rubis* class boats. For example, *Casabianca* – the latest member of the class to be withdrawn from service – had completed over 36 years of service when decommissioned in September 2023. Whilst this track record is a testament to the quality of construction and maintenance of these submarines, it also makes it clear why the arrival of the *Suffren* class is so eagerly awaited by the navy.

A computer-generated image of a *Suffren* class submarine. The 'Barracuda' project that gave rise to the class traces its origins to studies into a future SMAF submarine that were carried out in the 1990s and which subsequently progressed to a feasibility phase towards the end of that decade. After further design work – and considerable delays due to lack of funding – an order for the lead submarine was placed with what was then DCN (now Naval Group) in December 2006. *(Naval Group)*

PROJECT PROGRESSION

Programme Approval: In France, major armaments programmes are governed by a series of military programming laws that typically cover a period of up to six years. This *loi de programmation militaire* (LPM) system aims to reconcile the constitutional imperative of voting through an annual budget with the desirability of ensuring funding for longer-term investment in developing and acquiring major weapons systems. Orders for what was then still known as the SMAF were first included within the 1997–2002 LPM (approved in 1996). Although – as mentioned above – the next phase of design work was approved in 1998, plans for the swift award of construction contracts faced year-on-year slippage. Consequently, the order for the lead submarine of the new class placed in December 2006 fell within the lifespan of the following LPM 2003–2008. Whilst a class of six boats was envisaged to replace the *Rubis* class on a like-for-like basis, this initial award only included a firm contract for one boat, with the others subject to subsequent approval. Ultimately, however, the original plan was maintained, with the contract for the sixth and final *Suffren* class boat being placed in 2019.

Project Organisation: The order for each *Suffren* class submarine was placed by the DGA, an arm of the French Armed Forces Ministry. The DGA is therefore the principal contracting authority for the programme. With over 10,000 employees, it is also able to provide vital expertise across a range of relevant areas, such as hydrodynamics, acoustic signature and weapons. A submarine integrates systems such as weapons, sensors and communications equipment provided by a wide range of suppliers. By providing a comprehensive view of all aspects of the defence industry, the DGA can ensure that all these systems will interact efficiently; and also that the submarine will operate coherently with all other elements of the French armed forces. DGA's challenge is to ensure the overall cohesiveness of these various components so as to create an efficient defence tool.

A peculiarity of the *Suffren* class programme – due to its use of nuclear propulsion – is the presence of an additional contracting authority for the submarines' nuclear plant in the form of the Atomic Energy and Alternative Energies Commission; the *Commissariat à l'énergie atomique et aux énergies alternatives* (CEA). This public body's missions include the development of applications of nuclear energy; its Military Applications Directorate – *Direction des applications militaires* (DAM) – has responsibility for the nuclear propulsion systems used aboard aircraft carriers and submarines; it is also the DAM which is responsible for the nuclear warheads carried by French strategic missiles.

In a reflection of this division, development and production activities for the 'Barracuda' submarine programme are subject to a partnership of Naval Group (the prime contractor) and TechnicAtome. Naval Group is responsible for the project's management and has overall design responsibility. In this guise, it is answerable for the submarine – excluding the nuclear propulsion compartment – and its combat system, carrying out final integration at Cherbourg. Meanwhile TechnicAtome has responsibility for the design and construction of the submarine's nuclear plant, manufacturing the nuclear core and supplying key components.[7] Under this arrangement, Naval Group also supplies key elements of the propulsion system (e.g. the steam generators) and integrates the propulsion compartment. An integrated team encompassing programme supervisors

from the DGA and CEA, project managers from Naval Group and TechnicAtome, and representatives from the French Navy is responsible for ensuring the programme's delivery. It includes specialist teams deployed on site to monitor construction.

Construction: The construction of all 'Barracuda' programme submarines takes place at Cherbourg. Hull sections are fabricated in a workshop equipped with one of the world's most powerful (12,000-tonne) presses. After fabrication, the sections are transferred to the huge 'Laubeuf Hall', which was completed in 1989. Some 54m high – so as to handle the ballistic missile launch tubes used in strategic submarines – and some 190m in length, the hall is where submarine assembly takes place.

First steel cutting for *Suffren* took place on 19 December 2007. Subsequent construction was carried out in a modular manner, with hull segments between two to three metres in length being assembled to create five separate sections. These are outfitted as completely as possible: for example, whole deck modules are raft mounted inside the hull sections, with the rafts comprising large metal frames or cradles that are connected to the hull via sound and vibration damping elements. The largest raft, for propulsion machinery, is reported to weigh around 450 tonnes.

The complete propulsion plant is assembled in the Indret plant, which is located near Nantes on the banks of the River Loire. The nuclear reactor, all accessories and the propulsion machinery – the turbine, reduction gearing and auxiliaries – are mounted on their rafts and tested; as the reactor is not fuelled at this stage, steam is produced on site. When testing is completed, the modules are loaded on a barge which is towed to Cherbourg. The modules are then integrated into the submarine's aft section.

The class's building strategy relies significantly on digitalisation; a 3D virtual model including 700,000

Two photographs of the 'Barracuda' programme submarines *Duguay Trouin* and *Suffren* under construction in the giant Laubeuf building hall at Naval Group's Cherbourg shipyard. The submarines are constructed in five separate sections that are outfitted with various modules before being welded together to make a complete hull. The photograph of *Duguay-Trouin* (top) shows the forward section with its four 533mm torpedo tubes already in place. *(Naval Group)*

components of the submarine is available through tablets on site as part of a 'zero paper' submarine-building approach. Another important aspect is the use of augmented reality imaging: shipyard workers inside the submarine wearing special glasses can see the compartment as it is with the 3D model overlaid. This enables fitters to check that everything is in accordance with the digital plan and to place parts for installation with precision. In the cramped compartments that are typical of submarines, this is a great advantage.

Another significant step forward has been achieved through the use of so-called *plateformes d'intégration* (PFIs). These allow integration of hardware and software in shore-based facilities that have the same consoles, servers and cabling intended for the completed submarine, allowing as many systems to be tested and verified before they are placed in a submarine that is under construction. This saves Naval Group significant time during the onboard integration process and significantly reduces the need for testing after the hull has been assembled. PFIs also make it possible to train submarine crews ashore.

Once the various modules have been inserted into the hull sections, the five sections are joined together to form the complete hull; the final joining of all sections. The 'closing' of *Suffren*'s hull took place in 2016.

A large dock with a length of 161m and a width of 30m is located adjacent to the Laubeuf building hall. It is equipped with a platform type shiplift that is used to lower a new submarine gradually into the water once it has been completed. Transfer of the completed submarine – as well as movements of sections and large modules earlier in the construction process – is performed using hydraulically-driven 'walkers'. Twelve pairs are required for a completed *Suffren* class submarine. Once it has been lowered into the water, the submarine remains on the submerged platform and the sensitive operation of loading the reactor with nuclear fuel takes place. A mobile workshop structure is fitted to cover the insertion hatch which is located above the nuclear core; it is designed to comply with all relevant nuclear regulations. This fuelling area is under the DGA's control and security is very strict.

As previously mentioned, *Suffren* was publicly 'unveiled' by the President of the French Republic, Emmanuel Macron, on 12 July 2019 just in front of the building hall. It was transferred to the dock plat-

The 450-tonne electric propulsion module for *Rubis*, the fifth member of the *Suffren* class, seen in the course of being transported by barge from the Indret plant near Nantes to Cherbourg at the end of May 2024. Upon arrival at Cherbourg, the module will be integrated into the submarine's aft section. *(Bernard Prézelin)*

Suffren pictured around the time of her unveiling ceremony in July 2019. The twelve pairs of hydraulic 'walkers' used to transfer submarines from the building dock to that platform-type shiplift used to 'launch' the submarine are readily apparent. The photograph also gives a good impression of the *Suffren's* class overall design, including the 'X'-form control surfaces and (covered) pump-jet. Note that at this stage of build the submarine carried the hull number Q284. *(Naval Group)*

form a few days later prior to being lowered into the water on 1 August that year. After loading of nuclear fuel, the submarine's reactor went 'live' on 17 December 2019. The submarine was floated off the platform in February 2020 and performed its first dive – off Cherbourg – on 28 April 2020. By that time, the Covid-19 pandemic had arrived to complicate the trials' programme, with the need to quarantine crew and industry specialists before each testing campaign commenced.

Trials were carried out progressively through several test campaigns, commencing with dives at progressively deeper depths to check the watertightness of the hull. This was followed by trials of the propulsion system and auxiliaries, including the submarine's manoeuvrability. A second phase of tests focused on the performance of the combat system and associated equipment, leading finally to trials of the new boat's operational capabilities.

Suffren's maximum diving depth – officially classified and reported only as 'greater than 300 metres' – was achieved in June 2020. After a port call in Brest, *Suffren* arrived at its homeport of Toulon for the first time on 28 July 2020.

Table 3.3.1.

SUFFREN (S635) PRINCIPAL PARTICULARS

Building Information:	
Fabrication Commenced:	19 December 2007 Launched: 1 August 2019[1] Delivered: 6 November 2020
Builders:	Naval Group at its shipyard in Cherbourg, Normandy.
Dimensions:	
Displacement:	c. 4,800 tonnes surface displacement, c. 5,300 tonnes dived displacement.
Overall Hull Dimensions:	99.5m x 8.8m x 7.3m. Hull diameter is 8.8m.
Weapons Systems:	
Armament:	4 x bow 533mm torpedo tubes. Space for up to 24 torpedoes or equivalent. Weapons outfit includes: – Naval Group F21 'Artémis' heavyweight torpedoes. – MBDA MdCN cruise missiles. – MBDA SM39 Block 2 Mod 2 anti-surface missiles. – Capacity to lay naval mines.
Countermeasures:	Thales ESM. Naval Group Canto decoy launchers.
Principal Sensors:	Thales UMS 3000 bow and flank sonar arrays. Thales mine and obstacle avoidance sonar and Velox M-8 sonar interceptor. Thales ETBF DSUV 62C towed array. Safran Series 30 Search Optronic Mast and Attack Optronic Mast. Safran Series 10 LPI CSR low probability of intercept surveillance radar.
Combat System:	SYCOBS combat management system. Integrated communications including Thales Divesat. NATO Links 11, 16 and 22.
Propulsion Systems:	
Machinery:	Nuclear with hybrid steam and turbo-electric propulsion: 1 x K15 TechnicAtome pressurised water reactor producing up to 150MW of power. 1 x Thermodyne steam turbine for high-speed operation or 2 x Exail electric motors drawing power from 2 x Thermodyn-Jeumont turbo alternators for lower speeds. 1 x shaft and pump-jet. 2 x emergency MAN diesel generators. 1 x emergency retractable propeller.
Speed and Range:	Over 25 knots. Unlimited effective range.
Diving Depth:	Classified but in excess of 300m.
Other Details:	
Complement:	Normal crew is 65, including 11 officers. Two crews are usually assigned to each boat.
Class:	Six. Two – *Suffren* (S635) and *Duguay-Trouin* (S636) – are in service. *Tourville, De Grasse, Rubis* and *Casabianca* are being built.

Note

1. Corresponds to the date of the lowering of the shiplift into the water. A formal unveiling ceremony was held on 12 July 2019.

DESIGN DESCRIPTION

Principal particulars of the *Suffren* class submarines are set out in Table 3.3.1. *Suffren*'s surfaced displacement is around 4,800 tonnes, increasing to approximately 5,300 tonnes in submerged condition. This is almost double that of the preceding *Rubis* design. The boat's hull is 99.5m long and 8.8m in diameter compared with equivalent figures of 73.6m and 7.6m for *Rubis*. External innovations that are readily apparent when viewing the new boats are the 'X' form stern control planes and the placement of the forward diving planes on the hull rather than the fin (US Navy sail). The design of the stern planes reportedly improves manoeuvrability, while the forward diving planes can be retracted into the hull to reduce hydrodynamic noise.[8] The hull is fabricated from high strength HLES 80 steel alloy. This steel combines high yield strength – the capacity to resist permanent deformation – with the ability to be subject to welding.

The interior of the submarines comprise three levels, with the living and operational spaces being located on the upper and middle decks, and the lower deck being occupied by technical rooms and

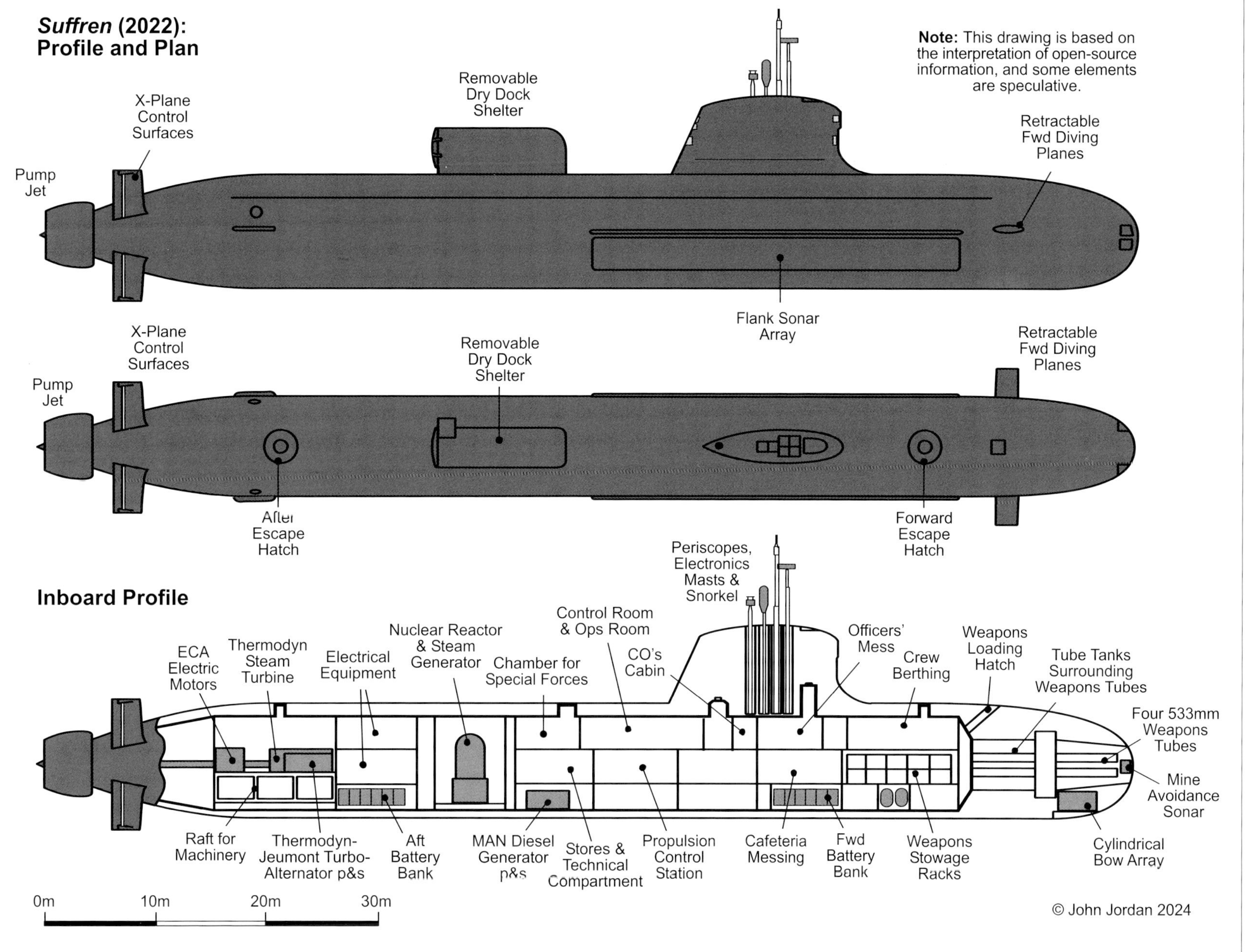

Displacing around 5,300 tonnes in full load condition, *Suffren* and her sisters are considerably larger than their *Rubis* class predecessors but still comparatively small when compared with current American and British designs. They also differ from their Anglo-Saxon counterparts in their use of civil grade, low-enriched uranium in their reactors. These two photographs taken off Brest in the summer of 2020 provide a good overview of the class's general appearance. *(Bernard Prézelin)*

facilities. In overall terms, the main functional areas from forward to aft comprise:

- The four weapons launch tubes.
- The crew berthing area (upper deck), with the weapons stowage area below.
- The control/operations room, placed after of the fin, with technical spaces below.
- The nuclear compartment.
- The propulsion compartment.

Living Quarters: The *Suffren* class's equipment and systems have been influenced by the objective of minimising crew size through automation and digitalisation. Their complement of sixty-five men and women, including eleven officers, reflects this objective, comparing favourably with the seventy-strong crew found in the smaller *Rubis*.

The submarine's increased dimensions, combined with a reduced crew, make it possible to offer better living conditions. There is a single cabin for the boat's commanding officer, with the other cabins having from two to six berths. There is also more storage space for each person, as well as more toilets and showers than previously. The class is designed to be operated by a mixed crew, with an area which includes cabins and toilets reserved for female submariners. Some *Suffren* class crews now include women, as is also the case aboard the strategic submarines. There is also provision to berth supernumeraries such as Special Forces aboard, with the level of comfort varying dependent on their number. Sufficient provisions are carried to support an endurance of 70 days before replenishment.

Each submarine is manned by two crews, 'blue' and 'red', alternating with each other. This same system – also used in the strategic submarines and the *Rubis* class – is intended to maximise a boat's use.

Propulsion System: The choice of nuclear propulsion was mandated at the very start of the programme considering the many advantages it provides; notably the provision of almost unlimited autonomy combined with the ability to sustain high speeds. The reactor is an evolution of the K15 type that is already fitted in the strategic submarines currently in service and – with two reactors – in the aircraft carrier *Charles de Gaulle*. As the *Suffren* class has a smaller hull diameter than the strategic submarines, the reactor needed to be adapted to the

The *Suffren* class's increased size and smaller crew mean that the boats' living quarters are an improvement on the somewhat austere accommodation provided in the *Rubis* class. These photographs show personnel eating a meal in the petty officers' wardroom and a briefing in the officers' wardroom. *(Rachel Bodier/Marine Nationale/Défense)*

size of the boats. The thermal power of this 'evolved' K15 reactor is classified but published data suggests that the similar units aboard the strategic submarines generate 150MW, or three times that of the K48 type used in the *Rubis* class. The K15 is a compact, pressurised water reactor (PWR) that is arranged so that the steam generator is located immediately above the reactor core. The design facilitates the use of natural circulation for cooling purposes over a wide range of reactor power. This limits the need to use primary pumps, benefiting acoustic stealth.

In contrast to the reactors installed aboard American and British submarines, the fuel used by the *Suffren* class's K15 reactor is 'civil grade', low-enriched uranium. This is the case for all reactors currently in French service. This choice has been driven by the ability to utilise the French civil nuclear fuel chain – France has a large number of nuclear power plants – to support fuel production and recycling. The drawback is the need to refuel the reactor periodically compared with the use of reactors that do not require refuelling during the service life of a vessel in the latest US Navy and Royal Navy submarines. However, extensive research and testing activity carried out with the support of the 'RES' research reactor located at the CEA's Cadarache research centre has helped to improve fuel management, extending the reactor refuelling cycle to ten years from the seven years that applied previously.

The *Suffren*'s class propulsion train is different from that found aboard the previous *Rubis* class SSNs, which used two turbo alternators to provide power for an electric motor. In contrast, *Suffren* utilises a hybrid system under which steam produced

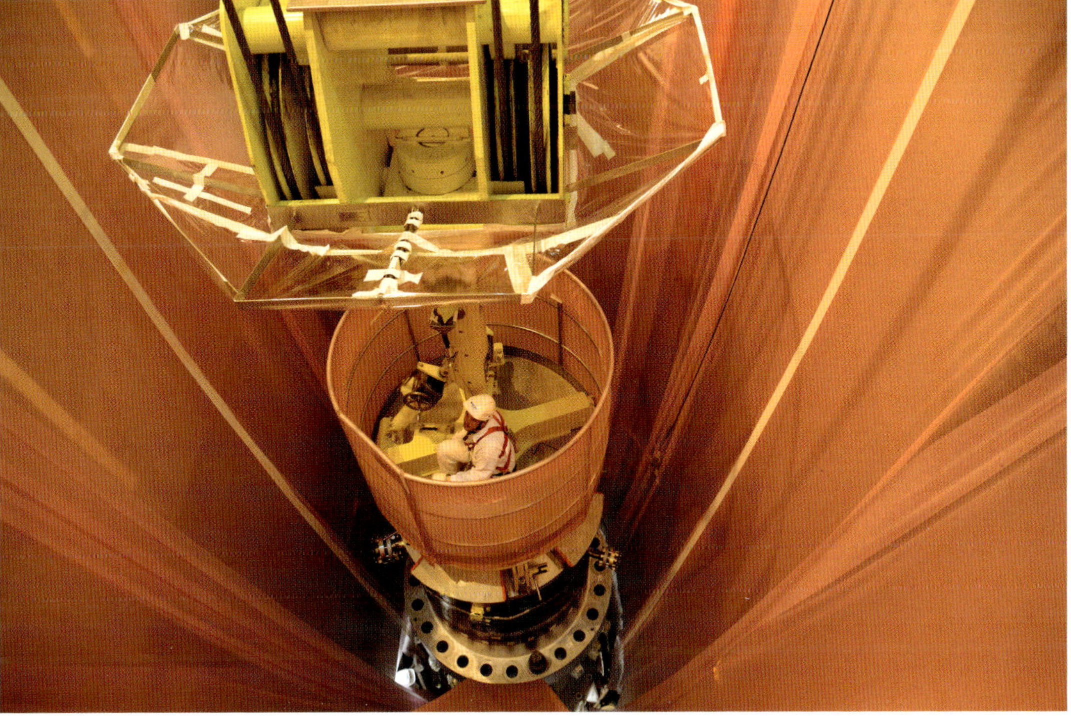

The *Suffren* class boats are powered by the latest iteration of the K15 pressurised nuclear reactor previously installed in the *Le Triomphant* class strategic submarines and the aircraft carrier *Charles de Gaulle*. This photograph shows the reactor's steam generator – located above the generator core – being installed during manufacture. *(TechnicAtome)*

The *Suffren* class submarines use a Thales SYCOBS combat management system that is also used aboard the French Navy's strategic submarines. Information gathered by the system is displayed on a total of ten multi-screen consoles located to the port and starboard sides of the control and operations room. A digital touch screen table is located in the centre of the room. Note that screens have been obscured in these official images for security purposes. *(Rachel Bodier/ Marine Nationale/Défense)*

by the reactor can be used to power either a similar turbo-electric arrangement utilising two Thermodyn-Jeumont turbo-alternators in conjunction with two Exail (formerly ECA Group) electric motors or a Thermodyn steam propulsion turbine in direct drive mode. In essence, the turbo-electric propulsion is used for stealthy operation at low to medium speeds, with the higher-power steam turbine arrangement being used when higher speeds are required. The boats' actual maximum speed is classified, being stated only as 'over 25 knots'.

The submarine is driven by a pump jet which has been the subject of extensive studies and tests to optimise its acoustic signature. An additional retractable propeller is located in the forepart of the submarine. This can be used to assist manoeuvring, as well as an emergency propulsion system. Two emergency diesel generators can be used to supply electrical power in the event of serious damage to the main propulsion system once a submarine is at snorkel depth.

The *Suffren* class's entire propulsion system, as well as its auxiliaries, are controlled from the main propulsion control station – *poste de contrôle propulsion* (PCP) – located just below the control room. This is a different location from previous submarines – where it was located closer to the reactor compartment, further aft – and facilitates communications with the control/operations room team. An integrated platform management system remotely controls and monitors all of the submarine's equipment. This level of automation is greater than in preceding classes.

Combat System: The *Suffren* class's combat system integrates a sonar suite, various other sensors, communications systems and weapons into a cohesive whole. The heart of the system is the SYCOBS combat management system; the common combat system for the 'Barracuda' and strategic submarines or *système de combat commun Barracuda SNLE.*[9] SYCOBS synthesises information gathered from the various sensors for display on ten multifunction consoles located in the control and operations room; the *poste central navigation opérations* (PCNO) in French terminology. The multi-screen consoles can be monitored from a commanding officer's position located on the centreline at the aft end of the control room. There is also a touch screen table in the centre of the control room that can display a wide range of information captured by the various sensors –

including video images from the optronic masts – to enhance situational awareness.

Sonar and Sensors: The class's primary sensor is arguably its Thales UMS 3000 multi-sensor sonar suite, encompassing bow and flank arrays. A fully digital system, its role is to detect, classify, locate and track potential threats and targets. The full sonar suite encompasses:

- A large cylindrical bow array located below the torpedo tubes.
- Flank array sonar panels located along the submarine's sides in a 'silent zone' in the forward part of the hull. They are fitted with ultra-thin (less than 70mm) polyvinylidene fluoride (PVDF) polymer elements to improve their sensitivity.
- A mine and obstacle avoidance sonar positioned forward between the torpedo tubes.
- A Velox M-8 broadband sonar interceptor used for threat detection.
- A NUSS-2F navigation echo sounder.

There is also provision for a towed-array sonar. It has been reported that the current Thales ETBF DSUV 62C model found on the *Rubis* class is used in the new boats but that a new array is under development.

The submarine's traditional main means of target detection – its optical periscopes – are no longer present aboard the *Suffren* class. Instead, two Safran optronic periscopes – a search optronic mast and attack optronic mast – are installed. More specifically these are:

- **A Safran Series 30 Search Optronic Mast (SOM):** This incorporates a HDTV colour camera, a thermal imager, and a low light level TV. A 'quick look round' function is fitted, rotating at high speed to provide a 360° surface and aerial vision. RESM electronic-warfare sensors are also fitted on the mast.
- **A Safran Series 30 Attack Optronic Mast (AOM):** This is of smaller diameter than the SOM, minimising its wake and reducing radar signature. It is fully compatible with the SOM and incorporates similar technology.

The use of optronic masts provides several advantages; for example, the images can be processed via different systems and displayed at multiple stations simultaneously whilst the pressure hull no longer needs to be penetrated. Notably, the use of this system provides flexibility as to where the control and operations room can be positioned. In *Suffren*'s case, the selected location aft of the fin has facilitated the layout of berthing and living areas, which are grouped together in the submarine's forward part.

This photograph of *Suffren*'s fin (sail) shows a number of important sensors. The foremost mast is used by the Safran Series 10 LPI CSR radar, whilst a Safran Series 30 optronic (non-penetrating) attack periscope is aft and to starboard. The array to its port is likely a Thales communications mast. What appears to be the retracted hoist for the snorkel used in conjunction with the emergency diesel generators is further aft. *(Bernard Prézelin)*

Safran also provides a Series 10 LPI CSR compact X (NATO I/J) band radar, which is used for navigation, intelligence gathering and tactical evaluation. The mast does not penetrate the hull, as the transmitter-receiver set is located in a watertight pod. A communications mast, a Thales 'Divesat' satellite mast and a snort mast for running the emergency diesel generators are also located on the fin. Two Sigma 40 XP inertial navigation systems from Safran are also fitted

Weapons Systems: *Suffren* can carry a variety of different weapons; namely torpedoes, anti-ship missiles, cruise missiles and mines. All are launched through the four 533mm bow tubes. Weapons are stowed in the weapons compartment aft of the launch tubes: there are racks for twenty munitions and a handling system that allows weapons to be stored and placed in the weapons launch tubes with limited human intervention. All tube-loading operations can be performed in a short space of time by just two crew members.[10]

The ability to deploy cruise missiles in the form of the *missile de croisière naval* (MdCN) is one of the greatest capability changes provided by the new submarines. The weapon is based on MBDA's SCALP (Storm Shadow) air-launched missile, which France chose to develop to equip frigates – launched from a vertical launch system – and submarines. *Suffren* carried out the first submarine launch on 20 October 2020. The 6.5m-long missile has a weight of c. 1,400kg and carries a c. 250kg payload at high subsonic speed. Whilst the seeker, navigation system and missile preparation software are similar to those used by SCALP, the MdCN required significant changes to its shape to allow launching from a torpedo tube, It also needs an acceleration and

Three official photographs of *Suffren* taken at speed whilst undertaking post-delivery trials with the *Marine Nationale* in the autumn of 2020. Her nuclear propulsion system provides almost unlimited endurance, whilst her integrated combat system provides the ability to deploy torpedoes, missiles and mines. *(Axel Manzano/Marine Nationale/Défense)*

tilting module – essentially a booster – as it does not benefit from the high initial speed provided by a jet. When launched from a submarine, MdCN is placed in a watertight capsule, from which it is separated on leaving the water. A Safran Microturbo TR50 turbojet provides a range in excess of 1,000km, significantly greater than the air-launched equivalent. The MdCN can use various navigation modes – inertial, GPS and terrain reference – during flight whilst its terminal guidance system includes target recognition through an infrared sensor that can recognise the target's shape.

The class's anti-ship missiles are the MBDA SM39 Block 2 Mod 2 submarine-launched iteration of the Exocet family. The 665kg, 4.7m-long missile has a range of 50km, which enables a submarine to launch the missile while remaining out of an enemy's detection range. In broadly similar fashion to the MdCN, the missile is housed in a watertight container – a *véhicule sous marin* (VSM) – until ejected when leaving the water. Operating at sea-skimming level, the missile uses an inertial navigation system followed by autonomous terminal guidance from an active RF seeker.

The torpedoes are the new Naval Group F21 heavyweight model developed under the 'Artémis' programme. Designed to neutralise enemy ships and submarines, they are faster and more agile than the French Navy's previous F17. Initially wire-guided, the torpedoes use acoustic homing technology provided by Thales in an engagement's later stages. Features include an advanced, self-guided mode; shallow and confined water capability; and incorporation of the latest generation of resistance against countermeasures. Operational attack depth has been reported as between 10m and 500m. Some 6m in length, the F21 uses electric propulsion to achieve an officially quoted range in excess of 50km at a speed of more than 50 knots. The propulsion system is provided by Atlas Elektronik and incorporates Saft-supplied silver oxide-aluminium (AgO-Al) electrochemical battery stacks. These reportedly deliver twice as much energy and power as conventional silver-zinc batteries for the same mass and volume. The AgO-Al cell chemistry is only activated when it comes into contact with seawater – which acts as the electrolyte – assisting the batteries' safe long-term storage.

Like previous submarines, *Suffren* also has the capacity to lay mines from its torpedo tubes. France says very little on these weapons but a new type of mine is possibly under development to replace old systems. However, no definitive information has been published.

Countermeasures: The 'Canto' anti-torpedo system – part of the 'Contralto' countermeasures system – forms part of the class's wider countermeasures suite. Once launched from the submarine, 'Canto' decoys generate a large number of false acoustic targets based on the dilution/confusion principle. This involves it acting as a jammer to create a dilution effect and as a false target generator for a confusion effect. The decoys are stored outside the pressure hull and launched by compressed air.

Dry Deck Shelter (DDS): An element of the *Suffren* class design which shows the importance that is now attached to undertaking missions from sea to shore in littoral areas is the possibility of embarking a DDS. Attached to the deck abaft of the fin, it allows Special Forces to avoid utilising the torpedo tubes as a means of exit, facilitating the deployment of them and their equipment. Accessible from inside the submarine by an airlock, the c. 11m-long DDS is flooded to allow divers to exit quickly and begin their mission.

A new swimmer delivery vehicle has been developed to use the new capabilities offered by the DDS. The PSM3G third-generation swimmer delivery vehicle was developed by Exail and is able to transport several divers. However, precise details regarding this very secret programme are scarce.

FIRST DEPLOYMENTS

Well before the French Navy took charge of *Suffren* for its first trials, the boat's crews had completed a long period of training ashore. As part of this programme, a set of simulators was installed at the Underwater Navigation School located in Toulon Naval Base. Here, the crews were trained to pilot the submarine on platforms mounted on jacks in order to reproduce the trim and list conditions of real-life operations as well as to manage the reactor, the other elements of the propulsion system, and its auxiliaries. Weapons systems operators also benefited from training using dedicated simulators

As previously mentioned, *Suffren* reached its base port of Toulon at the end of July 2020 after

The *Suffren* class submarines are capable of deploying with a dry deck shelter to facilitate the deployment of Special Forces without recourse to using the submarine's torpedo tubes. *(Marine Nationale)*

Table 3.3.2: *SUFFREN* NUCLEAR-POWERED ATTACK SUBMARINES: CLASS LIST

NAME	PENNANT[1]	ORDERED	FIRST STEEL CUT	TO SHIPLIFT	REACTOR LIVE	SEA TRIALS	DELIVERY	ACTIVE SERVICE
Suffren	S635	22 December 2006	19 December 2007	July 2019	17 December 2019	28 April 2020	6 November 2020	1 June 2022[2]
Duguay-Trouin	S636	26 June 2009	26 June 2009	26 November 2021	30 September 2022	27 March 2023	28 July 2023	4 April 2024
Tourville	S637	28 June 2011	28 June 2011	20 July 2023	24 April 2024	[Summer 2024]	[End 2024]	[2025]

Notes

1. French submarines have not shown any pennant numbers for some years, a decision now extended to all naval vessels.
2. An official ceremony was carried out on 3 June 2022.
3. *De Grasse* (S638) was ordered on 18 July 2014 and is due for delivery in 2026.
4. *Rubis* (S639) was ordered on 2 May 2018 and is due for delivery in 2028.
5. *Casabianca* (S640) was ordered on 12 July 2019 and is due for delivery in 2030.

completing an initial series of trials. This was followed by another series of tests, involving different elements of the submarine's weaponry. In the course of September and October 2020, launches of the MdCN cruise missile, Exocet SM39 anti-surface missile and F21 torpedo were carried out. Following completion of these tests, *Suffren* was formally accepted by the DGA from Naval Group on 6 November 2020.

Suffren then progressed to completing its verification of military capabilities – *vérification des caractéristiques militaires* (VCM) – before being admitted into active service. This process focuses on establishing that a vessel can fulfil the requirements that are expected of it; for example that it can integrate successfully with other units and that the reliability of its equipment is as anticipated. For the first vessel of a class, operating procedures and limits on use have to be specified and documented. As previously noted, an extended deployment navigating through different geographical and climatic zones is organised. The navy has not communicated the regions visited or the submarine's ports of call during this phase.

Suffren class crews have benefitted from extensive training at the French Navy's Underwater Navigation School in Toulon before embarking in the boats. The simulators are mounted on jacks to reproduce the trim and list conditions found during underwater operations. *(Lisa Bessodes/Marine Nationale/Défense)*

After admission into active service in June 2022, *Suffren* has been active in supporting France's naval interests. Notably, during the summer of 2023, she made another lengthy deployment that included a passage through the Suez Canal and a port call at Abu Dhabi. The dry deck shelter was fitted at this time.

As noted in Table 3.3.2, considerable progress is now being made with the rest of the programme. The second member of the class, *Duguay Trouin*, was delivered in July 2023, subsequently making a port call in the French Antilles during her long cruise. This was followed by admission into active service on 4 April 2024. Shortly after, on 18 April, it was announced that a synchronised MdCN firing had taken place involving the FREMM frigate *Aquitaine* and one of the SSNs – likely *Duguay Trouin* – to achieve a coordinated strike on a target located on a DGA test range. This was an important demonstration of the *Marine Nationale*'s ability to coordinate long-distance strikes on a single target using different vessels.

Like *Suffren*, *Duguay Trouin* is homeported at Toulon. The other four submarines in the class will also be based there in due course. Significant infrastructure work has been carried out at the naval base to support the class, including enhancements to piers and docking facilities. Docking facilities include arrangements for nuclear refuelling to be carried out as required.

The third member of the class, *Tourville*, left the Laubeuf Hall in July 2023 in preparation for transfer to the shiplift. Her nuclear reactor went live on 24 April 2024 and she is expected to commence

The support vessel *Garonne* pictured operating with *Suffren* during the course of the submarine's extended trials that culminated in her being accepted into operational service in June 2022. Her sister *Duguay-Trouin* is now also in service and the third member of the *Suffren* class, *Tourville*, is scheduled to commence sea trials soon. *(Benjamin Papin/Marine Nationale/Défense)*

sea trials during the summer of 2024. The other three *Suffren* class submarines are at various stages of construction at Cherbourg, with the last expected to enter service by the end of the current decade.

CONCLUDING WORDS

The words of Captain Cyril, the Marine Nationale's programme officer for the *Suffren* class, make a fitting conclusion to this chapter.[11] He said, 'With the *Suffren* class, France has made a significant step, which is like passing from primary school to high school. France is now in a very exclusive club of navies operating nuclear-powered submarines that are fitted with dry deck shelters and swimmer delivery vehicles, and that are able to fire cruise missiles while submerged.' He added, 'I have commanded two *Rubis* class submarines, and a *Le Triomphant* class strategic submarine. The *Suffren* is the boat that I have always dreamed about commanding.'

Notes

1. The *Marine Nationale*'s process of bringing a new warship into operation involves an additional series of trials after delivery to the navy that typically conclude with a lengthy cruise (*un déploiement de longue durée*) to 'shake down' the vessel's equipment prior to the unit being declared operational (*admis au service actif*).

2. It is worth noting that Cherbourg also sees the nuclear submarines constructed at the yard returned to the site for final decommissioning. The submarine section containing the nuclear plant is cut out for storage and separate treatment whilst the rest of the boat is then broken up for recycling.

3. These are *Émeraude, Améthyste* and *Perle*.

4. The *Rubis* class have undergone progressive modernisation since first entering service. In addition to combat system upgrades, the first four boats were reconfigured with a new hull design as part of the AMÉTHYSTE acoustic silencing programme. The final two boats were completed to this revised configuration.

5. These studies considered the possibility of collaboration with the British Royal Navy on the next generation, an idea that was abandoned because of different project requirements and timescales. The United Kingdom subsequently ordered its first batch of *Astute* class submarines in 1997.

6. The final, detailed design review was completed in January 2010, when the first boats of the class were already under construction.

7. TechnicAtome is a specialist designer and producer of compact nuclear reactors, largely for naval use. Just over 50 percent of its shares are directly owned by the French state, with the CEA and Naval Group being the other major shareholders.

8. Significant efforts have been made to reduce turbulence caused by the design's hull and to minimise hydrodynamic nose through computer simulation and model testing. This included trials with large scale, 5–6m-long models at the DGA's Lac de Castillon in south-east France.

9. SYCOBS was initially installed aboard strategic sub-marines during refits. It is currently in its third generation 3.0 version and further development is ongoing.

10. Maximum weapons capacity is therefore twenty-four if the tubes are also pre-loaded.

11. The Captain's full name was not disclosed for security reasons. The author would also like to thank Audrey Perret and Aspirant Noémie Schnoller of the *Marine Nationale*'s SIRPA Marine, Faiza Zaroual of Naval Group and Côme Cornuat of the DGA for their help with the production of this chapter.

4.1 TECHNOLOGICAL REVIEW

Author:
David Hobbs

WORLD NAVAL AVIATION

A Review of Recent Developments

A dominant emerging theme in world naval aviation, as elsewhere in the broader military sphere, is the significance of uncrewed aerial vehicles (UAVs). Notably, conflicts in Ukraine and across the Middle East have seen further increases in the use of uncrewed combat air vehicles (UCAVs) of many different sizes and capabilities as primary offensive weapons. Target acquisition and control have been facilitated by the rapid growth and application of digital technologies, especially artificial intelligence, many of them derived from the private sector. However, different priorities are seemingly emerging between the major navies. For example, the US Navy (USN) is taking a cautious approach to carrier-borne UAV acquisition, whilst the British Royal Navy (RN) is openly embracing new technologies as a means of increasing mass and capability within a limited budget. Given that UAVs are making the headlines as a major contemporary focus of naval warfare, this review supplements its normal geographic coverage with a look at both progress and changing attitudes to uncrewed aviation since the first, 2010, edition of *World Naval Review*.

F-35B strike fighters pictured operating from the Royal Navy aircraft carrier *Queen Elizabeth* in August 2021. The hovering jet – F35B ZM152 (BK-18) – was subsequently lost on 17 November 2021 in an accident that revealed deficiencies in the availability of sufficiently-trained maintenance personnel to support sustained F-35B operations at sea. *(Crown Copyright 2021)*

UNITED KINGDOM: ROYAL NAVY

Loss of F-35B Strike Fighter ZM 152: The full Board of Enquiry report into the loss of an F-35B from *Queen Elizabeth* on 17 November 2021 during the course of the CSG-21 deployment, otherwise known as Operation 'Fortis', was published on 10 August 2023.[1] The report identified issues about the operation of the type within a joint force organisation which has yet to produce a carrier-borne strike fighter squadron that is as effective and efficient as possible. The direct cause of the loss was due to the jet's engine failing to generate sufficient take-

off thrust because an intake blank had been left in the port intake duct; one of a number of items used to protect aircraft on deck known collectively as 'red gear'. Two separate inspections had failed to notice the blank, and there was no effective procedure in place to ensure the removal of all red gear before flight. The Board's damning conclusion was that a fundamental broader factor in the combination of minor errors that led to the loss of a serviceable aircraft was a lack of people with the necessary carrier operating experience within the embarked Royal Air Force (RAF) 617 Squadron, even towards the end of the CSG-21 deployment.[2]

US Marines with Marine Fighter Attack Squadron 211 (VMFA-211) pictured during the F-35B squadron's deployment aboard the Royal Navy aircraft carrier *Queen Elizabeth*. The maintenance support provided for the embarked American unit was on a more effective scale than that of its British 617 Squadron counterpart. *(US Navy)*

617 Squadron had embarked with 113 maintenance personnel for its eight aircraft. To achieve even this modest number, fifteen had been taken from the training squadron (207 Squadron) at Marham and a further fourteen had joined directly from Phase 2B training and lacked any operational experience.[3] Only a little over half of the squadron's technicians had ever operated from an aircraft carrier before and nearly a quarter had never completed the Embarked Forces Sea Survival Course (EFSSC), which is supposed to be a mandatory qualification for service at sea. Unlike RN aircraft technicians, their RAF counterparts had no flight line servicing qualification as part of their Phase 2B training and those that could not be fitted into the limited spaces available on RN courses had to carry out supervised on-the-job training once embarked, placing increased demands on the limited number of experienced personnel. The restrictions placed on the whole ship's company after an outbreak of Covid increased the level of fatigue still further and a high turnover of people made the situation even worse. There had been frequent changes in 617 Squadron's senior engineering officer in the lead up to CSG-21, whilst the senior warrant officer had only joined relatively recently and had never been to sea before. Out of the four key engineering management positions, only one person had completed more than one of the carrier work-up embarkations. Twelve technicians had to be repatriated without replacement during CSG-21 for personal or health reasons, whilst the report revealed other shortcomings which added up an unfortunate lack of familiarity with carrier operations.

The other F-35B unit embarked in *Queen Elizabeth* for CSG-21 provides an interesting contrast. The US Marine Corps' (USMC's) Marine Fighter Attack Squadron 211 (VMFA-211) embarked with 255 marines to support its ten F-35Bs, effectively 25 personnel per jet, contrasting with 617 Squadron's initial 14. If one accepts that the USMC used its greater operational experience to determine the technical support needed for sustained operations at sea, the British squadron began the deployment 44 percent understrength, even before the twelve were repatriated. It is also notable that, prior to CSG-21, *Queen Elizabeth* took part in Exercise 'Strike Warrior' during which it was found that 617 Squadron lacked sufficient technicians to carry out flying operations and aircraft rectification concurrently. Interestingly, it was only discovered due to the experience of CSG-21 that sustained carrier operations needed a larger engineering workforce compared to land-based operations. The officer responsible for the investigation into the F-35B's loss, Air Marshal Steve Shell RAF, concluded that the Lightning Force 'had not yet

809 Naval Air Squadron (NAS), the second operational F-35B Lightning squadron, was stood up on 8 December 2023. This photograph shows a F-35B painted in squadron colours to mark the event. *(Crown Copyright 2023)*

On 5 September 2023, a fixed-wing uncrewed aircraft was landed aboard *Prince of Wales* in a groundbreaking demonstration of drone technology. The aircraft – a W Autonomous Systems HCMC – is reportedly the first fixed-wing UAV to land and then take off from a British aircraft carrier. *(Crown Copyright 2023)*

reached the critical mass at which experience can be retained' and that, in the interim, it had to be recognised that there would be trade-offs between readiness, growth and safety.

The experience arguably reflects the broader problem that the Joint F-35B Force faces in that it is expected to perform two disparate, highly specialised roles concurrently. There is, thus, a constant tension between the need to generate a unit trained for extended carrier operations while also carrying out different mission profiles as part of a land-based tactical air force. The successful operation of a carrier air wing requires a focused mindset; the ship's company and squadrons must take every chance to work together as a team at sea. Alarmingly, however, in 2022 Joint Force F-35Bs were embarked in RN carriers for just 18 days. This reflects the previous experience of Joint Force Harrier, which also struggled because its squadrons were committed to operations ashore in Afghanistan and had only a few days a year left for embarkation. This was used mostly for 'ab initio' deck landing training, with no scope for the continuous, integrated tactical work a navy needs. The USN's aviation personnel have carrier operations in their DNA and strive to be the best they can be. The RN deserves no less.

Fixed-Wing Aircraft Developments: It is not all bad news. A notable development occurred in December 2023, with the commissioning of 809 Naval Air Squadron (NAS), the second operational Lightning squadron. Originally announced in 2013, this unit was to have been formed in April 2023 but manpower issues caused delays. It is due to achieve operational status in December 2024, with full operational capability for United Kingdom's carrier strike force scheduled for the following year. Whilst its formation restores one of the most historic Fleet Air Arm unit identities, it is another jointly-manned squadron, based at RAF Marham and operated in the same way as 617 Squadron with a mix of RN and RAF personnel.

Other potential capability enhancements continued to be studied. Colonel Phil Kelly, Royal Marines – the head of carrier strike and maritime aviation within the RN Develop Directorate – informed the Combined Naval Event 2023 conference at Farnborough that the RN is exploring the widespread deployment of uncrewed aircraft across the fleet – but with specific emphasis on carriers – as part of its Future Maritime Aviation Force (FMAF) vision.[4] One element, Project 'Ark Royal', is examining the phased introduction of aircraft launch and recovery systems to allow the operation of high-performance uncrewed aerial vehicles, together with the potential to operate crewed fixed-wing aircraft. The plan would be to spread cost and improve capability in incremental steps, beginning with an increase in the available deck run for uncrewed aircraft to take off. A move to short take-off but arrested recovery (STOBAR) would follow, allowing the operation of the large fixed-wing uncrewed air system that is identified as Project 'Vixen' within the FMAF. Finally, an assisted launch system capable of launching heavy fixed-wing aircraft would be installed. It seems that several assisted launch and recovery options have already been reviewed, including the Electromagnetic Aircraft Launch System (EMALS) and Advanced Arrester Gear (AAG) used aboard the USN *Ford* (CVN-78) class carriers and a development of the Electro-Magnetic Kinetic Induction Technology Demonstrator developed by GE Vernova Power Conversion in the United Kingdom. At present Develop Directorate is funding development and gathering evidence ready for the 2025 Integrated Defence Review.

A General Atomics Mojave UAV takes off from the flight deck of *Prince of Wales* in November 2023 during the aircraft carrier's 'Westlant 23' trials programme off the United States' eastern coast. The Mojave is the largest uncrewed aircraft yet launched from or recovered to a RN carrier. *(Crown Copyright 2023)*

Prince of Wales emerged from nine months of engineering repairs and capability enhancement in the second half of 2023, subsequently sailing for her delayed 'Westlant 23' trials programme off the United States' eastern seaboard. Whilst still operating off the Cornish coast on 5 September 2023, a fixed-wing uncrewed aircraft was landed aboard in a groundbreaking demonstration of drone technology. A W Autonomous Systems HCMC – capable of carrying a 100kg load over 620 nautical miles – flew from Predannack, Royal Naval Air Station (RNAS) Culdrose's satellite airfield in Cornwall, to deliver a symbolic payload before being launched for the return flight. Subsequently, in November, *Prince of Wales* carried out further uncrewed aircraft trials off the United States, this time with a General Atomics Mojave. Developed from the Reaper and Grey Eagle series of uncrewed aerial systems, the Mojave has a wingspan of 16m, a maximum take-of weight of 3.2 tonnes and a maximum endurance in excess of 25 hours. It can carry a wide range of weapons and sensors. The Mojave is the largest uncrewed aircraft yet launched from or recovered to a RN carrier. Rear Admiral James Parkin, Director Develop, described the trial as heralding '… a new dawn in how we conduct maritime aviation and another exciting step in the evolution of the RN carrier strike group into a mixed crewed and uncrewed fighting force'.[5]

In addition to progressing uncrewed operations, *Prince of Wales* also carried out landings to clear a range of USMC and US Coast Guard aircraft to operate from the *Queen Elizabeth* class. Another major aim of the deployment was to expand the F-35B's operating envelope. Designated as Development Test Phase 3 (DT-3), this saw aircraft of the F-35 Integrated Test Force based at Naval Air Station (NAS) Patuxent River carry out sorties with full internal and external loads of dummy weapons in a variety of weather conditions. Key tests included shipborne rolling vertical landings (SRVLs), in which the aircraft performs a running landing using a combination of wing lift and angled engine thrust. The technique allows recovery at greater weights than a vertical landing and means that the aircraft can land with a greater weight of unused weapons and fuel. It does, however, rely on using brakes to stop; on a wet deck at night this could be 'exciting' both for deck crews and the pilot. Sixty SRVLs were carried out in total; ten at night. Other trials included nearly 150 take-offs in various weather conditions and sea states during what was regarded as a highly successful deployment.

Queen Elizabeth's last 12 months have been more mixed. In February 2024, the carrier was due to sail to participate in the major NATO exercise 'Steadfast Defender 24' when pre-sailing checks revealed corrosion in one of the starboard propeller shaft couplings. This was described by the RN as a 'wear and tear' issue and completely unrelated to the problems found in *Prince of Wales* in 2022. However, it was deemed prudent to replace *Queen Elizabeth* with

The Royal Navy aircraft carrier *Prince of Wales* had to stand in for her sister *Queen Elizabeth* at short notice to lead the Royal Navy's carrier strike group during NATO Exercise 'Steadfast Defender 24' after corrosion was observed in one of the latter's shaft lines. Here F-35B strike fighters, as well as Merlin and Wildcat helicopters, are seen arrayed on *Prince of Wales*'s deck on 24 February 2024 as the strike group assembled. *(Crown Copyright 2024)*

Prince of Wales and carry out repairs. The latter had been at 30 days' notice preparing for a maintenance period but her ship's company did a remarkable job getting her ready for sea in just eight

Rotorcraft: In July 2023 the Crowsnest airborne surveillance and control system (ASaC) finally achieved initial operating capability (IOC) after considerable delay. Commander Chris Jones RN, commanding officer of 824 NAS, briefed the 'Anyface' Association of AEW/ASaC veterans in March 2024 that IOC was the positive outcome of years of hard work by engineers, aircrew and support staff. A new software 'drop' on the system had been delivered in time for aircrew to use it from *Queen Elizabeth* during the autumn CSG-23 (Operation 'Firedrake') deployment, in which Crowsnest Merlins achieved the most significant tactical integration of ASaC to date. They used the latest generation of Link 16 to share their situational awareness picture with ships and aircraft in live North Atlantic operations. Autumn 2023 also saw the return of live fighter control, using a Merlin ASaC as a controlling unit over the North Sea. During Exercise 'Strike Warrior', ASaC observers provided fighter control for Typhoons and F-35s in a series of complex situations against simulated aggressor forces. Whilst some might think that such control was no longer needed because of the mass of data available in contemporary aircraft, the capability was warmly received by pilots who debriefed that it helped them to focus on the essential aim. ASaC capability has at last taken a significant step forward and further enhancements are in train before full operating capability is achieved.

Meanwhile, the Wildcat HMA 2 sea control helicopter is progressing towards providing a mature capability. Although their Martlet and Sea Venom missile systems will not achieve full operational capability until 2025–2026, the Operational Advantage Centre (Maritime Warfare) – the lead RN organisation for tactical development – carried out extensive Martlet firing trials under a series of tests known as 'Triton's Arrow' in mid-2023. Using an 815 NAS Wildcat and involving both 744 and 825 NAS in support roles together with industry partners QinetiQ and Thales, the trials were intended to test the weapon system to its limits. Martlet was evaluated in a variety of circumstances, including engagements against small, fast-moving surface targets and a successful firing against an airborne target. The air-to-air firing was against a Banshee drone, confirming the Wildcat's ability to engage targets above, on and under the sea surface with its various weapon loads. By late 2023, Wildcats had amassed over 40,000 flying hours since entering service in 2015 and deployed on embarked operations around the world. Development continues, notably the installation of NATO Link 16 communications to improve access to digital information and enhance the helicopter's ability to interface with uncrewed systems.[6]

The RN is also experimenting with uncrewed rotorcraft. In September, BAE Systems and Malloy Aeronautics demonstrated the capacity of their T-600 heavy-lift uncrewed air system – an electrically-powered demonstrator capable of VTOL – to carry an inert Stingray torpedo during NATO Exercise REPMUS (Robotic Experimentation and Prototyping with Maritime Uncrewed Systems) 2023. The T-600 is being used to validate logistics resupply and anti-submarine warfare capabilities in advance of the improved T-650, which will offer a larger, 300kg payload and a rapid reconfiguration capacity. The RN also plan to operate the Peregrine (Schiebel S-100) miniature surveillance helicopter from January 2025.

The last year has also seen developments in RN amphibious operations. The Littoral Response Group (South) – LRG(S) – finally deployed East of Suez in 2024 after being held in the Eastern Mediterranean for a considerable time following the outbreak of the conflict between Hamas and Israel. It comprises the Royal Fleet Auxiliary (RFA) vessels *Argus* and *Lyme Bay*, with three Merlin HC 4 helicopters of 845 NAS embarked in the former. Whilst standing ready to evacuate British nationals from the region if necessary, the opportunity was taken to carry out exercises with regional allies. In January 2024 *Lyme Bay* delivered over 80 tonnes of humanitarian aid for Gaza into Port Said in Egypt. By late March 2024 the LRG had arrived in Chennai for a maintenance period in an Indian shipyard, after which a number of regional exercises are planned. In addition to her role as a helicopter carrier, *Argus* is

The Wildcat HMA 2 sea control helicopter is progressing towards providing a mature capability. This photograph shows nighttime maintenance being performed on a Wildcat assigned to the Type 45 destroyer *Dragon* during a deployment in the Black Sea in late 2021. *(Crown Copyright 2021)*

also a Level 3 Primary Casualty Receiving Ship equipped with advanced medical facilities.

The ability of the Merlin HC 4 to land LRG strike groups has been significantly enhanced by expanding the type's Ship Helicopter Operating Limits (SHOL). Since the Commando Helicopter Force (CHF) first received Merlins in 2016 they have operated largely within the SHOL released for the type's predecessor, the smaller and lighter Sea King HC 4. However, the new emphasis on raiding operations led to a SHOL trial being carried out in *Albion* during 2023, which was aimed at increasing the aircraft's capabilities to the maximum. Ship and aircraft were instrumented to monitor real-time performance and the Merlin was fitted with ballast, which was increased incrementally to study performance at various weights. The data gathered allowed the trials team to redefine the limits of the flight envelope, taking into account the combination of power required, wind over the deck and the turbulence encountered from the ship's superstructure to produce a new SHOL that still allows safe launch and recovery within the Merlin's engine and transmission limits. Ten days of tests included 350 deck landings under a variety of conditions including heavy landings facing forward into wind and through 360 degrees over the deck, running landings and demonstration of the type's ability to carry out heavy, limited-power recoveries safely. The expanded SHOL allows the Merlin HC 4 to carry up to twelve more marines or fuel for an extra two hours' flight. The latter could mean deeper penetration into hostile territory if necessary. Lieutenant Commander Tom Lofthouse RN, the Trial Detachment Commander, described the results as a 'game-changing' increase in CHF lift and a significant contribution to the growth of LRG capability.

UNITED STATES: USN AND USMC

Aircraft Carrier Acquisition and Deployment: The USN carrier fleet remains under extreme pressure. Delays to the completion of new ships and to the refuelling and complex overhaul (RCOH) of older hulls are responsible for the problem. Huntingdon Ingalls Industries' (HII's) shipbuilding facility at Newport News has more work in progress than at any time in the past 40 years. This includes new carrier construction, RCOH activity, and work on

A C-2A Greyhound from the 'Rawhides' of Fleet Logistics Support Squadron 40 (VRC-40) makes an arrested landing aboard *Gerald R. Ford* (CVN-78) on 15 December 2023. The temporary grounding of the fleet's CMV-22B Osprey logistics aircraft, which are scheduled to replace the Greyhounds, has made the veteran aircraft's sunset period particularly busy. *(US Navy)*

both the *Virginia* (SSN-774) and *Columbia* (SSBN-826) class submarine programmes. To alleviate some of the strain, the yard is outsourcing work on carrier hull construction to a facility at Hampton Roads owned by Fairlead, a private shipbuilding and repair business. The company has seized the opportunity to expand its operations and, in turn, has been rewarded with industrial base funds from the government. The company is set to build 10 percent of the steel structure of the carrier *Enterprise* (CVN-80), third ship in the *Ford* (CVN-78) carrier class, directly benefiting both the carrier and submarine programmes.[7]

Despite this initiative, USN FY2025 budget documents published in March 2024 revealed that *Enterprise* will now be delivered in September 2029; a year and a half later than previously planned. Workforce shortages, wider supply chain issues and the impact of the pandemic have all been referenced as reasons for the delay. The same documents revealed that the USN plans to postpone procurement of the future CVN-82 from 2028 to 2030, partly because of delays to previous ships. Predictably, the plan has been criticised by HII and the supplier Aircraft Carrier Industrial Base Coalition (ACIBC) as disrupting the production cycle. The USN is still considering a block buy of both CVN-82 and CVN-83 following a similar arrangement for *Enterprise* and *Doris Miller* (CVN-81) that is believed to have saved as much as US$4bn.[8] At the other end of the lifespan spectrum, the USN has established a new Nuclear-Powered Aircraft Carrier (CVN) Inactivation and Disposal Program Office (PMS 368), which has assumed responsibility for final disposal of the previous *Enterprise* (CVN-65). It is also tasked with preparing for the ultimate disposal of the *Nimitz* (CVN-68) and, presumably ultimately, *Ford* classes; a programme that is expected to last for over 100 years and cost billions of dollars. *Enterprise*'s disposal is regarded as being of particular importance since it provides a template for the later ships.[9]

Despite plans to emphasise carrier operations in the Indo-Pacific to counter China, events in the Middle East have inevitably had a major impact on the USN's carriers over the past year. The first global deployment of the new *Gerald R. Ford* was particularly affected. Having departed Newport News in May 2023 with Carrier Air Wing (CVW-8) for a supposed six-month deployment, the carrier was deployed to the Eastern Mediterranean from a position off Italy after Hamas' 7 October attacks on Israel to act as a deterrent against the involvement of Iran and its allies in the conflict. Although scheduled to be relieved by *Dwight D Eisenhower* (CVN-69), she remained in the Mediterranean after her replacement arrived in the region. With *Eisenhower* subsequently occupied in the Red Sea countering Houthi rebel drone attacks on commercial shipping from Yemen, *Ford*'s deployment was ultimately extended on three occasions before her final return to her homeport on 17 January 2024 after 239 days at sea. Ongoing instability in both Europe and the Middle East is likely to keep the US Navy's carrier force busy into 2025.

In November 2023 the crash of a US Air Force special operations CV-22B Osprey tilt-rotor based in Japan, killing all eight onboard, significantly disrupted USN and USMC use of the type. On 6 December, the US Armed Forces grounded all Osprey variants, including the new CMV-22B fleet logistics aircraft and the USMC's MV-22B. The decision forced the navy to surge its last remaining squadron operating fixed-wing C-2A Greyhound aircraft, the east coast-based Fleet Logistics Support Squadron 40 (VRC-40), to cover the gap. Fortunately the Navy still had fifteen of the 'legacy' Greyhounds available to support carrier onboard deliveries to ships operating in both the USN's 5th and 7th Fleets despite the retirement of the last west coast-based Greyhound unit, VRC-30, on 8 December 2023. Plans to finally retire the C-2 in 2026 remain unaltered, however, and the problem appeared to have been resolved in March 2024 when Naval Air Systems Command (NAVAIR) cleared USN and USMC Ospreys to resume flying operations.

Table 4.1.1: US NAVY PLANNED AIRCRAFT PROCUREMENT: FY2024–FY2029

TYPE	MISSION	FY2024 AUTHORISED[1]	FY2025 REQUESTED	FY2026 PLANNED	FY2027 PLANNED	FY2028 PLANNED	FY2029 PLANNED	FYDP[2] PLANNED
Fixed Wing (Carrier Based)								
F-35B Lightning II JSF	Strike Fighter (STOVL)	16 (16)	13	13	17	20	19	82
F-35C Lightning II JSF	Strike Fighter (CV)	19 (19)	13	14	17	14	24	82
E-2D Advanced Hawkeye	Surveillance/Control	0 (2)	0	0	0	0	0	0
Fixed Wing (Land Based)								
P-8A Poseidon	Maritime Patrol	0 (10)	0	0	0	0	0	0
KC-130J Hercules	Tanker	2 (3)	0	0	0	0	1	1
E-XX (TACAMO)[3]	Communications	0 (0)	0	0	0	6	6	12
T-45 Replacement[4]	Training	0 (0)	0	10	12	12	12	46
T-54A[5]	Training	26 (26)	27	0	0	0	0	27
Rotary Wing								
CH-53K King Stallion	Heavy-Lift	15 (15)	19	18	18	20	21	96
C/MV-22/B Osprey	Transport	0 (5)	0	0	0	0	0	0
Unmanned Aerial Vehicles								
MQ-25 Stingray	Refuelling	3 (0)	3	3	3	5	7	21
MQ-4C Triton	Maritime Patrol	2 (2)	0	0	0	0	0	0
MQ-9A Reaper	Surveillance/Strike	5 (5)	0	0	0	0	0	0
Totals FY2025: [Totals FY 2024]		N/A [88 (103)]	75 [94]	58 [72]	67 [75]	77 [81]	90 [N/A]	367 [410 (425)]

Notes:

1. The first set of FY2024 numbers reflect aircraft requirements set out in the Biden Administration's Presidential Budget Request of March 2023; figures in brackets reflect numbers actually funded in the Further Consolidated Appropriations Act signed into law on 23 March 2024. As is frequently the case, the US Congress added material numbers of aircraft over the original request.
2. Total five-year FYDP (Future Years Defense Program) numbers for FY2025–29 as at time of the FY2025 Presidential Budget Request.
3. E-XX TACAMO (Take Charge And Move Out) is a planned replacement for the E-6B Mercury aircraft that form part of the United States' system of survivable communications links that are used to maintain communications between decision-makers and the triad of strategic weapon delivery systems. It will be based on a C-130J Hercules variant.
4. Refers to replacement of the T-45 Goshawk training aircraft. Unlike the current aircraft, the replacement will reportedly only be required to perform touch-and-go landings on the US Navy's aircraft carriers.
5. The T-54A is the replacement for the T-44 Pegasus twin-engine turboprop trainer. Both are part of the King Air series of aircraft.

Aircraft Procurement: The future plans for USN and USMC aircraft procurement set out in the FY2025 Department of the Navy Presidential Budget request are summarised in Table 4.1.1. Delays in the US budgetary approvals process meant that they were published before agreement of the previous, FY2024 appropriations that were finally signed into law towards the end of March 2024. As usual, the approved FY2024 numbers included a number of additional aircraft over the budget request, including ten P-8A Poseidon maritime domain awareness aircraft, five CMV-22B carrier logistics aircraft and two E-2D Advanced Hawkeye airborne early warning (AEW) aircraft. These three additions slightly extended programmes that would have otherwise ended.

The FY2025 request will also cease acquisitions of the MQ-4C Triton and MQ-9A Reaper unmanned aerial vehicles. The MQ-4C programme – devised to provide a persistent maritime intelligence, surveillance, reconnaissance and targeting (MISR-T) capability to complement the P-8A Poseidon – was initially intended to extend to seventy aircraft but actual production will now be only twenty-seven, including five developmental airframes. This partly reflects a decision taken to reduce the surveillance orbits the type will carry out from five to three. Meanwhile, MQ-4Cs of Unmanned Patrol Squadron 19 (VUP-19) have returned to Guam for the squadron's second operational deployment. The type reached IOC on 3 August 2023 and has received significant updates, including an improved sensor suite, on the basis of lessons learned from the first deployment. In March 2024, a detachment from VUP-19 also commenced operations from NAS Sigonella near Naples for the first time.[10]

Although procurement of F/A-18 E/F Super Hornets ended in FY2023, it was only in late March 2024 that the USN finally announced a US$1.1bn contract modification with Boeing for purchase of the final batch, all in Block III configuration. The specific breakdown is for ten F/A-18Fs in Lot 46 plus two F/A-18Fs and five F/A-18Es in Lot 47. The first of these is expected to be delivered in 2026 and the last in 2027, after which the production line will close. A crucial part of the contract negotiation was the technical data package for the type's post-production sustainment. NAVAIR expects the Super

A US Navy MQ-4C Triton assigned to Unmanned Patrol Squadron 19 (VUP-19) prepares to take off from Marine Corps Air Station (MCAS) Iwakuni in Japan on 5 October 2022. The uncrewed surveillance aircraft achieved IOC in August 2023 but procurement of the type has now ended at levels far lower than initially envisaged. *(US Navy)*

Although the final order for US Navy Super Hornet strike fighters was placed in March 2024, the type will remain in the US Navy inventory for decades to come. Here a F/A-18F Super Hornet from Strike Fighter Squadron 103 (VFA-103) performs a touch-and-go landing aboard the *Nimitz* class aircraft carrier *George Washington* (CVN-73) on 6 December 2023. *(US Navy)*

Hornet to remain the predominant aircraft in carrier air wings into the 2040s when it is to be replaced by the future F/A-XX. Apparently, arguments with Boeing over the final unit cost of these aircraft, as well as negotiations over the rights to the technical data package, were the cause of the delay. One consequence was a reduction in the number of jets ordered compared with the twenty that had previously been approved.

The F/A-XX will form the focal point of a potential family of crewed and uncrewed air systems known as Next Generation Air Dominance (NGAD). Details of the F/A-XX programme remain a closely-guarded secret but the FY2024 budget request included more than US$1.5bn for its development. F/A-XX is also associated with an even more secretive project known as 'Link Plumeria', which possibly forms part of the wider proposed NGAD family. In spite of the F/A-XX's importance, the most recent FY2025 request envisages spending being reduced to just US$454m as part of a rephrasing of expenditure across the five year, Future Years Defence Program to prioritise shorter term readiness.[11]

The F-35 programme continues to dominate current procurement. Despite being a more than 20-year-old design, ongoing F-35 development still attracts criticism for its failure to deliver on time and meet cost estimates. Technology Refresher 3 (TR-3) has been singled out for especial criticism. This is a combination of hardware and software intended to give better displays, processing speed and computer memory but which is suffering an 18-month delay in delivery and a US$1bn cost overrun. Lieutenant General Michael Schmidt, the Program Executive Officer, briefed a House of Representatives subcommittee in December 2023 that there had been a history of failing to deliver software with new hardware because laboratories had proved unable to replicate what would happen when the aircraft is in flight at the start of testing. Jon Ludwigson, Director of Contracting and National Security Acquisition at the US General Accountability Office (GAO), provided written testimony that part of the problem was that there are only seven aircraft available to test both TR-3 and Block 4 modernisation upgrades. There is acceptance of this problem and allocation of seven further aircraft to test Block 4 capabilities is planned. Ludwigson also noted that it was difficult to form a clear picture of how new capabilities intended for the F-35 were generated and costed, with planned Block 4 capabilities increasing from an initial sixty-six to an estimate of eighty with a substantial rise in cost. Although the F-35 was finally cleared for full rate production in March 2024, it seems apparent that problems associated with development of the aircraft's software will be an ongoing issue throughout its service life.[12]

US Marine Corps Aviation: With some 348 MV-22B Osprey tiltrotors in service across 15 active and two reserve squadrons, the USMC was impacted on a far larger scale than the USN as a result of the type's grounding following the fatal crash in November 2023 referenced above. Whilst other helicopter types such as the CH-53E heavy lift helicopter were used to plug the gap, this workaround will inevitably have caused strain across the USMC's aviation fleet. The subsequent lifting of the Osprey's grounding mandate on 8 March 2024 might have been influenced by this backdrop. Press reports noted that, whilst there was very high confidence in which component had failed and how it had failed, it had not yet been established why this had happened. The Osprey has previously suffered from a series of clutch malfunctions but the latest incident was unrelated to these problems.[13]

Meanwhile, progress is being achieved in the construction of large-deck amphibious assault ships. In November 2023, HII received an advanced procurement contract valued at US$130m for long-lead items for LHA 10, the fifth member of the *America* (LHA-6) class. The vessel was subsequently assigned the name *Helmand Province* in May 2024. Like her two immediate Flight 1 predecessors, she will be built with a well deck capable of handling, inter alia, two landing craft air cushion (LCACs). This is in contrast to the first two, Flight 0, members of the class, which were built without well decks to provide extra space for fuel, ammunition and other logistics to prioritise aviation assets. In an era when US Navy and Marine Corps thinking is dominated by the development of distributed operations, it is difficult to understand how the well deck in the Flight 1 design outweighs the advantages of enhanced aviation support in the earlier ships. However, work is already underway on the two initial Flight 1 iterations, with *Bougainville* (LHA-8) launched in September 2023 and the keel of *Fallujah* (LHA-9) laid the same month.

In October 2023 the USMC conducted its first flight of a Kratos XQ-58A Valkyrie UAV from Eglin

A F-35C Lightning II from Strike Fighter Squadron 147 (VFA-147) prepares for take-off aboard the *Nimitz* class aircraft *George Washington* (CVN-73) in May 2024. Although the F-35 is now well established in both USN and USMC service, its development continues to be hindered by software issues. *(US Navy)*

Bougainville (LHA-8), the first of the Flight 1 *America* class amphibious assault ships, pictured in the course of float-out at Huntington Ingalls Industries' Ingalls Shipbuilding yard on 30 September 2023. In contrast to the previous two, Flight 0, iterations of the type, she sacrifices some aviation facilities for a well deck. *(Huntington Ingalls Industries)*

US Marines with Marine Unmanned Aerial Vehicle Training Squadron 2 (VMUT-2) conduct familiarisation training with a MQ-9A Reaper UAV at Marine Corps Air Station Cherry Point, North Carolina on 11 April 2024. The USMC's aviation community appears to be adopting uncrewed aircraft more quickly than its USN counterpart, with the MQ-9A achieving IOC with the corps in August 2023. *(US Marine Corps)*

Air Force Base, Florida, with support from the USN and USAF. Further flights evaluated the type's ability to conduct ISR, electronic support for manned platforms, assistance to combat air patrols, and other crewed/uncrewed teaming possibilities. The tests formed part of a wider USMC search for a highly autonomous, low-cost, tactical UAV capable of providing agile support for expeditionary operations in austere environments. The XQ-58A can operate without a runway and has a potential range of 3,000 nautical miles with a payload of sensors or weapons. Two are being tested under the Rapid Defence Experimentation Reserve Program, which allows services to test systems already in use in other arenas with an emphasis on the needs of Indo-Pacific operations. The specific USMC evaluation is named as the Penetrating Affordable Autonomous Collaborative Killer Programme (PAACK-P), which seeks to inform requirements for the Marine Air-Ground Task Force Unmanned Aerial System Expeditionary Tactical Aircraft, MUX. The XQ-58As are operated by Marine Unmanned Aerial Vehicle Squadron 3 (VMU-3), which has also reached IOC with the MQ-9A Reaper and has been seen using V-BAT and TRV-50 tactical resupply UAVs during exercises in the Western Pacific.[14]

AUSTRALIA: ROYAL AUSTRALIAN NAVY (RAN)

The previously-planned acquisition of Schiebel S-100 helicopters to meet the first stage or 'block' of the RAN's three-stage Project SEA 129 Phase 5 was quietly cancelled in September 2023. A version of the S-100 has been in service with the RAN since 2016, serving with 822X NAS from 2018. It had reportedly been selected for the expanded requirement because it would deliver IOC 18 months earlier than any competitor. The decision appears to have been taken as part of the wider fallout from Australia's 2023 Defence Strategic Review and leaves the future direction of the AU$1.3bn (c. US$860m) Project SEA 129 Phase 5 open to question. The RAN had planned to acquire three blocks of unarmed maritime drones, with each subsequent block delivering greater capability than its predecessor

A remotely-operated Schiebel Camcopter S-100 from the Royal Australian Navy's 822X Squadron. Plans to acquire more of the type to meet the first part of the three-stage Project SEA 129 Phase 5 were quietly cancelled in September 2023. *(Australian Department of Defence)*

In December 2023 the Australian Naval Institute learned that the forty-five Australian Army and RAN MRH-90 Taipan helicopters which had been retired from service early because they failed to meet operational and maintenance standards were being disassembled and buried rather than sold. These aircraft were intended, inter alia, to operate from Australia's *Canberra* class amphibious assault ships as part of a combined littoral force. The RAN is purchasing additional MH-60R Seahawk helicopters in lieu of its Taipans, whilst the army's helicopters are to be replaced by forty UH-60M Blackhawk helicopters under a AU$S3bn deal.[15]

CHINA: PEOPLE'S LIBERATION ARMY NAVY (PLAN)

By late 2023 defence analysts were observing that the new carrier *Fujian* was being prepared for sea trials, with radar aerials, weapons and other equipment in place. The new warship subsequently departed Shanghai for an initial trials period on 1 May 2024, returning to the Jiangnan shipyard on the 8th of the month.[16] On the basis of experience with the PLAN's previous carriers, it is believed that the trials programme is likely to last about a year and that the ship could, potentially, enter initial operational service in late 2025. Designated Type 003, she is the third Chinese aircraft carrier; by far the largest at 80,000 tonnes and the first to be designed completely in China. Unlike her two predecessors, she is designed to operate aircraft using catapults and arrester wires. The former are similar to the USN's EMALS type but designed in China. Sources differ as to whether the necessary electrical power is produced by an integrated power system or by dedicated generators.

Fujian's sea trials are expected to include initial 'at sea' evaluation of the Shenyang J-15B Flying Shark, a variant of the existing J-15 used aboard China's existing carriers but specifically developed for catapult launch with a nose-tow bar like that fitted to USN aircraft. Trials of the J-15B have been taking place for several years at the PLAN training airfield at Xingcheng in Liaoning province. Both the J-15B and the Xi'an KJ-600 AEW aircraft are likely to be ready for embarkation in *Fujian* from late 2025. US experts have suggested that the KJ-600 is a copy of the USN E-2D Advanced Hawkeye. It has a high-mounted, un-swept wing and is powered by two turboprop engines; there is a quad-fin tail plane, tricycle landing gear and an aft-mounted tail hook. What is believed to be an electronically-scanned array is mounted in a large dorsal radome. Whilst there is therefore an undeniable similarity, the constraints of designing a multi-crew, radar-equipped airframe with twin-engine safety capable of operating from a carrier would inevitably produce a design that could not differ greatly from the E-2D, the latest iteration of a type with the longest production run of any carrier-based aircraft in history. The PLA Navy's KJ-600 is expected to be capable of multi-domain, multi-platform joint connectivity, data transmission and targeting. An article published in the Chinese Government-backed *Global Times* newspaper recently described its ability to network with the J-15 carrier-borne fighter in which it was said to 'form a communications network, establish an information chain, detect and locate target radiation sources and guide the fighter jets to conduct attacks against targets at sea'.[16]

During an annual legislative meeting in Beijing, PLAN political commissar Yuan Huazhi suggested that China was also constructing its fourth carrier, the as yet un-named Type 004. Observing that he had not heard of any technical problems, he said that the ship was on schedule and that the public would soon find out if it would be nuclear-powered.

FRANCE: MARINE NATIONALE

France's sole aircraft carrier *Charles de Gaulle* spent the second half of 2023 undergoing a mid-cycle docking, having entered the Vauban dock at Toulon on 16 May 2023. The docking – which took place between two major refits – encompassed as many as 1,900 though-life support items and more than twenty major modifications, including a hospital refit, replacement of the TACAN air navigation system, renovation of areas dedicated to naval staff and crew living quarters, and replacement of two of the vessel's four seawater distillation systems.[17] Having returned to sea early in 2024, *Charles de Gaulle* subsequently departed Toulon for the Mediterranean Mission 'Ákila' in April that year. During part of this deployment, the French carrier operated under NATO command for the first time.

A Rafale M strike fighter lands on the French aircraft carrier *Charles de Gaulle* during exercises with the US Navy in the Mediterranean in November 2022. Under refit during the second half of 2023, the carrier has now returned to operational service. Meanwhile, the Rafale M looks set to serve with a second fleet following the Indian Navy's decision to acquire the type in July 2023. *(US Navy)*

An Indian Navy MiG-29K multi-role fighter carrying out deck-landing practice on the carrier *Vikramaditya* during dual carrier operations in the Indian Ocean in March 2024. The MiG-29K has been less than successful in Indian Navy service and new French Rafale M aircraft are now being acquired to strengthen the fleet's aviation capabilities. *(Government of India)*

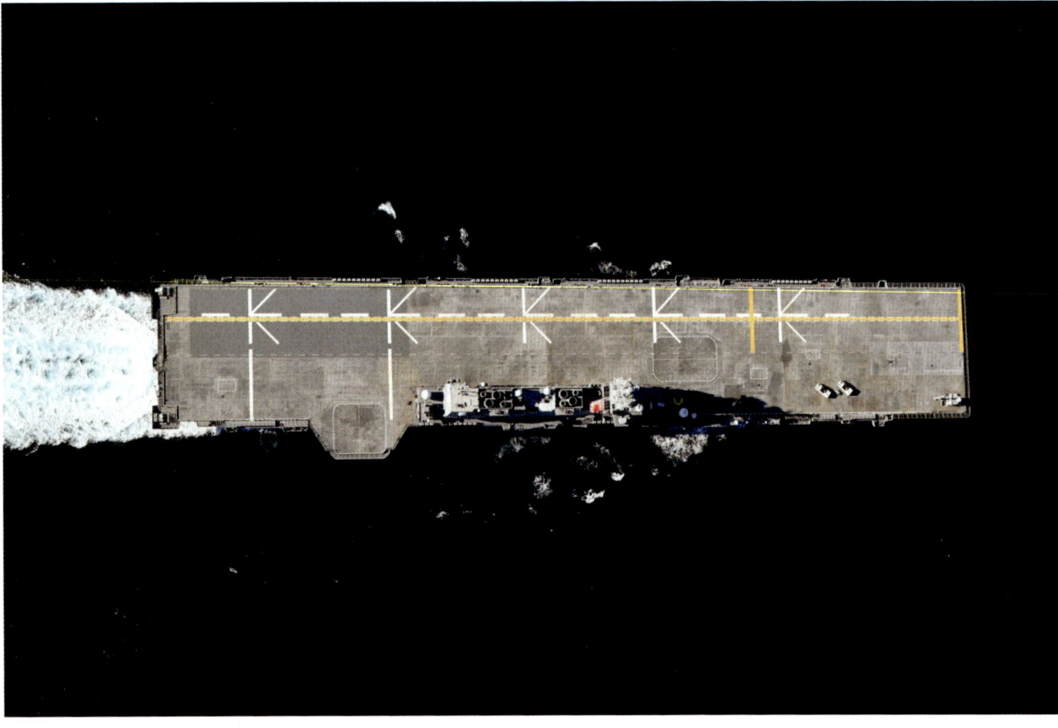

This overhead view of the JMSDF's 'multi-purpose destroyer' *Kaga* was taken in December 2023 following, inter alia, modifications to her bow structure to facilitate future operation of Japanese F-35 strike fighters. *(JMSDF)*

The French carrier strike group centred on *Charles de Gaulle* is set to deploy to the Pacific in late 2024 and will work closely with regional allies including the USA and Japan.

On current plans, *Charles de Gaulle* will be replaced in 2038 by the new *porte-avions de nouvelle génération* (PANG). In April 2024, France's defence procurement agency ordered the first items of long-lead equipment for the new vessel. The order related to the two new K22 nuclear reactors and associated steam generation equipment that will power the next-generation carrier.

INDIA: INDIAN NAVY (IN)

In June 2023 the Indian Navy (IN) carried out its first multiple carrier exercise for many years with more than thirty-five aircraft embarked in *Vikramaditya* and the new, first indigenously-built carrier *Vikrant*. *Vikramaditya* had returned to operational service earlier that year after a refit that had been extended by an onboard fire that had broken out during post-refit trials in July 2022. Further dual carrier operations took place in early 2024. By this time *Vikrant* had reportedly received equipment that had not been installed at the time of her initial commissioning after post-delivery work at builders Cochin Shipyard Limited (CSL).[18]

The IN has a stated goal of acquiring a third carrier to allow sustained operations. It appears to be winning the argument despite opposition from the Indian Air Force and other parts of India's defence establishment.[19] At present, the favoured option appears to be a slightly modified repeat *Vikrant*, although a larger and more capable design equipped with EMALS still has its proponents. CSL is expected to be the shipbuilder of choice regardless of which design is selected. It is already in the course of augmenting its facilities with a new 310m-long dry dock suitable for carrier construction that will be one of the largest in India.

The IN's carrier air wings are set to undergo significant change from the second half of this decade onwards. In July 2023, it was announced that Dassault Aviation's Rafale M had been selected to meet the navy's requirement for new fighter jets, winning out over Boeing's Super Hornet.

Negotiations to conclude the purchase of twenty-six Rafale Ms were still ongoing as of mid-2024, the requirement having been reduced from an initial plan for fifty-seven new aircraft due to cost constraints and, likely, a desire to prefer indigenous equipment in the longer term. India's Aeronautical Development Agency is working on a new Twin-Engine Deck-Based Fighter (TEDBF) design, which is in line with the government's drive for indigenous equipment. If successful, the TEDBF would likely enter operational service in the early 2030s. Other plans for new indigenous aircraft include the long-delayed Utility Helicopters Maritime (UHM) programme for over 100 rotorcraft and production of a naval version of the proposed larger Hindustan Aeronautics Ltd (HAL) indigenous multi-role helicopter.

The first IN MH-60R Seahawk squadron, 334 NAS, was commissioned at INAS Garuda in March 2024. Its helicopters will gradually replace the navy's Westland-built Sea Kings, which have been in service since the 1970s. All twenty-four Seahawks included in the deal are expected to be delivered by the end of 2025. Initial training for their air and ground crews was carried out in America from 2022 onwards. The deal includes the provision of Naval Strike Missile simulators and inert rounds for training but the IN has not yet confirmed that it intends to procure the missile for its Seahawks.

In February 2024 the US State Department approved the potential sale of thirty-one General Atomics MQ-9B UAVs to India. The US$3.9bn deal would reportedly include sixteen SeaGuardian variants for the IN. The SeaGuardian is a maritime variant of the MQ-9 equipped with radar and anti-submarine equipment. If the deal is completed, it will be used to enhance maritime awareness in the Indian Ocean region alongside the P-8I Poseidon. Two of the type have previously been evaluated by the IN under a lease deal concluded in 2020.

JAPAN: JAPAN MARITIME SELF DEFENSE FORCE (JMSDF)

A Japanese delegation led by Captain Tsuyoshi Sato JMSDF embarked in *Prince of Wales* to observe the DT-3 trials previously described, thereby making advance preparations for one of the two JMSDF *Izumo* (DDH-183) class carriers – officially multi-purpose destroyers – to carry out its own trials off the US East Coast in 2025.[20] The JMSDF does not at present have a fighter component within its naval air arm and it anticipated that units of the Japan Air Self Defense Force will be formed to embark in the *Izumo* class. Japan expects to receive its first six F-35B strike fighters during 2024/25 out of a total planned purchase of forty-two, with the first unit due to be formed at Nyutabaru Air Base. The delegation's embarkation in a British carrier is the latest step in the increasingly close working relationship that has developed between the JMSDF and RN over the past decade. Japan is also keen to learn lessons from other navies operating the F-35B and, in this vein, is likely to conduct operations with Italy's *Cavour* during the Italian carrier strike group's 2024 Indo-Pacific deployment.

In late 2023, *Izumo*'s sister *Kaga* (DDH-184) carried out sea trials after having her bow section modified into a square shape from the previous trapezoid. Accordingly, the forward part of her flight deck now resembles the USN's *Wasp* (LHD-8) and *America* classes. The work was carried out at Kure and also included reinforcing the flight deck and creating heat-resistant deck spots to allow vertical F-35B landings. New guidance lights and flight deck markings and other modifications were installed. The work is being carried out in two stages and *Kaga*'s next overhaul is scheduled to include modifications to the ship's internal compartments to support F-35B operations. *Izumo* has already received some of the relevant modifications but is to have the new bow fitted during the second phase. Both ships are expected to be fully ready for F-35B operations by 2027.

In February 2024 Japan Defence Minister Minoru Kihara announced that Japan is to carry out further trials of the MQ-9B SeaGuardian UAV in late 2024 from the Kanoya JMSDF air base. Earlier trials with a single SeaGuardian had been carried out from Hachinohe JMSDF air base but Kanoya is where Fleet Air Wing 1 of the JMSDF is based. The Wing's P-1s and P-3Cs routinely track and shadow Russian and Chinese warships as they pass through or conduct operations around Japan's south-west island chain. The purpose of the new trials is to evaluate the ability of UAVs to replace some of the missions flown by manned aircraft.[21]

NEW ZEALAND: ROYAL NEW ZEALAND NAVY (RNZN)

The RNZN is seeking a maritime helicopter to replace its SH-2G Super Seasprite from 2027. Identified as the Maritime Helicopter Replacement (MHR) project, the potential programme's request for information actually covers two distinct types. One is to be a manned helicopter capable of conducting a broad range of operations. The other would be an unmanned system able to complement the MHR and which might operate either alongside it or alone. A key element of the requirement is interoperability with Australia and other coalition partners and the RFI stresses the importance of robust through-life support arrangements, training and mission support. Early estimates put the cost of MHR at about NZ$1bn (c. US$625m). No. 6 Squadron Royal New Zealand Air Force (RNZAF), which operates the SH-2Gs, is said to be closely involved in defining MHR requirements. There is concern that the current Seasprite fleet might fail to achieve its intended out of service date due to the difficulty of obtaining spares, a concern that is driving New Zealand's focus on the sustainability of the type required under the MHR project. MHR is regarded as urgent because the SH-2Gs are the essential aviation component of the RNZN's naval combat force and, alongside the RNZAF's P-8A Poseidon aircraft, provide the New Zealand Defence Force with a rare offensive aerial capability.

PROGRESS WITH MARITIME UNMANNED AERIAL VEHICLES

In the 2010 edition of *World Naval Review* I wrote that the USN expected the Northrop Grumman X-47 Uncrewed Combat Air Vehicle (UCAV) to fly in late 2009 and to carry out deck landing trials in 2011. At that time a USN spokesman had said that the eventual replacement for the F/A-18E/F would be a UCAV likely to enter fleet service in 2025, by which time carriers would be able to operate both manned and unmanned aircraft in the same launch and recovery cycle. In 2025, however, there will still be no USN UCAVs at sea in a CVN and a cynical observer might say that there has been a lack of determination to drive their development forward. There are a number of reasons for this but they are not all technical; automated deck landing systems in manned aircraft have been available for decades and both the Super Hornet and Lightning have reliable systems fitted as standard. Pilots seldom use it, however, as they are graded on their 'hands-on' deck landing skill, with every landing monitored. It is easy to make the point that the system might fail and that manual skills have to be kept sharp, even though this requires a significant number of flying hours and expense. Landing Safety Officer (LSO) monitored deck landings are part of every fixed-wing USN pilot's DNA. Moreover, the introduction of autonomous UCAVs will inevitably lead to fundamental changes in both their numbers and career paths and this might not be viewed with enthusiasm.

The development of an unmanned carrier-capable UCAV began with research into a specifically naval type designated N-UCAV around the turn of the millennium. By 2006 the project had evolved into the Unmanned Combat Air System Demonstration (UCAS-D) programme, for which Northrop Grumman's X-47B was selected as its airborne technology demonstrator. It eventually carried out the world's first autonomous carrier landing by an uncrewed aircraft on 10 July 2013. The carrier was *George H. W. Bush* (CVN-77), fitted with appropriate electronics to support the trial which provided valuable data about command and control software, the necessary interface between the aircraft and the ship and the integration of unmanned aircraft into the deck operating cycle. Despite all this, UCAS-D went no further and the USN began to work on a new UCAV project known as the Uncrewed Carrier-Launched Airborne Surveillance and Strike (UCLASS) programme, leveraging UCAS-D technology. After a period of procrastination the UCAV's mission focus was changed, leading to further delay. In 2016 the USN announced that it was to be prioritised to act as an air-to-air refuelling tanker, the airborne element of the Carrier-Borne Airborne Refuelling System (CBARS). A slim list of requirements was accepted to get aircraft to sea quickly because the need to free F/A-18E/Fs from their secondary tanking role was considered urgent, although it was accepted that an aircraft large enough for this mission would also have a latent ISR capability in due course. The Boeing MQ-25A Stingray was selected but, despite early statements about the urgency of getting it to sea to prove the concept of integrating unmanned aircraft into the carrier air wing, production delays have meant that the first example was not handed over until March 2024. It is now considered unlikely that an operational unit will embark until late 2026 at the earliest. Moreover, the F/A-XX which is intended to replace the F/A-18E/F in the 2040s is now being described a manned, rather than unmanned, aircraft although it is expected to form part of a manned/unmanned team.

An unmanned Boeing MQ-25 T1 Stingray test aircraft, left, refuels a manned F/A-18F Super Hornet on 4 June 4 2021 in the first demonstration of such crewed/uncrewed teaming. Despite this initial progress, delivery of production model MQ-25 Stingrays into operational US Navy service is proving to be protracted. *(Boeing)*

Other major UCAV projects have also been delayed or cut back, partially due to a lack of enthusiasm in the communities that would operate them. As already mentioned, the MQ-4C Triton has had its programme of record significantly reduced, whilst the MQ-8C Fire Scout – which achieved IOC as recently as 2019 – will be retired from operational duties before the end of 2024 despite a reported US$1.5bn being spent on bringing the type into service. The MH-60R community still envisages a manned helicopter as the type's eventual replacement, albeit teamed with unmanned helicopters. The USMC, on the other hand, appears to recognise the importance of UCAVs and already uses a number of smaller battlefield examples to give marines on the ground their first view of the enemy as well as gathering wider intelligence. The Corps regards UCAV procurement as urgent.

In seeming contrast to the USN experience, the RN is turning to UCAVs with enthusiasm. This reflects a recent statement by James Cartlidge, the British Minister for Defence Procurement. Noting that the conflict in Ukraine is a very visible representation of a new way of war characterised by innovation and the rapid implementation of new technologies, he pointed to the deployment of uncrewed systems as a particularly clear example of delivering disproportionate impact on the battlefield.[22] The potential future line of development for the RN's carrier aviation suggests how this might be achieved. The British F-35Bs' dual tasking means that their embarked time is limited and it is, in any case, a very expensive aircraft to operate. A carrier-borne strike UCAV, on the other hand, would provide mass and could be embarked on a permanent basis. They would neither need to fly constantly to maintain aircrew proficiency nor need to be disembarked routinely while in harbour. Synthetic training for their control teams could be digitally provided at any time. The RN is deliberately seeking a coherent partnership with the UK industrial base to achieve these advantages and Cartlidge emphasised that collaborative developments 'will increasingly drive the mass of our armed forces'.

A US Navy MQ-8C Fire Scout UAV being prepared for deployment on the flight deck of the *Freedom* variant Littoral Combat Ship *Milwaukee* (LCS-5) in January 2022. Like many of the *Freedom* class, the MQ-8C is being consigned to the scrapheap after only a short period in operational service. *(US Navy)*

During 2024 the use of uncrewed systems in physically and electronically contested environments is unprecedented. They are being used for a wider range of tasks than ever before, especially in Ukraine, the Red Sea and the wider Middle East. Unlike the US, which has focused on large and expensive projects that are difficult to manage and control, the UK defence enterprise involves government and industry working collaboratively on the rapid development of relatively inexpensive commercial and military technologies. It is seemingly both responding to and learning from the need to provide immediate support for Ukraine against Russian aggression. Lessons relating to uncrewed technology and its application in this conflict are being assimilated quickly. However, UCAV development is about much more than the airborne platforms, most of which are fairly conventional. They require the integration of hardware, software and supporting secure communications networks together with new methods of rapid acquisition; and it is these that challenge conventional methods. Although Cartlidge did not say so, they also require a sharp operational focus on what is needed, why and over what timescale.

As well as learning about operations in Ukraine, the RN is using Project 'Vampire's' Banshee drones to help develop a cadre of skilled operators with knowledge of how best to operate UCAVs. Trials of uncrewed aircraft from *Prince of Wales* have demonstrated that carriers can integrate UCAV operations and the incorporation of assisted take-off and arrested recovery under Project 'Ark Royal' will broaden the number of types that can be operated without them being restricted to V/STOL. The operation of uncrewed helicopters from ships other than carriers from 2025 will provide data on which requirements for a future family of ship-borne crewed and uncrewed aircraft will be based, including UAVs used for logistic transfer and re-supply, weapon and sonobuoy release, and casualty evacuation. Cartlidge's vision is heartening and the UK certainly has the potential to be a leader in uncrewed system development at a time central to the types of warfare that are evolving in Europe and

The Royal Navy is looking to produce force mass by using uncrewed aerial vehicles to supplement limited numbers of crewed aircraft. Here a Banshee drone is pictured with a F-35B strike fighter aboard *Prince of Wales*. The Royal Navy is using Project 'Vampire's' Banshee drones to help develop a cadre of skilled operators with knowledge of how best to operate UCAVs. *(Crown Copyright 2021)*

the Middle East. Early UCAVs were limited by their lack of affordable artificial intelligence technology to give them a high degree of autonomy. Spurred on by the challenges of contemporary conflict, this is the area that is seeing the most rapid progress.

At least two nations are developing 'drone carriers', which they believe will offer a range of capabilities at far less cost than a conventional aircraft carrier.[23] Following Turkey's removal from the F-35 programme, the Turkish Navy is re-purposing the amphibious assault ship *Anadolu* to operate Bayraktar TB-3 UCAVs, which are to be capable of ISR and strike missions with smart weapons. Meanwhile, Iran is converting two container ships into drone carriers. One, *Shahid Mahdavi*, commissioned into the Islamic Revolutionary Guard Corps Navy in 2023 but the other, *Shahid Badheri*, is not yet in service. Whilst the large drones envisaged by the USN are complex and costly aircraft that commanders might hesitate to risk in a contested environment, the Turkish and Iranian drones are relatively inexpensive. At the same time, they pose a threat to more sophisticated and expensive systems, especially when used as a stream or swarm. Most UCAVs to date have been relatively low-performance aircraft but cheap to procure and fly. Sophisticated air defence systems can invariably destroy them but at a cost; ships only carry a limited number of surface-to-air missiles and, once fired, they have to return to a base to be

Conventional, crewed aircraft line the deck of the US Navy aircraft carrier *Ronald Reagan* (CVN-76) as the destroyer *Ralph Johnson* (DDG-114) comes alongside to conduct a replenishment at sea during operations in the Philippine Sea on 4 June 2024. Whilst the US Navy might not have adopted carrier-borne UCAVs as quickly as expected, this situation is likely to change in years to come. *(US Navy)*

replenished. Moreover, inexpensive 'kamikaze drones' can be produced in enormous numbers at far less cost than the missiles that oppose them. This has become a major issue, leading to the development of lasers such as the RN's Dragonfire, which is being developed under conditions of great urgency.

In summary, the advantages of sea-based UCAVs have been recognised for decades. However, prejudice has arguably slowed their acquisition in the USN. Their widespread use in conflicts in Europe and the Middle East has changed the nature of warfare both at sea and on land and stimulated an unprecedented rate of progress, especially in the digital technology that underpins their control, guidance and target acquisition. The RN has too few crewed aircraft and pilots to carry out its widespread tasks and therefore finds the wider application of UCAVs especially attractive. It has a number of projects in hand aimed at expanding their use over the next decade. Even large and sophisticated UCAVs are far less costly to operate than crewed aircraft because they only need to fly when required to do so operationally, reducing the fuel used and removing the need for pilot training. This is something even the USN must take note of given an increasingly tight budget. Whilst carrier-borne UCAVs might not yet have arrived at the point I anticipated 15 years ago, the reasons for acquiring them have never been more urgent, and the capability that underpins them has never been as effective. Accordingly, the next 15 years are more likely to see game-changing progress than the last.

Notes

1. See *Service Inquiry into the loss of F-35B Lightning ZM152 (BK-18)* (London: Defence Safety Authority, 2023). This section also draws on an article 'The F-35 accident report – a reality check for UK Carrier Strike' posted to the *Navy Lookout* site – navylookout.com – on 25 August 2023, as re-posted by the Australian Naval Institute under the title 'Report on F-35 loss has lessons for RAN' the following day.

2. Although formally a RAF squadron, 617 Squadron is jointly manned by RAF and RN personnel in line with the wider arrangements for operation of the United Kingdom's F-35B force.

3. Phase 2B training forms the second phase of specialist or professional training and is typically carried out in a workplace environment. Phase 2 training follows on from Phase 1 basic training that is common to all specialisations.

4. See Richard Scott, 'UK Explores Cats And Traps Retrofit To QEC Aircraft Carriers' posted to the *Naval News* website – navalnews.com – on 1 June 2023. It has subsequently been reported that the Future Maritime Aviation Force nomenclature is no longer in use.

5. See the press release 'Royal Navy's successful crewless aircraft trials offer 'glimpse into the future' of carrier operations' posted to the Royal Navy's website – royalnavy.mod.uk – on 17 November 2023.

6. See, 'Navy Wildcats gunning for their true potential in 2024' published on the Fleet Air Arm Officers Association site – fleetairarmoa.org – on 30 December 2023.

7. This news was reported in an article by Sam LaGrone entitled, 'Crowded Newport News Shipbuilding pushing carrier work to other yards' published on the *USNI News* site – news.usni.org – on 7 November 2023.

8. These developments were covered in another *USNI News* article, 'Aircraft Carrier Enterprise Delivery Delayed by 18 Months, Says Navy' posted by Mallory Shelbourne on 15 March 2024.

9. See the press release 'Navy marks ceremonial stand-up of CVN Inactivation and Disposal Program Office' posted to the Naval Sea Systems Command website – navsea.navy.mil – on 2 February 2024.

10. This development was covered in an article by Alison Bath, 'US Navy deploys its newest multi-intelligence drone to Sicily' posted to the *Stars and Stripes* site – stripes.com – on 5 March 2024.

11. See Justin Katz, 'Navy delaying next-gen F/A-XX fighter spending for near-term investments' posted to the *Breaking Defense* news site – breakingdefense.com – on 11 March 2024.

12. See John Grady, 'Wittman Criticizes F-35 Lightning II Joint Strike Fighter Program Delays' posted to the *USNI News* site on 13 December 2023.

13. Amongst numerous reporters commenting on the continued uncertainties relating to the Osprey crash was Eric Tegler in 'V-22s Will Fly Again With No Fix For The Problem That Grounded Them' posted to the *Forbes* site – forbes.com – on 10 March 2024.

14. See Aaron-Matthew Lariosо, 'Marine Corps Experimental "Loyal Wingman" Drone Makes First Flight' posted to the *USNI News* site on 5 October 2023.

15. The RAN's Taipans were withdrawn from service in April 2022 and the Australian Army's in September 2023; the latter being brought forward from the previously planned date of December 2024 following the type's grounding after a fatal crash on 28 July 2023 that claimed four lives. The accelerated withdrawal did not, however, presuppose or in any way suggest the outcome of crash investigations that remain ongoing.

16. The report on KJ-600 missions was contained in Liu Xuanzun's 'China's carrier-based fighter jets trains with early warning aircraft' posted to the *Global Times* site – globaltimes.cn – on 7 February 2024. The site also published another report on 8 May 2024 by Liu Xuanzun and Guo Yuandan – 'China's 3rd aircraft carrier completes maiden sea trials, to greatly empower PLA Navy' – covering *Fujian*'s initial trials.

17. See the Naval Group press release, '*Charles de Gaulle*: a closer look at the replacement of the "boilers"' posted to naval-group.com on 17 July 2023.

18. This news was reported by Adithya Krishna Menon in 'Indian Navy Conducts Dual Carrier Operations' posted to the *Naval News* site on 10 March 2024.

19. In May 2024, Indian Defence Minister Rajnath Singh stated that work on a third aircraft carrier would start soon. He added, 'We will not stop at that. We will make five, six more'. His remarks were reported by Ajay Banerjee in 'Work on third aircraft carrier to start soon, more to follow, says Rajnath Singh' in an article posted to *The Tribune*'s site – tribuneindia.com – on the 14th of that month.

20. See the Royal Navy press release, 'Japanese join HMS *Prince of Wales* to pave way for F-35 operations by their Navy' dated 1 November 2023.

21. This news was reported by Dzirhan Mahadzir in, 'Japan Set to Test MQ-9B Sea Guardian Later this Year', which was posted to USNI News on 16 February 2024.

22. Mr Cartlidge was introducing the UK's approach to drone systems, *Defence Drone Strategy: The UK's Approach to Defence Uncrewed Systems* (London: Ministry of Defence, 2024), currently available by searching gov.uk.

23. See Alexander Gale, 'Drone carriers and the future of naval aviation' posted to the *UK Defence Journal* site – ukdefencejournal.org.uk – on 20 October 2023.

4.2 TECHNOLOGICAL REVIEW

AN/SPY-6(V) RADAR

The US Navy's New Scalable Radar Family

Author:
Richard Scott

Jack H. Lucas (DDG-125), the first DDG-51 Flight III Aegis guided-missile destroyer, was commissioned into the US Navy on 7 October 2023 in a ceremony in Tampa, Florida. Evolved from the previous DDG-51 Flight IIA design, the Flight III is notable for being the first ship to enter service with the next-generation AN/SPY-6(V)1 Air and Missile Defence Radar (AMDR). Developed by Raytheon (part of RTX), the new S (NATO E/F)-band sensor integrates with the latest iteration of Aegis (Baseline 10) to provide the US Navy with what the service claims to be an unrivalled integrated air and missile defence (IAMD) capability.

Although the deckhouse and array faces on *Jack H. Lucas* appear little different from those on previous DDG-51 ships, the techniques and technology embodied within the AN/SPY-6(V)1 radar are, in fact, at least two generations removed from those of the legacy AN/SPY-1D(V) system long associated with Aegis, affording greater detection range, increased sensitivity and improved target discrimination performance. Furthermore, the same advanced solid-state technology implemented in the AMDR has now spawned a broader AN/SPY-6(V) family of radars scaled to suit the needs of the navy's aircraft carriers, major amphibious ships, new guided missile frigates, and earlier generation DDG-51 Flight IIA destroyers. The expectation is that AN/SPY-6(V) variants will be integrated into over sixty US Navy ships over the next decade.

Jack H. Lucas (DDG-125), the lead DDG-51 Flight III Aegis guided-missile destroyer, is the first ship to enter service with the next-generation AN/SPY-6(V1) Air and Missile Defence Radar. *(Huntington Ingalls Industries)*

AN/SPY-6(V) ORIGINS

The story behind the AN/SPY-6(V) family can be traced back over more than two decades. At its heart was a realisation that, despite a series of substantial technology and performance uplifts, the AN/SPY-1 phased-array radar that had been paired with the Aegis system since its inception was at the very limit of its development potential. The inherent constraints of its passive phased-array radar design – based on technologies originating in the late 1960s – limited the power available from the below-decks transmitter group, and meant large losses at the array face. There were also significant penalties to be paid with regard to energy management, weight, reliability, and life cycle costs. Accordingly, back in early 2000, the US Navy promulgated a so-called Surface Navy Radar Roadmap, which set out the service's vision of its future radar requirements. This document highlighted the need for a new IAMD radar with much-increased sensitivity to meet evolving ballistic missile defence (BMD) needs; increased clutter rejection to address small anti-air warfare

(AAW) targets in littoral environments; and a wide instantaneous bandwidth for BMD discrimination.

Johns Hopkins University Applied Physics Laboratory (JHU APL) – based in Laurel, Maryland – serves as the US Navy's key technical partner for radar and combat systems development. It played an important role in the development of the operational requirements and top-level system requirements that would ultimately shape the AMDR programme, and also completed an early digital array radar study that identified a distributed receiver and exciter radar architecture and digital beamforming as key enablers of a future IAMD radar system.

In 2003 a follow-on gap analysis defined the capability needs of the projected CG(X) next-generation guided missile cruiser and its associated multi-mission radar. The analysis of alternatives (AoA) that followed considered the cost, schedule and performance of various ship and radar alternatives, including different frequency bands and combinations, radar sensitivities, and architectural and technology solutions. The AoA concluded that the preferred option for a new radar was a large S-band radar sized for simultaneous BMD and area air defence, coupled with a smaller X (NATO I/J)-band radar sized for horizon search/self-defence needs.

Two years later, the Office of the Chief of Naval Operations directed the Above Water Sensors Directorate in Program Executive Office Integrated Warfare Systems (PEO IWS) to commence work on generating top-level radar performance (TLRP) requirements in preparation for a multi-phase acquisition program. PEO IWS is responsible for the acquisition and lifecycle support of above-water combat systems within the wider Naval Sea Systems Command (NAVSEA) organisation.[1]

Given the onerous demands of the IAMD mission, together with the cost and implied technology development required to engineer an advanced maritime radar, PEO IWS sponsored a multidisciplinary government team – with JHU APL providing technical leadership in several areas – to develop a concept architecture. This reference architecture was developed in parallel with the top-level requirement so as to underpin and validate the technical feasibility of the requirements then being established.

A Maritime Air and Missile Defense of Joint Forces (MAMDJF) Initial Capabilities Document endorsed by the Joint Requirements Oversight Council (JROC) in May 2006 affirmed the gaps in

This photograph of a replenishment at sea evolution being carried out aboard the US Navy destroyer *Higgins* (DDG-76) in June 2024 provides a good view of one of her four AN/SPY-1 radar arrays. Development of the AN/SPY-6(V) radar family traces its origins to the realisation that the AN/SPY-1 phased-array radar that had been paired with the Aegis system since its inception was at the very limit of its development potential. *(US Navy)*

AAW and BMD capability, and designated the navy as project lead. The Under Secretary of Defense for Acquisition, Technology, and Logistics (USD (AT&L)) directed the US Navy to proceed with an AoA for MAMDJF in June 2006. The Director of Program Analysis and Evaluation endorsed the radar portion (Phase I) of the AoA in October 2008.

This formalised the requirement for a next-generation phased-array radar for CG(X). The new radar would simultaneously support long-range, exo-atmospheric detection, tracking, and discrimination of ballistic missiles (demanding an increase in radar sensitivity and bandwidth to detect and track high speed targets at extended ranges) and area and self-defence against AAW threats (requiring improved sensitivity and a de-cluttering capability to pick out stressing, very-low-observable/very-low flying threats in the presence of heavy land, sea, and rain clutter).

However, the intention to procure a brand new class of surface combatant now came under intense scrutiny. A Radar/Hull Study performed by NAVSEA in 2009 compared different radar solutions, combat system architectures and hull designs in different combinations. The outcome of this evaluation led the navy to conclude that a suitably scaled AMDR suite could go to sea on an evolved (Flight III) version of the DDG-51 guided-missile destroyer and still meet AMDR requirements. As a result, the CG(X) programme was cancelled in April 2010.

With the conclusion of the Radar/Hull Study and cancellation of CG(X), the nominal capability and configuration of the AMDR 'suite' was established: the S-band AMDR-S would be optimised for volume search at range for air and ballistic missile defence; the X-band AMDR-X would offer improved discrimination and better low-elevation performance out to the horizon; and a Radar Suite Controller (RSC) would provide radar resource management, co-ordination, and the interface into the Aegis combat system. What the US Navy also identified was the importance of a scalable radar design (with respect to power and sensitivity) and modularity of both hardware and software. The service also stipulated open-architecture compliance to promote technology insertion and performance enhancement throughout the life of the system.

CONCEPT DEVELOPMENT AND TECHNOLOGY MATURATION

The top level radar performance (TLRP) requirement established the basis for a competitive concept studies phase lasting six months. In June 2009, NAVSEA awarded contracts to Lockheed Martin, Northrop Grumman and Raytheon for AMDR-S/RSC concept studies. Under these, all three companies reviewed and provided feedback on the navy's requirements documents; conducted system engineering trade studies; developed an initial system concept; and developed a draft technology prototype and demonstration plan to achieve what was known as Technology Readiness Level (TRL) 6. The navy used the outputs of these concept studies to refine performance requirements and identify technical risks in preparation for transition to the Technology Development (TD) phase. Subsequently, in September 2010, NAVSEA awarded parallel TD contracts, each valued at US$120m, to Lockheed Martin, Northrop Grumman and Raytheon.

These awards funded design concept refinement, technology maturation, and the demonstration of technology prototypes, culminating in the development of an initial system design to a level sufficient to conduct a preliminary design review. All three contractors were tasked to prove four critical technologies – high-power Gallium Nitride (GaN)-based amplifiers and Transmit/Receive (T/R) modules; active-array physical architectures; digital receiver/exciters; and large aperture digital beamforming and calibration – in order to demonstrate that these could achieve the TRL 6 maturity required for a 'Milestone B' acquisition approval. The TD phase additionally included the production and functional testing of radar algorithms in S-band active phased-array prototypes – populated by at least 1,000 transmit/receive (T/R) modules – with large aperture digital beamforming. Software development for multi-mission scheduling and discrimination was another important aspect of the TD phase. As one of the key requirements was to execute simultaneous detection and tracking of both ballistic missiles and air targets, the radar has to be able to perform both tasks in a certain amount of time.

A pre-solicitation notice addressing base-year engineering studies for AMDR-X – with options for engineering and manufacturing development (EMD) and low-rate initial production (LRIP) – was issued in July 2011. AMDR-X was envisaged to be a three-face X-band radar to provide horizon search, precision tracking, missile communications, and terminal illumination guidance. However, in December 2011, the US Navy announced it had re-examined its AMDR-X requirements and determined that the planned solicitation 'no longer reflects the present needs of the navy'. The following April the service announced that the X-band requirement would initially be met by the non-developmental AN/SPQ-9B X-band horizon search radar. A month later a Defense Acquisition Board acquisition decision memorandum directed a change to the programme structure to include only the AMDR-S-band radar and the RSC, confirming that the X-band capabilities in the original AMDR Capability Development Document would be addressed in a separate future Program of Record.[2]

TD activities for AMDR-S/RSC were concluded in September 2012, with NAVSEA subsequently releasing a request for proposals for the engineering and manufacturing development phase in June 2012. Offers were received in July 2012. AMDR successfully achieved Milestone B approval in September 2013 and was authorised to transition into the EMD phase. The following month, after a protracted and complex competitive source selection process, Raytheon was awarded a U$385.7m EMD contract covering the design, development, integration, test, and delivery of AMDR-S/RSC over a 48-month period.[3]

EMD funded the detailed design of the system and development of an affordable and executable manufacturing process, concluding with a 'Milestone C' decision to transition AMDR-S into initial production (the EMD phase contract including options for up to nine Low Rate Initial Production – LRIP – units). The EMD phase also included integration and test of a single-faced AMDR-S/RSC engineering development model (EDM) with an AN/SPQ-9B system at the land-based test site at the Pacific Missile Range Facility

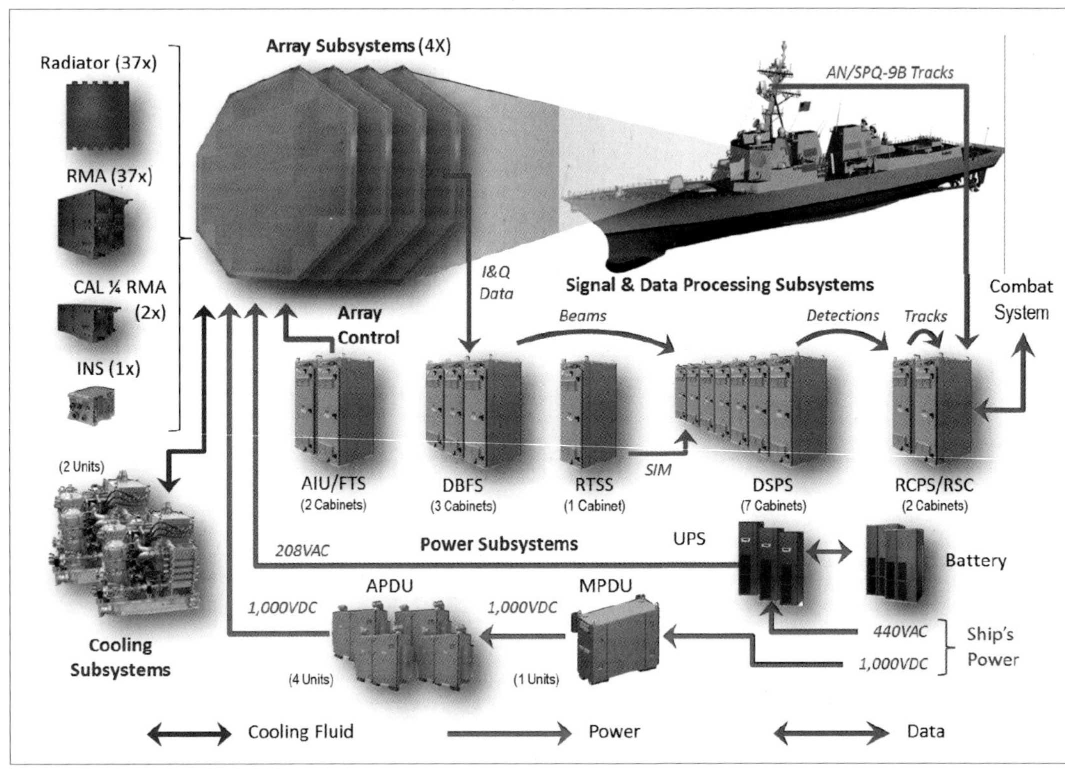

A Raytheon diagram showing the AN/SPY-6(V)1 Air and Missile Defense Radar's (ADMR's) architecture. Raytheon was one of three companies awarded concept and, subsequently, technology development contracts to bring the ADMR programme to a level of maturity where engineering and manufacturing could begin. *(Raytheon)*

(PMRF) in Kauai, Hawaii. In October 2014, the AMDR-S system was assigned the formal nomenclature AN/SPY-6(V)1.

MODULAR PHILOSOPHY

The modular and scalable AN/SPY-6(V) radar architecture proposed by Raytheon and selected by NAVSEA is founded on a series of 'building blocks', called Radar Modular Assemblies (RMAs), which can be stacked together and time/phase-synchronised. In this way, the radar aperture can be sized to meet specific mission needs of any class of ship, with cooling, calibration, power and logical interfaces all being scaled accordingly.

Each RMA is effectively a self-contained radar, containing 144 T/R modules, in a 2ft x 2ft x 2ft box. T/R modules are packaged into Transmit/Receive Integrated Multi-channel Module (TRIMM) assemblies. A single RMA hosts twenty-four TRIMMs, each of which hosts six T/R modules. This large number of T/R modules provides a high degree of fault tolerance through antenna redundancy and graceful degradation.

The AMDR-S requirement was SPY +15 dB, which is more than thirty times more sensitive than the SPY-1 radar. To achieve this requirement demands a 14.1ft x 13.6ft x 5ft array structure built up from thirty-seven RMAs (aggregating to 5,328 T/R modules per array face).

High power/high efficiency power amplifier technology was identified as a key enabler for AMDR at an early stage. T/R devices based on GaN wide bandgap semi-conductor material offer significant power, efficiency, size/weight, cost and reliability benefits over the Gallium Arsenide (GaAs) modules previously used in multifunction radars. Raytheon claims that radio frequency amplifiers manufactured using GaN are five times more powerful than other semiconductors, and provide power at a 34 percent lower cost than GaAs.

Raytheon also sought to emphasise availability, reliability and maintainability in its proposal (the operational tempo is assumed to be 180 days on station). For example, AN/SPY-6(V) requires 70 percent fewer line replaceable units (modular spare parts removed and replaced at the field level) than the legacy AN/SPY-1 radar, and close to 95 percent of array maintenance comes down to just a few unique parts. Technicians can swap out assemblies in just over five minutes, and are required to use just two tools. Obsolescence of commercial off-

AN/SPY-6(V)1 arrays inside the Radar Development Facility at Raytheon's Andover, Massachusetts, plant. The worker in the picture provides a sense of scale. Raytheon was awarded a U$385.7m contract covering the design, development, integration, test, and delivery of the Air and Missile Defence Radar in October 2013. *(Raytheon)*

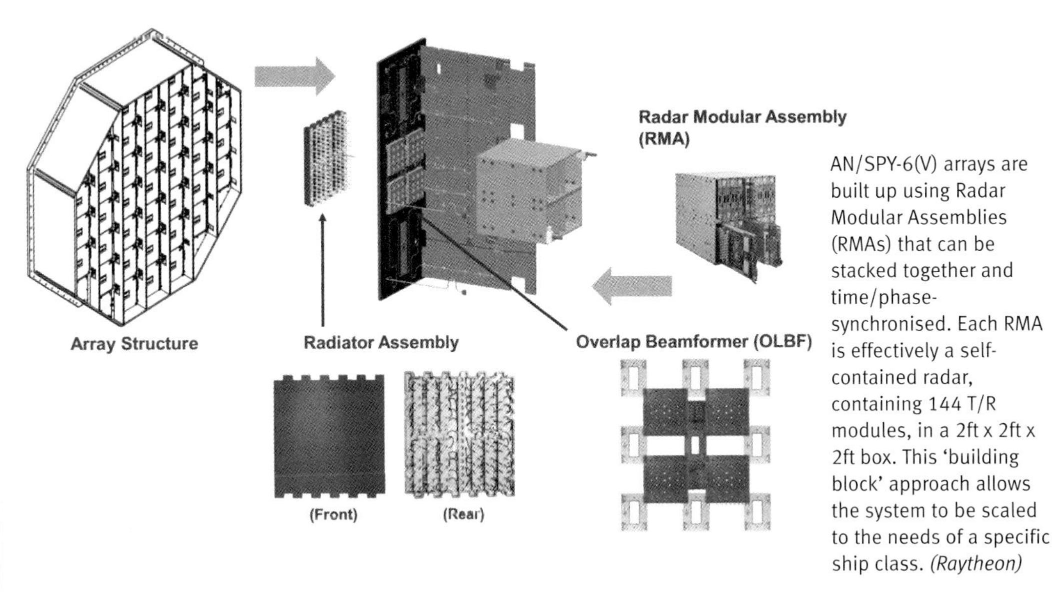

AN/SPY-6(V) arrays are built up using Radar Modular Assemblies (RMAs) that can be stacked together and time/phase-synchronised. Each RMA is effectively a self-contained radar, containing 144 T/R modules, in a 2ft x 2ft x 2ft box. This 'building block' approach allows the system to be scaled to the needs of a specific ship class. *(Raytheon)*

the-shelf processing equipment will be implemented using a 'refresh by attrition' approach, combined with an eight-year refresh cycle. The planned software sustainment strategy for AN/SPY-6(V) includes post-delivery routine software maintenance and software updates every two years.

DEMONSTRATION AND TEST

The AMDR-S EMD phase saw the construction of a production-representative, single-face engineering development model (EDM) and two RSC EDMs for testing at the Advanced Radar Detection Laboratory (ARDEL) at the PMRF in Hawaii. Other notable deliverables included an AMDR-S/RSC interface simulator – for delivery to the Naval Surface Warfare Center, Dahlgren Division – and an AMDR-S emulator. Near Field Range testing of the AN/SPY-6(V) single-face EDM radar was successfully completed in May 2016 in Sudbury, Massachusetts. The EDM system, integrated with the AN/SPQ-9B test system, was installed at the ARDEL site the following month.

A single-faced AMDR-S/RSC engineering development model was installed at a land-based test site at the Pacific Missile Range Facility in Hawaii. Live testing of the new array commenced in September 2016. *(Raytheon)*

Development Phase 3 (DT-3) live testing commenced in September 2016. The EDM was subsequently used to demonstrate functionality and performance – air, surface, electronic attack/electronic protection, BMD, IAMD, sphere targets, satellites and missile communications – in a series of live tracking experiments against increasingly complex targets. Outside of specific test events, the radar also demonstrated its capabilities against multiple targets of opportunity.

In October 2016, the AN/SPY-6(V)1 EDM first tracked multiple satellites through their orbits. The following month, the radar executed its first integrated air and missile defence track by simultaneously tracking aircraft and satellites. The EDM was also tested in a series of BMD tests. The first, 'Vigilant Hunter', conducted in March 2017 in conjunction with Standard Missile-3 Block IIA flight test SFTM-01, saw the system search for, acquire and track a medium-range ballistic missile target from launch through flight. A second BMD test, designated 'Vigilant Titan', was conducted in late July 2017. In this test, the radar successfully searched for, detected, tracked and discriminated a medium-range ballistic missile target. The third and most complex test – involving simultaneous air and ballistic missile targets – was performed at PMRF on 7 September 2017. During this flight test, designated 'Vigilant Talon', the AN/SPY-6(V)1 EDM searched for, detected and maintained track of a short-range ballistic missile target and multiple air-to-surface cruise missile targets throughout their trajectories.

In March 2018 the EDM failed a BMD tracking test ('Vigilant Janus') as a result of a defective software update that caused the array to stop tracking a live target. A software update was implemented to rectify the issue and the radar was re-tested at the end of January 2019 under a flight test designated 'Vigilant Nemesis'. According to PEO IWS, the 'Vigilant Nemesis' event proved the capability of the AN/SPY-6(V)1 to detect, track and discriminate an Aegis Readiness Assessment Vehicle-CZ complex short-range ballistic missile target and support the design of the Aegis Baseline 10 combat system. 'Vigilant Nemesis' marked the conclusion of BMD flight testing for the AN/SPY-6(V)1 radar.

It had originally been planned that the single-face EDM would be transferred to Lockheed Martin's Moorestown, New Jersey, site in the third quarter of 2018 to support Aegis Baseline 10 combat system testing. In the event, however, it was decided that the EDM would remain at PMRF for additional target of opportunity testing. Instead, PEO IWS took the decision to revise the acquisition schedule, and divert a new array to support Aegis Baseline 10/SPY-6(V)1 interface and power distribution testing at the Combat System Engineering Development Site in Moorestown, New Jersey.

Test activity using the EDM has continued. In December 2022, an early operational assessment (OA) of AN/SPY-6(V)1 performance was undertaken at ARDEL to evaluate the capability of the radar to detect and track fighter aircraft, anti-ship cruise missile surrogates, unmanned aerial vehicles, helicopters, airborne early warning and control aircraft, and small-boat targets. This OA was executed to identify modifications that could optimise system performance, albeit using an EDM that used obsolete TRIMMs not representative of the current production standard.

PRODUCTION START AND INITIAL DELIVERY

'Milestone C' approval for low-rate initial production (LRIP) was achieved in April 2017. The following month a US$327m contract option was exercised for three LRIP systems (long-lead material for the first production AN/SPY-6(V)1 had been authorised in December 2016). A contract for one additional LRIP radar was authorised in April 2018.

Successful completion of the 'Vigilant Nemesis' test event saw authorisation given for the award of up to five additional LRIP radar systems. The option for a further three AN/SPY-1(V)6 shipsets was exercised with Raytheon in March 2019, with the last two remaining options exercised in December 2019, bringing the total LRIP buy up to nine shipsets.

AN/SPY-6(V)1 radar materiel delivery (power and cooling equipment) to support the shipbuilding schedule for DDG-125 – the lead DDG 51 Flight III destroyer constructed by the Ingalls Shipbuilding Division of Huntington Ingalls Industries (HII) in Pascagoula, Mississippi – commenced in the third quarter of 2019. The four radar arrays followed into the Ingalls shipyard between July and October 2020. The programme supported the successful completion of the DDG-125 Aegis 'light-off' milestone in December 2021. Initial underway trials of AN/SPY-6(V)1 in *Jack H. Lucas* commenced in late 2022.

The US Navy accepted delivery of *Jack H. Lucas* in June 2023 and has subsequently conducted various sea trials with AN/SPY-6(V)1 as part of developmental testing. In late March 2024, the new destroyer participated in the Missile Defense Agency's Flight Test Aegis Weapon System-32 (FTM-32) off the coast of Hawaii. FTM-32 – also known as 'Stellar Laelaps' – saw *Preble* (DDG-88) successfully intercept a medium range ballistic missile target using a SM-6 Dual II (Block IA) interceptor with the latest software upgrades. *Jack H. Lucas* used AN/SPY-6(V)1 to 'observe' the FTM-32 flight test, and collect data in support of its Initial Operational Test and Evaluation campaign. Challenges have arisen, however. The Government Accountability Office's latest Weapon Systems Annual Assessment, published in June 2024, noted that 'major integration deficiencies' between AN/SPY-6(V)1 and Aegis had been identified in June 2023 during acceptance trials for *Jack H. Lucas*. Updated software has been developed to address these issues.

Initial capability for AN/SPY-6(V)1 is now planned to be achieved in FY 2027. The US Navy expects to continue operational testing into 2028.

ENTERPRISE AIR SURVEILLANCE RADAR

The same architecture and technology that has been developed to meet the AMDR requirement has subsequently been leveraged to serve as the foundation for a broader AN/SPY-6(V) family of radars designed to be scalable and adaptable across multiple US Navy ship classes and mission requirements. In the first instance, the Enterprise Air Surveillance Radar (EASR) covers rotating (Variant 1) and fixed array (Variant 2) iterations – designated AN/SPY-6(V)2 and AN/SPY-6(V)3 respectively – that are scaled to meet the specific needs of nuclear-powered aircraft carriers (CVNs) and large amphibious vessels (LHAs and LPDs).

EASR was driven by the need to introduce a non-developmental volume surveillance radar that could

Jack H. Lucas (DDG-125) left the Ingalls shipyard of Huntington Ingalls Industries (HII) in Pascagoula, Mississippi on 26 September 2023 en route for her homeport of San Diego, California. Accepted by the US Navy in June 2023, she was commissioned in October that year. The close-up picture shows one of the four AN/SPY-6(V)1 arrays that equip the ship. Whilst superficially similar to the previous AN/SPY-1, AN/SPY-6(V)1 represents a leap of at least two further generations of technology. *(Huntington Ingalls Industries/Raytheon)*

replace the legacy AN/SPS-48 and AN/SPS-49 radars, whilst integrating with the Ship Self-Defense System Baseline 12. By using the self-contained RMA as a 'building block', Raytheon was able to offer a solution that could be sized to meet the specific mission needs of carriers and amphibious ships while maximising 'back end' commonality to realise total ownership cost benefits through common spares, maintenance and training.

AN/SPY-6(V)2 and (V)3 are designed to simultaneously support air traffic control (ATC), situational awareness, and ship self-defence against both air and surface threats. For these missions, increased clutter capability, short-range detection and tracking, and special weather waveforms are needed. AN/SPY-6(V)2 is a rotating, single-face radar designed for new-build amphibious ships, and for back-fit to existing *Nimitz* (CVN-68) class carriers; AN/SPY-6(V)3, which features three fixed arrays, will equip *Ford* (CVN-78) class carriers from *John F. Kennedy* (CVN-79) onwards. Whereas the AN/SPY-6(V)1 uses thirty-seven RMA building blocks per array face, the AN/SPY-6(V)2 and AN/SPY-6(V)3 variants developed under the EASR programme are scaled to nine RMAs per face. While not offering the same performance as AN/SPY-6(V)1, this configuration still provides a radar with the same sensitivity as the legacy AN/SPY-1(V) radar.

AN/SPY-6(V)2 – one of the Enterprise Air Surveillance Radar variants – is a rotating, single-face radar featuring nine RMAs. The system is pictured here in one of the two near-field test facilities in Raytheon's Andover facility. *(Raytheon)*

In August 2016, Raytheon was awarded a US$92m, 42-month EMD contract covering the development, build, integration, and delivery of a single EASR EDM for testing at the Surface Combat System Center, Wallops Island, Virginia. The EMD contract also included production options for sixteen radars. The EASR EDM is a production-representative Variant 1 single-face array to support land-based testing. The rotating version was selected because the rotating positioner of the EDM could easily be stopped/secured to facilitate demonstration of fixed-array operation. After a year of intensive calibration and integration at Raytheon's Near Field Range in Massachusetts, the EDM was delivered to the Wallops Test Facility in March 2019 and mounted on a test tower. Live testing at the Wallops Test Facility began in mid-2019.

The EASR radar test programme proceeded at pace, reflecting the fact that the core software baseline was similar to that previously developed for AN/SPY-6(V)1. Testing also included some new functionality, including ATC and weather map, specific to the EASR baseline requirement. A production readiness review was concluded with PEO IWS at the end of 2019, clearing the way for the start of EASR production. Raytheon had in fact received initial long-lead funding in July of that year so as to have material in hand in preparation for LRIP production options to be exercised in 2020.

The first ship to receive an AN/SPY-6(V)2 radar is *Richard M. McCool Jr.* (LPD-29), the 13th and final LPD-17 Flight I amphibious transport dock built for the US Navy. She was handed over in April 2024. Next in line is the *America* (LHA-6) class multipurpose amphibious ship, *Bougainville* (LHA-8), which is currently fitting out at HII's Ingalls Shipbuilding division in Pascagoula. The future *John F. Kennedy*, currently in the final stages of testing at HII Newport News Shipbuilding in Newport News, Virginia, is the first unit to receive AN/SPY-6(V)3. She is scheduled for handover in 2025. IOC for AN/SPY-6(V)2 and (V)3 is planned for the last quarter of FY 2029. This will follow the completion of developmental testing/operational testing. Subsequent to the EASR acquisition initiative, the US Navy has determined that the AN/SPY-6(V)3 radar will also equip its new *Constellation* (FFG-62) class multi-mission guided-missile frigates.

Another variant of the AN/SPY-6(V) family is planned for back-fit to existing DDG-51 Flight IIA ships as a replacement for their current SPY-1D(V) radar. Given the nomenclature AN/SPY-6(V)4, this variant – which will be retrofitted together with Aegis Baseline 10 – will feature four array faces each populated with twenty-four RMAs. While this is a somewhat reduced RMA count compared to the AN/SPY-6(V)1 version equipping Flight III destroyers, it will nonetheless confer significantly improved IAMD performance within the constraints of the Flight IIA platform. The AN/SPY-6(V)4 back-fit solution will leverage and scale AN/SPY-6(V)1 capabilities for the DDG MOD (modernisation) programme.[4] Development testing at the ARDEL facility is planned to start in 2025, with a power and integration test to occur in Fiscal Year 2026. Under current plans, the first DDG 51 Flight IIA destroyer to receive the AN/SPY-6(V) 4 back-fit will begin its refit in late 2026.

HARDWARE PRODUCTION

While Raytheon is the incumbent for production of AN/SPY-6(V) family radars, the US Navy owns the Technical Data Package. This means it has the right to open up hardware manufacture and sustainment to more than one source in an effort to achieve cost efficiencies through competition.

In late 2019 NAVSEA promulgated its plans for SPY-6(V) hardware production and sustainment for the FY 2021–2025 period, stating that it intends to award up to two fixed-price type contracts – a so-called 'Leader' and a 'Challenger' – while reserving the right to place just one contract. In addition to hardware production, the Leader scope includes hardware sustainment for already fielded AN/SPY-6(V) systems.

In a pre-solicitation notice published in December that year, NAVSEA outlined plans to contract for up to sixty-one AN/SPY-6(V) variants across the five-year ordering plan. This total broke down to sixteen (V)1 variants, sixteen (V)2 variants, fourteen (V)3 variants, and fifteen (V)4 variants. According to the scope of this scheme, both the Leader and the Challenger would take responsibility for production, assembly, inspection, testing, and delivery of their assigned AN/SPY-6(V) quantities. The Leader would additionally be responsible for RMA sustainment support at the line replaceable unit (LRU) level of all previously delivered AN/SPY-6(V) systems. In the event, only Raytheon responded to the navy's solicitation. Potential competitors chose not to bid, largely because the structure of the competition, and the absence of a 'build-to-print' plan, would not allow them to mobilise production in an acceptable timescale

NAVSEA awarded a first full-rate hardware, production and sustainment contract to Raytheon in March 2022. Alongside the US$651m base contract, the award included options for additional AN/SPY-6(V) ship sets that could ultimately total US$3.16bn. Three options have been exercised to date. The most recent, confirmed in June 2024 and valued at US$677m, covers an additional seven radars. This takes the total number of ship sets under contract to thirty-eight systems. A further six radars are anticipated under option year four.

The navy has not given up on its ambitions to compete future hardware production. In a January 2024 market survey notice, PEO IWS presented plans for a new five-year procurement, starting in FY 2026, for a further thirty-one AN/SPY-6(V) shipsets. Various procurement strategies are being considered, including 'winner-take-all', 'Leader and Challenger', and/or breakouts of LRUs or subsystems as separate contract(s). Taking heed of the failure of the previous competition, PEO IWS intends to pursue a 'build-to-print' model that would stipulate producing hardware to the exact specifications, drawings, and design contained within the Technical Data Package: deviations would only be permitted for the purposes of addressing obsolescence, or reducing life-cycle cost

RADAR ROADMAP

One significant characteristic of the AN/SPY-6(V) radar is the way in which it has been engineered with an open architecture so as to accept technology updates (both hardware and software). A development roadmap has already been established under which a number of system enhancements are being pursued.

One part of this roadmap is the Network Cooperative Radar (NCR) programme. Successfully demonstrated in 2021, NCR is an advanced software-based radar system solution that supports the goal of creating a distributed sensing network.

The first ship to receive the AN/SPY-6(V)2 radar is the amphibious ship *Richard M. McCool Jr.* (LPD-29). She is pictured here in the course of sea trials early in 2024. *(Huntington Ingalls Industries)*

The AN/SPY-6(V)3 fixed-face variant will equip the US Navy's new *Constellation* (FFG-62) class frigates. Each of the three array faces will be made up of nine RMAs. *(US Navy)*

BUILDING THE AN/SPY-6(V) RADAR FAMILY

Raytheon is building AN/SPY-6(V) family radars in a new vertically integrated, advanced manufacturing facility built at the company's Andover, Massachusetts, site. Opened in 2018, and representing an investment of over US$70m, the 30,000ft² Radar Development Facility incorporates highly automated materials handling and a dual-robotic assembly line. Two near-field test ranges have also been built as part of the facility.

Raytheon describes the Radar Development Facility as a 'connected factory'. This means that it uses digital technology for seamless sharing of information among people, machines and sensors, including suppliers. The business is also harnessing automation – using robots to perform assembly typically done by hand, and to conduct automated optical inspections – to reap production efficiencies, and ensure a more accurate and highly repeatable manufacture process. Another way the business is gaining efficiencies is by using Radio Frequency Identification (RFID) technology to track material packages in real time as they move around the factory. Digital data encoded in RFID tags or smart labels means that inventory can be tracked from storage and around the factory floor.

The Andover site is also host to a military-grade GaN foundry where Raytheon develops, designs and manufactures GaN-based radar components, and conducts research and development in partnership with defence labs and innovation hubs.

Raytheon has invested in advanced automation at its Andover, Massachusetts facility to achieve production efficiencies, and ensure a more accurate and highly repeatable radar manufacture process. *(Raytheon)*

According to Raytheon, NCR functionality is an example of how AN/SPY-6(V) family radars will evolve as 'software-defined apertures' rather than traditional radars.

Raytheon has also worked with the ONR to mature the Advanced Distributed Radar (ADR) concept. This functionality – designed to improve multi-ship/inter-radar cooperative capabilities – is intended to enhance BMD detection performance, increase sensitivity at large scan angles, and insert core algorithms to enable AN/SPY-6(V)1 to operate in a 'receive-only' mode in cooperation with other radars. In addition to the BMD mission, ADR will also improve AAW capabilities and provide advanced electronic protection techniques.

On the hardware side, Raytheon was contracted by the ONR in 2023 to develop ASPIRE (an acronym of Agnostic Signal Processing for Increased Radar Efficiency) for the AN/SPY-6(V) family of radars. Under the contract, Raytheon is capitalising on the latest commercially-available computing to address hardware options for more flexible digital beamforming, advanced signal processing, and smaller digital receiver/exciter systems. As well as allowing the system to process more information faster, the ASPIRE hardware development also delivers efficiencies in radar size, weight, and power requirements.

Notes

1. NAVSEA is the US Navy command responsible for managing the design, construction, integration, delivery and support of surface ship and submarine platforms and combat systems.

2. This requirement is now planned to be met by a Future X-band Radar (FXR). The FXR programme is intended to deliver a new X-band multifunction radar system performing horizon search and track, surface search and track, periscope detection and discrimination, and missile communications. It will primarily replace the functional capabilities of the current mechanically scanning AN/SPQ-9B X-band radar, while also introducing an additional capability for missile communications and advanced electronic protection.

3. Lockheed Martin, a losing bidder, filed a bid protest with the Government Accountability Office shortly after contract award, forcing NAVSEA to issue a 'stop work' order to Raytheon. The protest was withdrawn on 9 January 2014, and the 'stop work' order rescinded.

4. Introduction of AN/SPY-6(V)4 will form part of the DDG MOD 2.0 programme alongside the Aegis Baseline 10 combat system, the AN/SLQ-32(V)7 electronic warfare system, and new high efficiency super-capacity chiller plant. An initial four DDG 51 Flight IIA ships – *Pinckney* (DDG-91), *Chung-Hoon* (DDG-93), *James E. Williams* (DDG-95) and *Halsey* (DDG-97) – will receive the upgrade package under a two-stage 'smart start' initiative. Full DDG MOD 2.0 refits will begin in FY2028 at a rate of two ships per year.

4.3 TECHNOLOGICAL REVIEW

OVERSEEING THE ROYAL NAVY'S REJUVENATION

Delivering the Type 26 and Type 31 Frigate Programmes

Author:
Conrad Waters

The British Royal Navy currently stands on the threshold of a much-needed period of major rejuvenation. This is particularly true with respect to its surface combatants, whose numbers have been steadily falling as existing warships reach life expiry. The Type 23 frigates that form the core of the navy's surface component were originally intended to serve for 18 years, but growing numbers have now passed their thirtieth birthdays. The cost and practicality of maintaining these elderly vessels has become an increasing challenge, with numbers slipping from thirteen to just nine in recent years as a consequence.[1] More positively, a significant programme of new construction has already been underway for several years that involves two separate frigate classes and aims to restore previous fleet numbers of the type. This will ultimately see eight Type 26 anti-submarine warfare (ASW) and five Type 31 general-purpose frigates delivered to the Royal Navy. Clearly,

Delays in replacing the Royal Navy's existing Type 23 frigates mean that the class are starting to be withdrawn from service as they reach life expiry, resulting in a decline in fleet numbers below previously planned levels. This photograph shows the Type 23 frigate *Montrose* returning to Devonport in December 2022 after an extended, near four-year-long deployment to the Middle East. She was subsequently decommissioned on 17 April 2023. *(Babcock International)*

These computer-generated images show the BAE Systems-built Type 26 ASW frigate (top) and its Babcock-constructed Type 31 general purpose frigate counterpart (bottom) whose delivery is being overseen by the Naval Ships Delivery Group. *(BAE Systems/Babcock International)*

there is a pressing need for these new warships to enter service as quickly as possible so as to halt – and then reverse – the surface fleet's decline.

This process of rejuvenation has not been without its hurdles. An upsurge in shipbuilding activity driven partly by the frigate programmes but also, for example, by heavy demand relating to submarine construction has stretched the capacity of Britain's shipbuilding sector. Whilst the need to modernise industrial infrastructure is part of the challenge, the imperative of expanding a highly skilled workforce is probably the greatest difficulty that has to be overcome. Perhaps reflecting some of these obstacles, the pace of new frigate construction has not been as rapid as initially expected. Notably, delivery of *Glasgow* – the lead ship of the Type 26 programme – is now expected in 2026 prior to declaration of initial operating capability in 2028; around 12 months later than first planned.

Perhaps inevitably, this seemingly slow rate of progress has produced much criticism, in which your editor has occasionally joined. Much of this opprobrium has been directed at the Defence Equipment & Support (DE&S) organisation; the major procurement arm of the UK Ministry of Defence. In July 2023, a House of Commons Defence Committee report stated, 'Moreover, DE&S' poor oversight of the Type 26 programme … has led to a "perfect storm", whereby barely half of the surface escort fleet – itself much reduced – is operationally available at any one time. In short, DE&S' distinctly sub-optimal management of surface ship refitting and new build programmes has become wholly unacceptable and is now crying out for fundamental reform.'[2] In truth, however, much of the criticism seems based on limited knowledge of the shipbuilding process and an inability to make effective comparisons with international programmes. Accordingly, this chapter aims to balance the record by examining the management of the Royal Navy's current frigate construction programmes and the very real progress that is being achieved.

THE NAVAL SHIPS DELIVERY GROUP

Responsibility for ensuring the delivery of the Royal Navy's two new frigate programmes currently rests with the Naval Ships Delivery Group (NSDG). Headed by retired Royal Navy Rear Admiral Mark Beverstock, NSDG forms part of the wider DE&S organisation headquartered at Abbey Wood near Bristol. The group forms part of DE&S's Ships Domain, which is under the leadership of Director General Ships.[3]

NSDG's role is to work on behalf of the Senior Responsible Owner (SRO) – the officer at Navy Command tasked with delivering the entirety of the Type 26 and Type 31 programmes to full operating capability – so as to bring the frigates to their acceptance stage. In essence, the SRO appointed to bring about the two projects provides NSDG with a budget and an equipment capability requirement. NSDG then has to ensure delivery of the equipment to the cost and timescale specified.

Actual implementation of the two frigate programmes is placed in the hands of the prime contractors assigned to carry out the projects. These are BAE Systems for the Type 26 frigates and Babcock International for the Type 31 class. As prime contractors, the two companies have contractual responsibility for undertaking the overall construction process, including management of the complex supply chain of sub-contractors contributing to the projects' realisation. In turn, NSDG oversees the contract and manages the risks to delivery that are inherent in the construction process, intervening as necessary to help negotiate a solution if problems arise.

NSDG currently has two separate teams dedicated to the management and oversight of, respectively, the Type 26 and Type 31 programmes.[4] Each team is headed by a team leader (project manager) and comprises a number of specialists in disciplines such as engineering, systems and commercial aspects to assess and manage programme risks. The size of each team is influenced by the complexity of their assigned project and the nature of the risks that need to be managed. As of early 2024, the Type 26 team comprised over 100 personnel, with that for the Type 31 around half this number. Some of these people provide direct oversight at the shipyard whilst others are based at the Bristol headquarters.

The lead Batch 2 'River' class offshore patrol vessel, *Forth*, seen arriving at Portsmouth naval base for the first time on 26 February 2018. Lessons learned from the class's construction programme have resulted in DE&S's Naval Ships Delivery Group increasing oversight over the Royal Navy's current construction programmes. *(BAE Systems)*

DELIVERING THE TYPE 26 PROGRAMME

Of the two programmes that NSDG manages, that for the Type 26 frigate is the longest established. The project has a lengthy and complicated history, tracing its origins to concept studies for replacing the Type 22 and Type 23 frigates that commenced in the mid-1990s. By 2010, these deliberations had progressed to the stage that a project assessment contract was in place for what was known as the Type 26 Global Combat Ship. However, ongoing discussions over ship numbers and costs meant that several more years were to elapse before a construction contract was placed. A £3.7bn (US$4.7bn) order for three of the new warships was finally placed in July 2017 and was followed by a £4.2bn (US$ 5.3bn) contract for a further five frigates in November 2022. Both awards were agreed with BAE Systems on a single-source, non-competitive basis. Collectively, the eight warships will replace those members of the Type 23 class that have been specifically configured for anti-submarine operations.[5]

Smoothing the Way Forward: Construction of the Type 26 frigates at BAE Systems' shipyards on the River Clyde in Glasgow was preceded by completion of the Batch 2 'River' class offshore patrol vessels. These were contracted to plug a gap in work between fabrication of blocks for the *Queen Elizabeth* class aircraft programme and the new frigates, as well as to rebuild the facilities' skills in integrating warships given the time that had elapsed since the previous Type 45 *Daring* class destroyers had been built. This 'de-risking' approach proved its value when the first patrol vessel, *Forth*, was handed over in 2018 with significant defects that were only identified after delivery. As a result, she had to be handed back to the shipbuilder to allow remedial work to be undertaken.

Whilst undoubtedly embarrassing, the Ministry of Defence learned valuable lessons from this experience that have stood them in good stead in terms of supervising frigate construction. In particular, the problems revealed that a previous belief that it was possible to take a 'light touch' approach to oversight – leaving responsibility largely with the contractor – was a mistake. As a result, steps were taken to increase the Ministry of Defence's presence on the 'waterfront', an approach that had already proved its

A picture of *Glasgow*, first of the new Type 26 frigates, on the hardstanding at BAE Systems' Govan shipyard in May 2021. Her planned delivery date has been delayed by approximately a year due to the emergence of a number of problems during the early stages of her construction. *(BAE Systems)*

This photograph shows *Glasgow* against the backdrop of BAE Systems' Govan shipyard on 25 November 2022 just prior to being loaded onto the semi-submersible barge that was used to carry out her launch. Although her construction has taken longer than first planned, significant efforts to de-risk important elements of the programme should assist subsequent trials and delivery. *(BAE Systems)*

worth by the time the patrol vessel programme was completed. By the time *Spey*, the final Batch 2 'River' class vessel, was delivered, the list of defects had been reduced to a single sheet of A4 paper. The move to adopt increased supervision has been maintained with respect to the current frigate programmes.

Supplier Challenges: The early stages of Type 26 construction were particularly notable for the need to manage problems in the broader supply chain. One significant challenge was driven by considerable delays encountered in delivery of the lead ship's main reduction gearbox. The design's focus on ASW operations and, accordingly, its emphasis on noise reduction, means that this is a critical piece of equipment whose acoustic qualities needed to be assured. Equally, its position deep within the ship meant that it was a key 'lock in' item that needed to be installed at an early stage in the construction process. For this reason, BAE Systems placed a design and development contract encompassing the first three gearboxes with David Brown Santasalo as early as 2013 following an international procurement competition. This was intended to ensure the equipment was ready once the construction order for the frigates was placed.

In the event, production of the first gearbox did not progress according to plan. Interestingly, the most significant problem arose from a risk-mitigation measure that involved the construction of a shore-based test rig at David Brown's Huddersfield factory to check the gearbox's performance against design requirements.[6] Testing revealed that the gearbox started vibrating as it moved towards operating at full power, a problem that was ultimately traced to the natural frequency of concrete plinths used in the text rig's design. It took a long time to understand the nature of this problem, threatening the overall production schedule of the lead ship. BAE Systems and NSDG worked proactively to minimise the delay's impact, devising a solution under which an opening was cut into *Glasgow*'s hull to slide the gearbox into the relevant compartment at a much later stage in the build process than was first envisaged. Although it was not possible to mitigate all of the lost time, the end result was far better than might otherwise have been the case.

More broadly, the investment in upfront testing has clearly proved its worth, also allowing a number of other minor issues to be identified and addressed.

Glasgow pictured transiting the River Clyde prior to being floated off the semi-submersible barge that BAE Systems now uses to conduct ship launches from its Clyde shipyards. Whilst *Glasgow* will have taken nine years to build by the time she is delivered, new infrastructure should reduce this to around five years by the time Type 26 frigate construction ends. *(Crown Copyright 2022)*

As a consequence, NSDG already has confidence that an important programme component that would only previously have been tested when *Glasgow* departed the River Clyde for sea trials will meet its performance parameters. This is particularly important given that any issues identified at a later stage would have had material consequences not only for the Royal Navy but also the foreign navies utilising the Global Combat Ship design. It is also worth noting that gearbox testing is only one aspect of the arrangements to de-risk important elements of the Type 26 programme. For example, the ships utilise an innovative mission bay and a fully representative load test and handling facility has been built to ensure it operates as intended. Another example is the use of GE Vernova's land-based electrical integrated test facility to put the electrical propulsion and distribution system that is being installed in the class through its paces. In this way the Ministry of Defence is learning lessons from past programmes to de-risk the delivery of future warships as quickly and effectively as possible.

Infrastructure Upgrades: The November 2022 award of the contract for an additional batch of five Type 26 frigates has unlocked further investment for future warship production. The longer-term visibility provided by the award has allowed BAE Systems to proceed with the construction of a new covered ship hall at the Govan yard in Glasgow that will allow the simultaneous assembly of two

BAE Systems is currently modernising its Govan yard with a new purpose-built ship hall, seen in the centre of this computer generated image. The facility will be used to assemble all Type 26 frigates from the third unit, *Belfast*, onwards. It forms an important part of efforts both to increase the shipyard's construction capacity and speed warship deliveries. *(BAE Systems)*

Type 26 frigates in a controlled, weather-tight environment. Currently being constructed by McLaughlin and Harvey, the facility measures 170m by 80m and will be equipped with two 100-tonne and two 20-tonne cranes and be able to accommodate 500 workers in each shift. The hall forms the centrepiece of a £300m (c. US$380m) programme of modernisation and digitalisation that BAE Systems reports is being made in its shipyards on the River Clyde.

To date, progress with the new facility has been remarkably rapid. NSDG notes that since BAE Systems received the second Type 26 contract, they have obtained all the permissions required for the new shipbuilding hall, awarded the contract for construction of the building, completed much of the basic erection work and are on track to commence assembly of the third Type 26, *Belfast*, in the facility by the winter of 2024. Final completion of the hall in 2025 is part of plans to accelerate the frigates' build time from the nine years required for the lead ship to as little as five years for the final vessel. This would bring construction schedules broadly in line with international competitors. It is also intended that the new ship hall will allow the interval separating the work on each ship to be reduced to 12 from 18 months.[7]

THE TYPE 31 FRIGATE: A DISRUPTIVE APPROACH

The other programme currently being overseen by NSDG is that for five Type 31 general-purpose frigates. This has been described as a 'deliberately disruptive programme' that was intended to increase competition in the supply of Royal Navy warships. The basis of the Type 31's procurement was to set a competitive price point and ask industry to make

A computer-generated image of Babcock's new 'Venturer Building' at the Rosyth shipyard near Edinburgh. Construction of the new ship hall – completed in November 2021 – is fundamental to Babcock's plans to deliver five Type 31 frigates under a 'deliberately disruptive programme'. *(Babcock International)*

Two photographs of the lead Type 31 frigate *Venturer* pictured in Babcock's eponymous ship hall at Rosyth in April 2024. The Type 31 frigate programme is still in the relatively early stages of construction and has yet to complete the most challenging integration stage. Nevertheless, progress to date has been impressive. *(Crown Copyright 2024)*

bids on the basis of the best capability that they could provide within the available budget. This requirement was combined with a very challenging ambition to be able to manufacture – by the end of the programme – a frigate from first steel cutting to delivery within a period of three years.[8] After a competitive acquisition process, a contract valued in excess of £1.25bn (US$1.6bn) – exclusive of certain government-furnished equipment – for the five ships was awarded by DE&S to Babcock International in November 2019. The so-called 'Inspiration' class is based on Babcock's 'Arrowhead 140' design and will replace those Type 23 frigates configured for general-purpose missions, completing the replacement programme.

Just as for the Type 26 frigates, the Type 31 programme has not gone entirely to plan. Notably, macroeconomic changes driving higher than anticipated inflation forced Babcock to take an initial £100m (US$125m) provision on the contract in April 2023 to cover the likely loss if the excess costs cannot be recouped. It is also worth noting that the construction of the 'Inspiration' class is still at a relatively early stage; assembly of the first two frigates – *Venturer* and *Active* – is currently underway but the lead ship had yet to be launched as of mid 2024. NSDG is open that they expect hurdles to overcome as the ships enter the most challenging, integration stage.

Nevertheless, the Type 31 programme has already been remarkable both for the scale of the ambition that has been set and for the progress that has already been achieved. A key element of Babcock's plan for delivering the new frigates has been their assembly in a new covered construction hall at their shipyard in Rosyth, near Edinburgh. Named the 'Venturer Building' after the first Type 31, this ship hall is similar to that currently being built by BAE Systems at Govan, providing a state-of-the-art shipbuilding facility that supports the latest manufacturing and information-management processes. It was completed in November 2021. Measuring 147m by 62m, it is equipped with two 125-tonne gantry cranes and can also support the simultaneous assembly of two frigates. Babcock believes that the assembly hall will benefit not only Type 31 delivery but also participation in subsequent British and international shipbuilding projects. Taken together, BAE Systems' and Babcock's investment programmes have essentially completed the wholesale recapitalisation of the United Kingdom's surface warship construction infrastructure in only a handful of years, the Covid-19 pandemic notwithstanding.

Like the Type 26 Global Combat Ship, the Type 31's 'parent' Arrowhead 140 design has also attracted export success, being selected as the basis for, first, the Indonesian Navy's 'Merah Putih' ('Red White') programme and, subsequently, Poland's 'Miecznik' ('Swordfish') class frigates. In addition to these initial contracts, Arrowhead 140 has formed the basis of a number of proposals to other countries incorporating construction options ranging from licensed build to full assembly at Rosyth. It also seems that the Type 31 programme is increasing Babcock's broader profile in the global market for warship design and construction. Notably, in May 2024, the British group announced that it had been selected by Saab to support the design for the development of the Swedish Navy's new *Luleå* class surface combatant.

LESSONS FOR THE FUTURE

It seems apparent from this brief overview that the criticism of the direction and oversight of the Royal Navy's two current major surface combatant programmes is overblown. There have undoubtedly been challenges in undertaking what – collectively – is the largest recapitalisation of the Royal Navy's surface fleet since the end of the Cold War. However, many of these difficulties can be traced to a sustained lack of investment in both infrastructure and skills during a period extending over multiple decades. The situation has also arguably been exacerbated by a seeming lack of government and industry focus on securing the export contracts that have been the saviour of many Continental European shipbuilding groups during this era of post-Cold War retrenchment.

Rectifying this situation is not an easy task, requiring continuous effort to revitalise shipbuilding facilities and the supply chain whilst, perhaps more importantly, training a new generation of shipbuilders with the necessary skillset. DE&S, in the form of NSDG, is playing a crucial part in this process, helping both to resolve problems when things inevitably go wrong as construction of the new frigates moves forward and also to learn important lessons for the future. This is being accompanied by broader efforts to encourage industry to invest in new infrastructure and the skills which go with it. Both BAE Systems and Babcock have developed extensive programmes to recruit and train large numbers of apprentices. NSDG is also putting considerable work into benchmarking current and expected performance against international competitors. The ultimate aim is to put British shipyards into the top quartile of performance in warship building internationally.[9]

When viewed in conjunction with the United Kingdom's National Shipbuilding Strategy (NSbS), which aims to drive a broader revitalisation of the shipbuilding sector, it is clear that considerable progress is being achieved with putting British naval shipbuilding onto a firmer footing. As well as driving progressive improvements in current frigate construction, this work is laying the foundations for the next generation of surface combatants, such as the proposed Type 83 destroyers and Type 32 frigates. It can only be hoped that NSDG and the wider shipbuilding enterprise will be allowed to sustain these achievements in a changing political environment. The Royal Navy's current rejuvenation depends on it.

Notes

1. The Type 23 frigate *Monmouth* was decommissioned on 30 June 2021 and her sister *Montrose* on 17 April 2023. On 14 May 2024, it was announced that *Westminster* and *Argyll* would also be retired.

2. See *It is broke – and it's time to fix it: The UK's defence procurement system HC 1099* (London, House of Commons, 2023), p. 15. A copy of the Defence Committee's report can currently be accessed at: committees.parliament.uk/publications/40939/documents/199440/default/

3. Director General Ships is responsible for two main directorates, one overseeing ship and ship systems acquisition; the other ship support. NSDG is one of a number of delivery groups within the acquisition directorate with, for example, another group overseeing semi-complex vessels such as the new fleet solid support ships. However, the overall DE&S structure is evolving, notably through the introduction of a new 'Gateway' in early 2024 that is described as providing a consistent, single-entry point into DE&S for all new capability needs. In essence, this will split the initial acquisition of new equipment up to contractual agreement from the subsequent management of the contract delivery stage. It is also worth noting that submarine projects fall outside the ambit of DE&S, being managed by the separate Submarine Delivery Agency.

4. As part of the ongoing process of DE&S reform, consideration is being given to creation of an integrated team so as to improve the ability to share expertise and experience across the common disciplines involved in the two programmes.

5. Variants of the Type 26 Global Combat Ship design have also been selected by Australia and Canada for their future frigate programmes.

6. NSDG states that this was the first time this had been done in a British warship production programme, reflecting a desire to prevent the emergence of problems late in the construction and trials process. This step reflected difficulties experienced in previous Royal Navy programmes, as well as – doubtless – problems reported with overseas projects, such as the German Navy K130 *Braunschweig* class corvettes and the *Freedom* (LCS-1) variant of the US Navy's Littoral Combat Ship.

7. Planned construction times were set out in an article by Richard Scott, 'First Type 26 Frigate Progresses Towards Completion' posted to the *Naval News* site – navalnews.com – on 24 April 2024.

8. It should be noted that it is not appropriate to make direct comparisons between planned Type 26 and Type 31 build times and costs, as the former's ASW specialisation make them more complex and expensive ships to construct.

9. NSDG utilise the internationally-recognised First Marine International consultancy – a business of the Dutch-headquartered Royal HaskoningDHV – as part of its benchmarking efforts.

10. The editor would like to thank the Head of the Naval Ships Delivery Group, Mark Beverstock, for providing many insights into the NSDG's work in an interview conducted in December 2023. This interview appears in the editor's 'Delivering the Royal Navy's future surface fleet' in *European Security & Defence 2/2024* (Bonn: Mittler Group, 2024) pp. 62–6. The assistance of Daniel Evans, Head of Media and Deputy Head of External Communications at DE&S, has also been essential in the production of this chapter.

4.4 TECHNOLOGICAL REVIEW

POST-COLD WAR NAVAL EVOLUTION

Technological Change since the Cold War's End

Author:
Norman Friedman

It is now more than 30 years since the end of the Cold War; and with it, the end of massive Western investments in navies, as in other military forces. Current Western navies resemble the ones in service in 1991 far more than the navies of, say, 1960 resembled those of the 1920s or 1930s. That was partly because the focus of Western naval development had shifted from the fleet-on-fleet emphasis that pertained before the Second World War to a combination of strike carrier aviation, strategic strike, and anti-submarine warfare. This, in turn, was because the Soviet fleet was so unlike the major fleets of the pre-Second World War period. The technology major navies embody has changed since the 1960s, but much more subtly than it did in the decades encompassed by the Second World War and the early Cold War. The Cold War was the main driver of Western technology throughout much of the period up to 1991. That no longer holds good. During the post-Cold War period, the emphasis in Western navies was expeditionary, as the main problems confronting the West came out of the Third World. Whilst that is still largely the case, the US Navy – at least – is now turning back towards an emphasis on great power conflict, this time with China.

The Italian Navy's Cold War era aircraft carrier *Giuseppe Garibaldi* pictured on exercises with the more modern FREMM-type frigate *Carlo Bergamini* and the British Royal Fleet Auxiliary's dock landing ship *Lyme Bay* in November 2020. The technology major navies embody has changed more subtly during the post-Cold War era than in previous periods, although the orientation of many Western fleets has become more expeditionary in nature. *(Crown Copyright 2020)*

THE COLD WAR'S AFTERMATH

Cold War research and development (R&D) built up a considerable momentum. This ensured that some Cold War programmes would continue in its immediate aftermath – albeit with generally reduced funding – even as the problems they addressed had changed. It took time for navies to decide what a post-Cold War naval world would look like, and what they needed to deal with it. As had been the case during the Cold War, the US Navy continued to dominate Western naval R&D, but on a far smaller scale.[1] As an indication of what was expected, the US Department of Defense pressed major contractors to merge on the theory that there would not be enough work for all of the existing companies. These mergers drastically reduced workforces, including those engaged in R&D.

The US Office of the Secretary of Defense also pressed the US Navy to abandon most in-house research and development in favour of contracts let to industry. There was hope that industry could innovate more effectively than US Navy laboratories and development activities. In ship design, this pressure was responsible for the development of two competitive Littoral Combat Ship (LCS) designs (although the decision that both would enter production was political). The failure of the LCS programme was responsible for a decision that the replacement new frigate should be based on an existing successful design. In the past, nearly all US Navy warship designs had begun with a preliminary design prepared within the naval shipbuilding organisation: BuShips, then NAVSEA. This in-house capacity is now nearly gone.

In all NATO countries after 1991, there was considerable pressure to realise a peace dividend. That generally involved large-scale decommissioning and scrapping, often of ships with considerable remaining lifetime. Building programmes were cut back or abandoned. Shipyards became considerably less viable, since exports could not take up the slack in national programmes and Western countries generally were not selling nearly enough merchant ships to make up the difference. As a consequence, it is now rather difficult for any Western country rapidly to reverse the process of decline. That is why the United States, for example, currently struggles to complete two nuclear attack submarines a year. Much the same is true of weapons and other naval systems production. To some extent the need to supply Ukraine is now recapitalising the defence sector. In some cases there is a serious attempt to use industry not formerly devoted to defence, for example to produce large numbers of unmanned vehicles.

CIVILIAN TECHNOLOGY AND COMPUTING POWER

To a considerable extent, a key post-Cold War trend has been to adapt rapidly-evolving civilian technology, particularly in computing power. Thus a major US Navy post-Cold War initiative in submarines was Acoustic Rapid COTS Insertion (ARCI); a programme that fitted submarines with computer servers which could be swapped out (refreshed) periodically to embody the current state of computing practice. The faster and faster servers ran new software which could not formerly have been embodied in the submarines' sonar systems.

The development of two competing Littoral Combat Ship designs – illustrated in this photograph of the then newly-built *Independence* (LCS-2) and *Freedom* (LCS-1) in May 2012 – was influenced by a hope that transfer of much in-house R&D to industry would help to drive more effective innovation. The experience of the Littoral Combat Ship in practice makes it questionable that this hope was realised. *(US Navy)*

The *Virginia* class submarine *Texas* (SSN-775) prepares to undock from Dry Dock No. 3 at Portsmouth Naval Shipyard on 20 February 2024 in the course of a scheduled overhaul. The adoption of commercial 'off the shelf' (COTS) technology has meant that US Navy submarines have been able to enhance their sonar performance by accessing rapid enhancement in computing power, reducing the need for investment in a new generation of sonar systems. *(US Navy)*

ARCI was a response to straitened finances which could not support a new generation of submarine sonars, although in fact the *Virginia* (SSN-774) class does have some new sonars. It turned out that at the end of the Cold War the navy was relying heavily on newer and larger sonar transducers without making full use of the ones it already had. ARCI proved quite successful, and similar COTS (commercial off the shelf) technology insertion has been extended throughout the fleet. Whilst this proved somewhat difficult with respect to the Aegis system – in which computers and radars were very tightly bound together – it has worked there as well.

The trend towards exploiting rapidly-evolving commercial technology is revealed in descriptions of current command and control systems. During the Cold War, such systems were relatively static. Brochures would describe them in terms of concrete capabilities, such as the number of tracks they could handle. By the 2010s, such brochures typically claimed that the software of a new command and control system could run all of the software formerly run on other systems. Specifications no longer typically included numbers of tracks or similar statistics. It turned out to be very difficult to characterise software in anything like the way that hardware used to be described. The systems offered in brochures were difficult or impossible to distinguish, much as in the world of commercial software. Certainly some are a lot better than others, although no one but a user is likely to be able to tell.

The explosion of computing power, certainly in the West, has made autonomous unmanned vehicles more and more effective. Their power is being

The explosion of computing power has made autonomous unmanned vehicles increasingly effective, with variants of various shapes and sizes performing a steadily growing range of missions on, above and under the waves. This is a Huntington Ingalls Industries' REMUS 100 unmanned underwater vehicle (UUV), which has seen widespread naval use for mine countermeasures and underwater surveying. *(Huntington Ingalls Industries)*

demonstrated again and again in Ukraine, for example in the Ukrainians' very successful use of unmanned surface vehicles based on jet-skis and the like to attack Russian surface ships. Airborne drones have become ubiquitous, both for sensing and for attack (as 'kamikazes'). In both cases, the drones are relatively inexpensive largely because the computer chips which control them are so cheap.[2] As a consequence, drones can be deployed in far larger numbers than had been imagined before the outbreak of the war in Ukraine. Swarms of drones make saturation attacks practicable, at least at short ranges, on a previously unimagined scale. That has important implications for shipboard air defences.

Another consequence of exploding computing power and, hence, of artificial intelligence is a shift in the technology of mine countermeasures. The principal technique is still minehunting. In 1991, that meant using a minehunter, with a dramatically reduced signature, to examine suspicious objects on the sea bed one-by-one. Typically the minehunter deployed a vehicle which safely examined a potential mine before planting an explosive to neutralise it. The minehunter had to examine mines carefully because an error could be fatal. As computing power increased, alternatives were raised. The problem had always been to distinguish mines from non-mines on the seabed despite marine growth which might disguise real mines. The simplest possibility was to have an autonomous vehicle – which was too small to cause a mine to explode – swim through a potential minefield to determine whether possible mines were present at all. The US Navy developed, but apparently did not deploy, a submarine-borne underwater vehicle. Now it appears that autonomous vehicles may be intelligent enough to distinguish mines and indicate their positions so that some other vehicle, such as a helicopter, can drop munitions to neutralise them. Autonomous vehicles made it possible to clear Iraqi ports rapidly in 2003.

Civilian technology has also become prominent in what used to be military reconnaissance space systems. It is not that such bespoke systems are gone, but that much of the capability formerly associated with high-end space-based reconnaissance is now available on a relatively inexpensive civilian basis. Merchant ships now generally employ the Automatic Identification System (AIS), which can be read from space. This post-Cold War capability may considerably limit the 'sea sanctuary' which navies had usually enjoyed in the past; the reality that once a ship was beyond the horizon she was essentially invisible. At the least, AIS may make it a lot easier to sift a radar picture of ships at sea to limit it largely to warships. On the other hand, with the rise of autonomous vehicles, it may be easier to create believable decoys.[3]

The end of the Cold War saw Western navies significantly scale back their 'blue water' specialised anti-submarine warfare (ASW) forces. This is the US Navy's FFG-7 class frigate *Doyle* (FFG-39) on a visit to Portsmouth, United Kingdom in 2008, a few years before her final withdrawal. *(Conrad Waters)*

THE LURE OF THE LITTORAL

Strategically, the end of the Cold War revealed a deep chasm in Western naval thinking. The US Navy had pursued a Maritime Strategy designed to fight a major war – if one broke out – largely with a general-purpose fleet. This would be as much at home projecting power into the Third World as fighting in the Norwegian Sea. Most other large Western navies, with the important exception of the French, were far more specialised. Typically, they were oriented towards an anti-submarine campaign against the Soviets and their large submarine force or towards defending the Baltic against a Soviet amphibious attack.

After the end of the Cold War, NATO navies generally dramatically cut their specialised anti-submarine warfare (ASW) forces. Thus the US Navy retired its *Perry* (FFG-7) class and earlier frigates without direct replacement. The Royal Netherlands Navy eventually sold nearly all its frigates, whilst the Royal Navy quickly discarded many of its specialised Type 22s. All of these ships had been widely applauded for their optimisation for anti-submarine warfare. Similarly, the Royal Swedish Navy discarded most of its fast attack craft, replacing them with much larger ones capable of more distant operations. Within a few years overall American naval strength was more than halved, although the strike carrier force suffered less dramatic cuts. Other NATO navies were cut even more deeply.

Naval needs hardly vanished, but they changed substantially. Initially the US Navy expected that it would find itself engaged in littoral warfare, the littoral being the strip of water influenced by events ashore, plus the strip of adjoining shore influenced directly from the sea. Most people in the world live in littoral areas. The expectation was that the collapse of the Soviet Union would unfreeze a wide variety of local problems; analysts joked about the 'new world disorder' as President Bush spoke of a 'new world order' making for widespread peace and prosperity. The 1991 war against Iraq fitted this expectation.

This littoral idea had real implications. Ships operating in the offshore strip would face sudden attacks from pop-up missile launchers ashore. Their defensive systems had to react very rapidly. The only fast-reaction defensive system in US Navy service was Aegis. Non-Aegis ships were discarded, even those which had just been subject to the New Threat Upgrade (NTU). Although NTU was conceived to counter saturation air attacks, it did not provide the kind of quick reaction a ship close offshore might need. Discarding NTU ships was also attractive because nearly all of them had steam power plants, which required many more personnel than gas turbines. Personnel were already very expensive, and they were likely to become scarcer in a post-Cold War world. Most other NATO navies had already retired their steam-driven ships. The need for quick reaction also favoured vertical launchers over mechanical ones. That choice raised a new issue: how vertically-launched missiles might be replenished at sea. Despite many proposals, this problem has not been solved.

The littoral idea justified eliminating long-range carrier strike aircraft, on the ground that mass air strikes would be needed only in the littoral strip, to support ground operations there. For anything further inland, the navy could rely on Tomahawk cruise missiles and the Air Force. Experience has showed that this was a bad bet. Tomahawk proved extremely effective, for example in the war in Serbia, but it was not a mass weapon. In surface ships it had to share vertical launch cells with air defence missiles whilst submarines had very limited numbers of Tomahawks on board. With the shift towards orientation against China, it seems that future hypersonic anti-ship missiles will require much larger launchers. This will leave ships with fewer weapons that are still virtually impossible to replenish at sea.

The focus of anti-submarine warfare changed, from the deep-water fight against high-performance nuclear submarines to an inshore (littoral) fight

A Tomahawk cruise missile training round is lowered aboard the US Navy *Los Angeles* class submarine *Springfield* (SSN-761) in April 2022 whilst in Western Australian waters. The post-Cold War era saw considerable reliance on Tomahawk as a long-range precision strike weapon but only limited numbers can be deployed at sea. The photograph also shows the difficulties that would need to be overcome to replenish the current generation of missiles at sea. *(US Navy)*

One important aspect of the post-Cold War naval environment was a switch in the emphasis of anti-submarine operations to focus on stealthy diesel-electric submarines loitering in littoral waters. The Brazilian submarine *Riachuelo*, which has been constructed to the French Naval Group 'Scorpène' design, is a good example of this type of threat. *(ICN-Naval Group)*

against small numbers of capable non-nuclear submarines. Unlike their nuclear counterparts, such submarines can sit on the bottom, waiting for targets to appear.[4] Early post-Cold War US Navy ASW efforts included means of discerning such bottomed submarines. In addition, diesel-electric submarines do not produce the characteristic sound signatures so important in Cold War ASW against nuclear submarines. Active sonars therefore became more important, although they lack the range of Cold War passive arrays. The low-frequency active sonars developed during the latter part of the Cold War, such as the British Type 2087, were valued because they could detect diesel-electric submarines at long range, despite silencing.

An aspect of anti-submarine warfare which survived the Cold War was the attempt to counter enemy torpedoes. Late in the Cold War it became evident that Soviet anti-ship torpedoes were wake-followers rather than, as in the West, homers on the sound produced by a ship target. Since every country Western navies now face uses Russian-supplied weapons (or weapons copied from Russian prototypes), the need to counter wake-followers has become urgent. Unfortunately it is extremely difficult (or impossible) to simulate a ship's wake in a way that a torpedo will follow. A variety of hard-kill countermeasures have been proposed but they do not seem to have been very successful. The US Navy recently abandoned a programme involving a half-size lightweight anti-torpedo torpedo (6.75in diameter). An alternative would be an air-flight weapon, which would dive towards a torpedo target. Its advantage would be very quick time of flight, but on the other hand it would not home on the target torpedo, so it would need precise targeting. An Israeli company displayed a concept for such a weapon at the 2022 Euronaval show.

OPERATIONAL EXPERIENCE

The first big Western naval campaign of the post-Cold War period was the Gulf War of 1990–1. For the US Navy, an important lesson was that the proliferation of ballistic missiles could badly affect power projection from the sea. The great bulk of equipment and ammunition which supported the fight against Iraq came through a single pier at Jeddah. The Iraqis fired a Scud tactical ballistic missile at it, but missed. Had a Scud with a chemical warhead hit the pier, it could have disrupted the whole operation. This experience drove forward the Aegis ballistic missile defence programme, which now includes a capability to deal with far more sophisticated threats, such as intercontinental ballistic missiles (ICBMs). The programme has now given the US Navy the ability to deal with at least some hypersonic threats. Its success was demonstrated when US Navy Aegis-equipped ships defeated Houthi anti-ship ballistic missiles fired at merchant ships and warships in the Red Sea. The Gulf War was followed by the NATO campaigns against Serbia, in which land-attack Tomahawk missiles were successfully used in quantity to hit land targets precisely.

The next war demonstrated something startling. On 9/11 (2001) a subnational group (Al-Qaeda) based temporarily in Afghanistan managed to kill over 3,000 people in the United States without having to use any kind of sophisticated technology. For the US Navy, the attack showed that the United States had to be able to deal with multiple foreign crises simultaneously, and also that it would sometimes have to deal with target areas far inland of the littorals. During the Cold War, it had been assumed, apparently correctly, that the Soviets, the main threat, would never confront the United States and the West in more than one place at a time, for fear of generating an uncontrollable reaction. The US Navy now posited a need to spread its power much more widely. Major warships could not be built rapidly, but the existing ones could become the cores of a larger number of combat formations. The amphibious ships which normally worked with carrier strike groups (and shared their escorts) could instead become the cores of new Expeditionary Strike Groups (ESGs). New Surface Action Groups could be created. Many more surface warships were needed to fill out the new formations. This perception was the origin of the Littoral Combat Ship (LCS).

The number of LCS required was about the same as the total of smaller US naval combatants, mainly mine and patrol ships. The idea, then, was that LCS would replace these ships wholesale, on a one-for-one basis. To do that, LCS had to have a modular payload so that it could perform many missions. The modular payloads in turn were linked with a programme of unmanned vehicles, both undersea and airborne. In effect the LCS became the mother ship for an unmanned system in much the same way that an aircraft carrier or other air-capable ship 'mothers' manned or unmanned aircraft (although it would mother only a single system). The LCS modules were largely sensing devices, with the LCS transmitting their data to a central command which could operate on that basis. In theory, the terrain, above and below water, of a littoral area would preclude wide-area sensing by any single ship or device, so that sensors would have to be multiplied.[5] The LCS itself would exploit data it gathered using an unmanned vehicle such as a helicopter or UUV. This concept of operations made it possible for an LCS to function, for example, as a minehunter. There is now some question as to whether the LCS can be truly multi-functional, or whether individual units will have to specialise permanently. That is largely a question of crew training and replacement. It appears that many of the LCS now being retained – drawn from *Independence* (LCS-2) class – will function largely as minehunters.

The next war carrying major naval lessons seems to have been the lengthy war involving the Houthis in Yemen. This began in 2014 as a civil war against a Yemeni regime backed by Saudi Arabia. From 2015 onwards the Houthis began occasional attacks on ships moving along their part of the Red Sea coast, using – inter alia – both anti-ship cruise missiles and drones. The Houthis had received missiles, including ballistic land-attack weapons, from Iran. During this phase of the conflict, US Navy vessels were attacked by cruise missiles on a number of occasions and several incoming missiles were shot down by Aegis-directed surface-to-air weapons.

The Iranians subsequently developed simple anti-ship homing devices for ballistic missiles, which they supplied to the Houthis. After the war in Gaza broke out in late 2023, the Houthis began a more intensive phase of attacks against merchant ships and warships in the Red Sea and in its narrow neck, the Bab-el-Mandeb, using these new weapons in conjunction

The extent of the emphasis on littoral operations in the post-Cold War years is demonstrated by the emergence of the Littoral Combat Ship design. This was essentially envisaged as a 'mothership' for a range of modular systems, many unmanned. Here a MQ-8B Fire Scout unmanned aerial vehicle (UAV) is seen operating from *Billings* (LCS-15) during a deployment in the Caribbean in June 2022. Early operational experience has suggested that issues around crew training have acted as a significant limitation on the LCS type's ability to use modular systems to achieve a truly multi-functional capacity, leading to ships being designated to perform more discrete missions. Other ships of the type have been retired after only comparatively short periods of service. *(US Navy)*

These two photographs were taken onboard the *Arleigh Burke* class destroyer *Carney* (DDG-64) on 19 October 2023 when the Aegis-equipped vessel engaged a combination of Houthi missiles and unmanned aerial vehicles in the Red Sea. The recent engagements in the Red Sea have demonstrated the effectiveness of Western air defences but have also highlighted some important questions. *(US Navy)*

with cruise missiles and drones. The US Navy, the British Royal Navy and France's *Marine Nationale* were amongst a number of fleets deploying warships to combat these attacks. The Aegis system performed effectively, demonstrating its anti-ballistic missile capability using both SM-2 and, almost certainly, the Evolved Sea Sparrow Missile (ESSM). Both the French and Royal Navy also engaged ballistic missiles with Aster surface-to-air missiles directed, respectively, by Herakles and Sampson phased-array radars. In both cases there does not seem to have been much question that the missiles have been quite successful.

A notable feature of the Houthi campaign – and one that has only occasionally been pointed out – is that ballistic missiles fired over the horizon need targeting information. That they have been receiving such information is evident in the fact that favoured ships, such as those flying Chinese flags, were only rarely attacked. It has been claimed that an Iranian vessel has been helping to provide the necessary data to Houthi forces. If so, it is unclear whether or not any attempt has been made to jam its communications. Western governments have certainly been unwilling to attack it directly, confining their counter-attacks to the Houthis themselves.

The attacks highlighted some important questions. Ballistic missiles are relatively inexpensive, and the drones which supplemented them are really quite cheap. However, sophisticated air defence missiles are expensive, and ships carry them in only limited numbers; a Type 45 destroyer, for example, has only forty-eight cells for its Aster missiles. An Aegis destroyer has more than twice as many missile cells – some of which may be quad-packed with four ESSMs – but she probably also carries a few Tomahawks. How much does it cost to exhaust her magazine, particularly if the standard practice is to fire two missiles at each target? Can cheap attack drones saturate an air defence system? The problem is not that too many will appear at once, but rather that the numbers available will eventually exhaust magazine capacity.[6]

This is not a new question. Several navies, including the US Navy and the Royal Navy, are currently working on directed-energy (mainly but not entirely lasers) air defence weapons, presumably primarily to destroy drones. Since the 'bullets' involved are pulses of energy, magazine capacity is in effect unlimited. For years, since at least the 1980s, effective anti-missile lasers have been considered imminent. Their time may finally be coming, at least against relatively flimsy drones. At the least, if drones have to be made survivable, their unit cost will rise to the point that they are no longer so easy to use in swarms. On the other hand, it may be that automatic guns like the existing Phalanx are effective enough against slow-moving drones, so the exhaustion problem may have been overstated.

THE OTHER SIDE OF THE HILL

It is difficult to characterise the naval development programmes of the countries opposed to the West, mainly Russia, China, and Iran. When the Soviet Union broke up, the Russians were confronted by a problem created by the previous Soviet rulers. They had deliberately dispersed key industry in hopes of tying their country together. Thus, for example, the post-breakup Russian navy found that its gas turbines were made in Ukraine. Investment in most forms of naval R&D seems to have been very low. For example exhibits on display as late as the 2010 St. Petersburg naval exhibition were recognisably mainly things which had been either in existence or under development in 1991. The two most prominent exceptions were long-range nuclear weapons and hypersonic missiles; the latter still being developmental at the time. Western navies are now reacting to live hypersonic threats while developing their own hypersonic anti-ship missiles. In the past, they had generally preferred stealthy subsonic anti-ship missiles to supersonic ones. For example, the French found that a proposed supersonic successor to Exocet did not sell.

China has pioneered in the development of long-range ballistic anti-ship missiles, parading weapons it calls carrier-killers. The Chinese have built a dummy aircraft carrier in a desert to act as a target. However, to date they appear not to have demonstrated the ability actually to track and hit a moving ship well offshore. For its part, the US Navy has deployed the SM-6 missile on board Aegis-equipped ships and has tested it against hypersonic targets in an extension of the Aegis anti-ballistic missile programme.

The ongoing war in Ukraine has caused several Western countries to increase defence spending, although the nature of that war has arguably made for an emphasis on land and air forces rather than naval ones. At the least, the war has encouraged interest in hypersonic missiles, both as weapons and as threats.

The US Navy launches a hypersonic missile during a Navy Strategic Systems Programs and Army Hypersonic Project Office test from the NASA Wallops Flight Facility in Virginia on 26 October 2022. Western navies are now reacting to live hypersonic threats while developing their own hypersonic anti-ship missiles. *(US Navy)*

Notes

1. In this chapter, the 'West' is taken to include NATO and closely aligned countries, such as Australia, Japan, New Zealand and Taiwan.

2. The economics involved have shifted. Software is expensive to write, but cheap to reproduce, so that a very capable unmanned aerial vehicle (UAV) may be expensive to develop but very inexpensive to produce. At least in theory, this economic shift should affect a computer-intensive aircraft like the F-35, which should benefit from the economics of scale in production.

3. Of course, warships can spoof AIS. Many civilian craft, such as large fishing vessels operating illegally, routinely either spoof the system or turn off their transceivers. Interestingly, AIS is heavily dependent on the use of the Global Positioning System (GPS) which is a good example of a reverse shift towards civilian uses of formerly restricted military technology. Initially GPS was conceived as a navigational system which would offer its best precision only to the military. The United States' Clinton Administration reversed that decision. GPS has been a key enabler of unmanned vehicles, particularly over the trackless sea.

4. Nuclear submarines generally do not bottom because they can be disabled by mud sucked into their condensers.

5. Apparently the initial LCS ASW concept was that an unmanned helicopter launched by the LCS would lay sensing barriers which would make it possible to track a diesel submarine on the basis of the flow noise it generated over its hull. Because sensing was entirely passive, the submarine would be unaware that it was being tracked. A manned or unmanned helicopter could be directed to attack the submarine on this basis. This idea seems not to have worked. The ASW module was changed to use a variable-depth sonar but was then cancelled due to cost overruns.

6. It is not clear to what extent close-in weapons systems were used to counter the supplementary drone attacks but it is known that (costly) missiles have been used on many occasions. Clearly, the imbalance between a very expensive air defence missile and a very cheap UAV is striking.

Contributors

Jean François Auran: Jean François Auran was a member of the French Army for 37 years. He received training first as a specialist in air defence, then as a staff officer, and ultimately as a logistics specialist. He served in NATO (JC Lisbon) and Africa (Angola, Chad, DRC, and Ivory Coast), including in Angola as the Defence Attaché. He writes for the magazines *Marines et Forces Navales*, *European Security and Defence* and *Defense Expert* on a regular basis. This is his first contribution to *Seaforth World Naval Review*. He holds a PhD in contemporary history. He lives with his wife Palmira, in Lille (Hauts de France).

Sidney E. Dean: An international affairs specialist by training, Sidney E. Dean is a freelance writer focussing on strategic studies, military technology and military history. He writes extensively for the publications of the Mittler Group and numerous other journals. He is founder and president of Transatlantic-Euro-American Multimedia LLC, and past editor of *Hampton Roads Military History Quarterly* and *Hampton Roads International Security Quarterly*. Having spent considerable time living in Europe and on both coasts of the United States, he currently makes his home in south-eastern Virginia.

Norman Friedman: Norman Friedman is one of the world's best-known naval historians and the author of over forty books. He has written widely on issues of military interest, including an award-winning account of the Cold War, and with respect to warship development. Amongst recent works, *Winning a Future War: War Gaming and Victory in the Pacific War* – a description of how war gaming at the US Naval War College helped the US Navy prepare for the Pacific War – produced for the Naval History & Heritage Command is a notable contribution to naval history. His latest book, *British Coastal Forces*, forms part of a wider series on British warship types. In 2022, he received the Anderson Medal for lifetime achievement from the Society for Nautical Research, and also the Dudley W. Knox medal for lifetime achievement in naval history from the (US) Naval Historical Foundation. The holder of a PhD in theoretical physics from Columbia, Dr. Friedman is a regular commentator on television and lectures widely on defence issues. He resides with his wife in New York.

David Hobbs: David Hobbs is a naval historian with an international reputation. He has written over twenty books, the most recent of which, *The Fleet Air Arm and The War in Europe 1939–1945*, was published by Seaforth in 2022. He has also written for several journals and magazines and in 2005 won the award for the Aerospace Journalist of the Year, Best Defence Submission, in Paris. He also won the essay prize awarded by the Navy League of Australia in 2008. He has lectured on naval subjects worldwide and has been broadcast in several countries. He served in the Royal Navy for 33 years and retired with the rank of Commander. He is qualified as both a fixed and rotary wing pilot and his log book contains 2,300 hours with over 800 carrier deck landings, 150 of which were at night. For eight years he was the Curator of the Fleet Air Arm Museum at Yeovilton. His next book, *Aircraft of the Royal Navy since 1908*, describes over 450 types of fixed wing, rotary wing and lighter-than-air aircraft and is due to be published in 2024. He lives in Northumberland with his wife Jandy, a former WRNS Officer.

Bruno Huriet: Bruno Huriet is a French merchant navy officer, holding a dual bridge & engine certificate. After a few years on bulk carriers he worked ashore as ship superintendent on a major naval export contract. Subsequently – over a period extending for more than 20 years – he has been employed by companies in insulation and interior outfitting for both civilian and naval projects. Having worked on several naval projects in different countries, he is particularly interested in comparing the varying design solutions adopted by different navies. He is a long-standing contributor to *Seaforth World Naval Review*.

Bradley Martin: Brad Martin is a senior policy researcher at the RAND Corporation, where he has worked since November 2012. His work has emphasised issues of vulnerability resulting from economic interdependence, strategic readiness impacts from logistics and infrastructure shortfalls, and the overlap between geopolitics and supply chain exposure. He is also serving as Director of the RAND Supply Chain Security Institute, where his work includes table-top exercises and war games with private and public stakeholders. Prior to joining RAND, he served in the US Navy as a surface warfare officer, retiring after 30 years of service as a Captain. He has a doctorate in political science from the University of Michigan, which he achieved prior to joining the navy.

Josiah Martin: Josiah Martin is a current doctoral student in Terrorism Studies at American University's School of Public Affairs, where he worked as a research assistant to Dr. Bryan Arva. His research interests include Grey Zone Warfare, counterinsurgency, and the connections between terrorism and organised crime. Josiah earned a Bachelor's and a Master's in Criminal Justice from George Mason University, where he wrote his thesis on mapping the Terrorism-Piracy Nexus. He is currently applying for Officer Candidate School with the intention of becoming a Surface Warfare Officer in the US Navy.

Mrityunjoy Mazumdar: Mr Mazumdar, who studied applied physics & mechanical engineering, has been a regular contributor to *Seaforth World Naval Review* since its inception. His interests are the sea services of South and Southeast Asian countries, as well as the lesser known naval and air forces around the world. His words, pictures, and research have appeared in many naval and military aircraft publications including *Janes Navy International*, IQPC's *Defence Industry Bulletin*, *Shephard Media*, *Ships of the World*, *Warship Technology* and *Air Forces Monthly* as well as the standard naval reference books. Having grown up in India and Nigeria, Mr Mazumdar lives in the 'wine country' north of San Francisco with his wife.

Richard Scott: Richard Scott is a UK-based analyst and commentator who has specialised in coverage of naval operations and technology for over 25 years, with particular interests in the fields of naval aviation, guided weapons and electronic warfare. He has held a number of editorial positions with Jane's, including the editorship of *Jane's Navy International* magazine, and is currently group Consultant Editor – Naval. Mr Scott is also a regular contributor to other periodicals, including the *AOC Journal of Electromagnetic Dominance* and *Warship World*.